Historical Society of Alberta
Vol. III

THE FORMATION OF ALBERTA:

A DOCUMENTARY HISTORY

Introduction by
L. G. THOMAS and L. H. THOMAS

Edited by
DOUGLAS R. OWRAM

General Editor
R. C. MACLEOD

Alberta Records Publication Board
HISTORICAL SOCIETY OF ALBERTA
1979

Copyright 1979 by the Historical
Society of Alberta, Calgary, Alberta

All rights reserved

Published with the assistance of grants from the
Alberta Historical Resources Foundation, the Alberta
Department of Culture and the 75th Anniversary
Commission.

ISBN 0-88864-987-8

TABLE OF CONTENTS

LIST OF DOCUMENTS

PREFACE

This volume is the third in the series of works by the Alberta Records Publications Board of the Historical Society of Alberta and has been timed to coincide with the 75th anniversary of Alberta's creation as a Province. In order to help commemorate that anniversary it was decided to try to organize and publish a documentary history of the events leading to Provincial status.

The creation of Alberta as a Province in 1905 was marked not only by intense political and constitutional controversy but as well by a tremendous outpouring of documents, correspondence, speeches and newspaper editorials. The vast collection of material available to the historian thus necessarily renders this volume illustrative rather than definitive. Nevertheless, in the selection of material an attempt has been made to provide a reasonably detailed record of the process leading to Provincial status. In particular, an effort was made to include the great bulk of official and semi-official material which passed between the federal and territorial governments in the years between 1900 and 1905. This, combined with a more selective use of newspaper editorials, private correspondence, and material from before 1900 will, it is hoped, provide the reader with some understanding of the politics and stages that culminated in the formation of Alberta. The introduction by

Lewis H. Thomas and Lewis G. Thomas acts as an essential supplement to this documentary material and helps both to fill in gaps and to provide an integrated overview of events.

The history of the formation of Alberta as a Province is to a large extent inseparable from the history of the changing constitutional position of the North-west Territories as a whole. Thus many of the documents included are as applicable to Saskatchewan as to Alberta. Wherever possible, however, the selection process took into account the Alberta perspective of this volume. The debate on Alberta separation in the 1890's, the fight over the site of the capital and the use of Alberta newspapers for editorial opinion reflect this perspective.

The same deliberate decision to take an Alberta perspective was used in assessing the importance to give various facets of the issue. This fact is perhaps most obvious in the treatment of the controversy over the educational clauses in the autonomy bills. In the East, particularly in Ontario, these clauses were by far the most important of the issues raised by the creation of new Provinces in the West. In the North-west Territories, however, there are clear indications that the education question, while important, was only one of many controversies. Control of natural resources, the capital question, the political future of the new Province and, above all, the principle of Provincial autonomy were of equal or greater importance to Albertans. While trying to give adequate coverage to the schools question as a central issue in the whole controversy I have thus tried equally to place it in the context of the times and in the myriad of controversies which were involved in the constitutional alterations of 1905.

In the preparation of this work I have received assistance from a number of people. Stan Gordon and Janice Dickin McGinnis undertook the initial research and collecting of documents. Their thoroughness and initiative left me with a vast and balanced set of documents from which the final selections were made. Stan Gordon also had what can only be termed the misfortune to be around during the process of selection and I often imposed on him for assistance and advice. Rod Macleod, general editor of the series, has throughout acted as a liaison between myself and the Board and has as well provided useful advice and assistance. Olive Baird, Rhennie Casement and Rhona Thomas typed the documents with their usual mixture of efficiency, accuracy and good humour—not an easy task given the length of this collection and the fact that it was given to them with little warning. Lillian Wonders of the

Department of Geography drew the maps for this work. Finally, publication is made possible by a grant from the Alberta Historical Resources Foundation, whose generosity has sustained the series since its inception.

Doug Owram
August, 1979

INTRODUCTION
Lewis H. Thomas and Lewis G. Thomas

The Province of Alberta was born in an atmosphere of great political turbulence, which continued beyond the date of the passage of the Alberta and Saskatchewan Acts, which were assented to on July 20, 1905. The chief protagonists were Prime Minister Wilfrid Laurier and F.W.G. Haultain, premier of the North-West Territories. Other personalities involved in the creation and definition of the boundaries of the two new provinces were Frank Oliver, Liberal member of parliament for Edmonton, R.B. Bennett, then a member of the Northwest Assembly, Clifford Sifton, Minister of the Interior, and Walter Scott, Liberal member of parliament for Assiniboia West.[1]

Alberta derived its name and origin from the Provisional District of Alberta, one of four districts in the Territories. Their creation was originally suggested by J.S. Dennis, Deputy Minister of the Interior in a memorandum to Sir John A. Macdonald, dated October 15, 1881. Macdonald, then Minister of the Interior, accepted Dennis' suggestion which was embodied in an Order-in-Council of May 8, 1882.[2] The Order was submitted to Parliament the same day and was approved. The publicly stated reason for this action was "for the convenience of settlers and for postal purposes."[3] Nevertheless, the real purpose was to create districts whose boundaries would justify their establishment as provinces at a later date. Memoranda by Macdonald refer to these districts as provinces, or provinces to be. The reason for hiding the true intent was probably Macdonald's fear of raising the expectations of Westerners, since his government was not prepared to speed the movement toward provincial autonomy.[4]

In the years after 1882 a distinct district consciousness developed.[5] This became apparent when the Territorial Assembly defined constituencies in each district. Another illustration is provided by an editorial of June 4, 1890, in the *Saskatchewan Herald*, which objected to the immigration policy of members of the Assembly for Assiniboia. "This sense of frustration", the editor wrote, "would produce district consciousness which would make itself felt in many diverse ways". The belief that Alberta was a distinct entity is evident in the formation of a special committee of the Alberta members which would memorialize the federal government on matters principally affecting the District of Alberta.[6]

In 1886 Parliament granted representation to the North-West Territories, with Assiniboia receiving two seats and Saskatchewan and Alberta one each. The Territories first participated in federal elections in 1887. This involved the organization of federal political party organizations, and inevitably by the turn of the century, many members of the territorial Assembly were to think in party terms. In the election of 1896, Frank Oliver was returned as the Liberal member of parliament for Alberta. He had already established a reputation as a critic of the Conservative party, and a spokesman for increased powers for the legislative Assembly.

The dominant personality in the Assembly from 1888 to 1905, was a young lawyer from Ft. Macleod, F.W.G. Haultain. The editor of the Calgary *Herald* once wrote of him:

> He is a man of academic training and large, clear perception; straightforward and manly even towards his enemies. In some respects, he is the most finished debater ever heard on a Western platform, arraying his facts in crisp, clear-cut sentences, and then pressing home his argument with logic and force.[7]

In 1896 the Legislative Assembly endorsed a lengthy memorial to the federal government. The memorial contained the following pronouncement:

> The Assembly is of the opinion that . . . it is not necessary to have recourse to the granting of full Provincial status. They believe that till the time arrives, which may be at a not distant day, when the Territories should be taken into Confederation (as one or more provinces) the passing of a few amendments to the North West Territories Act will allow for, subject to disallowance of other Ordinances 'to exclusively make laws in relation to matters' already within their legislative jurisdiction.[8]

During the debate on the resolution to approve this memorial, Dr. R.G. Brett of Calgary argued for provincehood for Alberta, including Athabasca. This proposal had previously been advocated by the Calgary *Herald*. A committee had been formed in that city which issued a pamphlet, *Provincial Government for Alberta, Its Meaning and Necessity*.[9] Haultain opposed Brett's argument, arguing that the Territories were "One single united country, and would remain so." They should have, Haultain continued, "A good strong Province" with a diversity of resources.[10]

Late in December, 1896, the new Liberal Minister of the Interior, Clifford Sifton, announced his support for responsible government. The legislation which he introduced in 1897 provided for the establishment on October 1, 1897, of "The Executive Council of the Territories" whose members were to be chosen by the Lieutenant Governor—it being understood that their status and tenure of office would conform to the well-understood principles of responsible government. "The Bill", he said "will give the people of the Territories a government which shall not have the full powers of the provincial government, but insofar as they have power to deal with subjects, they shall do it the same way as other provinces. They will have Ministers who are responsible to the Legislature, and the rules and precedents that apply to the Provincial governments will apply to the government of the Territories."[11]

As soon as the Act came into force the Lieutenant-Governor called on Haultain to form a government. Haultain was unyielding in his opposition to the introduction of party politics in the territorial Assembly.[12] Although himself a Conservative in federal politics, his Cabinet included men who were both Liberals and Conservatives, the notable Liberals being J.H. Ross and G.V.W. Bulyea. In Haultain's view, eastern political loyalties and principles were irrelevant to the concerns of the Assembly in coping with the unique conditions of an area which was evolving so rapidly. Moreover, the Assembly should present a united front in its relations with Ottawa.

The other provisions of the Act of 1897 and the financial arrangements of that year did not meet the Assembly's request. The extensions of legislative authority, particularly the power to borrow money on the public credit, were denied, except in some minor respects. The proposal for a federal annual subsidy was also denied. Haultain commented:

> Constitutionally we have approached close to provincial basis but financially we are a long distance from that basis . . . if the arbitrary amounts voted by Parliament are to be based not upon present requirements but upon the worn out estimates of earlier requirements then [we] will go in for full provincial establishment in order to get financial recognition.[13]

It was a comment that gave clear warning that not all territorial grievances had been removed and hinted at a factor which would play a major role in moving Haultain to support Provincial Autonomy. This legislation for the Territories was given Royal assent on June 29, 1897.[14]

In the years following 1897 the Territorial population rose sharply as a result of federal immigration policy administered by Clifford Sifton. The annual number of homestead entries increased from 2,384 in 1897 to 8,167 in 1901. The census of 1901 indicated a total population of 165,555. Five years later it was 417,956. The sums expended by the Territorial government for roads, bridges, and school district grants, produced a precarious budget, since federal annual grants always were less than territorial requirements. Recollecting those years, Haultain commented that "The immigrant was a distinct asset to the Dominion and, at that time, a distinct liability to the Territories, with their increased need for local improvements".

Haultain and his Cabinet were not without their critics, although there were no party lines in the Assembly. This nonpartisan principle was embodied in Haultain's choice of cabinet ministers who were both Liberal and Conservative in Federal politics.[15] Haultain's chief critic was R.B. Bennett, the member for Calgary West, first elected in 1898. During the debates in the Assembly, Bennett was critical of various actions of the local administration. He was motivated by personal rivalry with Haultain; they disagreed on the principle of non-partisanship in the Assembly and on the question of creating a western province, whose capital would be Calgary. Although not officially the leader of the opposition, Bennett was, except for Haultain, by far the ablest member of the Assembly.

The combination of growing financial pressures and an increasingly effective opposition led Haultain to follow the implication of his statement of 1897 through to its logical conclusion. On May 2, 1900, on Haultain's initiative, the Legislative Assembly approved a memorial to the federal government which began by reciting the constitutional progress of the Territories and lamenting the "intermittent and insufficient addition to the annual grant, the provision so made by the Parliament of Canada never bearing any adequate provision to the financial obligations" which the government of the Territories incurred. The memorial concluded with the request that enquiries "be made and accounts taken with a view to the settlement of the terms and conditions upon which the Territories or any part thereof shall be established as a Province. . . ."[16] The Federal response to the memorial was a routine acknowledgement sent two months later by the Acting Under Secretary of State indicating that "the matter shall receive attention." During the budget debate of 1900 Haultain delivered a speech which was the longest and most brilliant of his entire career. Among other points which he advanced was the following:

> They had been accorded very largely the duties of a province. The part given was of more importance than the part withheld. They had arrived at a time when something more was necessary, some larger power given, and then left to work out their own salvation. . . . They were driven and driven by necessity, both by their financial conditions and constitutional position, to consider the assumption of provincial institutions.[17]

On January 30, 1901, Haultain wrote to Sifton in even stronger terms than those of the Assembly Memorial of the previous year:

> While financial embarrassments rather than constitutional aspirations have led the North-West Government and

> Legislature to discuss the provincial status I think that
> sufficient practical reasons can be given for the early estab-
> lishment of provincial institutions in the West.[18]

Sifton responded on March 21, 1901, with the following
conciliatory reply:

> Without at the present moment committing myself to any
> positive statement I am prepared to say that the time has
> arrived when the question of organising the Territories on
> the Provincial basis ought to be the subject of full con-
> sideration. It would appear to me that the better way of
> bringing the matter to a more definite position would be
> to arrange for a conference upon the subject between the
> representatives of your Government and a committee of
> Council representing the Federal Government. I shall be
> pleased to bring about arrangements for such a conference
> at any time that is mutually convenient.[19]

The Conference to which Sifton had alluded was held on
October 25, 1901. Haultain and A.L. Sifton represented the
Territorial government and the Federal Cabinet Committee
included Laurier, Cartwright, Clifford Sifton, W.S. Fielding,
J.I. Tarte and Senator R.W. Scott. Haultain repeated his arguments for provincehood, in view of the financial problems
which the territorial government was facing. The federal representatives argued that it would be premature to grant provincial status at this time. Laurier invited the delegation to submit
their case in writing, so that it could be considered by the whole
Cabinet.

After his return to Regina Haultain wrote a long and
cogently argued letter to Laurier on December 7, 1901,[20] in
which he pointed out that he was submitting on behalf of his
Government a "statement of the present position as it appears
to us, together with such remarks as seem to be necessary to
properly set forth the reasons which led the Assembly to request
that enquiries be made and accounts be taken with a view to the
establishment of provincial institutions within that portion of
the North-West Territories lying between the Provinces of
Manitoba and British Columbia. . . . Put in the briefest possible form the position is simply this: The population of the
Territories has been and is increasing so rapidly as the result of
efforts put forth by the Immigration Branch of the Interior
Department that the means at the command of the Territorial

Government are far from being sufficient to enable it to properly administer the affairs of the country. The increase in the population has increased our work and expenditures by a rate far greater than can be measured by the mere increase in the number of the people. . . ."

Haultain proceeded to point out the comparable financial position of the original provinces at Confederation:

> After all is done and said the real and most successful immigration agent is the contented settler, and a heavy rate of taxation, no matter how necessary, is not calculated to satisfy the man who is struggling to make a home in this undeveloped country. Then again, to require the people of the Territories to carry on the work of opening up and developing the country would not be to treat the early settlers in the North-West in the manner in which the people of the older Provinces have been treated.

His government, Haultain continued, sought provincial status on the basis of the British North America Act. In response to the discussions at the conference in Ottawa the previous October he submitted a draft bill embodying the views of the Executive Council of the Territories. This consisted of 24 sections, each section being accompanied by an explanatory memorandum. Section one of the bill defined the area of the proposed province (unnamed) as comprising all of the provisional districts lying south of the 57th parallel of latitude. With regard to the section of the bill relating to the claim for ownership and control of the natural resources, Haultain's memorandum asserted:

> As Great Britain has divested herself, for the benefit of her Colonies, of all her proprietary rights in the public domain within those Colonies, so, it is thought, Canada should do with respect to any claim that may be preferred on behalf of the Dominion to the beneficiary interest in the public domain within that part of the North-West Territories to be included in any Province to be established.[21]

There was no section in the draft bill relating specifically to education. The only protection for the rights of a minority would, in Haultain's view, be provided by section 93 of the British North America Act. This was a questionable protection in view of Haultain's stand that the Territories had become part of Canada in 1870 when no school legislation existed for the area. "[he] would work," he had declared in 1891, "and vote against it [the separate school system] as hard as he could". This view, reinforced by his anti-Catholic and anti-French prejudices derived from his Ontario, Protestant background, inevitably created fear for the security of the existing separate school system in the minds of Roman Catholics as the time for provincial autonomy drew nearer.

At the Parliamentary session earlier in the year the autonomy question was raised for the first time by Walter Scott, the Liberal member for West Assiniboia. His speech was quite long and borrowed from Haultain's observations in the Assembly and elsewhere. He argued that the present was an opportune time to begin negotiations, quoting from Sifton's letter to Haultain during the previous year. He noted that in his view there should be only one province, and that it should possess its natural resources.

Meanwhile, an agitation developed in Manitoba for the westward extension of its borders, leaving one new province between it and British Columbia. This proposal was overwhelmingly rejected by the territorial legislature in May.

The territorial press began to discuss the autonomy issue, and this provoked reaction among some members of the Assembly. The member for St. Albert declared for two provinces which, he pointed out, was favored by the six members from the District of Saskatchewan, and the Edmonton Board of Trade. On November 2, T.O. Davis, Liberal member of Parliament for Saskatchewan, stated that he favored two provinces, one bounded by the southern boundary of the District of Saskatchewan and extending to British Columbia, with Battleford as the capital, and the southern one with Regina as the capital.[22]

The Calgary *Herald* pointed to an issue which was to arise in acute form in 1905:

> It is the opinion of many eminent jurists that if we are granted Provincial status the land of the Province, or Provinces, is our inalienable heritage and, if an attempt should be made to deprive us of it, the Government and people of the Territories should combat the matter to the last ditch.[23]

On March 27, 1902, Haultain received a letter from Sifton containing the following pronouncement:

> It is the view of the Government that it will not be wise at

the present time to pass legislation forming the North-West Territories into a Province or Provinces. Some of the reasons leading to this view may be found in the fact that the population of the Territories is yet sparse; that the rapid increase in population now taking place will in a short time alter the conditions to be dealt with very materially; and that there is a considerable divergence of opinion respecting the question whether there should be one province only or more than one province. Holding this view, therefore, it will not be necessary for me to discuss the details of the draft bill which you presented as embodying your views.[24]

Sifton's blunt refusal came as a shock to an Assembly and populace that had taken earlier correspondence to indicate a positive attitude on the part of the Dominion. It was thus in a tone of surprise and regret that Haultain replied on April 2nd. With regard to the controversy over the number of provinces he wrote:

> With regard to the divergence of opinion as to one or more Provinces, I might say that there is a difficulty which will always exist, and which any postponement of action will not remove.[25]

Sifton's letter arrived while the Assembly was still meeting, which permitted Haultain to reinforce his argument for autonomy by having the Assembly endorse the following resolution:

> Whereas the larger powers and income incidental to the Provincial status are urgently and imperatively required to aid the development of the *Territories* and to meet the pressing necessities of a large and rapidly increasing population:
> BE IT RESOLVED, That this House regrets that the Federal Government has decided not to introduce legislation at the present Session of Parliament with a view to granting provincial institutions to the Territories.[26]

Dr. Patrick of Yorkton, in the District of Assiniboia, and a member of the opposition, moved an amendment advocating two provinces with east-west boundaries at the 57th parallel running from Manitoba to British Columbia for the southern province and at the 60th parallel for the northern boundary of the northern province.[27] He was supported in his two-province argument by Thomas McKay, MLA for Prince Albert, and by R.B. Bennett of Calgary. This amendment, however, was defeated 22 to 7.

In May the Territorial general election was held. Haultain's government "party" elected 24 members; 6 oppositionist and 5 independents were returned. Haultain's election program read in part as follows:

> At the present time the Government of the Territories is engaged in negotiations with the Dominion Government leading to the establishment of a part of the Territories upon the provincial basis. Apart from all other considerations, financial necessity has forced this question to the front. A rapidly increasing population has caused the present revenues of the Territories to become totally inadequate to meet the public demands and in the opinion of the Government the only solution of the difficulties now being met with is to be found in the larger powers and income which go with the Provincial status upon proper terms: . . . Action upon the whole question has been postponed by the Dominion Government principally upon the ground that there is a "divergence of opinion respecting the question whether there should be one Province only or more than one Province"—a question which in the last resort is one for the Dominion Government to settle. The opinion of the Territorial Government is based upon the fact that in the past one Government and one Legislature have found no difficulty in conducting the affairs of the country. . . . There is a widespread and well founded opinion existing throughout Canada against what has been called "over-Government," or "multiplicity of Governments." . . . It [the government] does not consider the question of one or more Provinces to be of paramount importance in view of the magnitude of the other questions involved. They are briefly—
>   (1) Equal rights with all the other Provinces of the Dominion and the same financial consideration that has been given to those Provinces;
>   (2) Control of the public domain in the West, by the West and for the West;
>   (3) Compensation for the alienation of any part of the public domain for purely federal purposes.[28]

Although the school system was not referred to in this platform, it was Haultain who introduced in an otherwise lack-lustre campaign in 1902 the issue of separate schools. He challenged Sifton to state the government's policy in this regard. Sifton did not respond, probably realizing that it was too sensitive an issue to risk public comment.

In the Parliamentary session in the spring of 1902 provincial autonomy was discussed at some length for the first time, when the estimates for the Government of the North-West Territories were under consideration. Walter Scott led off with a long, detail-packed discussion of the financial difficulties of the local government in meeting the requirements of a rapidly growing population. As in his speech the previous year he urged early action on the autonomy issue. Oliver of Alberta, was vigorous in demanding an increased grant, but was silent on the constitutional issue. Rev. J.M. Douglas of Assiniboia East, elected as a Patron of Industry with Liberal support but rapidly moving into the Liberal camp, endorsed the remarks of Sifton and Oliver. "This question of an increased subsidy," he declared, "is a very important one in the estimation of the people generally. We should have either an increased subsidy or provincial autonomy. As far as I have given the matter atten-tion, I think it would be much better for the country, in its exist-ing circumstances, to receive an increased subsidy at present rather than provincial autonomy."[29]

It was the Conservative opposition, which became the champions of autonomy, and henceforth it became a national political issue. "The Government might just as well admit" one opposition member from Manitoba declared, "that the delay is caused by the question of the schools, the question of language, and do not think for a moment that the people in the North-west are not pretty well aware of that. You might just as well face the question now, and the less people you have in the territories the more easily it can be dealt with."[30] Borden, the leader of the opposition, said:

> I do not see that the financial question, or the question of making an arrangement on a per capita basis, if it is an adequate reason now, will not be an adequate reason in the future for preventing these territories from having self-government.[31]

Sifton began his lengthy rebuttal by noting the understandable divergence of opinion among the members from the North-West:

> It does not very often happen that any legislative assembly has to deal with a question involving the constitutional status of a territory such as that which we are now discussing. The committee, perhaps, hardly realizes the fact that we are discussing the questions of the financial and constitutional status of a territory which has almost as much fertile land as the continent of Europe, and which bids fair, under existing circumstances, to be an enormously important factor in the development of the business, not only of Canada, but of the North American continent before very many years pass away.[32]

The whole constitutional discussion was of very recent origin,[33] he claimed, and "There is still some difference of opinion among the people. There is some sentiment in favour of the district [of Assiniboia] being united to the province of Manitoba; but the prevailing sentiment is that it should remain a part of the Northwest Territories. If you go to the district of Saskatchewan, you will find an entirely different sentiment prevailing among the people there. They are not in favour of the territories' being formed into one province, and they are not in a hurry for provincial autonomy; but when it comes they do not want their district to be united with the territory to the south."[34]

At the end of January, 1903, Haultain was again writing Sifton in anticipation of the spring session of Parliament. He reviewed the correspondence which had passed between them and with Sir Wilfrid Laurier since 1900. Continuing, he said:

> ... I have heard and read with great concern your opinion to the effect that it is desirable to postpone action upon the Memorial of the Legislative Assembly of May 2, 1900, and the claims of the Territories founded thereon. The necessities are so urgent and the movement in favour of Provincial Institutions is so unanimous, that I should like, if possible, to convey to your mind an adequate appreciation of the significance of the movement and of the unfortunate effect which its neglect or repression will have upon the North-West.[35]

To demonstrate support of the stand taken by the Assembly and by him, he reproduced his election platform of 1902. The result of the election "has justified my statement that it could only demonstrate and accentuate the fact that there undoubtedly is some divergence of opinion in the Territories upon the one or more Province question. There are probably a few members of the new Legislature who support the view of two Provinces but they are not united as to the manner in which the Territories should be divided . . . an overwhelming majority of the constituencies has pronounced in favour of one Province."[36] He concluded this cogent dispatch as follows:

> In a letter, addressed to you on January 30, 1901, I said "that financial embarrassments rather than constitutional aspirations" led us to request the full Provincial powers. I might now say that we are driven by both reasons. Financial necessities have developed constitutional aspirations, but apart from the purely financial aspect of the case we demand that system of government under which we shall have as full opportunities for the exercise of our citizenship as our fellow citizens in the Province.[37]

In order to give fuller force to these representations, Haultain indicated that his Commissioner of Agriculture and Territorial Secretary, G.H.V. Bulyea, would present his dispatch to him and to Laurier. Bulyea was a Liberal in federal politics, and would, he hoped, receive a sympathetic reception.

On February 3rd the Territorial premier wrote to Laurier contending that in view of the sharp increase in the Territorial population since he had written the Prime Minister on December 7, 1901, that there should be an increase in parliamentary representation (14 instead of the existing 10) and also on the debt allowance for the new province. During the month it became apparent that while the federal government was prepared to discuss financial matters, it would not consider constitutional questions.

Shortly after sending his February letter, Haultain became involved in the proceedings of the first convention of the Conservatives in the Territories. It had long been known that he was a Conservative in federal politics, although firmly committed to opposing the drawing of party lines in the Assembly. The March 25th convention was convened by Borden as a result of representation by prominent Territorial Conservatives. The convention passed a number of resolutions,[38] one of them commending Borden for "his unequivocal support of the Territorial claims to full autonomy." Another resolution favoured "the immediate grant of full Provincial autonomy—including the ownership of public land, mines and minerals and compensation for land alienated for Federal purposes." Another resolution favoured the running of the next Territorial election on party lines. Haultain refused to be bound by this resolution. Despite his opposition to the introduction of party politics in the Legislative Assembly, Haultain was named honorary president of the Association.

The year 1903 saw the emergence of the autonomy issue as the major element in the parliamentary debates of that year, in the correspondence which passed between the Territorial government and Ottawa, and in the newspaper press of the prairies. Following his letter of January 31, 1903, to Sifton, a sub-committee of the Cabinet met with Bulyea and himself in Ottawa, but no decision was communicated to Haultain, with the result that he was placed at a disadvantage in presenting a budget to the Assembly which was to meet on April 6th. At this time Sifton was in London and Haultain was forced to communicate with the Prime Minister "not only for a large increase in our grant for the coming Dominion fiscal year but for a substantial supplementary Vote to meet the actual necessities of the present moment". To sum up he said, "I beg to ask for an early reply to our request: First, for the granting of Provincial Institutions to the Territories; Secondly, for a Vote supplementary to the North-West grant for the current year; and Thirdly, for a largely increased Vote for the year 1903-1904."[39] A reply came from Fielding, the Federal Minister of Finance, promising the supplementary vote and an advance on capital account of up to $500,000 for Public Works, two of them being bridges which the federal government had authorized; but he said nothing about constitutional matters. To this Haultain replied as follows:

> Supplementary vote quite satisfactory if made supplementary to current year. Other propositions absolutely unsatisfactory in method and amount. Conditions here require large increase to annual grant for coming Dominion fiscal year apart from question of capital advance, for which we have made no request. In case capital advance is made unrestricted disposal by local legislature must be allowed, and we should strongly protest against any part of cost of replacing Macleod and Lethbridge bridges, both Federal undertakings, being charged.[40]

While the constitutional issue did not figure in the government's response to Haultain, it did move to increase territorial representation in the House of Commons as part of the Redistribution Act of 1903.[41] The existing territorial population did not justify this move, except, Laurier stated, in the following terms:

> . . . The population of the North-west Territories was 158,940 according to the last census. According to the unit of representation, they are entitled to only six members. But we are not bound by the letter of the constitution so far as representation of the North-West Territories is concerned. Therefore, we propose to give to those Territories a representation in this House of ten members.[42]

The throne speech of the April—June session of the Territorial Assembly urged the claims of the Territories to provincial status. On April 24, 1903, the Assembly unanimously endorsed a memorial to the federal government which reiterated the Territorial claim to provincial powers "upon fair and just terms analogous to those upon which the old Provinces have been dealt with."[43] On June 8, 1903 Laurier wrote to Haultain:

> With regard to your further request that legislation be introduced this session conferring on the Territories full provincial organisation, I have had the honour to discuss the matter with the members of the House of Commons from the Territories. I have asked them to consider whether it would be advisable to have such legislation introduced this year.[44]

To this, Haultain responded a week later:

> With all deference to the opinion expressed by you, I cannot see that the representation proposed to be given to the Territories under the Redistribution Bill could be in any way affected by the passing of concurrent legislation granting the Provincial status to the Territories.[45]

Laurier had written to A.C. Rutherford, a leading Alberta Liberal, stating that the government had made a "very liberal offer to the North-West Territories Government." He regretted that Haultain's answer was so negative and hoped that when the federal terms were communicated to the Assembly "they will be found more than satisfactory by the friends of the Liberal party in that body".[46]

At the October—November session of the Assembly another memorial to Ottawa was endorsed reaffirming the terms of the memorial passed at the spring session. On June 16th Bulyea wrote to Laurier dealing with Liberal prospects in the Territories, which would be influenced by the financial arrangements made with the Territorial government and stated:

> I have had considerable correspondence with the Federal members representing the Territories, who were kind enough to apprize me of the general representations they had made in your Government, and I advised them that I consider that if such were adopted it would reasonably satisfy the general public in the Territories, and would put your candidates and your supporters in the coming election in a position in which they could fight with zeal and, I am pleased to say, with every prospect of success.[47]

T.O. Davis, Liberal MP for Saskatchewan, gave an interview to the correspondent of the Toronto *Globe* on July 10th declaring:

> . . . The question of Provincial autonomy is not troubling the people of the Territories to any great extent. The whole agitation is confined to a small band of politicians who have more to gain than the public by a change in the status of the Territories. He did not see that they had very substantial grievances.[48]

This was a reversal of his earlier stand in favour of two provinces, probably motivated by his perception that the cause of autonomy would be endorsed by the Federal Conservative party.

In July, D.J. Goggin, former Superintendent of Education in Regina, and a hard-nosed proponent of national schools, emphasized in a statement in the Toronto *News* that the niggardly response to Territorial financial claims ignored the real needs of the Territories. The delay in dealing with the constitutional question he described in the following terms:

> There are those who assert that the delay is owing to difficulties anticipated in connection with separate schools and the use of the French language. It is said that the

Legislature will insist upon being left perfectly free to deal
with these as with all other questions of internal administration, though I have not seen any declaration to that
effect by the Premier or the Legislature. It is hinted that
certain powerful political influences, operating outside
the Territories, have made it clear to our rulers at Ottawa
that a guarantee of separate schools and dual language
must be an integral part of any autonomy measure.[49]

James Clinkskill, MLA from Saskatoon, also was reported in
the same paper. He stated that the existing system of separate
schools was working satisfactorily in the view of the laity "but
it was said the Hierarchy wanted a clause in an Act granting
Provincial autonomy which would give them absolute control
over these schools".[50] Later in the year the *News* was told by
G.H.V. Bulyea that the support for autonomy and one
province was overwhelming in the election of 1902.

It was not only the Territorial press which concerned itself
with the autonomy issue. The Toronto *News* was an outspoken
supporter of the immediate grant of autonomy for the Territories, a position endorsed as well by the Winnipeg *Telegram*.
The Liberal press, on the other hand—the Manitoba *Free Press*,
the Ottawa *Free Press*, and the Brantford *Expositor* favoured
delay.[51] On October 31st the *News* claimed that the real reason
for delay was that "the Government dare not act for it fears the
raising of the Separate School issue by the Hierarchy of
Quebec."[52]

The attitude of the national press, coupled with the sympathetic attitude of Borden and other Conservative spokesmen
in the House of Commons the previous year, led the four
members from the Territories, all Liberals, to advocate indefinite postponement of provincial status. Only the two senators
for the Territories, Perley and Lougheed, both Conservatives,
stood firm for autonomy. In the debates in the House of
Commons during the session of 1903 Borden, in a two hour
speech, supported Haultain's arguments as contained in the
letters which he had sent to Ottawa, which had been tabled in
the House. Borden castigated the government for its negative
response and concluded his peroration with the following
words:

The time has arrived when the same power of local self-
government should be granted to the people of the North-
west Territories as that enjoyed by the people of the older

provinces of Canada, and that this government, in com-
pliance with the prayer of the legislature of the North-
West Territories twice repeated, should take immediately,
without any further delay whatever, such steps as may be
necessary to accomplish that purpose, which I believe, to
be not only a wise but a just one.[53]

Borden was followed by Frank Oliver, who refused to vote for
Borden's motion that the autonomy question should be
considered and acted on as promptly as possible. He said that
he would not support the motion for granting provincial institutions to the Territories unless he knew exactly the terms on
which autonomy would be granted. He claimed that the
opposition was attempting to make political capital out of the
issue. Walter Scott also rejected the motion on the ground that
he would not wish the matter to be discussed unless Sifton were
present "for the purpose of guiding the discussion" which was
necessary for the rights of the people of the North-West to be
protected. T.O. Davis of Saskatchewan was more emphatic in
opposing Haultain's ideas, with which, he claimed he had
never agreed. The people in the District of Saskatchewan, he
asserted, were opposed to the grant of provincial autonomy.
Walter Scott, who in previous years had been a spokesman for
autonomy, now reversed his position and urged delay, ration-
alizing it on the grounds that the matter of C.P.R. tax exemptions was now before the courts, and the outcome would affect
the Territorial budget. But he spent most of his time castigat-
ing the opposition, who, he alleged, had made the question a
political issue.

On the same day as his letter to Laurier, the territorial
Premier wrote a long letter to Sifton discussing the income and
grant needs of the territories, concluding as follows: "Under all
circumstances, and in view of the inadequate amount supplied
last year, I feel I am quite within the mark and making a very
modest request when I ask for an increase of $400,000, at least,
for the coming Dominion year."[54]

There was no discussion of autonomy during the parliamentary session of 1904, which met from March to July. No
Constitutional discussion took place between the federal and
territorial government in 1904 until mid April when there was
a meeting between the federal authorities and Haultain,
Bulyea, and J.J. Young, MLA. On April 13, 1904 Haultain was
reported in the Toronto *Star* to the effect that they were "simply
urging the necessity, in our progress for self government

similar to the older provinces".[55] During the spring session of
the Assembly D.H. McDonald, the leader of the opposition,
advocated division of the Territories into two provinces. There
was some variation in the attitude of the Territorial newspapers on the question of the number of provinces. The Lethbridge *News* favoured one province, whereas the Edmonton
Bulletin and most papers in the western part of the Territories
favoured two provinces with a boundary running north and
south. In Prince Albert the *Advocate* and Mr. T.H. McGuire of
that town, and a former territorial judge, favoured three
provinces.[56] The southernmost was to include Assiniboia and
southern Alberta; north of this to the 60th parallel would be
Alberta; Saskatchewan would include the District of Saskatchewan and the eastern part of the District of Athabasca and
extending on the far east to Hudson Bay. Territorial and
Toronto papers also raised the question of separate schools, in
which they detected a conspiracy on the part of the Roman
Catholic church to recognize the principle of separate schools
in the constitution of the new province or provinces.

On June 1 Haultain wrote the strongest letter he had ever
sent to Laurier. He noted that:

> the Members of the Legislative Assembly are closely in
> touch with the people of this country, and they, one and
> all, have repeatedly expressed opinions entirely contrary
> to those which have apparently determined your action on
> this question. Further—and I make this statement advis-
> edly—of the 35 members of the Assembly one-half are well
> known to be in active sympathy with yourself and your
> Government, and these gentlemen are in full accord with
> the other members of the House upon this subject. . . . I
> think it becoming to mention these matters at this time, as
> it seems to me that they are in themselves evidence that the
> advice tendered to you by some of your supporters in
> Parliament from the Territories has not been in accord
> with the desires of the people as they are giving expres-
> sion to them.[57]

He demanded on behalf of the territorial government that
negotiations be opened to settle accounts, and to organize a
province in "that portion of the North-West Territories lying
between the western boundary of Manitoba and the eastern
slope of the Rocky Mountains, and extending northward from
the International boundary and the Northern boundary of

Manitoba as far into the district of Athabasca as may be decided upon."[58] The new province would have, in addition to adequate parliamentary representation, control of the public domain (the natural resources).

This supplemented an earlier and equally combative letter to the Prime Minister on May 19th, in which he had said that if the increase in parliamentary representation for the territories under the Redistribution Act of 1902 "is to be regarded as a set-off to our demand for provincial powers we have not received that representation . . . to which we are entitled."[59] Haultain argued that according to the figure given by the Department of the Interior, the territorial population was about 450,000, which entitled the territories to have 18 members in the House of Commons.

On September 24, 1904, the Territorial Assembly opened with a speech from the Throne containing the following pronouncement: "I have to express the regret of my government that the movement towards the establishment of the territories upon a provincial basis has not been materially forwarded during the past year. All correspondence upon the subject will be submitted to you."[60]

At long last, on September 30th, Haultain received a reply to his letter to Laurier of May 19th. The Prime Minister contested Haultain's arguments and then proceeded as follows:

> You will have learned prior to the receipt of this letter that Parliament has been dissolved. The new House of Commons will contain not four but ten representatives of the North-West Territories who coming fresh from the people will be entitled to speak with confidence as to the views and requirements of those whom they represent. Should my Government be sustained we will be prepared immediately after the election to enter upon negotiations for the purpose of arriving at a settlement of the various questions involved in the granting of provincial autonomy with a view to dealing with the question at the next session of Parliament.[61]

Haultain, who campaigned vigorously against the Liberals in the general election of 1904, criticized Laurier's reply to his letter of May 19th as justifying the attitude which he and Borden had long maintained; he noted that Laurier remained silent on the terms on which provincehood would be based. Borden, he pointed out, had promised control over public lands and other natural resources. The school question, however, was not a public issue in the territories during the campaign.

Haultain must have been keenly disappointed with the results of the election, held on November 3rd. It not only brought defeat for Borden, but only three Conservatives were returned in the 10 seats assigned to the North West.

Late in the year Laurier invited Haultain and Bulyea to a Conference with the federal authorities on the subject of the autonomy acts. On January 5, 1905 the conference began, which lasted until February 4, between Haultain, Bulyea, Laurier, Sir William Mulock, Postmaster General, Charles Fitzpatrick, Minister of Justice, and Senator R.W. Scott. Sifton was absent throughout the conference on account of ill health. During the period of the conferences Laurier corresponded with Sifton, asking for his views on Haultain's claim for the public lands and asking for his advice on the names for the two new provinces. Sifton replied emphasizing the traditional federal government policy of retaining the lands under federal control to insure the continuation of rapid immigration, on which his fame as the Minister of the Interior was based. On the question of names he favoured Alberta for the western province, and Assiniboia for the eastern, although he would not oppose the choice of Saskatchewan. The proceedings of the conference were private and no minutes were kept. Some impression of the conversations are to be found, however, in press reports and in the Laurier papers. It is clear that there was a difference of opinion between the federal and territorial authorities on natural resources, and funds for payment for the resources previously alienated. The territorial government request for the creation of one province was also contentious, since the federal government favoured two. It appears that there was little or no reference to education.

The autonomy bills were introduced by Laurier on February 21, 1905, and the debate on them was one of the longest, if not the longest, to take place in the House of Commons—ten weeks, including 28 days of solid discussion. On the first reading of the bills Laurier gave perhaps the greatest speech of his entire political career. He began with a comparison between the progress of Canada and the United States during the 19th century. With regard to social and constitutional development, he noted that Canada had been "satisfied with slower progress. Our institutions in our new Northwest have been developed by gradual stages so as to insure at all times among these new communities law and order, and the restraints and safeguards of the highest civilization." The time had arrived, he stated, when the final step could be taken "to complete the passage of the Northwest Territories from what was once necessary tutelage into the fullness of the rights which under our constitution appertain to provinces."[62]

Laurier noted that two years previously a request for the immediate grant of provincial status was made in the North-West, but the government had decided that the time was premature. In the devising of provincial institutions four questions were involved: the number of provinces, the ownership of public lands, the financial relations between the provinces and the federal government, and the school system.

With regard to the number of provinces, Laurier described the problem at length. He set forth the various geographical divisions within the Territories, and the agitation for the expansion of the boundaries of Manitoba. He then proceeded to present the argument in favour of two provinces running north and south from the 49th parallel to the 60th parallel of latitude, separated by a purely arbitrary line, the 4th meridian, to be named Saskatchewan and Alberta, comprising 255,000 square miles for Alberta and 251,000 square miles for Saskatchewan.

In the preparation of the bills some difficulty had been encountered on the selection of the capitals of the two provinces. Laurier then said: "As to the capital of the province of Saskatchewan, the difficulty is easily solved, it will be as it is at present, Regina. But as to the capital of Alberta, the selection was not so easy. There were three claimants for it— Calgary, Red Deer and Edmonton, each of which had a good claim. We have decided that we cannot make any final selection, leaving the final selection to the province itself. In the meantime, if you look at the map you will see Edmonton seems to be the most central point, and therefore we propose to make Edmonton the capital for the present."

With regard to the natural resources issue, Laurier began by distinguishing between Saskatchewan and Alberta and the older provinces which had come into Confederation. These, he argued, were crown colonies with their own crown lands departments, whereas the lands in the North-West had been the property of the federal government since 1870. To buttress his argument he used the words of Sir John A. Macdonald in an order-in-council in 1884, which took issue with the claims of the province of Manitoba. The order stated in part:

> The great attraction which the Canadian government now offers, the impression to the mind of man contemplating immigration is that a well-known and recognized government holds unfettered in its own hand the land which it offers free, and that government has its agencies and organizations for directing, receiving, transporting and placing the immigrant upon the homestead which he may select.

Laurier pointed out that provincial control of the resources might produce a variety of policies with regard to the disposal of public land and therefore clash with the federal government's efforts to increase immigration. He admitted that this would deprive the new provinces of an important source of income:

> realizing that fact, it is the duty of parliament to make ample, even generous, provision which will compensate the provinces for the retention of the land by the federal government.

He then proceeded to discuss the financial relations between the federal government and the two new provinces. He summed up the proposals in the following terms. For civil government the $50,000 annually; for the per capita allowance, $200,000 with provision for increase until the population of the province reached 800,000; for debt allowance $405,375; for land compensation for the year 1905 $375,000, for a total of $1,030,375; and $62,500 annually to provide for buildings and public works. Most important of all, there was to be compensation for the absence of control over the public lands of $1,125,000.

Turning to education, Laurier declared that:

> This question is perhaps under existing circumstances the most important of all that we have to deal with.

He then proceeded to describe the history of separate schools in the province of Canada and subsequently the province of Ontario. He dealt at some length with the views of George Brown who, he said, had struggled all his life against the separate school system, but who in the interests of achieving Confederation was prepared to compromise.

He then proceeded to deal with the provision for separate schools in the North-West Territories Act of 1875:

> I am not here to advocate separate schools as an abstract proposition but we have introduced into this bill the two propositions, that the minority shall have the power to establish their own schools and that they shall have the right to share the public monies. It is the law today. It is in accord with the constitution, with the British North America Act.

Laurier then concluded his presentation of the educational section as follows:

> If I were to speak my mind upon separate schools, I would say that I never could understand what objection there could be to a system of schools wherein, after secular matters have been attended to, the tenets of the religion of Christ, even with the divisions which now exist among His followers, are allowed to be taught. We live in a country wherein the seven provinces that constitute our nation either by the will or by the tolerance of the people, in every school christian morals and christian dogmas are taught to the youth of the country.

The key phrase here was "after secular matters have been attended to", implicit in the concept of national schools and also in the Territorial school system of 1905, which conformed to the spirit of national schools, and to the existing system of territorial schools.

The subject of French language rights was not included in the bills, because Laurier had concluded that there was already enough feeling against separate schools which he was determined to defend, and he did not wish to introduce a second contentious issue. Hence the new provinces were not to be bilingual. The section of the bill relating to the school question included the following clause:

> 16. The provisions of section 93 of *The British North America Act*, 1867, shall apply to the said Province as if, at the date upon which this Act comes into force, the territory comprised therein were already a Province, the expression

"the Union" in the said section being taken to mean the said date.

Subsection 2 of this clause re-enacted section 11 of the North-West Territories Act of 1875 relating to education with its provisions for separate schools, thus making it apply to the new provinces. This was coupled with the following third subsection:

> 3. In the appropriation of public moneys by the Legislature in aid of education, and in the distribution of any moneys paid to the Government of the said Province arising from the school fund established by *The Dominion Lands Act*, there shall be no discrimination between the public schools and the separate schools, and such moneys shall be applied to the support of public and separate schools in equitable shares or proportion.[63]

Before the second reading of the autonomy bills, Clifford Sifton resigned from the Laurier ministry on February 27th, in protest against section 16, which he feared would permit the restoration of the Quebec-style system of dual education introduced in the territorial education ordinance of 1884.[64] The key phrase was "in continuance of the principles heretofore sanctioned under the North-West Territories Act", which Sifton feared might permit the restoration of the 1884 ordinance creating a dual system. This fear seems exaggerated, since it assumes that Fitzpatrick, Senator Scott, Henri Bourassa, Laurier, and the Papal delegate to Canada, (Mgr. Sbaretti) the spokesman for the Canadian hierarchy, all believed they could force the provincial legislative assemblies to re-enact the 1884 school law. The inevitable failure of such an effort would force Roman Catholics to rely on federal remedial legislation, or slow moving and uncertain court action. All this would seem to support Laurier's contention that he was simply protecting the rights of the minority which they possessed in 1905. Nevertheless the Liberal members were convinced by Sifton, and a period of intensive intra-party negotiations began, culminating in the submission to the government of a proposed amendment to section 16. Sifton also submitted an amendment on March 11th, which had an effect on the final draft of the new education clause, which Laurier introduced on March 22nd.

On March 15th, during the debate on the estimates in the House of Commons, Borden attacked the government in a lengthy speech objecting to the hasty procedure followed by Laurier in introducing the Bills while Sifton and Fielding were absent from the House. He complained about the "indecent haste" which was involved in the introduction of the Bills, particularly since it was now three weeks since the second reading debate had begun. Laurier in his reply to Borden, noted that the education clause had been considered on February 17, so that Haultain knew in advance about section 16 in the Bill which he had introduced on the 21st. Haultain, he implied, had no reason to complain of the procedures which had been followed. M.S. McCarthy, the Conservative member for Calgary, protested the procedures as well, noting that it was clear that cabinet ministers paid more attention to issues in central Canada than the rights of the people living two or three thousand miles away.

On March 11th, Haultain addressed a long open letter to Laurier outlining his opinion on various aspects of the autonomy bills with which he disagreed, and again complained about Laurier's failure to consult him and Bulyea before the bills were introduced.

Debate on the 2nd reading of the autonomy bill began on March 22nd. Laurier led off with a lengthy defence of the original school clause which included a response to Haultain's open letter. Towards the end of his address, however, he made a startling announcement:

> . . . it has been objected to us that the language used in section 16 was too broad, too vague, and that if it were adopted, it would create trouble and confusion instead of certainty as to the rights of the minority. . . . We therefore thought it was preferable to have the law made absolutely certain and in order to do that we have incorporated the ordinances under which the law as it is today has been established. It may be disappointing to some, but we believe that on the whole it is preferable to have a clear understanding on this subject so that the minority shall have the privilege of exercising control over their schools as they have today, . . .

The amended section embodying this principle appears in the Alberta and Saskatchewan acts. It should be observed that the amendment contained no reference to the North-West Territories Act of 1875—the source of his disagreement with Sifton.

Borden followed Laurier in a long and tedious speech concluding with an amendment:

> Upon the establishing of a province in the Northwest Territories of Canada as proposed by Bill (#69) the legislature of such provinces subject and in accordance with the provisions of the British North America Act 1867 to 1886, is entitled and should enjoy full powers of Provincial self-government including power to exclusively make laws in relation to education.[66]

Borden twitted Laurier for his abandonment of the principle of provincial rights, and made it the basis of Conservative opposition to the substitute amendment. He was most effective in supporting Haultain's contention that the North-West Territories had been admitted to the Union in 1870 and not in 1905. The difference was vital, since in 1870 separate schools did not exist *by law* in the Territories.

It was not until March 24 that Sifton participated in the debate. He began by stating that he was severing his connection with the Liberal party. His resignation from the Cabinet was in protest against the education clause whose terms had not been communicated to him prior to the introduction of the autonomy bills. With regard to the other provisions of the bills, he agreed on the number and size of the provinces, although claiming that there were good reasons for extending their boundaries to the Arctic ocean as soon as possible. Concerning public lands, he also agreed with government policy on the retention by the federal government of the lands to insure an uninterrupted flow of immigration. A mistake in the bill in section 20 conveyed the impression that the provinces, rather than the federal government, were the beneficial owners of the land. There would, Sifton predicted, be continuous claims submitted to parliament in future years. Haultain, he noted, had already made this claim in his open letter to Laurier.

Sifton then turned to the education clause, both the original and the amended versions, embarking first on a long, involved discussion of the original education clause of the North-West Territories Act of 1875 which, he claimed, permitted ecclesiastical control of Roman Catholic school districts. The Territorial ordinance of 1892 which repealed the school ordinance of 1884, and abolished the Board of Education and substituted secular control of education by the Territorial executive, was in defiance of the act of 1875. Then he came to the nub of the matter and the reason for his resignation. Laurier's original clause 16 began by declaring that,

> The provisions of section 93 of the British North America Act, 1867, shall apply to the said province as if, that the date upon which this act comes into force, the territories comprised therein were already a Province, the expression "the Union" in the said section being taken to mean the said date.
>
> Subject to the provisions of the said section 93, and in continuance of the principles heretofore sanctioned under the North-West Territories Act it is enacted that the Legislature of the said Province shall pass all necessary laws with respect to education. . . .

This reference to the *North-West Territories Act*, in Sifton's view, continued the act of 1875 in force, and would permit the re-introduction by the provinces of the dual system of 1884. Such a development may not have been in Laurier's mind:

> My right hon. friend the Prime Minister says it was his intention by the legislation which he proposed, to continue the existing system in the Northwest Territories; and I accept that statement, of course, as expressing his intentions . . . the draughtsman either wholly misunderstood his instructions or he possessed a most remarkable faculty for covering things which were not covered by his instructions.

Sub-section 3 of Laurier's bill was equally objectionable:

> We would earmark that fund for ever, and would compel the legislatures of these provinces to divide that money, and in all probability to constitute one of the greatest endowments of sectarian education that has ever been proposed.[67]

Turning to the amended section 16, he praised it for its clarity and intelligibility. He stressed that the amendment "preserves the right of the Protestant or Roman Catholic minority to have their school, a separate school in name, but a public school in fact, in a separate building if they wish. That is the right it preserves. It preserves, secondly, the right of the

Protestant or Roman Catholic minority in such school to have
religious teaching from 3:30 to 4 o'clock in the afternoon.''[68]

After describing at length his involvement in the Manitoba
school dispute of 1890-1897 he worked up to his concluding
declaration:

> To the extent which is embodied in the proposition before
> this House I am willing to go. I am willing to go that far
> because I believe that the essential principles of a first-
> class, thoroughly national school system are not impaired,
> and the taint of what I call ecclesiasticism in schools, and
> which in my judgment always produces inefficiency, will
> not be found in the school system of the Northwest under
> this legislation, unless the people of the Northwest choose
> to have it, in which case it is their business and not ours . . .
> therefore I have to say, having given the subject the best
> consideration that I am capable of giving it, and having
> given it that consideration not only from the standpoint of
> the position of affairs in this parliament but from the
> standpoint of the position of affairs in the Northwest
> Territories in time to come, that I can, though not with
> very much enthusiasm, and with some degree of reluctance,
> give my support to the Bill.[69]

It is obvious that the protestant furor against separate
schools in 1905 expressed in the eastern Canadian English
speaking press and the pronouncements in numerous branches
of the Orange Lodge, of the Protestant clergy and church
bodies, was politically inspired. None of the protesting bodies
had previously evinced an interest in the territorial school
system originally established in 1884.

Walter Scott's speech on March 31st on the autonomy bill
was long and eloquent. He discounted Haultain's claim that he
had not been consulted on the education clause:

> Mr. Haultain came here just after New Year's and was here
> almost continually until the 21st of February when this
> measure was brought down. There were consultations
> going on nearly every day. If there were no discussions
> between the members of the Government and the repre-
> sentatives of the North-West Territories with regard to
> Education whose was the fault? Was there any prohibition
> resting on Mr. Haultain against bringing the matter of

Education into the conference? I will point out to you a little later, Mr. Speaker, that in not bringing up the matter of Education Mr. Haultain was doing exactly what he had been doing in the North-West Territories. For years he had been discussing this Autonomy matter, and yet until the time of the general election last October you will fail to find any reference he ever made in any discussion to the subject of Education.[70]

Unlike most of the participants in the debate, Scott dealt at some length with the number of provinces and their boundaries. He rejected the one-province argument of Haultain. He himself preferred a division along the eastern boundary of the district of Alberta instead of the 4th meridian, as more equitable, since he argued that Alberta had a large arable area in the north, unlike Saskatchewan. Turning to other questions he endorsed the proposal for representation in the House of Commons and Senate. He also approved the federal financial commitments to the new provinces, elaborating on the details of the revenues and expenditures. On the question of federal retention of control of public lands, he thought the government had devised a generous method of compensating the provinces for the deprivation of potential revenue.

Turning to the educational clause he lamented the "totally disproportionate amount of attention . . . given to what is only a phase of the educational matter"[71] But since the matter had been raised in such a contentious form, he felt obligated to discuss it, which he did at some length with numerous quotations from newspaper editorials and speeches by Conservative politicians. For his own part, he endorsed the amended clause. He concluded his speech on the following eloquent note:

> I repeat, in conclusion, that I am satisfied with the propositions contained in these Bills and that they are the most important that ever have been presented to this parliament nobody disputes. I am satisfied that they will result not only in the immediate future, but in the intermediate future as well as in the far future, in the existence of two provinces in no sense inferior to, in every way equal with, their sister provinces—enjoying absolute religious equality, full provincial rights, an efficient free, public or common, non-sectarian school system controlled by the state and on a plan guaranteeing the perfect autonomy of every conscience and scruple—in a word, enjoying freedom

in every reasonable and British sense of the term;—and that the provisions of these Bills will enable the people of these new provinces to carry on their great work and fulfil the duties that fall upon them as self-governing provinces in this Dominion with every measure of success.[72]

Other features of the autonomy bills caused relatively little comment, despite their importance. There was some discussion of the merits of the 4th meridian as the boundary line. Ranching spokesmen in southeast Alberta argued that the dividing line should be 75 miles farther east to unify the region occupied by that industry. The government's policy on public (Crown) lands has already been noted. It was Borden who took up the issue—a much more important question for the future development in the provinces than the school question. Public lands included not only the surface resources (soil and forest), but also all sub-surface coal and minerals. All the other provinces—except Manitoba—possessed their Crown land before Confederation, and this arrangement was sanctioned by section 109 of the British North America Act. Borden argued strongly for provincial control on several occasions, notably when the bills were introduced and during the third reading debate. Yet it is surprising that few other Conservative members took up the issue. Walter Scott, speaking as a Liberal, defended the bill because of the financial terms for the withholding of control of the lands. An acrimonious discussion took place on the constituency boundaries for the first election. The Conservatives claimed that the seats were gerrymandered to favour the Liberals. The bill provided for an equal division of the assets and liabilities of the Territories between the two provinces. The debate on second reading lasted until May 3rd, when Borden's amendment was defeated by a vote of 59 to 140, one of the largest majorities on record. The vote on second reading on the same day, 140 to 59, split the Conservative party, 13 supporting the government.

The debate dragged on interminably for the next two months, until the bill was passed on third reading on July 6th. There had been 17 amendments by private members and 4 by Borden, all of them defeated by large majorities. The length of the debate postponed the inauguration of the provinces from July 1st to September 1st.

With the passage of the Autonomy Bill on July 6, the way was clear for the appointment, in effect by the Prime Minister, of Lieutenant-Governors for the two provinces to be formally inaugurated on September 1. These appointments were crucial, for it would be the responsibility of the Lieutenant-Governor to choose the provincial premiers who would create and control the machinery of government in the new provinces after their inauguration, at least until the first meeting of the new legislatures.

It was assumed[73] that A.E. Forget, Lieutenant-Governor of the Territories since 1898, would continue his office in one of the provinces. This left Laurier some room for manoeuvre. Many territorial politicians had identified themselves with federal Liberalism, though for local purposes they had been more or less content to work in the non-partisan framework dominated by Haultain. They were naturally concerned to make provision for their future and their concern is reflected in their correspondence.[74]

Laurier's most difficult decisions hinged on the future of Haultain himself. As territorial premier he had led the struggle for autonomy and autonomy could be regarded in large measure as his achievement. Yet Haultain, as the advocate of a single province and of the maintenance of provincial rights in the critical fields of education and resources, was severely critical of Laurier's federal legislation. He had waged his battle for autonomy on non-partisan lines but, in federal politics, he had increasingly identified himself as a Conservative. He had a useful foothold in both provinces, for he had begun his political career in southern Alberta, a region that had Conservative proclivities. As premier of either province he would at best maintain his non-partisan position, at worst use his unquestioned powers and prestige as a declared Conservative. Neither prospect was attractive to those Liberals determined to maintain their party strength in the prairie west. Haultain's participation on behalf of the Conservatives in the Ontario bye-elections of June, 1905 was probably decisive in resolving Laurier's hesitations. The Prime Minister finally decided that Haultain must be excluded. On July 25, 1905, he invited G.H.V. Bulyea, a committed Liberal, to accept office as Lieutenant-Governor of Alberta.[75] It was taken for granted that Forget would continue at Regina as Lieutenant-Governor of Saskatchewan.[76] Neither was expected to summon Haultain to form a provincial government.

Haultain's political future was not the only imponderable with which the jugglers of political advantage had to cope. Among the Alberta politicians none had a better claim to an invitation to form a Liberal cabinet than Frank Oliver, the pioneer Edmonton journalist who was now an Alberta Member of Parliament. Oliver, however, had another goal in view. The resignation of Clifford Sifton as Minister of the Interior, a post of particular significance for the west because of its administration of natural resources, overcame any populist scruples Oliver might have had, and his appointment to the vacated ministry was announced on April 8.[77]

After Oliver the strongest claim as a Liberal premier was Peter Talbot's, but as early as May 29, 1905, he had made it clear that he would prefer the comforts of the Senate or, if the worst came to the worst, the office of Sheriff at Red Deer, convenient to his farm home near Lacombe.[78] None of the influential southern Alberta Liberals, C.A. Stuart, Arthur L. Sifton, Clifford's older brother, or D.L. Scott, seems to have been a serious contender, and Dr. L.G. De Veber of Lethbridge was perhaps the only one to take his own prospects seriously.[79] Sifton and Scott, of course, were already on the Territorial bench. Oliver and Talbot both supported the choice of Alexander Cameron Rutherford, a popular Edmonton lawyer with experience as a member of the Territorial Assembly. On August 13 the Liberal convention at Calgary chose him their leader, and on September 2 Bulyea named him as premier.[80] By that time Haultain had committed himself to Saskatchewan and a non-partisan defence of provincial rights.

Though Laurier had kept his Alberta friends on tenterhooks until nearly the end of July, both Liberals and Conservatives had begun to organize on the assumption that the election scheduled for November 9 would be fought on conventional party lines. The modest splendours of the inauguration ceremonies on September 1 were barely concluded when Lieutenant-Governor Bulyea announced that he had called upon Rutherford to form a government and on September 9 his new cabinet was gazetted.[81] Rutherford was Minister of Education and Provincial Treasurer as well as premier. The Attorney-General was Charles Wilson Cross, a youthful, vigorous and popular Edmonton lawyer, whose influence in Edmonton Liberalism was second only to that of Frank Oliver. William Henry Cushing, Minister of Public Works, was a substantial Calgary businessman. William Thomas Finlay, Minister of Agriculture and Provincial Secretary, an Ulsterman who had settled at Medicine Hat, where he had served as Mayor, had also been a member of the territorial assembly. So had Leverett George De Veber, Minister without Portfolio, who was born in New Brunswick in 1849 and had served in the Mounted Police and practised medicine at Macleod and Lethbridge. De Veber went to the coveted seat in the Senate on March 8, 1906.

Small though his cabinet was, Rutherford had managed to produce a reasonably balanced representation of its centres of population. It also represented the most influential elements in an Alberta which by 1905 was launched on a period of rapid growth. All its members belonged to the business and professional classes, though Finlay had an interest in the Medicine Hat Ranching Company. All had some attachment to churches in the main stream of Canadian Protestantism, though the Anglican De Veber had married a Roman Catholic. Rutherford was a McGill graduate, Cross a graduate of the University of Toronto and De Veber had studied at King's College, Windsor, Nova Scotia, Harvard, St. Bartholomew's Hospital in London and at the University of Pennsylvania. Except for Finlay, the Ulsterman, all had come to the west from the older provinces to the east of the Great Lakes.

Both the traditional Canadian parties had held conventions and issued platforms before the province was formally inaugurated, the Liberals at Calgary on August 13, the Conservatives at Red Deer on August 16. The Liberals, having elected Rutherford President on the understanding that this implied his leadership and his endorsement as prospective premier, produced a platform[82] that essentially supported the federal legislation on which autonomy was to be based. Its references to "the principle of Provincial rights" and the maintenance of "an efficient system of common schools" were discreet enough to cause minimal embarrassment to Laurier's government at Ottawa.

The Conservatives could afford to be more intransigent and "emphatically" protested "against our natural resources being unjustly withheld from us and exploited by any political party at Ottawa." They demanded the surrender to Alberta of "the public domain of which it has been 'unfairly and unjustly' deprived" and compensation for lands already alienated "for purely Federal purposes."[83] They declared for public ownership of public utilities, where the Liberals asserted only that "the desirability of retaining or acquiring control of all provincial franchises should be kept steadily in view." In spite of demands in some Conservative quarters for the abolition of separate schools, and the importance which this issue assumed in Saskatchewan, no direct reference to the controversy over the educational clauses in the autonomy legislation appeared in the platform.

At the same convention at which they adopted this platform the Conservatives had elected as their provincial leader Richard Bedford Bennett. A Calgary lawyer, and an associate of Senator James Lougheed, the leading Alberta Conservative, Bennett had served in the territorial assembly from 1898 to 1905 except for an interval in 1900 when he ran unsuccessfully for Parliament. His association with the Canadian Pacific Railway was a central issue in the campaign.[84]

The campaign of 1905 indeed turned largely upon personalities. Obviously neither party could run upon its record in provincial administration. Both promised much the same things in their platforms. Though the Conservatives were more critical of the autonomy legislation, autonomy was an accomplished fact. "The issue in the election thus tended to resolve itself into a question, not of measures, but of men. Could Rutherford and his government carry out their promises more effectively than Bennett and the Conservatives?"[85]

Narrow regional and local interest, though very much in the minds of both the electors and the candidates, obviously had to be glossed over in the party interest. Neither party could possibly commit itself in its platform on such a matter as the location of the capital, only provisionally set at Edmonton. It could be assumed that any successful candidate in Edmonton or Calgary would press for a permanent location in his own city. A similar assumption could be made by the voters in or near other claimants to consideration, whether in Red Deer, Banff or Vegreville. Rational judgement demanded consideration here of the candidate's potential influence in the legislature, only partially a matter of his party label.

In the election of November 19, 1905, the Liberals won an overwhelming victory, carrying all but two of the twenty-five seats. Bennett was narrowly defeated by Cushing in Calgary. Liberal majorities were larger in the north than in the south, where more votes were cast against the government candidates than for them, owing to the presence of a number of Independent, Socialist and Labour contenders. The vote in the constituencies south of, and including, Red Deer was substantially higher than in those of the north.

The outcome of the election suggested that any dissatisfaction with the autonomy legislation was far outweighed by Liberal control over the machinery of government, federal as well as provincial. In Edmonton, a Conservative candidate, who had campaigned largely on the separate schools issue, lost his deposit. Conservatives attributed such defeats to the votes of

Roman Catholics and new settlers of non-Anglo-Saxon origin, whom they saw as the captives of a Liberal party dependent on Quebec and the immigrant vote. This diagnosis suggests that the Conservatives were not only disorganized but were still caught up in a mythology of politics borrowed from the Canadian past. Many Alberta voters in 1905 had only the most tenuous connection with that past, for Alberta was changing rapidly. The comfortable dependency of the southern Alberta rancher on his good connections with Ottawa had given way to a much more complicated relationship with central Canada, based for the moment on the development of cereal agriculture. To Alberta farmers and businessmen the Liberals, with their aggressive railway and immigration policies, and their relative openness to proposals for change in such matters of economic importance as the tariff, seemed much more in tune with the times than the Conservatives they identified with the old order of privilege for powerful interests like the ranching companies and the Canadian Pacific. In 1905 Albertans were caught up in headlong development, a development with which Laurier and the Liberals appeared to identify. Alberta voters were prepared to forgive any temporary restrictions on provincial control of education and natural resources the federal legislation imposed. Alberta perceived itself as part of the west that was supplying the thrust behind the dynamic growth of Canada in the new century. The Liberals, under Laurier at Ottawa or Rutherford in Alberta, were the party that the majority of Alberta voters saw as most likely to promote, or least likely to impede, the movement of the last best west into the full enjoyment of its rich heritage.

The first meeting of the legislature did not open until March 15, 1906. Meanwhile Rutherford and his cabinet had time to carry on with the establishment of governmental machinery begun well before the election. The basis was, of course, the territorial civil service. Similarly in the new legislature there was a basis of past experience, much of it in the territorial assembly, though the Clerk of the House could boast a more exotic background as a former member of the Isle of Man's House of Keys.[86] It was a youthful legislature, the average age near forty-five, lawyers and the Ontario born were prominent on its membership, agriculture and small business were well represented. Most of the members were, by the standards of their various constituencies, prominent and successful citizens, men whose abilities had enabled them to take full advantage of the opportunities offered by an Alberta well launched upon a period of rapid development.

By the time the first legislature was dissolved early in the spring of 1909, it had adapted the territorial legal and educational structures to the needs of the new province. It had carried out, again building upon the territorial foundation, an extensive programme of public works, including the acquisition and development of a government owned telephone system. It had settled the capital at Edmonton and created the legislative basis for a provincial university at Strathcona, Edmonton's rival city across the North Saskatchewan. Though the capital and university decisions gave great offence to Calgary, the Liberal majority remained undivided and, in successive bye-elections, the Conservatives offered no effective challenge. The Liberals were less successful in coping with labour problems, especially in the troubled coal fields, and, in a bye-election at Lethbridge in 1909, a labour candidate, Donald McNabb, was elected by acclamation.[87]

In its last session early in 1909, the legislature adopted the government's ambitious scheme of guarantees for railway lines, to be built, not only by established companies like the Canadian Northern and the Grand Trunk Pacific, but by a new company, the Alberta and Great Waterways. On this policy and on its record of achievement the Rutherford government appealed to the province for its support in the election of March 22, 1909. It was again overwhelmingly sustained but the name of the Alberta and Great Waterways railway was to echo through the politics of Alberta even after the crushing defeat of the Liberals in the Alberta election of 1921.

Looking back at the sequence of events which culminated in the emergence of the province of Alberta in 1905, one is impressed by the fact that they were organically related to a much more remote past than the early years of the new century. This is clearly evident in the collection of documents which follow. Evident too is the fact that the autonomy movement involved some of the most persistent issues of our national political life.

Finally, the actors in this historical drama included most of the leading statesmen of the day, on both the national and local levels. And, as is invariably the case, their responses were not always rational and betray misunderstandings, frustrations, mistakes, and inadequacies. But there is no doubt that the final result was a noteworthy example of collaborative statesmanship, set in a tradition created by earlier administrations, and pragmatically modified by the actors on a later stage.

FOOTNOTES TO INTRODUCTION

(The numbers in parentheses which appear at the end of some of the footnotes refer to documents included in this volume.)

1. See Lewis H. Thomas, *The North-West Territories 1870-1905.* C.H.A. Booklet No. 26, (Ottawa, 1870), 17-18.
2. See Department of the Interior file No. 37906 P.A.C., and Order-in-Council, May 8, 1882. (I-11, I-12)
3. *House of Commons Debates* (hereinafter referred to as *Commons Debates*), 1882, 1567-68.
4. See Lewis H. Thomas, *The Struggle for Responsible Government in the North-West Territories, 1870-97.* (Toronto, 1956), chaps. 7 and 8.
5. See the Regina *Leader*, Mar. 15, 1887 and July 22, 1897, and Prince Albert *Times*, Nov. 19, 1886 and Apr. 1, 1887.
6. *Journals of the Legislative Assembly of the North-West Territories, 1891-92*, 35, 61-65.
7. Calgary *Herald*, May 3, 1902, cited in *Canadian Annual Review*, (hereinafter cited as *C.A.R.*), 1902, 71.
8. *Journals of the 2nd Session of the Legislative Assembly of the North-West Territories 1896*, 68.
9. See Thomas, *op. cit.*, 256-58. (II-11)
10. *Ibid.*, 258.
11. *Commons Debates*, 1897, cols. 2797, 4115. (I-21)
12. *C.A.R.* 1902, 6970.
13. Regina *Leader*, Dec. 9, 1897. (II-24)
14. 60-61 Vict., c. 28. (I-22)
15. See C.C. Lingard, *Territorial Government in Canada: The Autonomy Question in the Old North-West Territories* (Toronto, 1946), 119-20.
16. E.H. Oliver, *The Canadian North-West. Its Early Development and Legislative Records.* Hereinafter cited as Oliver, (Ottawa, 1915), Vol. II, 1157. (II-31)
17. Regina *Leader*, May 17, 1900. (I-30)
18. Oliver, *op. cit.*, 1158-59 (III-I)
19. *Ibid*, 1160. (III-2)
20. *Ibid*, 1163-95. (III-7)
21. *Ibid*, 1884. (III-7)
22. *C.A.R.*, 1901, 485. (III-9)
23. *Ibid*, 484.
24. Oliver, *op. cit.*, 1202. (III-14)
25. *Ibid*, 1204. (III-15)
26. North-West Territories, *Journals of the Legislative Assembly*, 1902, 18. (III-17)
27. See *Ibid*, 19.
28. Quoted in Haultain to Sifton, Jan. 31, 1903, Oliver, *op. cit.*, 1208-09. (IV-5)
29. *Commons Debates*, 1902, col. 3074.
30. *Ibid*, col. 3085.
31. *Ibid*, col. 3113. (III-18)
32. *Ibid*, col. 3098. (III-18)
33. *Ibid*, col. 3101. (III-18)
34. *Ibid*, col. 3104.
35. Haultain to Sifton, Jan. 31, 1903, Oliver, *op. cit.*, 1206. (IV-5)

36. *Ibid*, 1210. (IV-5)
37. *Ibid*, 1211. (IV-5)
38. *C.A.R.*, 1903, 196-97. (IV-6)
39. See Oliver, *op. cit.*, 1218. (IV-11)
40. *Ibid*, 1219. (IV-13)
41. 3 Edward VII, Chap. 60.
42. *Commons Debates*, 1903, col. 774.
43. North-West Territories, *Journals of the Legislative Assembly*, 1903. (IV-10)
44. Oliver, *op. cit.*, 1224-25. (IV-20)
45. *Ibid*, 1225. (IV-21)
46. Laurier to Rutherford, May 28, 1903, Rutherford Papers, University of Alberta Archives. (IV-15)
47. *C.A.R.*, 1903, 202. (IV-18)
48. *Ibid*. (IV-18)
49. Toronto *News*, July 13, 1903, in *C.A.R.*—1903, 203.
50. *Ibid*.
51. *Ibid*, 203-04.
52. *Ibid*, 205.
53. *Commons Debates*, 1903, col. 13, 883. (IV-24)
54. Oliver, *op. cit.*, 1240.
55. *C.A.R.*, 1904, 343.
56. Letter dated Dec. 26, 1904, published in the Toronto *Globe*, Jan. 3, 1905.
57. Oliver, *op. cit.*, 1235. (IV-31)
58. *Ibid*.
59. *Ibid*, 1237. (IV-30)
60. North-West Territories, *Journals of the Legislative Assembly*, 1904, 8.
61. Oliver, *op. cit.*, 1243. (IV-34)
62. *Commons Debates*, 1905, 1422. The subsequent quotations from Laurier's speech introducing the bills will be found in cols. 1423 to 1459. (V-18)
63. A copy of the original school clause will be found in the Laurier Papers, P.A.C. (V-20)
64. See D.J. Hall, "A Divergence of Principle: Clifford Sifton, Sir Wilfrid Laurier and the North-West Autonomy Bills, 1905," *Laurentian University Review*, Vol. 7, No. 1 (November 1974), 3-24. (V-24, V-25)
65. *Commons Debates*, 1905, col. 2925. (V-36)
66. *Ibid*, col. 2979. (V-37)
67. *Ibid*, col. 3106. (V-38)
68. *Ibid*, col. 3107. (V-38)
69. *Ibid*, col. 3120. (V-38)
70. *Ibid*, col. 3622-23.
71. *Ibid*, col. 3610.
72. *Ibid*, col. 3647.
73. L.G. Thomas, *The Liberal Party in Alberta: A History of Politics in the Province of Alberta, 1905-1921*. Toronto, University of Toronto Press, 1959, 17.
74. See Section VI, documents number 11 to 23.
75. Laurier Papers, Laurier to Bulyea, July 25, 1905, 100389-91. (VI-18)
76. J.W.C. Brennan, *A Political History of Saskatchewan, 1905-1929* Unpublished Ph.D. thesis, University of Alberta, 1976, 50.
77. L.G. Thomas, *Liberal Party*, 15-16. (V-42)
78. Rutherford Papers, Talbot to Rutherford, May 29, 1905.

79. L.G. Thomas, *Liberal Party*, 18.
80. *Ibid*, 18-19. (VI-36)
81. *Ibid*, 21-22.
82. Edmonton *Bulletin*, August 5, 1905. (VI-27)
83. *C.A.R.*, 1905, 229-230. (VI-28)
84. L.G. Thomas, *Liberal Party*, 26.
85. *Ibid*, 26.
86. *Ibid*, 34.
87. *Ibid*, 49.

Section I
Early Constitutional Development, 1670-1897

The region of which Alberta would become a part had a long recorded history before the name Alberta was even known. Equally, in the years before the idea of provincial status became a major theme, there was a considerable evolution of the area's constitutional sphere. The first formal government, if it can be termed such, of the region came in 1670 with the granting of the Charter to the Company of Adventurers Trading into Hudson's Bay. This fur trading firm was, for two centuries, the only overarching authority in the region and it was under its auspices that the first exploration by Europeans of the future Province of Alberta took place.

In 1867 the creation of the Dominion of Canada opened the way for the next stage in the region's evolution. In 1870 Rupert's Land and the North West Territory was formally transferred to Canada and what was to become the future province of Alberta was governed under the basic constitution as set out in the Act for the Temporary Government of Rupert's Land and the Manitoba Act designed primarily to create the Province of Manitoba. These Acts and the government they established clearly indicate that initially the Dominion looked to only the most rudimentary form of government for the 'North West Territories'. In fact, the government of the Territories was not even resident in the region, meeting instead in Manitoba. Real power and real services in the Territories remained centred at Ottawa.

The North West, however, was growing through these years of Dominion rule and before long the existing constitution proved inadequate for the proper government of the region. Thus, in 1875, the Territories got its own Act and a resident government. Later years saw the gradual evolution of both the authority and complexity of that government as it kept pace with developing territorial aspirations. By 1888 elected representatives had replaced appointed members and by 1897, after years of disagreement between Ottawa and the Territorial government, full responsible government was accorded to the North West by the new Liberal government under Wilfrid Laurier. In less than three decades the region had evolved from the most rudimentary governmental structure possible to a full fledged parliamentary system with the necessary civil service apparatus to provide effective service within its sphere of responsibility. As several observers pointed out at the time there was only one step left to take and that was to full Provincial Autonomy.

I — 1

THE ROYAL CHARTER INCORPORATING THE HUDSON'S BAY COMPANY, 1670.

CHARLES THE SECOND, by the grace of God King of England, Scotland, France and Ireland, Defender of the Faith, &c., TO ALL to whom these presents shall come, greeting: WHEREAS our dear and entirely beloved Cousin Prince Rupert, Count Palatine of the Rhine, Duke of Bavaria and Cumberland, &c.; Christopher Duke of Albemarle, William Earle of Craven, Henry Lord Arlington, Anthony Lord Ashley, Sir John Robinson, and Sir Robert Vyner, Knights and Baronets; Sir Peter Colleton, Baronet; Sir Edward Hungerford, Knight of the Bath; Sir Paul Neele, Knight; Sir John Griffith and Sir Philip Carteret, Knights; James Hayes, John Kirke, Francis Millington, William Prettyman, John Fenn, Esquires; and John Portman, Citizen and Goldsmith of London; have, at their own great cost and charges, undertaken an expedition for Hudson's Bay, in the north-west part of America, for the discovery of a new passage into the South Sea, and for the finding some trade for furs, minerals and other considerable commodities, and by such their undertaking have already made such discoveries as do encourage them to proceed further in pursuance of their said design, by means whereof there may probably arise very great advantage to us and our kingdom: AND WHEREAS the said Undertakers, for their further encouragement in the said design, have humbly besought us to incorporate them, and grant unto them and their successors the sole trade and commerce of all those seas, straits, bays, rivers, lakes, creeks and sounds, in whatsoever latitude they shall be, that lie within the entrance of the straits, commonly called Hudson's Straits, together with all the lands, countries and territories upon the coasts and confines of the seas, straits, bays, lakes, rivers, creeks and sounds aforesaid, which are not now actually possessed by any of our subjects, or by the subjects of any other Christian Prince or State: NOW KNOW YE, that we, being desirous to promote all endeavours tending to the public good of our people and to encourage the said undertaking, HAVE, of our especial grace, certain knowledge and mere motion, given, granted, ratified and confirmed, and by these presents, for us, our heirs and successors, DO give, grant, ratify and confirm, unto our said Cousin, Prince Rupert, Christopher Duke of Albemarle, William Earle of Craven, Henry Lord

Arlington, Anthony Lord Ashley, Sir John Robinson, Sir Robert Vyner, Sir Peter Colleton, Sir Edward Hungerford, Sir Paul Neele, Sir John Griffith and Sir Philip Carteret, James Hayes, John Kirke, Francis Millington, William Prettyman, John Fenn and John Portman, that they, and such others as shall be admitted into the said society as is hereafter expressed, shall be one body corporate and politic, in deed and in name, by the name of "The Governor and Company of Adventurers of England trading into Hudson's Bay," and them by the name of "The Governor and Company of Adventurers of England trading into Hudson's Bay," one body corporate and politic, in deed and in name, really and fully for ever, for us, our heirs and successors, WE DO make, ordain, constitute, establish, confirm and declare by these presents, and that by the same name of Governor and Company of Adventurers of England trading into Hudson's Bay, they shall have perpetual succession, and that they and their successors, by the name of "The Governor and Company of Adventurers of England trading into Hudson's Bay," be, and at all times hereafter shall be, personable and capable in law to have, purchase, receive, possess, enjoy and retain lands, rents, privileges, liberties, jurisdictions, franchises and hereditaments, of what kind, nature or quality soever they be, to them and their successors; and also to give, grant, demise, alien, assign and dispose lands, tenements and hereditaments, and to do and execute all and singular other things by the same name that to them shall or may appertain to do; and that they and their successors, by the name of "The Governor and Company of Adventurers of England trading into Hudson's Bay," may plead and be impleaded, answer and be answered, defend and be defended, in whatsoever courts and places, before whatsoever judges and justices, and other persons and officers, in all and singular actions, pleas, suits, quarrels, causes and demands whatsoever, of whatsoever kind, nature or sort, in such manner and form as any other our liege people of this our realm of England, being persons able and capable in law, may or can have, purchase, receive, possess, enjoy, retain, give, grant, demise, alien, assign, dispose, plead, defend and be defended, do, permit and execute; and that the said Governor and Company of Adventurers of England trading into Hudson's Bay, and their successors, may have a common seal to serve for all the causes and businesses of them and their successors, and that it shall and may be lawful to the said Governor and Company, and their successors, the same seal, from time to time, at their will and pleasure, to break, change, and to make anew or alter, as to them shall seem expedient: AND FURTHER WE WILL, and by these presents, for us, our heirs and successors, WE DO ordain, that there shall be from henceforth one of the same Company to be elected and appointed in such form as hereafter in these presents is expressed, which shall be called the Governor of the said Company; and that the said Governor and Company shall or may elect seven of their number, in such form as hereafter in these presents is expressed, which shall be called the Committee of the said Company, which Committee of seven, or any three of them, together with the Governor or Deputy Governor of the said Company for the time being, shall have the direction of the voyages of and for the said Company, and the provision of the shipping and merchandizes thereunto belonging, and also the sale of all merchandizes, goods and other things returned, in all or any the voyages or ships of or for the said Company, and the managing and handling of all other business, affairs and things belonging to the said Company: AND WE WILL, ordain and grant by these presents, for us, our heirs and successors, unto the said Governor and Company, and their successors, that they the said Governor and Company, and their successors, shall from henceforth for ever be ruled, ordered and governed according to such manner and form as is hereafter in these presents expressed, and not otherwise; and that they shall have, hold, retain and enjoy the grants, liberties, privileges, jurisdictions and immunities only hereafter in these presents granted and expressed, and no other: And for the better execution of our will and grant in this behalf, WE HAVE ASSIGNED, nominated, constituted and made, and by these presents, for us, our heirs and successors, WE DO ASSIGN, nominate, constitute and make our said Cousin, PRINCE RUPERT, to be the first and present Governor of the said Company, and to continue in the said office from the date of these presents until the 10th November then next following, if he, the said Prince Rupert, shall so long live, and so until a new Governor be chosen by the said Company in form hereafter expressed: AND ALSO WE HAVE assigned, nominated and appointed, and by these presents, for us, our heirs and successors, WE DO assign, nominate and constitute, the said Sir John Robinson, Sir Robert Vyner, Sir Peter Colleton, James Hayes, John Kirke, Francis Millington and John Portman to be the seven first and present Committees of the said Company, from the date of these presents until the said 10th day of November then also next following, and so until new Committees shall be chosen in form hereafter expressed: AND FURTHER

WE WILL and grant by these presents, for us, our heirs and successors, unto the said Governor and Company, and their successors, that it shall and may be lawful to and for the said Governor and Company for the time being, or the greater part of them present at any public assembly, commonly called the Court General, to be holden for the said Company, the Governor of the said Company being always one, from time to time to elect, nominate and appoint one of the said Company to be Deputy to the said Governor, which Deputy shall take a corporal oath, before the Governor and three or more of the Committee of the said Company for the time being, well, truly and faithfully to execute his said office of Deputy to the Governor of the said Company, and after his oath so taken shall and may from time to time, in the absence of the said Governor, exercise and execute the office of Governor of the said Company, in such sort as the said Governor ought to do: AND FURTHER WE WILL and grant by these presents, for us, our heirs and successors, unto the said Governor and Company of Adventurers of England trading into Hudson's Bay, and their successors, that they, or the greater part of them, whereof the Governor for the time being or his Deputy to be one, from time to time, and at all times hereafter, shall and may have authority and power, yearly and every year, between the first and last day of November, to assemble and meet together in some convenient place, to be appointed from time to time by the Governor, or, in his absence by the Deputy of the said Governor for the time being, and that they being so assembled, it shall and may be lawful to and for the said Governor or Deputy of the said Governor, and the said Company for the time being, or the greater part of them which then shall happen to be present, whereof the Governor of the said Company or his Deputy for the time being to be one, to elect and nominate one of the said Company, which shall be Governor of the said Company for one whole year then next following, which person being so elected and nominated to be Governor of the said Company as is aforesaid, before he be admitted to the execution of the said office, shall take a corporal oath before the last Governor, being his predecessor or his Deputy, and any three or more of the Committee of the said Company for the time being, that he shall from time to time well and truly execute the office of Governor of the said Company in all things concerning the same; and that immediately after the same oath so taken, he shall and may execute and use the said office of Governor of the said Company for one whole year from thence next following:

And in like sort we will and grant, that as well every one of the above-named to be of the said Company or Fellowship, as all others hereafter to be admitted or free of the said Company, shall take a corporal oath before the Governor of the said Company or his Deputy for the time being to such effect as by the said Governor and Company, or the greater part of them, in any public court to be held for the said Company, shall be in reasonable and legal manner set down and devised, before they shall be allowed or admitted to trade or traffic as a freeman of the said Company: AND FURTHER WE WILL and grant by these presents, for us, our heirs and successors, unto the said Governor and Company, and their successors, that the said Governor or Deputy Governor, and the rest of the said Company, and their successors for the time being, or the greater part of them, whereof the Governor or Deputy Governor from time to time to be one, shall and may from time to time, and at all times hereafter, have power and authority, yearly and every year, between the first and last day of November, to assemble and meet together in some convenient place, from time to time to be appointed by the said Governor of the said Company, or in his absence by his Deputy; and that they being so assembled, it shall and may be lawful to and for the said Governor or his Deputy, and the Company for the time being, or the greater part of them, which then shall happen to be present, whereof the Governor of the said Company or his Deputy for the time being to be one, to elect and nominate seven of the said Company, which shall be a Committee of the said Company for one whole year from then next ensuing, which persons being so elected and nominated to be a Committee of the said Company as aforesaid, before they be admitted to the execution of their office, shall take a corporal oath before the Governor or his Deputy and any three or more of the said Committee of the said Company, being their last predecessors, that they and every of them shall well and faithfully perform their said office of Committees in all things concerning the same, and that immediately after the said oath so taken, they shall and may execute and use their said office of Committees of the said Company for one whole year from thence next following: AND MOREOVER, our will and pleasure is, and by these presents, for us, our heirs and successors, WE DO GRANT unto the said Governor and Company, and their successors, that when and as often as it shall happen, the Governor or Deputy Governor of the said Company for the time being, at any time within one year after that he shall be nominated, elected or sworn to the office of the Governor of the said Company, as is aforesaid, to die or to be removed from the said office, which Governor or Deputy Governor not demeaning himself well in his said office, WE WILL to be removable at the pleasure of the rest of the said Company, or the greater part of them which shall be present at their public assemblies, commonly called their General Courts holden for the said Company, that then and so often it shall and may be lawful to and for the residue of the said Company for the time being, or the greater part of them, within a convenient time after the death or removing of any such Governor or Deputy Governor, to assemble themselves in such convenient place as they shall think fit, for the election of the Governor or Deputy Governor of the said Company; and that the said Company, or the greater part of them, being then and there present, shall and may, then and there, before their departure from the said place, elect and nominate one other of the said Company to be Governor or Deputy Governor for the said Company, in the place and stead of him that so died or was removed; which person being so elected and nominated to the office of Governor or Deputy Governor of the said Company, shall have and exercise the said office for and during the residue of the said year, taking first a corporal oath, as is aforesaid, for the due execution thereof; and this to be done from time to time so often as the case shall so require: AND ALSO, our will and pleasure is, and by these presents, for us, our heirs and successors, WE DO grant unto the said Governor and Company, that when and as often as it shall happen any person or persons of the Committee of the said Company for the time being, at any time within one year next after that they or any of them shall be nominated, elected and sworn to the office of Committee of the said Company as is aforesaid, to die or to be removed from the said office, which Committees not demeaning themselves well in their said office, we will to be removable at the pleasure of the said Governor and Company, or the greater part of them, whereof the Governor of the said Company for the time being or his Deputy to be one, that then and so often, it shall and may be lawful to and for the said Governor, and the rest of the Company for the time being, or the greater part of them, whereof the Governor for the time being or his Deputy to be one, within convenient time after the death or removing of any of the said Committee, to assemble themselves in such convenient place as is or shall be usual and accustomed for the election of the Governor of the said Company, or where else the Governor of the said Company for the time being or his Deputy shall appoint: And that the said Governor and Company, or the greater part of them, whereof the Governor for the time being or his Deputy to be one, being then and there present, shall and may, then and there, before their departure from the said place, elect and nominate one or more of the said Company to be of the Committee of the said Company in the place and stead of him or them that so died, or were or was so removed, which person or persons so nominated and elected to the office of Committee of the said Company shall have and exercise the said office for and during the residue of the said year, taking first a corporal oath, as is aforesaid, for the due execution thereof, and this to be done from time to time, so often as the case shall require: And to the end the said Governor and Company of Adventurers of England trading into Hudson's Bay may be encouraged to undertake and effectually to prosecute the said design, of our more especial grace, certain knowledge and mere motion, WE HAVE given, granted and confirmed, and by these presents, for us, our heirs and successors, DO give, grant and confirm, unto the said Governor and Company, and their successors, the sole trade and commerce of all those seas, straits, bays, rivers, lakes, creeks, and sounds, in whatsoever latitude they shall be, that lie within the entrance of the straits, commonly called Hudson's Straits, together with all the lands and territories upon the countries, coasts and confines of the seas, bays, lakes, rivers, creeks and sounds aforesaid, that are not already actually possessed by or granted to any of our subjects, or possessed by the subjects of any other Christian Prince or State, with the fishing ,of all sorts of fish, whales, sturgeons, and all other royal fishes in the seas, bays, inlets and rivers within the premises, and the fish therein taken, together with the royalty of the sea upon the coasts within the limits aforesaid, and all mines royal, as well discovered as not discovered, of gold, silver, gems and precious stones, to be found or discovered within the territories, limits and places aforesaid, and that the said land be from henceforth reckoned and reputed as one of our plantations or colonies in America, called "Rupert's Land:" AND FURTHER, WE DO by these presents, for us, our heirs and successors, make, create and constitute the said Governor and Company for the time being, and their successors, the true and absolute lords and proprietors of the same territory, limits and places aforesaid, and of all other the premises, SAVING ALWAYS the faith, allegiance and sovereign dominion due to us, our heirs and successors, for the same, TO HAVE, HOLD, possess and enjoy the said territory, limits and places, and all and singular other the premises hereby granted as aforesaid, with their and every of their rights, members, jurisdictions, prerogatives, royalties and appurtenances whatsoever, to them the said Governor and Company, and their successors for ever, TO BE HOLDEN of us, our heirs and successors, as of our manor of East Greenwich, in our county of Kent, in free and common soccage, and not in capite or by Knight's service; YIELDING AND PAYING yearly to us, our heirs and successors, for the same, two elks and two black beavers, whensoever and as often as we, our heirs and successors, shall happen to enter into the said countries, territories and regions hereby granted: AND FURTHER, our will and pleasure is, and by these presents, for us, our heirs and successors, WE DO grant unto the said Governor and Company, and to their successors, that it shall and may be lawful to and for the said Governor and Company, and their successors, from time to time, to assemble themselves, for or about any the matters, causes, affairs or businesses of the said trade, in any place or places for the same convenient, within our dominions or elsewhere, and there to hold court for the said Company, and the affairs thereof; and that, also, it shall and may be lawful to and for them, and the greater part of them, being so assembled, and that shall then and there be present, in any such place or places, whereof the Governor or his Deputy for the time being to be one, to make, ordain and constitute such and so many reasonable laws, constitutions, orders and ordinances as to them, or the greater part of them, being then and there present, shall seem necessary and convenient for the good government of the said Company, and of all governors of colonies, forts and plantations, factors, masters, mariners and other officers employed or to be employed in any of the territories and lands aforesaid, and in any of their voyages; and for the better advancement and continuance of the said trade or traffic and plantations, and the same laws, constitutions, orders and ordinances so made, to put in use, and execute accordingly, and at their pleasure to revoke and alter the same or any of them, as the occasion shall require: And that the said Governor and Company, so often as they shall make, ordain or establish any such laws, constitutions, orders and ordinances in such form as aforesaid, shall and may lawfully impose, ordain, limit and provide such pains, penalties and punishments upon all offenders, contrary to such laws, constitutions, orders and ordinances, or any of them, as to the said Governor and Company for the time being, or the greater part of them, then and

there being present, the said Governor or his Deputy being
always one, shall seem necessary, requisite or convenient for
the observation of the same laws, constitutions, orders and
ordinances; and the same fines and amerciaments shall and
may, by their officers and servants from time to time be
be appointed for that purpose, levy, take and have, to the use of
the said Governor and Company, and their successors, without
the impediment of us, our heirs or successors, or of any the
officers or ministers of us, our heirs or successors, and without
any account therefore to us, our heirs or successors, to be made:
All and singular which laws, constitutions, orders and ordinances, so as aforesaid to be made, WE WILL to be duly observed
and kept under the pains and penalties therein to be contained;
so always as the said laws, constitutions, orders and ordinances,
fines and amerciaments, be reasonable, and not contrary or
repugnant, but as near as may be agreeable to the laws, statutes
or customs of this our realm: AND FURTHERMORE, of our
ample and abundant grace, certain knowledge and mere
motion, WE HAVE granted, and by these presents, for us, our
heirs and successors, DO grant unto the said Governor and
Company, and their successors, that they and their successors,
and their factors, servants and agents, for them and on their
behalf, and not otherwise, shall for ever hereafter have, use and
enjoy, not only the whole, entire and only trade and traffic, and
the whole, entire and only liberty, use and privilege of trading
and trafficking to and from the territory, limits and places
aforesaid; but also the whole and entire trade and traffic to and
from all havens, bays, creeks, rivers, lakes and seas, into which
they shall find entrance or passage by water or land out of the
territories, limits or places aforesaid; and to and with all the
natives and people inhabiting, or which shall inhabit within
the territories, limits and places aforesaid; and to and with all
other nations inhabiting any the coasts adjacent to the said
territories, limits and places which are not already possessed as
aforesaid, or whereof the sole liberty or privilege of trade is not
granted to any other of our subjects: AND WE, of our further
royal favour, and of our more especial grace, certain knowledge
and mere motion, HAVE granted, and by these presents, for us,
our heirs and successors, DO grant to the said Governor and
Company, and to their successors, that neither the said
territories, limits and places, hereby granted as aforesaid, nor
any part thereof, nor the island, havens, ports, cities, towns or
places thereof or therein contained, shall be visited, frequented
or haunted by any of the subjects of us, our heirs or successors,

contrary to the true meaning of these presents, and by virtue of our prerogative royal, which we will not have in that behalf argued or brought into question: WE STRAITLY charge, command and prohibit, for us, our heirs and successors, all the subjects of us, our heirs and successors, of what degree or quality soever they be, that none of them, directly or indirectly, do visit, haunt, frequent or trade or adventure, by way of merchandize, into or from any of the said territories, limits or places hereby granted, or any or either of them, other than the said Governor and Company, and such particular persons as now be or hereafter shall be of that Company, their agents, factors and assigns, unless it be by the license and agreement of the said Governor and Company in writing first had and obtained, under their common seal, to be granted, upon pain that every such person or persons that shall trade or traffic into or from any of the countries, territories or limits aforesaid, other than the said Governor and Company and their successors, shall incur our indignation, and the forfeiture and the loss of the goods, merchandizes and other things whatsoever, which so shall be brought into this realm of England, or any the dominions of the same, contrary to our said prohibition, or the purport or true meaning of these presents, for which the said Governor and Company shall find, take and seize in other places out of our dominions, where the said Company, their agents, factors or ministers shall trade, traffic or inhabit by virtue of these our letter patent, as also the ship and ships, with the furniture thereof, wherein such goods, merchandizes and other things shall be brought and found; the one-half of all the said forfeitures to be to us, our heirs and successors, and the other half thereof WE DO by these presents clearly and wholly, for us, our heirs and successors, give and grant unto the said Governor and Company, and their successors: AND FURTHER, all and every the said offenders, for their said contempt, to suffer such other punishment as to us, our heirs and successors, for so high a contempt, shall seem meet and convenient, and not to be in anywise delivered until they and every of them shall become bound unto the said Governor for the time being in the sum of One thousand pounds at the least, at no time then after to trade or traffic into any of the said places, seas, straits, bays, ports, havens, or territories aforesaid, contrary to our express commandment in that behalf set down and published: AND FURTHER, of our more especial grace, WE HAVE condescended and granted, and by these presents, for us, our heirs and successors, DO grant unto the said Governor and Company, and their successors, that we, our heirs, and successors, will not grant liberty, license or power to any person or persons whatsoever, contrary to the tenor of these our letters patent, to trade, traffic or inhabit, unto or upon any the territories, limits or places afore specified, contrary to the true meaning of these presents, without the consent of the said Governor and Company, or the most part of them: AND, of our more abundant grace and favour to the said Governor and Company, WE DO hereby declare our will and pleasure to be, that if it shall so happen that any of the persons free or to be free of the said Company of Adventurers of England trading into Hudson's Bay, who shall, before the going forth of any ship or ships appointed for a VOYAGE or otherwise, promise or agree, by writing under his or their hands, to adventure any sum or sums of money towards the furnishing any provision, or maintenance of any voyage or voyages, set forth, or to be set forth, or intended or meant to be set forth, by the said Governor and Company, or the more part of them present at any public Assembly, commonly called their General Court, shall not within the space of twenty days next after warning given to him or them by the said Governor or Company, or their known officer or minister, bring in and deliver to the Treasurer or Treasurers appointed for the Company, such sums of money as shall have been expressed and set down in writing by the said person or persons, subscribed with the name of said Adventurer or Adventurers, that then and at all times after it shall and may be lawful to and for the said Governor and Company, or the more part of them present, whereof the said Governor or his Deputy to be one, at any of their General Courts or General Assemblies, to remove and disfranchise him or them, and every such person and persons at their wills and pleasures, and he or they so removed and disfranchised not to be permitted to trade into the countries, territories and limits aforesaid, or any part thereof, nor to have any adventure or stock going or remaining with or amongst the said Company, without the special license of the said Governor and Company, or the more part of them present at any General Court, first had obtained in that behalf, any thing before in these presents to the contrary thereof in anywise notwithstanding: AND OUR WILL AND PLEASURE IS, and hereby we do also ordain, that it shall and may be lawful to and for the said Governor and Company, or the greater part of them, whereof the Governor for the time being or his Deputy to be one, to admit into and to be of the said Company all such servants or factors, of or for the said Company, and all such others as to them or the most part of them present, at any court held for the said Company, the Governor or his Deputy being one, shall be thought fit and agreeable with the orders and ordinances made and to be made for the government of the said Company: AND FURTHER, our will and pleasure is, and by these presents, for us, our heirs and successors, WE DO grant unto the said Governor and Company, and to their successors, that it shall and may be lawful in all elections and bye-laws to be made by the General Court of the Adventurers of the said Company, that every person shall have a number of votes according to his stock, that is to say, for every hundred pounds by him subscribed or brought into the present stock, one vote, and that any of those have subscribed less than One hundred pounds may join their respective sums to make up One hundred pounds, and have one vote jointly for the same, and not otherwise: AND FURTHER, of our especial grace, certain knowledge and mere motion, WE DO, for us, our heirs and successors, grant to and with the said Governor and Company of Adventurers of England trading into Hudson's Bay, that all lands, islands, territories, plantations, forts, fortifications, factories or colonies, where the said Company's factories and trade are or shall be, within any the ports or places afore limited, shall be immediately and from henceforth under the power and command of the said Governor and Company, their successors and assigns; SAVING the faith and allegiance due to be performed to us, our heirs and successors as aforesaid; and that the said Governor and Company shall have liberty, full power and authority to appoint and establish Governors and all other officers to govern them, and that the Governor and his Council of the several and respective places where the said Company shall have plantations, forts, factories, colonies or places of trade within any the countries, lands or territories hereby granted, may have power to judge all persons belonging to the said Governor and Company, or that shall live under them, in all causes, whether civil or criminal, according to the laws of this kingdom, and to execute justice accordingly; and in case any crime or misdemeanor shall be committed in any of the said Company's plantations, forts, factories or places of trade within the limits aforesaid, where judicature cannot be executed for want of a Governor and Council there, then in such case it shall and may be lawful for the chief Factor of that place and his Council to transmit the party, together with the offence, to such other plantation, factory or fort where there shall be a Governor and Council where justice may be executed, or into this kingdom of England, as shall be thought most convenient, there to receive such punishment as the nature of his offence shall deserve: AND MOREOVER, our will and pleasure is, and by these presents, for us, our heirs and successors, WE DO GIVE and grant unto the said Governor and Company, and their successors, free liberty and license, in any case they conceive it necessary, to send either ships of war, men or ammunition, unto any their plantations, forts, factories or places of trade aforesaid, for the security and defence of the same, and to choose commanders and officers over them, and to give them power and authority, by commission under their common seal, or otherwise, to continue or make peace or war with any prince or people whatsoever, that are not Christians, in any places where the said Company shall have any plantations, forts or factories, or adjacent thereunto, as shall be most for the advantage and benefit of the said Governor and Company, and of their trade; and also to right and recompense themselves upon the goods, estates or people of those parts, by whom the said Governor and Company shall sustain any injury, loss or damage, or upon any other people whatsoever that shall any way, contrary to the intent of these presents, interrupt, wrong or injure them in their said trade, within the said places, territories, and limits granted by this Charter: And that it shall and may be lawful to and for the said Governor and Company, and their successors, from time to time, and at all times from henceforth, to erect and build such castles, fortifications, forts, garrisons, colonies or plantations, towns or villages, in any parts or places within the limits and bounds granted before in these presents unto the said Governor and Company, as they in their discretion shall think fit and requisite, and for the supply of such as shall be needful and convenient, to keep and be in the same, to send out of this kingdom, to the said castles, forts, fortifications, garrisons, colonies, plantations, towns or villages, all kinds of clothing, provision of victuals, ammunition and implements necessary for such purpose, paying the duties and customs for the same, as also to transport and carry over such number of men, being willing thereunto, or not prohibited, as they shall think fit, and also to govern them in such legal and reasonable manner as the said Governor and Company shall think best, and to inflict punishment for misdemeanors, or impose such fines upon them for breach of their orders, as in these presents are formerly expressed: AND FURTHER, our will and pleasure is, and by these presents, for us, our heirs and successors, WE DO grant unto the said Governor and Company, and to their successors, full power and lawful authority to seize upon the persons of all such English, or any other our subjects which shall sail into Hudson's Bay, or inhabit in any of the countries, islands or territories hereby granted to the said Governor and Company, without their leave and license in that behalf first had and obtained, or that shall condemn or disobey their orders, and send them to England; and that all and every person or persons, being our subjects, any ways employed by the said Governor and Company, within any the parts, places and limits aforesaid, shall be liable unto and suffer such punishment for any offences by them committed in the parts aforesaid, as the President and Council for the said Governor and Company there shall think fit, and the merit of the offence shall require, as aforesaid; and in case any person or persons being convicted and sentenced by the President and Council of the said Governor and Company, in the countries, lands or limits afore-said, their factors or agents there, for any offence by them done, shall appeal from the same, that then and in such case it shall and may be lawful to and for the said President and Council, factors or agents, to seize upon him or them, and to carry him or them home prisoners into England, to the said Governor and Company, there to receive such condign punishment as his cause shall require, and the law of this nation allow of; and for the better discovery of abuses and injuries to be done unto the said Governor and Company, or their successors, by any servant by them to be employed in the said voyages and planta-tions, it shall and may be lawful to and for the said Governor and Company, and their respective President, Chief Agent or Governor in the parts aforesaid, to examine upon oath all factors, masters, pursers, supercargoes, commanders of castles, forts, fortifications, plantations or colonies, or other persons, touching or concerning any matter or thing in which by law or usage an oath may be administered, so as the said oath, and the matter therein contained, be not repugnant, but agreeable to the laws of this realm: AND WE DO hereby straitly charge and command all and singular our Admirals, Vice-Admirals, Justices, Mayors, Sheriffs, Constables, Bailiffs, and all and singular other our officers, ministers, liege men and subjects whatsoever, to be aiding, favouring, helping and assisting to the said Governor and Company, and to their successors, and to their deputies, officers, factors, servants, assigns and ministers, and every of them, in executing and enjoying the premises, as well on land as on sea, from time to time, when any of you shall thereunto be required; ANY STATUTE, act, ordinance, proviso, proclamation or restraint heretofore had, made, set forth, ordained or provided, or any other matter, cause or thing whatsoever to the contrary in anywise notwithstanding. IN WITNESS WHEREOF we have caused these our Letters to be made Patent. WITNESS OURSELF at Westminster, the second day of May, in the two-and-twentieth year of our reign.

By Writ of Privy Seal.

Pigott.

I — 2

Peter Fidler Visits the Athabasca District, 1791: Hudson's Bay Company Archives, E. 3/1 Peter Fidler's Journals and Surveys, 1790-1806.

June 19, 1791: . . . went down the river [Clearwater], along shore and at 8½ P.M. we returned back to our people—and found that it is very bad to go down, being nearly all the way we have seen . . . a continual rapid, . . . Found great quantities of Bitumen a kind of liquid tar oozing out of the Banks on both sides [of] the river, in many places which has a very sulphurous smell and quite black like real Tar, and in my opinion would be a very good substitute for that useful Mineral. . . . Saw along the northern shore of the river several Salt springs some of an exceeding Salt taste that in my opinion it would require but a little while to evaporate, before it became pure good Salt, in one or two places in particular. 2 springs would spring up not more than 8 yards from each other—and one would be exceedingly salt and the other quite fresh and pure water—singular! We also found particularly in a deep bay in the river, that the waters in former ages has scooped out and now left dry, several curious kind of Shells, some in the middle of Solid Stone and several in hard earth, the exact figure remaining and some appeared as if they had been petrified to a solid stone, such as Cockles, Muscles and other kind of shells frequently found in the interior parts of this Country . . .

June 21, 1791: . . . An island of Stones with a few willows upon it about 300 yards long and a creek and E[astern] side flowing with pure Bitumen or liquid Tar about 10 inches deep—which

I walked thro bare legged, but in less than half an hour I was obliged to use pease and soup to wash it off, it caused such an intolerable burning heat in my legs . . .

I — 3

Paul Kane Visits Fort Edmonton: Wanderings of an Artist Among the Indians of North America (London, 1859), 92-93, 260-263.

September 26, 1846

Edmonton is a large district: as it has to furnish many other districts with provisions, a large supply is always kept on hand, consisting entirely of dried meat, tongues, and pemmican. There are usually here a chief factor and a clerk, with forty or fifty men with their wives and children, amounting altogether to about 130, who all live within the pickets of the fort. Their employment consists chiefly in building boats for the trade, sawing timber, most of which they raft down the river from ninety miles higher up, cutting up the small poplar which abounds on the margin of the river for fire-wood, 800 cords of which are consumed every winter, to supply the numerous fires in the establishment. The employment of the women, who are all, without a single exception, either squaws or half-breeds, consists of making moccasins and clothing for the men, and converting the dried meat into pemmican.

December, 1847

The fort at this time of year presented a most pleasing picture of cheerful activity; every one was busy; the men, some in hunting and bringing in the meat when the weather permitted, some in sawing boards in the sawpit, and building the boats, about thirty feet long and six feet beam, which go as far as York Factory, and are found more convenient for carrying goods on the Saskatchewan and Red River than canoes. They are mostly built at Edmonton, because there are more boats required to take the peltries to York Factory than is required to bring goods back; and more than one-half of the boats built here never return. This system requires them to keep constantly building.

The women find ample employment in making mocassins and clothes for the men, putting up pemmican in ninety-pound bags, and doing all the household drudgery, in which the men never assist them. The evenings are spent round their large fires in eternal gossiping and smoking. The sole musician of the establishment, a fiddler, is now in great requisition amongst the French part of the inmates, who give full vent to their national vivacity, whilst the more sedate Indian looks on with solemn enjoyment.

No liquor is allowed to the men or Indians; but the want of it did not in the least seem to impair their cheerfulness. True, the gentlemen of the fort had liquor brought out at their own expense; but the rules respecting its use were so strict and so well known, that none but those to whom it belonging either expected, or asked, to share it.

On Christmas day the flag was hoisted, and all appeared in their best and gaudiest style, to do honour to the holiday. Towards noon every chimney gave evidence of being in full blast, whilst savoury steams of cooking pervaded the atmosphere in all directions. About two o'clock we sat down to dinner. Our party consisted of Mr. Harriett, the chief, and three clerks, Mr. Thebo, the Roman Catholic missionary from Manitou Lake, about thirty miles off, Mr. Rundell [sic], the Wesleyan missionary, who resided within the pickets, and myself, the wanderer, who, though returning from the shores of the Pacific, was still the latest importation from civilized life.

The dining-hall in which we assembled was the largest room in the fort, probably about fifty by twenty five feet, well warmed by large fires, which are scarcely ever allowed to go out. The walls and the ceiling are boarded, as plastering is not used, there being no limestone within reach but these boards are painted in the style of the most startling barbaric gaudiness, and the ceiling filled with centre-pieces of fantastic gilt scrolls, making altogether a saloon which no white man would enter for the first time without a start, and which the Indians always looked upon with awe and wonder.

The room was intended as a reception room for the wild chiefs who visited the fort; and the artist who designed the decorations was no doubt directed to 'astonish the natives.' If such were his instructions, he deserves the highest praise for having faithfully complied with them, although, were he to attempt a repetition of the same style in one of the rooms of the Vatican, it might subject him to severe criticisms from the fastidious. No tablecloth shed its snowy whiteness over the board; no silver candlebra or gaudy china interfered with its simple magnificence. The bright tin plate and dishes reflected jolly faces, and burnished gold can give no truer zest to a feast.

*With the confederation of the Dominion of Canada in 1867
the way was opened for the development and settlement of the
vast areas under Hudson's Bay Company jurisdiction. Expansion of Canada westward was a basic part of the Confederation
movement and was reflected in the British North America Act
itself. Nor did Canada and the United Kingdom waste time in
preparing for the transfer. The required Canadian address
requesting the transfer was passed at the first Session of the
Parliament of the new Dominion. The United Kingdom
responded with the Rupert's Land Act of 1868 and Canada
prepared to assume the government of the Territories in the Act
for the Temporary Government of Rupert's Land, passed in
1869. Parallel with these developments negotiations were being
carried on with the Hudson's Bay Company and, by the middle
of 1869, it looked as if the way was cleared for the region to be
transferred to Canada and, henceforth, to be governed as a unit
until settlement warranted alterations.*

I — 4

British North America Act, Section 146.

It shall be lawful for the Queen, by and with the advice of Her
Majesty's Most Honourable Privy Council, on Addresses from
the Houses of Parliament of Canada, and from the Houses of
the Respective Legislatures of the Colonies or Provinces of
Newfoundland, Prince Edward Island, and British Columbia,
to admit those Colonies or Provinces, or any of them, into the
Union, and on Address from the Houses of Parliament of
Canada to admit Rupert's Land and the Northwestern Territory,
or either of them, into the Union, on such Terms and Conditions in each Case as are in the Addresses expressed and as the
Queen thinks fit to approve, subject to the Provisions of this
Act; and the Provisions of any Order in Council in that Behalf
shall have effect as if they had been enacted by the Parliament of
the United Kingdom of Great Britain and Ireland.

I — 5

Address to Her Majesty the Queen from the Senate and House of Commons of the Dominion of Canada, Canada. Journals of the House of Commons, 1867-68, p. 108.

Most Gracious Sovereign,

We, your Majesty's most dutiful and loyal subjects, the Senate and Commons of the Dominion of Canada in Parliament assembled, humbly approach your Majesty for the purpose of representing:—

That it would promote the prosperity of the Canadian people and induce to the advantage of the whole Empire, if the Dominion of Canada, constituted under the provisions of the 'British North America Act, 1867,' were extended westward to the shores of the Pacific Ocean.

That the colonization of the fertile lands of the Saskatchewan, the Assiniboine, and the Red River districts; the development of the mineral wealth which abounds in the region of the North-west; and the extension of commercial intercourse through the British possessions in America from the Atlantic to the Pacific, are alike dependent on the establishment of a stable government for the maintenance of law and order in the North-western Territories.

That the welfare of a sparse and widely scattered population of British subjects of European origin, already inhabiting these remote and unorganized territories, would be materially enhanced by the formation therein of political institutions bearing analogy, as far as circumstances will admit, to those which exist in the several Provinces of this Dominion.

That the 146th section of the 'British North America Act, 1867' provides for the admission of Rupert's Land and the North-western Territory, or either of them, into union with Canada, upon the terms and conditions to be expressed in addresses from the Houses of Parliament of this Dominion to your Majesty, and which shall be approved by your Majesty in Council.

That we do therefore most humbly pray that your Majesty will be graciously pleased, by and with the advice of your Most Honourable Privy Council, to unite Rupert's Land and the North-western Territory with this Dominion, and to grant to the Parliament of Canada authority to legislate for their future welfare and good Government; and we most humbly beg to express to your Majesty that we are willing to assume the duties and obligations of government and legislation as regards these territories.

That in the event of your Majesty's Government agreeing to transfer to Canada the jurisdiction and control over the said region, the Government and Parliament of Canada will be ready to provide that the legal rights of any corporation, company or individual within the same shall be respected, and placed under the protection of Courts of competent jurisdiction.

And furthermore that, upon transference of the territories in question to the Canadian Government, the claims of the Indian tribes to compensation for lands required for purposes of settlement will be considered and settled in conformity with the equitable principles which have uniformly governed the British Crown in its dealings with the aborigines.

All which we humbly pray your Majesty to take into your Majesty's Most gracious and favourable consideration.

The Senate, Tuesday, December 17th, 1867
(signed), Joseph Cauchon, Speaker.
House of Commons, Monday, December 16th, 1867.
(signed), James Cockburn, Speaker.

I — 6

Rupert's Land Act, 1868. Statutes of the United Kingdom, 1868, Chapter 105.

An Act for enabling Her Majesty to accept a Surrender upon Terms of the Lands, Privileges, and Rights of "The Governor and Company of Adventurers of England trading into Hudson's Bay," and for admitting the same into the Dominion of Canada.

[31st July, 1868.]

WHEREAS by certain letters Patent granted by His late Majesty King Charles the Second in the Twenty-second Year of His Reign certain Persons therein named were incorporated by the Name of "The Governor and Company of Adventurers of England trading into Hudson's Bay," and certain Lands and Territories, Rights of Government, and other Rights, Privileges, Liberties, Franchises, Powers, and Authorities, were thereby granted or purported to be granted to the said Governor and Company in His Majesty's Dominion in North America:

And whereas by the British North America Act, 1867, it was (amongst other things) enacted that it should be lawful for Her Majesty, by and with the Advice of Her Majesty's most Honorable Privy Council, on Address from the Houses of the Parliament of Canada, to admit Rupert's Land and the North-Western Territory, or either of them, into the Union on such Terms and Conditions as are in the Address expressed and as Her Majesty thinks fit to approve, subject to the provisions of the said Act:

And whereas for the Purpose of carrying into effect the Provisions of the said British North America Act, 1867, and of admitting Rupert's Land into the said Dominion as aforesaid upon such Terms as Her Majesty thinks fit to approve, it is expedient that the said Lands, Territories, Rights, Privileges, Liberties, Franchises, Powers, and Authorities, so far as the same have been lawfully granted to the said Company, should be surrendered to Her Majesty, Her Heirs and Successors, upon such Terms and Conditions as may be agreed upon by and between Her Majesty and the said Governor and Company as hereinafter mentioned:

Be it therefore enacted by the Queen's most Excellent Majesty, by and with the Advice and Consent of the Lords, Spiritual and Temporal, and Commons, in this present Parliament assembled, and by the Authority of the same, as follows:

1. This Act may be cited as "Rupert's Land Act, 1868."

2. For the Purpose of this Act the Term "Rupert's Land," shall include the whole of the Lands and Territories held or claimed to be held by the said Governor and Company.

3. It shall be competent for the said Governor and Company to surrender to Her Majesty, and for Her Majesty by any Instrument under Her Sign Manual and Signet to accept a Surrender of all or any of the Lands, Territories, Rights, Privileges, Liberties, Franchises, Powers, and Authorities whatsoever granted or purported to be granted by the said Letters Patent to the said Governor and Company within Rupert's Land, upon such Terms and Conditions as shall be agreed upon by and between Her Majesty and the said Governor and Company; provided, however, that such Surrender shall not be accepted by Her Majesty until the Terms and Conditions upon which Rupert's Land shall be admitted into the said Dominion of Canada shall have been approved of by Her Majesty, and embodied in an Address to Her Majesty from both the Houses of the Parliament of Canada in pursuance of the One hundred and forty-sixth Section of the British North America Act, 1867; and that the

said Surrender and Acceptance thereof shall be null and void unless within a Month from the Date of Such Acceptance Her Majesty does by Order in Council under the Provisions of the said last recited Act admit Rupert's Land into the said Dominion; provided further, that no Charge shall be imposed by such Terms upon the Consolidated Fund of the United Kingdom.

4. Upon the Acceptance by Her Majesty of such Surrender all Rights of Government and Proprietary Rights, and all other Privileges, Liberties, Franchises, Powers, and Authorities whatsoever, granted or purported to be granted by the said Letters Patent to the said Governor and Company within Rupert's Land, and which shall have been so surrendered, shall be absolutely extinguished; provided that nothing herein contained shall prevent the said Governor and Company from continuing to carry on in Rupert's Land or elsewhere Trade and Commerce.

5. It shall be competent to Her Majesty by any such Order or Orders in Council as aforesaid, on Address from the Houses of the Parliament of Canada, to declare that Rupert's Land shall, from a Date to be therein mentioned, be admitted into and become part of the Dominion of Canada and thereupon it shall be lawful for the Parliament of Canada from the Date aforesaid to make, ordain, and establish within the Land and Territory so admitted as aforesaid all such Laws, Institutions, and Ordinances, and to constitute such Courts and Officers, as may be necessary for the Peace, Order, and good government of her Majesty's Subjects and others therein: Provided that, until otherwise enacted by the said Parliament of Canada, all the Powers, Authorities, and Jurisdiction of the several Courts of Justice now established in Rupert's Land, and of the several Officers thereof, and of all Magistrates and Justices now acting within the said Limits, shall continue in full force and effect therein.

I — 7

An Act for the Temporary Government of Rupert's Land and the Northwestern Territory when united with Canada: Statutes of Canada, 1869, Chapter 3.

Whereas it is probable that Her Majesty the Queen may, pursuant to the "British North America Act, 1867," be pleased to admit Rupert's Land and the North-Western Territory into the Union or Dominion of Canada, before the next Session of the Canada Parliament: And whereas it is expedient to prepare for the transfer of the said Territories from the Local Authorities to the Government of Canada, at the time appointed by the Queen for such admission, and to make some temporary provision for the Civil Government of such Territories until more permanent arrangements can be made by the Government and Legislature of Canada; Therefore, Her Majesty, by and with the advice and consent of the Senate and House of Commons, enacts as follows:

1. The said Territories when admitted as aforesaid, shall be styled and known as 'The North-West Territories.'

2. It shall be lawful for the Governor, by any Order or Orders, to be by him from time to time made, with the advice of the Privy Council, (and subject to such conditions and restrictions as to him shall seem meet) to authorize and empower such Officer as he may from time to time appoint as Lieutenant-Governor of the North-West Territories, to make provisions for the administration of Justice therein, and generally to make, ordain, and establish all such Laws, Institutions and Ordinances as may be necessary for the Peace, Order, and good Government of Her Majesty's subjects and others therein; provided that all such Orders in Council, and all Laws and Ordinances, so to be made as aforesaid, shall be laid before both Houses of Parliament as soon as conveniently may be after the making and enactment thereof respectively.

3. The Lieutenant-Governor shall administer the Government under instructions from time to time given him by Order in Council.

4. The Governor may, with the advice of the Privy Council, constitute and appoint, by Warrant under his Sign Manual, a Council of not exceeding fifteen nor less than seven persons, to aid the Lieutenant-Governor in the administration of affairs, with such powers as may be from time to time conferred upon them by Order in Council.

5. All laws in force in Rupert's Land and the North-Western Territory, at the time of their admission into the Union, shall so far as they are consistent with 'The British North America Act, 1867,'—with the terms and conditions of such admission approved of by the Queen under the 146th section thereof,— and with this Act,—remain in force until altered by the Parliament of Canada, or by the Lieutenant-Governor under the authority of this Act.

6. All Public Officers and Functionaries holding office in Rupert's Land and the North-Western Territory, at the time of their admission into the Union, excepting the Public Officer or Functionary at the head of the administration of affairs, shall continue to be Public Officers and Functionaries of the North-West Territories with the same duties and powers as before, until otherwise ordered by the Lieutenant-Governor under the authority of this Act.

This Act shall continue in force until the end of the next Session of Parliament.

Plans for the transfer of the territory did not work out as intended. In Red River the Metis, under the leadership of Louis Riel, insisted on the recognition of certain rights. The Canadian government was thus forced to alter the original intention of one very basic structure of government for the whole of the territory and to create a new Province in Manitoba. The Manitoba Act was also important for what would later become Alberta in two ways. First, the Act provided for the government of the rest of the North West. Second, it set a precedent that would be controversial in the discussion of additional provinces when it maintained all lands in the federal rather than provincial jurisdiction. These complications and delays meant that it was June of 1870 before the British government finally undertook the formal transfer of the North West to Canada.

I — 8

The Manitoba Act. Statutes of Canada, 1870, Chapter 3

Whereas it is probable that Her Majesty The Queen may, pursuant to the British North America Act, 1867, be pleased to admit Rupert's Land and the North-Western Territory into the Union or Dominion of Canada, before the next Session of the Parliament of Canada:

And Whereas it is expedient to prepare for the transfer of said Territories to the Government of Canada at the time appointed by the Queen for such admission:

And Whereas it is expedient also to provide for the organization of part of the said Territories as a Province, and for the establishment of a Government therefor, and to make provision for the Civil Government of the remaining part of the said

Territories, not included within the limits of the Province:

Therefore Her Majesty, by and with the advice and consent of the Senate and House of Commons of Canada, enacts as follows:

1. On, from and after the day upon which the Queen, by and with consent of Her Majesty's Most Honourable Privy Council, under the authority of the 146th Section of the British North America Act, 1867, shall, by Order in Council in that behalf, admit Rupert's Land the North-Western Territory into the Union or Dominion of Canada, there shall be formed out of the same a Province, which shall be one of the Provinces of the Dominion of Canada, and which shall be called the Province of Manitoba. . . .

30. All ungranted or waste lands in the Province shall be, from and after the date of the said transfer, vested in the Crown, and administered by the Government of Canada for the purposes of the Dominion, subject to, and except and so far as the same may be affected by, the conditions and stipulations contained in the agreement for the surrender of Rupert's Land by the Hudson's Bay Company to Her Majesty . . .

35. And with respect to such portion of Rupert's Land and the North-Western Territory, as is not included in the Province of Manitoba, it is hereby enacted, that the Lieutenant-Governor of the said Province shall be appointed, by Commission under the Great Seal of Canada, to be the Lieutenant-Governor of the same, under the name of the North-West Territories, and subject to the provisions of the Act in the next section mentioned.

36. Except as is hereinbefore enacted and provided, the Act of Parliament of Canada, passed in the now last Session thereof, and entitled, 'An Act for the Temporary Government of Rupert's Land, and the North-Western Territory when united with Canada,' is hereby re-enacted, extended and continued in force until the first day of January, 1871, and until the end of the Session of Parliament then next succeeding.

In 1871 the Act for the Temporary Government of Rupert's Land was, in substance re-enacted in An Act to make further provision for the government of the North West Territories (Statutes of Canada, 1871, Chap. XVI).

I — 9

Order of Her Majesty in Council admitting Rupert's Land and the North-Western Territory into the Union.

At the Court at *Windsor*, the 23rd day of *June*, 1870.

PRESENT:

The QUEEN'S Most Excellent Majesty.
Lord President.
Lord Privy Seal.
Lord Chamberlain.
Mr. Gladstone.

WHEREAS by the *"British North America Act*, 1867," it was (amongst other things) enacted that it should be lawful for the Queen, by and with the advice of Her Majesty's Most Honorable Privy Council, on Address from the Houses of Parliament of Canada, to admit Rupert's Land and the North-Western Territory, or either of them, into the Union on such terms and conditions in each case as should be in the Addresses expressed, and as the Queen should think fit to approve, subject to the provisions of the said Act. And it was further enacted that the provisions of any Order in Council in that behalf should have effect as if they had been enacted by the Parliament of the United Kingdom of Great Britain and Ireland:

And whereas by an Address from the Houses of Parliament of Canada, of which Address a copy is contained in the Schedule to this Order annexed, marked A, Her Majesty was prayed, by and with the advice of Her Most Honorable Privy Council, to unite Rupert's Land and the North-Western Territory with the Dominion of Canada, and to grant to the Parliament of Canada authority to legislate for their future welfare and good government upon the terms and conditions therein stated:

And whereas by the *"Rupert's Land Act*, 1868," it was (amongst other things) enacted that it should be competent for the Governor and Company of Adventurers of England trading into Hudson's Bay (hereinafter called the Company) to surrender to Her Majesty, and for Her Majesty, by any Instrument under Her Sign Manual and Signet to accept a surrender of all or any of the lands, territories, rights, privileges, liberties, franchises, powers, and authorities whatsoever, granted or purported to be granted by certain Letters Patent therein recited to the said Company within Rupert's Land, upon such terms and conditions as should be agreed upon by and between Her Majesty and the said Company; provided, however, that such surrender should not be accepted by Her Majesty until the terms and conditions upon which Rupert's Land should be admitted into the said Dominion of Canada should have been approved of by Her Majesty and embodied in an Address to Her Majesty from both the Houses of the Parliament of Canada, in pursuance of the 146th Section of the *"British North America Act*, 1867:"

And it was by the same Act further enacted that it should be competent to Her Majesty, by Order or Orders in Council, on Addresses from the Houses of the Parliament of Canada, to declare that Rupert's Land should, from a date to be therein mentioned, be admitted into and become part of the Dominion of Canada:

And whereas a second Address from both the Houses of the Parliament of Canada has been received by Her Majesty praying that Her Majesty will be pleased, under the provisions of the hereinbefore recited Acts, to unite Rupert's Land on the terms and conditions expressed in certain Resolutions therein referred to and approved of by Her Majesty, of which said Resolutions and Address copies are contained in the Schedule to this Order annexed, marked B, and also to unite the North-Western Territory with the Dominion of Canada, as prayed for by and on the terms and conditions contained in the hereinbefore first recited Address, and also approved of by Her Majesty:

And whereas a draft surrender has been submitted to the Governor-General of Canada containing stipulations to the following effect, viz.:—

1. The sum of 300,000£ (being the sum hereinafter mentioned) shall be paid by the Canadian Government into the Bank of England to the credit of the Company within six calendar months after acceptance of the surrender aforesaid, with interest on the said sum at the rate of 5 per cent, per annum, computed from the date of such acceptance until the time of such payment.

2. The size of the blocks which the Company are to select adjoining each of their forts in the Red River limits, shall be as follows:—

> Upper Fort Garry and town of Winnipeg, including the inclosed park around shop and ground at the entrance of the town 500
> Lower Fort Garry (including the farm the Company now have under cultivation)........................ 500

White Horse Plain 500

3. The deduction to be made as hereinafter mentioned from the price of the materials of the Electric Telegraph, in respect of deterioration thereof, is to be certified within three calendar months from such acceptance as aforesaid by the agents of the Company in charge of the depots where the materials are stored. And the said price is to be paid by the Canadian Government into the Bank of England to the credit of the Company within six calendar months of such acceptance, with interest at the rate of 5 per cent. per annum on the amount of such price, computed from the date of such acceptance until the time of payment:

And whereas the said draft was on the fifth day of July, one thousand eight hundred and sixty-nine, approved by the said Governor-general in accordance with a Report from the Committee of the Queen's Privy Council for Canada; but it was not expedient that the said stipulations, not being contained in the aforesaid second Address, should be included in the surrender by the said Company to Her Majesty of their rights aforesaid or in this Order in Council.

And whereas the said Company did by deed under the seal of the said Company, and bearing date the nineteenth day of November, one thousand eight hundred and sixty-nine, of which deed a copy is contained in the Schedule to this Order annexed, marked C, surrender to Her Majesty all the rights of government, and other rights, privileges, liberties, franchises, powers and authorities granted, or purported to be granted to the said Company by the said Letters Patent herein and hereinbefore referred to, and also all similar rights which may have been exercised or assumed by the said Company in any parts of British North America not forming part of Rupert's Land, or of Canada or of British Columbia, and all the lands and territories (except and subject as in the terms and conditions therein mentioned) granted or purported to be granted to the said Company by the said Letters Patent:

And whereas such surrender has been duly accepted by Her Majesty, by an instrument under her Sign Manual and Signet, bearing date at Windsor the twenty-second day of June, one thousand eight hundred and seventy:

It is hereby Ordered and declared by Her Majesty, by and with the advice of the Privy Council, in pursuance and exercise of the powers vested in Her Majesty by the said Acts of Parliament, that from and after the fifteenth day of July, one thousand eight hundred and seventy, the said North-Western Territory shall be admitted into and become part of the Dominion of Canada upon the terms and conditions set forth in the first herein-before recited Address, and that the Parliament of Canada shall from the day aforesaid have full power and authority to legislate for the future welfare and good government of the said Territory. And it is further ordered that, without prejudice to any obligations rising from the aforesaid approved Report, Rupert's Land shall from and after the said date be admitted into and become part of the Dominion of Canada upon the following terms and conditions, being the terms and conditions still remaining to be performed of those embodied in the said second address of the Parliament of Canada, approved of by Her Majesty as aforesaid:—

1. Canada is to pay to the Company 300,000£, when Rupert's Land is transferred to the Dominion of Canada.

2. The Company are to retain the posts they actually occupy in the North-Western Territory, and may, within twelve months of the surrender, select a block of land adjoining each of its posts within any part of British North America not comprised in Canada and British Columbia, in conformity, except as regards the Red River Territory, with a list made out by the Company and communicated to the Canadian Ministers, being the list in the Schedule of the aforesaid Deed of Surrender. The actual survey is to be proceeded with, with all convenient speed.

3. The size of each block is not to exceed [10] acres round Upper Fort Garry, [300] acres round Lower Fort Garry; in the rest of the Red River Territory a number of acres to be settled at once between the Governor in Council and the Company, but so that the aggregate extent of the blocks is not to exceed 50,000 acres.

4. So far as the configuration of the country admits, the blocks shall front the river or road by which means of access are provided, and shall be approximately in the shape of parallelograms, of which the frontage shall not be more than half the depth.

5. The Company may, for fifty years after the surrender, claim in any township or district within the Fertile Belt, in which land is set out for settlement, grants of land not exceeding one twentieth part of the land so set out. The blocks so granted to be determined by lot, and the Company to pay a rateable share of the survey expenses, not exceeding 8 cents Canadian an acre. The Company may defer the exercise of their

right of claiming the proportion of each township for not more than ten years after it is set out; but their claim must be limited to an allotment from the lands remaining unsold at the time they declare their intention to make it.

6. For the purpose of the last Article, the Fertile Belt is to be bounded as follows:— On the south by the United States boundary; on the west by the Rocky Mountains; on the north by the northern branch of the Saskatchewan; on the east by Lake Winnipeg, the Lake of the Woods, and the water connecting them.

7. If any township shall be formed abutting on the north bank of the northern branch of the Saskatchewan River, the Company may take their one-twentieth of any such township, which for the purpose of this Article shall not extend more than five miles inland from the river, giving to the Canadian Dominion an equal quantity of the portion of lands coming to them of townships established on the southern bank.

8. In laying out any public roads, canals, &c., through any block of land reserved to the Company, the Canadian Government may take, without compensation, such land as is necessary for the purpose, not exceeding one twenty-fifth of the total acreage of the block; but if the Canadian Government require any land which is actually under cultivation, or which has been built upon, or which is necessary for giving the Company's servants access to any river or lake, or as a frontage to any river or lake, they shall pay to the Company the fair value of the same, and shall make compensation for any injury done to the Company or their servants.

9. It is understood that the whole of the land to be appropriated within the meaning of the last preceding clause shall be appropriated for public purposes.

10. All titles to land up to the eighth day of March, one thousand eight hundred and sixty-nine, conferred by the Company are to be confirmed.

11. The Company is to be at liberty to carry on its trade without hindrance in its corporate capacity, and no exceptional tax is to be placed on the Company's land, trade or servants, nor any import duties on goods introduced by them previous to the surrender.

12. Canada is to take over the materials of the electric telegraph at cost price—such price including transport, but not including interest for money, and subject to a deduction for ascertained deterioration.

13. The Company's claim to land under agreements of Messrs. Vankoughnet and Hopkins is to be withdrawn.

14. Any claims of Indians to compensation for lands required for purposes of settlement shall be disposed of by the Canadian Government with the Imperial Government; and the Company shall be relieved of all responsibility in respect of them.

15. The Governor in Council is authorized and empowered to arrange any details that may be necessary to carry out the above terms and conditions.

And the Right Honorable Earl Granville, one of Her Majesty's principal Secretaries of State, is to give the necessary directions herein accordingly.

I — 10

The North-West Territories Act, 1875: Statutes of Canada, 1875, Chap. 49

An Act to amend and consolidate the Laws respecting the
North-West Territories
[Assented to 8th April, 1875]

WHEREAS it is expedient to amend and consolidate the laws respecting the North West Territories; Therefore, Her Majesty, by and with the advice and consent of the Senate and House of Commons of Canada, enacts as follows:—

GOVERNMENT AND LEGISLATION

1. The Territories formerly known as "Rupert's Land" and the North-Western Territory, (with the exception of such portion thereof as forms the Province of Manitoba), shall continue to be styled and known as the North-West Territories; and the word "Territories," in this Act, means the said Territories.

(2.) For the North-West Territories there shall be an officer styled the Lieutenant-Governor, appointed by the Governor General in Council, by instrument under the great seal of Canada, who shall hold office during the pleasure of the Governor General; and the Lieutenant-Governor shall administer the government under instructions from time to time given him by Order in Council, or by the Secretary of State of Canada:

2. Every Lieutenant-Governor so appointed shall, before

assuming the duties of his office, make or subscribe before the Governor General or some person duly authorized to administer such oaths, an oath of allegiance or office similar to those prescribed to be taken by a Lieutenant-Governor, under *"The British North America Act,* 1867."

3. The Governor-General, with the advice of the Queen's Privy Council for Canada, by warrant under his privy seal, may constitute and appoint such and so many persons from time to time, not exceeding in the whole five persons,—of which number the Stipendiary Magistrates hereinafter mentioned shall be members *ex officio,*—to be a Council to aid the Lieutenant-Governor in the administration of the North-West Territories, with such powers, not inconsistent with this Act, as may be, from time to time, conferred upon them by the Governor General in Council; and a majority shall form a *quorum.*

4. The seat of government of the North-West Territories shall be fixed, and may, from time to time, be changed by the Governor General in Council.

5. There shall be payable out of the Consolidated Revenue Fund of Canada, the following sums, annually, that is to say:—

To the Lieutenant-Governor, not exceeding $7,000

To the Stipendiary Magistrates, each,
not exceeding 3,000

To two members of Council, each, not exceeding . . . 1,000

To the Clerk of the Council, who shall also act as and perform the duties of Secretary to the Lieutenant-Governor,
not exceeding 1,800

Together with such sums of money as may, from time to time, be fixed by the Governor in Council in respect of travelling allowances for any of the officers above named.

6. All laws and ordinances now in force in the North-West Territories, and not repealed by or inconsistent with this Act, shall remain in force until it is otherwise ordered by the Parliament of Canada, by the Governor in Council, or by the Lieutenant-Governor and Council under the authority of this Act.

7. The Lieutenant-Governor, by and with the advice and consent of the Council of the North-West Territories, may make, ordain and establish ordinances as to matters coming within the classes of subjects next hereinafter enumerated, that is to say:—

(1.) Taxation for local and municipal purposes;

(2.) Property and civil rights in the Territories;

(3.) The administration of justice in the Territories, including maintenance and organization of courts, both of civil and criminal jurisdiction, and including procedure in civil matters in these courts, but the appointment of any judges of the said courts shall be made by the Governor General in Council;

(4.) Public health;

The licensing of inns and places of refreshment;

Landmarks and boundaries;

Cemeteries;

Cruelty to animals;

Game and wild animals and the care and protection thereof;

Injury to public morals;

Nuisances;

Police;

Roads, highways and bridges;

The protection of timber;

Gaols and lock-up houses;

(5.) Generally, all matters of a merely local or private nature;

(6.) The imposition of punishment, by fine or penalty or imprisonment, for enforcing any ordinance of the Territories made in relation to any matter coming within any classes of subjects herein enumerated;

(7.) Provided that no ordinance to be so made by the Lieutenant-Governor with the advice and consent of the Council of the said Territories, shall,—(1) be inconsistent with or alter or repeal any provisions of any Act of the Parliament of Canada in Schedule B. of this Act, or of any Act of the Parliament of Canada, which may now, or at any time hereafter, expressly refer to the said Territories, or which or any part thereof may be at any time made by the Governor in Council applicable to or to be in force in the said North-West Territories; or, (2.) impose any fine or penalty exceeding one hundred dollars;

(8.) And provided that a copy of every such ordinance made by the Lieutenant-Governor and Council shall be mailed for transmission to the Governor General within ten days after its passing, and may be disallowed by him at any time within two years after its passing; provided also, that all such orders in Council, and all ordinances so to be made as aforesaid, shall be laid before both Houses of Parliament as soon as conveniently may be after the making and enactment thereof respectively.

8. The Governor in Council may, by proclamation, from time to time, direct that any Act of the Parliament of Canada, or any part or parts thereof, or any one or more of the sections of

any one or more of any such Acts shall be in force in the North-West Territories generally, or in any part or parts thereof to be mentioned in the said proclamation for such purpose.

9. Provided further, that when and so often as any electoral district shall be established as hereinafter provided, the Lieutenant-Governor by and with the consent of the Council or Assembly, as the case may be, shall have power to pass ordinances for raising within such district by direct taxation, or on shop, saloon, tavern or any other such licenses, a revenue for local and for municipal purposes of such district, and for the collection and appropriation of the same in the promotion of such purposes respectively.

10. Whenever any electoral district shall be found to contain not less than one thousand inhabitants, the Lieutenant-Governor, by and with the consent of the Council or Assembly, as the case may be, may pass ordinances erecting the same into a municipal corporation or corporations as they may think fit: and thenceforth the power of the Lieutenant-Governor and Council or Assembly as herein conferred in respect of taxation for municipal purposes shall cease; and every such municipal corporation shall thenceforth have the right to pass by-laws for raising within such municipality by taxation a revenue for municipal purposes in such district, and for the collection and appropriation of the same in the promotion thereof; and the Lieutenant-Governor and Council or Assembly, as the case may be, shall pass an ordinance or ordinances prescribing the powers and authorities which may be exercised by any such municipal corporation and the mode and extent of such taxation: Provided that the power herein given to the Lieutenant-Governor and Council or Assembly, as the case may be, of taxation for local purposes of such district shall not be prejudiced by the erection of the same into a municipality or municipalities, but such power shall continue vested in them in respect of local purposes not comprised within such municipal purposes as to which powers may be conferred by any ordinance or ordinances as aforesaid.

11. When, and so soon as, any system of taxation shall be adopted in any district or portion of the North-West Territories, the Lieutenant-Governor, by and with the consent of the Council or Assembly, as the case may be, shall pass all necessary ordinances in respect to education; but it shall therein be always provided, that a majority of the ratepayers of any district or portion of the North-West Territories, or any lesser portion or sub-division thereof, by whatever name the same may be

known, may establish such schools therein as they may think fit, and make the necessary assessment and collection of rates therefor; and further, that the minority of the ratepayers therein, whether Protestant or Roman Catholic, may establish separate schools therein, and that, in such latter case, the rate-payers establishing such Protestant or Roman Catholic separate schools shall be liable only to assessments of such rates as they may impose upon themselves in respect thereof.

12. Any copy of any proclamation or order made by the Governor in Council, or ordinance, proclamation or order made by the Lieutenant-Governor and Council or Assembly, as the case may be, of the North-West Territories, printed in the *Canada Gazette*, or purporting to be printed by the Queen's Printer at Ottawa or Printer to the Government of Manitoba at Winnipeg, or to the Government of the North-West Territories, shall be *prima facie* evidence of such proclamation or order, and that it is in force.

ELECTION OF MEMBERS OF COUNCIL OR ASSEMBLY

13. When and so soon as the Lieutenant-Governor is satisfied by such proof as he may require, that any district or portion of the North-West Territories, not exceeding an area of one thousand square miles, contains a population of not less than one thousand inhabitants of adult age, exclusive of aliens or unenfranchised Indians, the Lieutenant-Governor shall, by proclamation, erect such district or portion into an electoral district, by a name and with boundaries to be respectively declared in the proclamation, and such electoral district shall thenceforth be entitled to elect a member of the Council or of the Legislative Assembly, as the case may be.

(2.) The Lieutenant-Governor shall thereafter cause a writ to be issued by the Clerk of the Council in such form and addressed to such Returning Officer as he thinks fit; and until the Lieutenant-Governor and Council of the Province otherwise provides, he shall by proclamation prescribe and declare the mode of providing voters' lists, the oaths to be taken by voters, the powers and duties of Returning and Deputy Returning Officers, the proceedings to be observed at such election and the period during which such election may be continued, and such other provisions in respect to such election as he may think fit.

(3.) The persons qualified to vote at such election shall be the *bona fide* male residents and householders of adult age, not being aliens, or unenfranchised Indians, within the electoral district, and shall have respectively resided in such electoral district for at least twelve months immediately preceding the issue of the said writ.

(4.) Any person entitled to vote may be elected.

(5.) When and so soon as the Lieutenant-Governor is satisfied as aforesaid, that any electoral district contains a population of two thousand inhabitants of adult age, exclusive of aliens or unenfranchised Indians, he shall issue his writ for the election of a second member for the electoral district.

(6.) When the number of elected members amounts to twenty-one, the Council hereinbefore appointed shall cease and be determined, and the members so elected shall be constituted and designated as the Legislative Assembly of the North-West Territories, and all the powers by this Act vested in the Council shall be thenceforth vested in and exercisable by the said Legislative Assembly.

(7.) The number of members so to be elected, as hereinbefore mentioned, shall not exceed twenty-one, at which number the representation shall remain; the members so elected shall hold their seats for a period not exceeding two years . . .

REGISTRATION OF DEEDS

54. The Governor may appoint a Registrar of Deeds in and for the North-West Territories, who shall hold office during pleasure, and who shall reside and keep his office in a place to be named for that purpose in his commission, or at such other place as may be appointed for that purpose from time to time by the Governor in Council, and who shall register all deeds and other instruments relating to lands situated in any part of the North-West Territories, and which have been laid out and surveyed by the Crown: and the Governor in Council may order an annual salary, not exceeding two thousand dollars, to be paid to the said registrar: and the Lieutenant-Governor and Council shall fix the fees to be paid for the registration of all such deeds and instruments,—which fees shall be collected by the registrar, and being first verified on oath, shall by him be paid over to the Lieutenant-Governor, at the end of every quarter in each year, on account of the Consolidated Revenue Fund of Canada; and the forms incident to, and effect of such registration shall be governed by laws to be made under this Act.

55. The Governor may appoint a Sheriff in and for the North-West Territories, who shall hold office during pleasure,

and who shall reside, and keep his office in a place to be named for that purposed in his commission; or at such other place as may, from time to time, be named by the Governor in Council, and who shall perform the duties of such office under the laws then in force in the said Territories. The Governor in Council may order an annual salary not exceeding twelve hundred dollars to be paid to such sheriff.

56. The Lieutenant-Governor shall, (but subject to any orders in that behalf from time to time of the Governor General), have the local disposition of the Police Force in and for the North-West Territories, established under *"An Act respecting the Administration of Justice, and for the establishment of a Police Force in the North-West Territories,"* and of any Act passed or to be passed in amendment thereof; and may exercise such power in aid of the administration of civil and criminal justice, and for the general peace, order and good government of the said Territories, and for or in aid of the performance of all duties which are now, or may at any time, by any law or ordinance, or by order of the Lieutenant-Governor, be assigned to sheriff's officers, bailiffs, constables or other officers in connection with the orders or process of any Justice of the Peace, Stipendiary Magistrate, or court.

57. The Lieutenant-Governor may appoint Justices of the Peace for the North-West Territories, who shall have jurisdiction as such throughout the same.

58. The Lieutenant-Governor and Council or Assembly, as the case may be, may, by ordinance, subject to the provisions of this Act, from time to time, set apart any portion of the said Territories as and for a judicial district, and may, from time to time, alter the limits and extent of any such district.

59. A Court or Courts of Civil and Criminal Jurisdiction shall be held in the said Territories, and in every judicial district thereof when formed, under such names, at such periods and at such places as the Lieutenant-Governor may from time to time order.

60. For every such court there shall be a clerk, who may be appointed by the Governor, who shall hold office during pleasure, and be paid an annual salary, not exceeding five hundred dollars.

61. The Governor may, from time to time, appoint by commission under the great seal, one or more fit and proper person or persons, not exceeding three, to be and act as Stipendiary Magistrate or Stipendiary Magistrates within the North-West Territories, who shall hold office during pleasure,

and who shall reside at such place or places as may, from time to time, be ordered by the Governor in Council.

62. Each Stipendiary Magistrate shall have jurisdiction throughout the North-West Territories, as hereinafter mentioned, and shall also have jurisdiction and may exercise within the North-West Territories, the magisterial, judicial and other functions appertaining to any Justice of the Peace, or any two Justices of the Peace under any laws or ordinances which may, from time to time, be in force in the North-West Territories.

63. Each Stipendiary Magistrate shall preside over such courts in the North-West Territories as shall, from time to time, be assigned to him by the Lieutenant-Governor, and to qualify him to do so, he shall take the following oath before the Lieutenant-Governor or any Stipendiary Magistrate, that is to say:—

"I do swear that I will truly and faithfully execute the several powers, duties and trusts committed to me by or under '*The North-West Territories Act*, 1875,' without fear, without favor, and without malice. So help me God."

64. The Chief Justice or any Judge of the Court of Queen's Bench of the Province of Manitoba, with any one of the Stipendiary Magistrates as an associate, shall have power and authority to hold a court under section fifty-nine, and therein to hear and determine as hereinafter mentioned, any charge preferred against any person for any offence alleged to have been committed within the North-West Territories, viz:—

(1.) In any case in which the maximum punishment for such offence does not exceed five years' imprisonment,—in summary way, and without the intervention of a jury;

(2.) In any case in which the maximum punishment for such offence exceeds five years' imprisonment but is not punishable with death,—then either in summary way and without the intervention of a jury, if the accused assents thereto; or, if the accused demands a jury, then with the intervention of a jury not exceeding six in number, who shall be then and there, or as soon thereafter as can be, chosen and sworn by the judge or Stipendiary Magistrate, as a jury in such case;

(3.) In any case in which the punishment for such offence is death,—then with the intervention of a jury not exceeding eight in number, who shall be then and there or as soon thereafter as can be, chosen and sworn by the judge as a jury in such case;

(4.) And every such court shall be a court of record; and if imprisonment in gaol for not less than two years in a penitentiary, be awarded in any case, the court may order the convict to be imprisoned in the North-West Territories, or to be conveyed to the penitentiary in the Province of Manitoba; and he shall in any such case, undergo such punishment therein, as if convicted in the Province of Manitoba;

(5.) The Lieutenant-Governor and Council or Assembly, as the case may be, may, from time to time, make any ordinance in respect to the mode of calling juries, and when and by whom and how they may be summoned or taken, and in respect of all matters relating to the same; but no grand jury shall be called in the North-West Territories;

(6.) On the first day of January and June in each year, each Justice of the Peace, Stipendiary Magistrate, and other Judge residing in the North-West Territories, or who has presided at any court therein, shall send in to the Lieutenant-Governor, in such form as he may prescribe, a return shewing all trials and proceedings, civil and criminal, had before him during the preceding six months.

65. A person convicted of any offence punishable by death may appeal to the Court of Queen's Bench of Manitoba, which shall have jurisdiction to confirm the conviction or to order a new trial; and the mode of such appeal and all particulars relating thereto, shall be determined from time to time by ordinance of the Lieutenant-Governor and Council or Assembly, as the case may be.

66. Any Stipendiary Magistrate of the said Territories, or the Chief Justice or any Judge of the Court of Queen's Bench of the Province of Manitoba, shall have power and authority to commit and cause to be conveyed to gaol in the Province of Manitoba, for trial by the Court of Queen's Bench according to the laws of criminal procedure in force in the said Province, any person or persons at any time charged with the commission of any offence against any of the laws or ordinances in force in the North-West Territories, punishable by death or imprisonment in the penitentiary; and the said Court of Queen's Bench or any judge thereof, shall have power and authority to have any person arraigned before the said court on any such charge; and the jury laws and laws of criminal procedure of the said Province shall apply to any such trial, except that the punishment to be awarded upon conviction of any such person, shall be according to the laws in force in the North-West Territories: and the sentence may be carried into effect in a penitentiary or other place of confinement in the North-West Territories, or in

the said Province, as if the same were in the North-West Territories.

67. Whenever any convict or accused person is ordered to be conveyed to gaol or to the penitentiary in Manitoba, and constable or other person in whose charge he is to be so conveyed, shall have the same power to hold and convey him, or to retake him in case of an escape, and the gaoler or warden of the penitentiary in Manitoba shall have the same power to detain and deal with him, in the said Province, as if it were within the North-West Territories, or as if the said convict or accused person had been ordered to be conveyed to such gaol or penitentiary, by some competent court or authority in the said Province.

68. Where it is impossible or inconvenient in the absence or remoteness of any gaol or other place of confinement, to carry out any sentence of imprisonment, any Justice of the Peace, or Stipendiary Magistrate, or the Chief Justice or any Judge of the Court of Queen's Bench of Manitoba, may, according to their several powers and jurisdictions, sentence such person so convicted before him or them, and sentenced, as aforesaid, to such imprisonment, to be placed and kept in the custody of the police force of the North-West Territories, with or without hard labour, the nature and extent of which shall be determined by the Justice of the Peace or Stipendiary Magistrate or Judge, by or before whom such person was convicted.

69. The Governor in Council may cause to be erected, in any part or parts of the North-West Territories, any building or buildings, or enclosure or enclosures, for the purpose of a gaol or lock-up, for the confinement of prisoners charged with the commission of any offence, or sentenced to any punishment therein; and confinement or imprisonment therein shall be held lawful and valid, whether under sentence of imprisonment in a penitentiary, gaol or other place of confinement.

70. Whenever in any Act of the Parliament of Canada in force in the North-West Territories any officer is designated for carrying on any duty therein mentioned, and there shall be no such officer in the North-West Territories, the Lieutenant-Governor and Council may order by what other person or officer, such duty shall be performed; and anything done by such person or officer, under such order, shall be valid and legal in the premises; or if it be in any such Act ordered that any document or thing shall be transmitted to any officer, court, territorial division or place, and there is then in the said North-

West Territories no such officer, court or territorial division or place, then the Lieutenant-Governor and Council may order to what officer, court or place such transmission shall be made, or may dispense with the transmission thereof.

ADMINISTRATION OF CIVIL JUSTICE

71. Every Stipendiary Magistrate of the said Territories, and the Chief Justice and any Judge of the Court of Queen's Bench of Manitoba or any one of them, shall respectively have power, jurisdiction, and authority to hear and determine within the North-West Territories, and at a court held under section fifty-nine, any claim, dispute or demand as hereinafter mentioned viz:—

(1.) Where the claim, dispute or demand is for a tort, wrong or grievance, in which the amount claimed does not exceed five hundred dollars, or if for a debt or on contract, in which the amount claimed does not exceed one thousand dollars, in a summary way and without the intervention of a jury;

(2.) In all other claims, disputes or demands than those above-mentioned, or for the recovery of the possession of real estate, if neither party demands a jury, in a summary way and without the intervention of a jury; but if either party demands a jury, then with the intervention of a jury not exceeding six in number, who shall be returned instantly by the clerk of the court to try the facts of the matter in dispute; and the Stipendiary Magistrate or Judge shall make such orders, judgments or decrees as appear to him just and agreeable to equity and good conscience: but neither the Stipendiary Magistrate nor any other judge or the court shall have cognizance of any action for any gambling debt or for any intoxicating liquor or intoxicant, or of any action by any person on a note of hand or other document, the consideration or any part of the consideration for which was for a gambling debt or for any such intoxicating liquor or intoxicant.

72. Every judgment of the Stipendiary Magistrate or presiding judge shall be openly pronounced in court as soon as may be after the hearing of the case, except that in any case where the Stipendiary Magistrate is not prepared to pronounce judgment *instanter*, he may postpone judgment and name a subsequent day and hour for the delivery thereof at the clerk's office in writing; and at such day and hour it shall be lawful for the clerk to read the judgment to the parties or their agents if present,

and if not, then to enter the said judgment in their absence; and such judgment shall be as effectual as if rendered in court at the trial:

(2.) Execution of any such judgment shall be carried into effect in the manner prescribed by any ordinance of the Lieutenant-Governor and Council or Assembly, as the case may be,—or if no such ordinance be then in force, then in like manner as a judgment to the same amount in the Province of Manitoba.

73. Any person feeling himself aggrieved by the decision of any Stipendiary Magistrate, or presiding judge, or court, in a claim, dispute or demand under the second sub-section of the seventy-first section of this Act, may appeal to the Court of Queen's Bench of Manitoba, which shall have jurisdiction to confirm the decision or to order a new trial; and the mode of such appeal and all particulars relating thereto, shall be determined from time to time by ordinance of the Lieutenant-Governor and Council or Assembly, as the case may be.

PROHIBITION OF INTOXICANTS

74. Intoxicating liquors and other intoxicants are prohibited to be manufactured or made in the said North-West Territories, except by special permission of the Governor in Council, or to be imported or brought into the same from any Province of Canada, or elsewhere, or to be sold, exchanged, traded or bartered, except by special permission in writing of the Lieutenant-Governor of the said Territories: and if any such intoxicating liquor or intoxicant is imported or manufactured or made in the said Territories, or brought into the same, or is sold, exchanged, traded or bartered, in contravention of this Act, it shall be absolutely forfeited, and may be seized by any officer of the customs or excise, or by any constable or other duly qualified person wheresoever found; and on complaint made before him, any Judge, Stipendiary Magistrate, or Justice of the Peace, may, on the evidence of one credible witness that this Act has been contravened in respect thereof, order the said intoxicating liquor or intoxicant so seized, to be forthwith destroyed; or in case of the same not having been seized, then on complaint as aforesaid, such Judge, Stipendiary Magistrate, or Justice of the Peace, may issue a search warrant, as in cases of stolen goods under the Acts in force respecting the duties of Justices of the Peace out of Sessions in relation to persons charged with indictable offences, and upon the same being

found, may cause them to be forthwith destroyed and the still, machinery, keg, barrel, case, box, package or receptacle whence or in which any intoxicating liquor or intoxicant has been manufactured, imported or made, sold, exchanged, traded or bartered, and as well that in which the original supply was contained as the vessel wherein any portion of such original supply was supplied as aforesaid, and the balance of the contents thereof, if such still, machinery, barrel, keg, case, box, package, receptacle or vessel aforesaid, respectively, can be identified, may be seized by any officer of the customs or excise, or by any constable or other duly qualified person, wheresoever found within the said Territories; and on complaint before any Judge, Stipendiary Magistrate or Justice of the Peace, he may on the evidence of any credible witness, that this Act has been contravened in respect thereof, declare such intoxicating liquor or intoxicant, still, machinery, vessel, or receptacle forfeited, and cause the same to be forthwith destroyed: and the person in whose possession any of them were found may be condemned to pay a penalty not exceeding one hundred dollars, nor less than fifty dollars, and the costs of prosecution; and one-half of such penalty shall belong to the prosecutor, and the other half to Her Majesty.

(1.) Any person who manufactures, makes, imports, sells, exchanges, trades or barters any intoxicating liquor, or intoxicant, except by special permission as aforesaid, or in whose possession, or on whose premises such intoxicating liquor or intoxicant of any kind may be or may have been found, shall be liable to a penalty not exceeding two hundred dollars, nor less than fifty dollars,—one-half of which shall go to the informer.

(2.) Any person who knowingly has in his possession any article, chattel, commodity or thing purchased, acquired, exchanged, traded or bartered, either wholly or in part, for any intoxicating liquor or intoxicant, shall forfeit and pay for each offence a penalty not exceeding two hundred dollars, nor less than fifty dollars,—one-half of which shall go to the informer.

(3.) Every article, chattel, commodity or thing, in the purchase, acquisition, exchange, trade or barter of which, the consideration either wholly or in part may be any intoxicating liquor or intoxicant, shall be forfeited to Her Majesty, and shall be seized as hereinbefore mentioned, in respect to any receptacle of any intoxicating liquor or intoxicant.

(4.) Every person who refuses or neglects to aid any constable, sub-constable, or other duly authorized person, in the execution of any act or duty required by this section, or who knowingly refuses to give information, or gives false information in respect to any matter arising therefrom, shall be subject to a penalty not exceeding two hundred dollars, nor less than fifty dollars,—one-half of which shall go to the informer.

(5.) The expression "intoxicating liquor" shall mean and include all spirits, strong waters, spirituous liquors, wines, fermented or compounded liquors, or intoxicating fluids; and the expression "intoxicant" shall include opium, or any preparation thereof, and any other intoxicating drug or substance, and tobacco or tea mixed, compounded or impregnated with opium, or with any other intoxicating drug, spirit or substance, and whether the same or any of them be liquid or solid.

(6.) Any penalty incurred under this section shall be recoverable, with costs of prosecution, by summary conviction on the evidence of one credible witness, before any Judge, Stipendiary Magistrate or Justice of the Peace having jurisdiction in the North-West Territories,—who shall, on payment of the same, pay the informer his share thereof; and in case of non-payment of the penalty and costs immediately after conviction, the convicting Judge, Magistrate or Justice may, in his discretion, levy the same by distress and sale, or commit the person so convicted and making default in payment of the said penalty and costs, to any common gaol or house of correction or lock-up house within the North-West Territories for a period not exceeding six months, unless the said penalty and costs be sooner paid.

(7.) And upon conviction for a second offence, the offender shall be liable to a penalty, not less than two hundred and not exceeding four hundred dollars, and, in the discretion of the convicting judge, magistrate or justice, to imprisonment for a period not exceeding six months.

(8.) No seizure, prosecution, conviction or commitment under this Act shall be invalid on account of want of form so long as the same is according to the true intent and meaning of this Act.

(9.) Intoxicating liquors imported or brought into the North-West Territories from any Province of Canada or elsewhere, by special permission in writing of the Lieutenant Governor of the said Territories, are subject to the several customs and excise laws of Canada, if in excess of one gallon.

75. Nothing in this Act shall affect the provisions of an Act passed in the thirty-seventh year of Her Majesty's reign, entitled *"An Act to amend certain laws respecting Indians, and to extend certain Laws relating to matters connected with Indians, to the Provinces of Manitoba and British Columbia."*

76. The several Acts and parts of Acts mentioned and contained in Schedule A., of this Act, if not expired, are hereby repealed; but such repeal shall not affect any duty accrued, right acquired, or penalty, forfeiture or liability incurred under the said Acts, or any of them, or any offence committed under any or either of them.

77. The several Acts and parts of Acts mentioned and contained in Schedule B, of this Act, as limited in the said schedule, shall apply to and be in force in the North-West Territories; but except the Acts mentioned and contained in Schedule B to this Act, and except such Acts of the Parliament of Canada or any part or parts thereof as may, under the eighth section of this Act, be made applicable to the North-West Territories, no Act of the Parliament of Canada heretofore passed, and no part thereof, shall apply to or be in force in the said Territories; and no Act of Parliament hereafter to be passed and no part thereof, shall apply to or be in force in the said Territories, unless the same be, by any such Act or under the eighth section of this Act, made applicable to or of force in the said Territories.

78. This Act shall come into force and effect upon, from and after such day as shall be named in a proclamation to be issued by the Governor in Counci for that Purpose.

79. This Act may be cited as *"The North-West Territories Act, 1875."*

One of the more prosaic developments of the Territorial era proved to be an important precursor to the formation of Alberta. In 1882, on the recommendation of J.S. Dennis, Deputy Minister of the Department of the Interior, the North West was divided into postal districts. The westernmost of these districts was named after the wife of the Governor General. Alberta, as will be seen, was not a unanimously popular name but the creation of the division proved the first step in the development of a district awareness that foreshadowed a sense of distinctiveness from not only the east but from other parts of the North West Territories.

Map A referred to by Dennis is Map Number 1 in this volume and Map B is number 2.

I — 11

The Creation of the Provisional Districts: Memorandum by J.S. Dennis, October 15, 1881. Public Archives of Canada, Records of the Department of the Interior, Vol. 264, File 37906.

The undersigned, in 1876, at the request of the then Minister of the Interior, submitted informally a scheme for dividing the North-West Territories into Provinces. The plan then proposed is shewn on map (A) herewith.

The line of the Canadian Pacific Railway through the Northwest selected by Mr. Sandford Fleming, had at that time been practically adopted by the Administration of the day, and Battleford had been fixed upon as the seat of government of the Territories. As this line passed north of Fort Pelly and the Elbow of the Saskatchewan River, and thence continued westerly to the Mountains via Edmonton, the arrangement of Provinces as then submitted, shewn on Map (A), was such as to enable each to share equally the advantages of the Railway, which it will be seen would have crossed them all at right angles about their respective centres.

The abandonment of Mr. Fleming's route, and the construction of the Railway by the existing chartered Company westerly from Winnipeg, passing south of Fort Ellice and Qu'Appelle, and thence towards the Mountains by the valley of the South Branch of the Saskatchewan has however so altered the whole situation in the Territories, as to render it expedient that a different sub-division of the country should be proposed, especially as regards the boundaries of the Provinces numbered 1 and 2; and the scheme shown on map (B) is therefore submitted for consideration in place of that shewn on map (A).

The undersigned recommends this scheme as in his opinion exhibiting—considering the important changes in many respects caused by the final selection of the southerly route for the Railway—the most desirable and politic division of the country. The great objects to be aimed at in devising the most expedient apportionment of the Territories, with a view to self-government in the future, are:—

1. Reasonable areas for the different Provinces.

2. The equalization of such areas as far as practicable.

3. Securing for each Province as nearly as possible an equal share of the great natural resources of the Territories.

The undersigned is of opinion that in the scheme now

submitted the several objects mentioned here at all events have been well considered.

1. The areas of the Provinces of Quebec, Ontario, and Manitoba, as at present constituted, are respectively as follows: Quebec, 193,355 square miles; Ontario, 109,480 square miles; Manitoba, 150,000 square miles. The several areas of the proposed new Provinces stand as follows: No. 1, 95,000 square miles; No. 2, 95,000 square miles; No. 3, 100,000 square miles; No. 4, 122,000 square miles.

A comparison of these with the areas of the older Provinces mentioned shows that the extent of each of the new Provinces would be only reasonable.

2. Although in area Nos. 1 and 2 are less than the others, there can be little doubt, from the information in the possession of the Government, that the greater extent of Nos. 3 and 4 is more than counter-balanced—in No. 3, by the existence of a very considerable amount of unavailable land, embraced in the mountains, and in the swampy country said to exist on the head waters of the Athabaska River; and in No. 4 by the large tract of swampy country said to exist within the height of land, north of Lesser Slave Lake, and between the Athabaska and Peace Rivers.

Taken altogether, therefore, and as Nos. 1 and 2 would have comparatively little waste land within their limits the undersigned thinks that the practically useful areas of the several proposed Provinces would be found not to materially differ.

3. The scheme submitted would give each Province a fair share of the natural and prospective advantages of the country as a whole. For instance, No. 1 is traversed its whole length by the Canadian Pacific Railway, which passes nearly through its centre, and it must benefit very largely by the formation of the commercial emporiums which will arise along the line of the Railway, created by the trade of the branch lines from the north which will probably be constructed to connect with the main road, and by the business which will be brought to the Railway via the South Branch of the Saskatchewan River.

The magnificent and extensive tracts of farming land extending from the Assiniboine River to Long Lake, and embracing the Touchwood Hills, the Fishing Lakes, The Qu'Appelle Valley and the Moose Mountains region, also the valuable country in the vicinity of Wood Mountains and the easterly and south-easterly slope of the Cypress Hills, and the most easterly exposures of lignite are all in Province No. 1.

No. 2 is intersected lengthwise and nearly centrally through its whole extent from west to east by the North Branch of the Saskatchewan River and includes not only the splendid valley of that river, but also the Valleys of the Carrot and Red Deer Rivers on the Southeast, the South Branch of the Saskatchewan River on the south, and the Battle River on the southwest, all of which is known to be exceptionally valuable country. On the north side of the North Branch of the Saskatchewan, this Province would embrace all the vast extent of farming and timbered country extending northwesterly from that River below Fort la Corne to the head waters of the Beaver River near Lac la Biche. Battleford, Carleton, and Prince Albert, are conveniently situated within its boundaries and either of them would be eligible as the permanent seat of government. It should not be forgotten, however, that while the land at Battleford—the present seat of government for the Territories—is the property of the Dominion, such is not the case with the other two points mentioned. The Hudson's Bay Company own the land at Carleton, and at Prince Albert most of the property situated on the River is claimed to have been settled upon previous to the Transfer.

The resources of No. 3 [Alberta] are varied and most valuable. It is splendidly watered, the North Saskatchewan and its tributaries intersecting its northern portions, and the headwaters of the Southern Branch of that River, and the Milk River—a tributary of the Missouri—its southern portions. Coal, or rather lignite of a character hardly distinguishable from true coal, either as regards appearance or value for fuel, abounds, and under conditions involving but little expense in mining. Timber of good quality is plentiful along the sources of the streams flowing from the Mountains; and in most of those streams are found the most delicious trout. The land in the southerly section, as well as that near the Hay Lakes and in the Battle River Valley—in fact all of the country not specially adapted for grain growing—is exceptionally valuable for the raising and grazing of cattle; while in the valley of the Saskatchewan proper, and northerly and northwesterly of Edmonton, is found one of the most productive and promising fields for general farming purposes contained in the whole Northwest. There is reason to believe, too, that the Eastern slope of the Mountains will prove to be rich in the precious metals. Lastly, this Province would be intersected, nearly through its centre, by the Canadian Pacific Railway.

No. 4—the Peace River Country. The Government is in

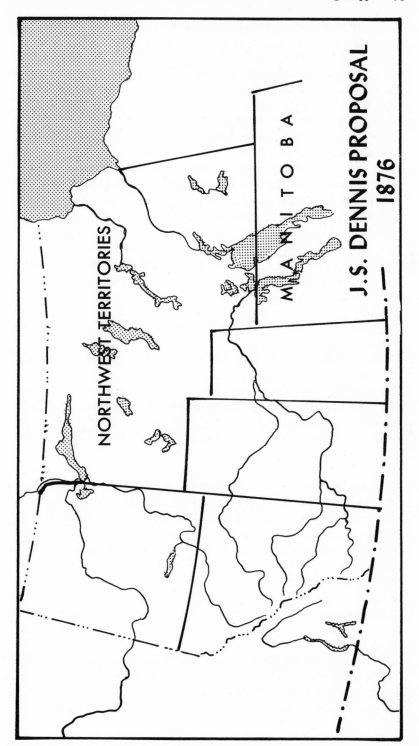

NORTHWEST TERRITORIES

M A N I T O B A

J.S. DENNIS PROPOSAL
1876

possession of a less amount of reliable information with respect to the lands embraced within the limits of this Province than as regards the others. It is, however, known to have great capabilities both for grain-growing and grazing. The climate is good, and coal and timber are abundant. The Peace River, which traverses the whole Province from southwest to northeast, is navigable for steamers for hundreds of miles. Mineral tar is found in great quantities in springs extending for many miles along the west bank of the Athabaska River.

The blue line laid down on map (B) shews approximately the northerly limit of the area of the Territories within which the climate will admit of cereals being grown to advantage.

All of which is respectfully submitted.

> (signed), J.S. Dennis,
> Deputy Minister of the Interior

I — 12

The Creation of Provisional Districts: Orders in Council, May 8, 1882

On a Memorandum from the Minister of the Interior, hereto annexed, submitting that for the convenience of settlers and for postal purposes, a portion of the North-West Territories should be divided into provisional districts and their boundaries defined.

The Committee concur in the recommendations contained in the said Memorandum, and submit the same for Your Excellency's approval.

> John J. McGee

———————

Ottawa, May 8, 1882

The undersigned has the honour to report:

That in his opinion, it is expedient for the convenience of settlers in the North-West Territories, and for postal purposes, that a portion of such Territories should be divided into provisional districts, and he recommends that four such districts be at once described and their boundaries settled.

He recommends the four such districts be named *Assiniboia, Saskatchewan, Alberta,* and *Athabasca.*

He further recommends that the boundaries of such districts shall be as follows:

1st Assiniboia

The district of Assiniboia, about 95,000 square miles in extent, to be bounded on the south by the international boundary line, the 49th parallel; on the east by the western boundary of Manitoba; on the north by the 9th correction line of the Dominion lands sytem of survey into townships, which is near the 52nd parallel of latitude; on the west by the line dividing the 10th and 11th ranges of townships, numbered from the fourth initial meridian of the Dominion Lands system aforesaid.

2nd Saskatchewan

The District of Saskatchewan, about 114,000 square miles in extent, to be bounded on the south by the district of Assiniboia and Manitoba; on the east by Lake Winnipeg and the Nelson River, flowing therefrom into Hudson's Bay; on the north by the 18th correction line of the Dominion Lands Survey system; and on the west by the line of that system dividing the 10th and 11th ranges of townships numbered from the fourth initial meridian.

3rd Alberta

The District of Alberta, about 100,000 square miles in extent, to be bounded on the south by the international boundary; on the east by the District of Assiniboia; on the west by the Province of British Columbia; and on the north by the 18th correction line before mentioned, which is near the 55th parallel of latitude.

4th Athabasca

The District of Athabasca, about 122,000 square miles in extent, to be bounded on the south by the District of Alberta; on the east by the line between the 10th and 11th ranges of Dominion Lands townships, before mentioned, until, in proceeding northward, that line intersects the Athabasca Lake and Slave River to the intersection of the last with the northern boundary of the district, which is to be the 32nd correction line of the Dominion Lands township system, and is very nearly on the 60th parallel of north latitude westward to British Columbia.

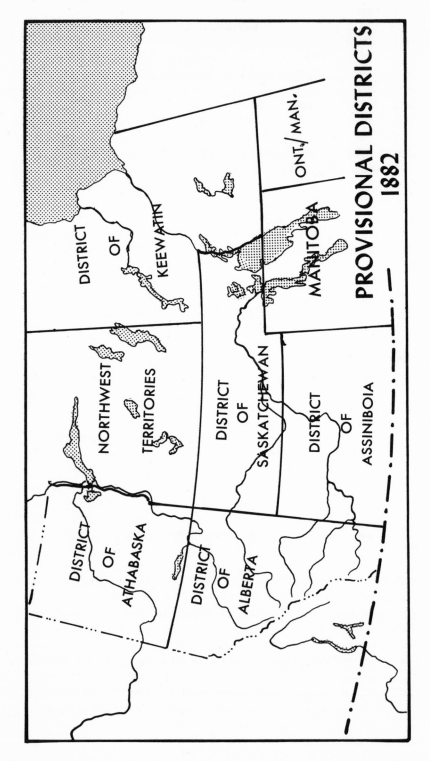

PROVISIONAL DISTRICTS
1882

A map of the proposed districts is herunto annexed.
All of which is recommended.

(Signed) John A. Macdonald
Minister of the Interior

I — 13

The Naming of Alberta: Princess Louise to J.D. Higinbotham, September 18th, 1924.

I have been very much interested in receiving your letter of 8th August.

You are perfectly correct in your belief that the beautiful, sunlit and prosperous Province of Alberta was named after me by my husband, the Marquis of Lorne, when Governor-General of Canada. He was asked to name it, as it was wished that the name should be associated with his tenure of office. There being various objections to my first name, owing to the difficulty of keeping it quite original, he decided to call it after my last name, Alberta, of which he was very fond. Indeed, he mostly called me by it, or abridged it to Alba.

I am intensely proud of this most beautiful and wonderful Province being called after me, and that my husband should have thought of it. It would, it strikes me, be a pity not to stick to historical facts, and I do not understand what other interpretation the Press could have found, to which you refer in your letter. I was named Alberta after my father. . . .

I — 14

'Our Province': The Edmonton Bulletin, July 1, 1882

The names of Manitoba, Assiniboia, Saskatchewan and Athabasca sound well and are very appropriate, but the same can hardly be said for the remaining district. Alberta may be a very nice name for a baby girl, although that is a matter of opinion, but there can scarcely be two opinions as to its being inappropriate as the name of a great province of a great country. It is not usual to name places after persons unless those persons are exceedingly great or are in some way connected with the place named after them. To name this province after any man who has yet appeared in Canada is too much honor for the amount of good any one of them has done this country. Surely in a region having such grand and varied features as this, some natural characteristic could be found that could give an appropriate and pleasant sounding name to the whole. Of course it is much easier to find fault than to suggest improvement but it would be much better to perpetuate the name of the animal which once overran the province and which will soon be extinct, by calling his favorite feeding grounds after him, than to give the country a name which reminds only of some paltry individual, or means nothing at all. Many names could be found some appropriate but none less so than Alberta.

Whatever the Bulletin *thought of the name, Alberta it remained and served as a means of focussing a growing sense of district consciousness. This sense of local identity was further encouraged because as government institutions expanded in the North-West, the provisional districts tended to be useful for more than postal purposes. Typical was the division of electoral districts when, in response to a long standing grievance, the North-West was given representation in the federal parliament in 1886. Henceforth Alberta not only had its own name but as well its own political representative.*

I — 15

An Act respecting the representation of the North-West Territories in the Parliament of Canada: Statutes of Canada, 1886, Chapter 24.

Whereas it is expedient to make provision for the representation of the inhabitants of the North-West Territories in the House of Commons of Canada as hereinafter provided: Therefore Her Majesty, by and with the advice and consent of the Senate and House of Commons of Canada, enacts as follows:—

1. This Act may be cited as 'The North-West Territories Representation Act, 1886.'
2. The Provisional Districts of Saskatchewan and Alberta, in the said Territories, as they were respectively constituted by an Order in Council, bearing date the eighth day of May, one thousand eight hundred and eighty-two, shall each be an

electoral district and shall each return one member to the House of Commons of Canada.

3. The provisional district of Assiniboia as it was constituted by the said Order in Council shall be divided into two electoral districts, each of which shall return one member to the said House of Commons. . . .

I — 16

An Act to amend the Revised Statutes of Canada, chapter fifty, respecting the North-West Territories: Statutes of Canada, 1888, Chapter 19.

Whereas it is expedient to amend *"The North-West Territories Act"* as hereinafter provided: Therefore Her Majesty, by and with the advice and consent of the Senate and House of Commons of Canada, enacts as follows:—

1. Sections seven, eight and ten and sections eighteen to twenty-five, both inclusive, of the Act cited in the preamble are hereby repealed.

2. There shall be a Legislative Assembly for the North-West Territories which shall have the powers and shall perform the duties heretofore vested in and performed by the Council of the North-West Territories, and shall be composed of twenty-two members elected to represent the electoral districts set forth in the schedule to this Act, and of legal experts, not exceeding three in number, appointed by the Governor in Council:

(2.) Such legal experts shall retain their seats for the whole term of the Legislative Assembly in the course of which they are appointed; they may take part in the debates and shall have the like privileges as the elected members of the Legislative Assembly, except that they shall not be entitled to vote:

(3.) Any judge of the Supreme Court of the North-West Territories may be appointed as such legal expert and may receive the sessional allowance hereinafter mentioned, notwithstanding anything contained in section forty-four of the Act above cited:

(4.) In each session of the Legislative Assembly there shall be allowed to each member attending such session the sum of five hundred dollars, and to each legal expert likewise attending the same two hundred and fifty dollars, together with his actual travelling expenses, payable out of the Consolidated Revenue

Fund of Canada; but such sessional allowance shall be subject to a proportionate reduction for any days on which any such member or legal expert does not attend a sitting of the Legislative Assembly during the session thereof; and the amount of such reduction and also of the travelling expenses above mentioned shall be ascertained in such manner as the Governor in Council prescribes.

3. Every Legislative Assembly shall continue for three years from the date of the return of the writs for choosing the same and no longer; and the first session thereof shall be called at such time as the Lieutenant Governor appoints.

4. There shall be a session of the Legislative Assembly at least once in every year, so that twelve months shall not intervene between the last sitting of the Assembly in one session and its first sitting in another session; and such Assembly shall sit separately from the Lieutenant Governor, and shall present Bills passed by it to the Lieutenant Governor for his assent, who may approve or reserve the same for the assent of the Governor General.

5. Until the Legislature of the North-West Territories otherwise provides, as it may do, the law in force therein at the time of the passing of this Act relating to the election of members of the Council of the North-West Territories shall, subject to the provisions of this Act, apply to the election of members of the Legislative Assembly.

6. The Lieutenant Governor shall, when occasion requires, cause writs to be issued by the Clerk of the Legislative Assembly, in such form and addressed to such returning officers as he thinks fit.

7. The persons qualified to vote at an election for the Legislative Assembly, shall be the male British subjects, by birth or naturalization (other than unenfranchised Indians), who have attained the full age of twenty-one years who have resided in the North-West Territories for at least the twelve months, and in the electoral district for at least three months, respectively, immediately preceding the time of voting.

8. Any British subject by birth or naturalization shall be eligible for nomination and election.

(2.) No nomination at any election shall be valid and called upon unless at or before the time of nomination a sum of one hundred dollars is deposited in the hands of the Returning Officer; and the receipt of the Returning Officer shall in every case, be sufficient evidence of the payment herein mentioned.

(3.) The sum so deposited shall be returned to the person by whom the deposit was made in the event of the candidate, by or on whose behalf it was so deposited, being elected or of his obtaining a number of votes at least equal to one-half the number of votes polled in favor of the candidate elected,— otherwise it shall belong to Her Majesty for the public uses of the Territories; and the sum so paid and not returned as herein provided, shall be applied by the returning officer towards the payment of the election expenses, and an account thereof shall be rendered by him to the Lieutenant Governor.

9. Elected members of the Legislative Assembly shall take and subscribe, before the Lieutenant Governor, or before such person as is designated by the Governor in Council, the following oath of allegiance:—

"I, A.B., do swear that I will be faithful and bear true allegiance to Her Majesty, her heirs and successors."

10. A majority of the members of the Legislative Assembly, including the members appointed by the Governor in Council, shall form a quorum for the transaction of business.

11. The Legislative Assembly, on its first assembling after a general election, shall proceed with all practicable speed to elect one of its elected members to be Speaker.

(2.) In case of a vacancy happening in the office of Speaker by death, resignation or otherwise, the Legislative Assembly shall proceed, with all practicable speed, to elect another of its elected members to be Speaker:

(3.) The Speaker shall preside at all meetings of the Legislative Assembly:

(4.) Until the Legislative Assembly otherwise provides in case of the absence for any reason of the Speaker from the chair of the Assembly for forty-eight consecutive hours, the Assembly may elect another of its members to act as Speaker, and the member so elected shall, during the continuance of such absence of the Speaker, have and execute all the powers, privileges and duties of Speaker.

12. Questions arising in the Legislative Assembly shall be decided by a majority of voices other than that of the Speaker, and when the voices are equal, but not otherwise, the Speaker shall have a vote.

13. The Lieutenant Governor shall select from among the elected members of the Legislative Assembly four persons to act as an advisory council on matters of finance, who shall severally hold office during pleasure; and the Lieutenant

Governor shall preside at all sittings of such advisory council and have a right to vote as a member thereof, and shall also have a casting vote in case of a tie.

14. The Legislative Assembly shall not adopt or pass any vote, resolution, address or bill for the appropriation of any part of the public revenue, or of any tax impost, to any purpose that has not been first recommended to the Assembly by message of the Lieutenant Governor in the session in which such vote, resolution, address or bill is proposed.

15. The Speaker of the Legislative Assembly shall receive a salary of five hundred dollars per annum, payable out of the Consolidated Revenue Fund of Canada.

16. The Governor in Council may appoint a Clerk of the Legislative Assembly, who shall act as and perform the duties of secretary to the Lieutenant Governor, and who shall take before the Lieutenant Governor the oath of allegiance, and such oath of office as the Governor in Council prescribes, and who shall receive a salary of two thousand dollars per annum; and such salary shall be paid out of the Consolidated Revenue Fund of Canada.

17. So much of section one hundred and six of the Act hereby amended as provides for the payment of any sum to the members or to the clerk of the Council of the North-West Territories is hereby repealed.

18. Section ninety-four of the Act hereinbefore cited is hereby amended by adding the following sub-section thereto:—

(2.) Every vehicle on which any such intoxicating liquor or intoxicant is imported or conveyed into or through or over any portion of the Territories, contrary to the provision of this Act, shall, together with the horses or other cattle employed in drawing any such vehicle as aforesaid, be forfeited to Her Majesty and may be seized and dealt with accordingly.

19. This Act shall be construed as one Act with the Act hereby amended.

I — 17

**Two Views of the North-West Territories Act of 1888:
David Mills, House of Commons Debates, 1888, 454-455.**

The people in that country have made desirable progress in number and in the development of that country, and a government a little more approaching that of a Province than

that which at present exists is no doubt required; but in all of
our Provinces we have Parliamentary responsible government,
and I do not understand from the hon. gentleman's observations
how he proposes that the executive government shall be carried
on. The proposition he has made relates purely to matters of
legislation . . . Does he propose that the Lieutenant Governor of
the Territories shall have an executive council to advise him
with regard to the administration of affairs of the Territories?
For you will observe that the powers possessed by the Governor
in Council there, now are not purely legislative powers, but
administrative and executive powers as well. How are these
administrative and executive powers to be exercised? Are they
to be exercised by the Executive of the Territories, acting under
the advice and approval of the majority of those whom the
people have elected to represent them? Does the hon. gentleman propose they shall act on the advice which they may, from
time to time, receive from the Government here? Now, I say that
these are matters of the very first importance, and that before we
are asked to take any step in advance in the legislative and
governmental development of that country, we should note
precisely what we are called upon to do; for it seems to me
rather extraordinary to admit that the people of the Territory
are so far advanced, by way of organisation, into a political and
social community, as to make it necessary that they should have
what may be considered a mature system devised for the
purposes of legislation, and yet that the legislative and administrative affairs of the country should be in the hands of an
irresponsible body . . .

**John A. Macdonald, House of Commons Debates, May 16,
1888, 1474.**

The North-West Act provided that when there were 21
elective members the Governor should cease to be a portion of
the Council and become Lieutenant Governor proper and
withdraw from the Council, but there is no provision in the Act
by which there is any executive or responsible government, or
by which the system that obtains in the Provinces should be
carried out. The true theory, as I think, of the territorial system,
so long as it continues, both here and in the United States, is
that Government proceeds from here. That is the principle on
which the original Act was based, and until the territory evolves
from its present condition into that of a full grown Province we
should, owing to its sparse population and the fact that

considerable assistance must be given from the central power, the Parliament of this Dominion, and there must be *ex necessitate* very considerable aid given to the country, responsible government in its accepted sphere would be premature.

David Mills' comments on the ambiguities of the 1888 Act were well taken. The new Legislature of the North-West Territories had scarcely been elected when members began to demand the formation of a full fledged executive commanding the support of and responsible to the majority of the Legislature. The Dominion government resisted and thus found itself in the position of resisting a movement that British North America had earlier wrested from a reluctant Great Britain. The result was a complex series of political crises and minor concessions before full responsible government was finally conceded.

Related to the issue of responsible government was the nature of finances for the North-West Territories. The dependence on annual grants from Ottawa was found increasingly irksome to the Territorial government as the years went by. In the period before 1897 the nature of the grant system tended to be a subordinate issue, dominated by the constitutional question of responsible government. The concern over the grants in these years, however, is significant in that the problem would not be resolved in 1897 and would prove to be a major factor in leading the Assembly and its powerful leader, F.W.G. Haultain, to move beyond territorial responsible government and to accept the growing demand for full provincial status.

I — 18

The Constitutional Question: Extract from Address in reply to Lieutenant-Governor Royal, November 14, 1890.

We take the liberty of pointing out to your Honor that this difference of opinion was not as to the right of your Advisory Council to control these funds, as might be inferred from your Honor's Message, but as to the right of control possessed by the House over them, and incidentally over the Advisory Council as well.

The reasons upon which the House bases the assertion of its right to control the moneys voted from year to year by the

Parliament of Canada for expenses of Government in the North-West are as follows:—

1. They are in general terms appropriated for the purposes of the local Government, which Government we understand the North-West Act to declare must be carried on by and with the advice and consent of this Assembly.

(b) In particular, they are apportioned to purposes which are controlled by, or dependent upon, the action of this House, that is to say: To give effect to our education laws; to pay for the printing which our proceedings render necessary; to pay for public improvements upon which we, as representatives of the people, are best fitted to advise, and as a matter of necessity do advise; to pay salaries of clerks and officials to meet the general expenses necessarily incurred in carrying on the Territorial Government—by and with our advice and consent—as the Act provides.

2. If there is a doubt as to the availability of funds for any desired purpose of legislation, that legislation is likely to remain unenacted, to the public inconvenience and loss, and if there is a hope of financial aid which is not realized when desired legislation is enacted, loss and inconvenience to the public again results, as well as discredit to this Assembly and its several Members. It therefore appears to us that if our legislation is to be of full benefit to the people of the Territories, we must be made aware from year to year of the amount of funds which can be depended upon to give effect to that legislation, and we can only properly become aware by the exercise of concurrent, if not absolute, control.

The Assembly further claims the right of the control of these funds on the ground that they must be considered as of the same nature as the subsidies received from the Federal Treasury by the several Provinces—that is, as a return, for the support of the local Government, on taxes paid by the people to the Federal Treasury—and therefore quite as much the property of the people of the North-West Territories, and quite as properly at the sole disposal of the local Government, as that part of the local revenues derived directly from the people by means of enactments of this Assembly.

We desire to point out that the fact of these funds not being raised under the authority of the North-West Government does not prevent them from properly being placed under the control of Your Honor, by and with the advice and consent of this Assembly; for the revenues derived from the issue of liquor permits and beer licenses under authority of Your Honor as Administrator of the North-West Government under instructions from Ottawa—which permits and licenses are in no way under the control of this Assembly, or issued on its responsibility —are still held to be subject to account to and appropriation by this House.

To sum up: The Assembly bases its claim to control: 1st, On the intent expressed in plain terms by the title of the vote in Parliament; 2nd, On the necessities of the case, as it affects the people of these Territories through the legislation of this Assembly; and 3rd, on the absolute right of the people of the North-West Territories—according to the scheme of Confederation—to the full control of their own funds.

The Assembly must point out that at its first Session Your Honor used such expressions and took such action as led us to believe that your views at that date fully agreed with those we now hold on this question. In Your Honor's Speech at the opening of the first Session on Oct. 31st, 1888, You were graciously pleased to say:

"It affords me much pleasure in opening the First Session of the Legislative Assembly of the North-West Territories, to be able to congratulate you upon the general prosperity of the country, and the completeness of its representation in our Legislature, which I regard as the preceding step to Provincial organization. In the progressive evolution of our present constitution towards thoroughly representative Government, you will find that I am in full accord with your legitimate aspirations. . . ."

I — 19

The Financial Question: Statement on behalf of the Executive Committee by Mr. Haultain, August 23, 1892 as Reported in Regina Standard, August 26, 1892.

Mr. Campbell asked the Executive Committee the following Questions:—

1. What action, if any, has been taken in respect of the Resolution passed at the last Session of this Assembly, with reference to the annual appropriation made by the Parliament of Canada for the Government of the Territories?

2. What has been the result, if any, in regard to that Resolution?

Mr. Haultain, on behalf of the Committee, replied as follows:—

The Memorial passed by the Legislative Assembly at the Session of 1891-92 with reference to the annual appropriation made by the Parliament of Canada for the Government of the Territories and the deficit in amount required for Schools was duly forwarded to the Prime Minister of Canada and the Honorable the Ministers of Finance and the Interior.

The Executive Committee on the 29th February sent further Memorials to the Governor-General-in-Council with regard to these two subjects copies of these Memorials are hereto attached.

In consequence of these Memorials in the beginning of March, '92, Mr. Haultain, a Member of the Committee, was requested by the Government of Canada to go to Ottawa and confer with the Government with regard to the financial claims of the Territories.

On Mr. Haultain's arrival in Ottawa a Sub-Committee of the Privy Council, consisting of the Ministers of Finance and the Interior, was appointed to confer with him on the subject-matter of the Assembly and Executive Committee Memorials. As a result of several conferences, the Sub-committee reported in favour of granting an amount by way of subsidy, to the Territories, of $250,000, in addition to provision by separate Votes for those special services administered by the Departments of Justice and the Interior, as well as for the Office of the Lieutenant-Governor and the statutory expenditure under the North-West Territories Act, making in all, a total Vote for the Territories of over $300,000, or within about $50,000 of the subsidy claimed by the Assembly.

The Report of the Sub-committee was not adopted by Council, and Mr. Haultain was requested to make an alternative proposition to the Assembly Memorial already under consideration. He, however, did not feel at liberty to make any proposition not based on the Memorials above mentioned, but requested to be heard by Council before a final decision on the Sub-committee Report was arrived at. The Privy Council added the First Minister and the Minister of Justice to the Sub-committee, and further conference was held with the Sub-committee thus enlarged. The Privy Council decided finally not to accept the Report of the Sub-committee in favor of a subsidy, on the ground that it was not desirable to give the Territories a Provincial status by granting a subsidy, and again asked Mr. Haultain for an alternative proposition.

Mr. Haultain then suggested that, instead of an itemized Vote for the Territories, Parliament should vote a lump sum for expenses of Government in the North-West Territories, to be transferred under Order in Council similar to provisions to that of 8th December, 1891.

The Sub-committee considered this latter proposition favorably, and the result is shown by the Order in Council of the 25th July, 1892, sent down by Message of His Honor to this House on the 13th day of August instant, and which will appear in the Journals of this House of that date.

By this Order in Council a bulk sum of $193,200 is placed under the control of the Assembly, the expenditure of which involves the control of the following services:—

Schools, Light and Fuel, Legislative Hall, Elections, Travelling Expenses, Roads and Bridges, Clerical Assistance, Contingencies, Printing and Advertising, Newspapers, Well-boring Machines, Caretakers and Messengers, Stationery, Telegrams, etc., and Advertising Sittings of Court.

The other subject dealt with in the Memorials of the House and Executive Committee was the deficit in School money.

The Memorials of the Assembly and Committee were the basis of Mr. Haultain's recommendations to the Government.

After submitting the whole matter to the Minister of the Interior, he recommended a supplementary Vote for the amount requested, and subsequently Parliament voted the sum of $26,700, as a supplementary Vote for Schools in the Territories, being slightly more than the amount claimed.

It will be seen that the lump Vote transferred by Order in Council of the 25th July, 1892, includes the item for light and fuel for the Legislative Hall, and all items asked for in the Executive Committee Memorial except that for Legal Adviser.

The total amount of the item transferred by the Order in Council of the 8th December, 1891, was $142,660.58. The total amount transferred by the Order in Council of the 25th July, 1892, available for the current year, is $193,200, or an increase of over $50,000.

The new services placed under the control of the Assembly are "Clerical Assistance," "Light and Fuel," "Caretakers and Messengers" and "Contingencies."

Last Session the amounts for each service were specified by an itemized Vote. Now the Assembly apportions the lump Vote at its discretion and according to the actual necessities of the Country. Last Session the amounts of the several Votes had to be expended upon the service indicated by the Vote, or lapse.

Now the whole amount of the lump Vote is available for any purpose.

It may be proper to mention, in conclusion that all expenses in connection with Mr. Haultain's trip in Ottawa were borne by the Federal authorities.

Provincial Autonomy was not supported by Haultain in these years but he had some difficulty in making that fact apparent to the Dominion Minister of the Interior. The confusion exhibited in the following documents may help to illustrate the frustrations faced by the Territorial government in the face of an indifferent and often ill-informed federal government.

I — 20

Autonomy versus Provincial Status. Correspondence between F.W.G. Haultain and T. Daly: Legislative Assembly Ordinances and Unpublished Sessional Papers of the Council and Legislative Assembly of the North West, 1894, Sessional Paper No. 1.

Daly to Haultain, June 29th, 1894.

I notice, however, that in one voice you people shout for Provincial autonomy, in another you say you don't want it. You have got the nearest approach to it that can be given without your having the full authority that is vested in the Legislative Assemblies of the different Provinces . . .

Haultain to Daly, July 18, 1894.

You say that in one voice we shout for provincial autonomy and in another say we do not want it.

We have never shouted for provincial autonomy, but have consistently said we do not want it. Allow me to suggest that 'provincial autonomy' is not the only sort of autonomy suitable to these Territories. We want the autonomy of any self-governing organization, be it School District, Municipal Council or Territory.

In your haste to make us inconsistent you fall into the common mistake of losing sight of the substance and looking altogether at the form.

We do not want provincial forms, but we do want that substantial control of our own affairs which is enjoyed by all autonomous bodies. Make the circle of our powers and our duties large or small, but let us have complete autonomy within that circle . . . I am sorry to take up your time going over all this old ground again, but your letter calls for reply and I wish to be in a position to explain to the House and later to the people of the Territories that it was not for want of pressing on our part that the practical needs of the Country has been given so little or rather such unfriendly consideration by the Government.

Daly to Haultain, July 28, 1894.

It seems to me that you have all the control of your affairs that is necessary under the circumstances. You say 'make a circle of our powers and our duties, large or small, but let us have complete autonomy within that circle.' It seems to me that the Act meets your wishes in this respect. You cannot have complete autonomy without responsible Government. You say you do not want responsible Government, and yet in your letter to Mr. Davin of 25th June you say 'when we have as a precedent a familiar form of constitution, well understood, in operation in all the Provinces, as well as in the Dominion, why should we be saddled with a bastard form of Government, which presents difficulties and defies analogy at every turn?' This seems to me an extraordinary statement in view of the fact that the familiar form of constitution in operation in the Provinces represents autonomy or responsible Government in its fullest form. There is no analogy whatever between the present constitutional condition of the Territories and that of any Province in the Dominion and there cannot be until such time as you are given full autonomy . . .

Haultain to Daly, August 5, 1894.

Your letter of the 26th July still seems to me to confound the substance with the form. Because we ask for autonomy does not mean that we are asking for those mere accidents of autonomy, provincial institutions. Quite the contrary, we want autonomy but we do not want provincial institutions.

I did not say that we do not want responsible Government. We *do* want responsible Government, not provincial Government.

What we want is management of our own affairs, be they large or small. That management can best be had by means of a responsible body chosen in the same way as responsible advisors are chosen, either in the Dominion or the Provinces.

Our Executive machinery, within well defined limits, can be exactly the same as that of a Province, can be conducted by analogy and worked according to precedent, without any other approach to provincial institutions or the elaborate establishment and extensive jurisdiction of a Province.

I — 21

Clifford Sifton on Responsible Government for the North-West: House of Commons Debates, June 15, 1897, cols. 4115-4116.

The Minister of the Interior.

The Bill will give the people of the Territories a government which shall now have the full powers of a provincial government, but in so far as they have power to deal with subjects, they shall do it in the same way as other provinces. They will have Ministers who are responsible to the legislature, and the rules and precedents that apply to the provincial governments will apply to the government of the Territories.

. . . .

Mr. Bergeron (Conservative M.P. for Beauharnois).

I do not see that there is much object in this Bill. I believe that as soon as we can, we should constitute the North-West Territories into a province, and give them a responsible government in a complete form.

The Minister of the Interior.

That is what we are doing.

Mr. Bergeron.

Not at all.

The Minister of the Interior.

The Bill goes in that direction. . . . The principle upon which I acted is this. I met the representatives of the territorial government, and they explained to me—as of course I knew before— that there has been in the Territories for some years, an agitation in favour of what is called provincial autonomy. Now, it is a subject with which it would be extremely inconvenient to deal until it takes some shape in the public mind. I fancy that any Government that undertook to form an organization there, without something more defined to go by would find very considerable difficulty. But I said that if they wanted something of a practical character which would assist them in carrying on their business, no doubt their wishes in that respect could be met. They suggested, therefore, that a Bill such as I have presented to the House would, for the present, meet the views of the people; and I have not thought it advisable to go further at the present time, but to allow matters to develop. At a future time the House may be called on to deal with the question of the organization of a provincial constitution.

House of Commons Debates, June 15, 1897, cols. 4115-4116.

I — 22

An Act further to amend the Acts respecting the North-west Territories: Statutes of Canada, 1897, Chapter 28.

[Assented to 29th June, 1897.]

Her Majesty, by and with the advice and consent of the Senate and House of Commons of Canada, enacts as follows:—

1. In this Act, unless the context otherwise requires, the expression "the said Act" means The North-west Territories Act, chapter fifty of the Revised Statutes.

2. The paragraph lettered (c.) of section two of the said Act is hereby repealed and the following substituted therefor:—

"(c.) The expression 'Lieutenant-Governor in Council' means the Lieutenant-Governor of the Territories, by and with the advice and consent of the Executive Council of the Territories, or in conjunction with the Executive Council of the Territories, as the case may be."

3. The said section two is hereby further amended by adding the following paragraph thereto:—

"(g.) The expression 'Legislative Assembly' means the Legislative Assembly of the Territories composed, under the provisions of this Act, of the members elected to represent the several electoral divisions into which the Territories are or from time to time may be divided."

4. Section eleven of the said Act is hereby amended by adding at the end thereof the words "or of the Legislative Assembly."

5. Section twelve of the said Act is hereby amended by striking out the words "Lieutenant-Governor in Council" herein, and substituting in lieu thereof the words "Legislative Assembly."

6. The section substituted for section thirteen of the said Act by section six of chapter twenty-two of the statutes of 1891 is hereby amended by striking out the words "at any time in force in" in the fifth line thereof, and substituting in lieu thereof the words "declared to be applicable to," and by repealing subparagraph (c) of paragraph (7) of subsection one of the said section thirteen.

7. Section sixteen of the said Act is hereby repealed and the following substituted therefor:—

"16. The Legislative Assembly may, from time to time, make ordinances in respect to the mode of calling juries, other than grand juries, in criminal as well as civil cases, and when and by whom and the manner in which they may be summoned or taken, and in respect to all matters relating to the same."

8. Section seventeen of chapter seventeen of the statutes of 1894 is hereby repealed and the following substituted therefor:—

"17. There shall be a Council to aid and advise in the government of the Territories, to be styled the Executive Council of the Territories; and the persons who are to be members of that Council shall be, from time to time, chosen and summoned by the Lieutenant-Governor and sworn in; and members thereof may be, from time to time, removed by the Lieutenant-Governor.

"2. All powers, authorities and functions which, under any Act of the Parliament of Canada or Ordinance of the Territories, are vested in or exercisable by the Lieutenant-Governor with the advice, or with the advice and consent, of the Executive Committee of the Territories, or in conjunction with that Committee, shall, upon the passing of this Act, be vested in, and shall or may be exercised by the Lieutenant-Governor with the advice, or with the advice and consent of, or in conjunction with, the Executive Council of the Territories, subject, nevertheless, to be abolished or altered by competent legislative authority."

9. Section eighteen of chapter seventeen of the statutes of 1894 is hereby repealed and the following substituted therefor:—

"18. No person holding any office, commission or employment to which an annual salary from the Crown is attached, shall be eligible as a member of the Legislative Assembly, or shall sit or vote therein, during the time he holds such office, commission or employment; but nothing herein contained shall render ineligible any member of the Executive Council of the Territories, by reason of any salary, fee, allowance, emolument or profit of any kind or amount attaching to such membership, from being a member of the Assembly, or shall disqualify him from sitting or voting therein: Provided he is elected while holding such office, and is not otherwise disqualified."

10. Subsection one of section fifty-six of the said Act, as amended by section eight of chapter twenty-two of the statutes of 1891, is hereby repealed, and the following substituted therefor:—

"56. For each judicial district the Governor in Council may appoint a sheriff and the Lieutenant-Governor in Council may appoint a clerk of the court and may respectively name the place at which such sheriff and clerk, respectively, shall reside and keep an office; and the clerk of the district within which the seat of government of the Territories is situate, shall be registrar of the court sitting in banc."

11. Subsection one of the section substituted for section sixty-four of the said Act by section seven of chapter seventeen of the statutes of 1894 is hereby repealed and the following substituted therefor:—

"64. The Lieutenant-Governor may appoint justices of the peace for the Territories, who shall have jurisdiction as such throughout the same; but, until the Legislative Assembly otherwise provides, no person shall be appointed a justice of the peace for the Territories, or shall act as such, who is not the owner in fee simple for his own use and benefit of lands lying and being in the Territories of and above the value of three hundred dollars over and above what will satisfy and discharge all encumbrances affecting the same and over and above all rents and charges payable out of or affecting the same and who has not resided in the Territories for a period of at least three years."

12. Subsection two of the section substituted for section sixty-four of the said Act by section seven of chapter seventeen of the statutes of 1894 is hereby amended by adding the following words thereto: "or such other oath or oaths as the Legislative Assembly from time to time prescribes."

13. Subsection four of the section substituted for section sixty-four of the said Act by section seven of chapter seventeen of the statutes of 1894 is hereby amended by striking out all the words after "years" in the fourth line thereof.

14. Paragraph (a) of subsection one of section sixty-six of the said Act is hereby amended by striking out the word "larceny" in the first and second lines, and substituting therefor the word "theft," and by striking out the word "feloniously" in the third line of the said paragraph.

15. Subsection one of section eighty-eight of the said Act is hereby amended by striking out the words "Lieutenant-Governor" in the third line thereof, and substituting the words "Legislative Assembly" in lieu thereof.

16. Section ninety of the said Act is hereby amended by striking out the words "Lieutenant-Governor in Canada" therein and substituting the words "Legislative Assembly" in lieu thereof.

17. Section sixteen of chapter nineteen of the statutes of 1888, is hereby repealed.

18. Section one hundred and seven of the said Act is hereby repealed and the following substituted therefor:—

"107. All road allowances in townships now or hereafter surveyed and subdivided in the Territories, and all road allowances set out on block lines now or hereafter surveyed in the Territories, the plans of survey whereof have been duly approved, shall be subject to the direction, management and control of the Lieutenant-Governor in Council, for the public use of the Territories, subject to any ordinance made or to be made with respect thereto."

19. The section substituted for section one hundred and eight of the said Act by section seventeen of chapter twenty-two of the statutes of 1891 is hereby repealed and the following substituted therefor:—

"108. On the Minister of the Interior receiving notice from the Lieutenant-Governor in Council of any particular thoroughfare or public travelled road or trail in the Territories, which existed as such prior to the subdivision of the land into sections and which it is desired to have transferred to the Territories, the Governor in Council may pass an order authorizing the survey of such road or trail by a Dominion land surveyor, such survey to be made under instructions from the Lieutenant-Governor in accordance with manual of instructions regarding the manner of making such surveys approved by the Surveyor General of Dominion lands; and upon approval of the returns of such survey by the Surveyor General, one copy thereof shall be filed in the Department of the Interior and one in the Land Titles Office for the district within which such road or trail is situated, and such road or trail may then be transferred by the Governor in Council for the use of the Territories, subject to any rights which may have been acquired under letters patent issued previous to such transfer.

"2. The width of such road or trail shall be one chain or sixty-six feet; and in making the survey, the surveyor shall make such changes in the location of the road or trail as he finds necessary for improving it, without, however, altering its main direction."

20. Subsection one of section twenty-one of chapter seventeen of the statutes of 1894 is hereby repealed and the following substituted therefor:—

"21. Subject to any ordinances made with respect thereto, the Lieutenant-Governor in Council may close up any road allowance or trail which has been transferred to the Territories, or vary its direction, and may open and establish any new highway instead thereof, and may deal with the land in any road allowance, public travelled road or trail so closed as he sees fit."

21. The Lieutenant-Governor in Council may cause to be surveyed and marked on the ground such roads or trails as are from time to time deemed necessary to aid in the development of any district which cannot be served by existing road allowances or by old trails mentioned in the section substituted for section one hundred and eight of the said Act by section nineteen of this Act.

2. Such roads shall be laid out one chain or sixty-six feet in width; and in making the survey the manual of instructions mentioned in the said section shall be followed, and one copy of the returns of such survey shall be filed in the Land Titles Office for the district within which such trail is situated and a second copy in the offices of the North-west Government at Regina.

22. Section six of chapter fifteen of the statutes of 1892 is hereby repealed.

23. This Act shall come into force on the first day of October, in the year one thousand eight hundred and ninety-seven.

Section II
The Growth of the Demand
for Provincial Status, 1890-1900

*Anyone who confined their reading to the official documents
of the Territorial period would be left with the impression that
the movement for responsible government was neatly separated
chronologically from the movement for Provincial status.
Equally, the idea of Alberta as a separate province would seem,
even after the development of an official movement for
provincial status, to have been rather weak given all the Territorial figures who called for one new Province. As will be seen
in the following section, however, the idea of a Province of
Alberta existed before responsible government was achieved.
As early as 1890 the Calgary* Herald *began to editorialize on the
subject. Initially the movement was a local one but, by the later
1890's, had developed into a widespread popular idea, especially
in southern Alberta.*

*There is a certain irony in the way in which this campaign
evolved. Initially the separation of Alberta was as important, if
not more important, than the constitutional question of
provincial status. Nevertheless, this separatist movement provided one of the major forces behind a Territory-wide demand
for constitutional alteration quite apart from any separation.
Also, the driving force behind many Calgarians' demands for
Alberta provincehood was the desire to make their city the capital. Eventually, as will be seen, Calgary was to lose in this contest to Edmonton, a city which in the early stages had been
unenthusiastic about the idea of provincial autonomy.*

II — 1

**'Wanted—A New Territory—The Territory of Alberta.
Calgary Herald, September 20, 1890:**

The time has come when the question of a division of the
North-West Territories should be, first, seriously considered,
and then, with a proper scheme matured, pushed vigorously
until the desired result has been accomplished.

What is needed in the interests of the western section of the
Territories is a division which will throw together those
portions of the vast country that have interests in common as a
country for ranching, mining and mixed farming. That is to
say: the territory east of British Columbia and west of a line
drawn north through Medicine Hat or Swift Current should be
formed into the Territory of Alberta, with Calgary as its capital,
leaving all east of this line to form a separate territory with its

capital wherever its inhabitants please to place it. The new territory would include in addition to the towns on the C.P.R. railway, such points as Edmonton, Macleod and Lethbridge. If Swift Current were to be selected as the dividing line, Battleford would fall into the new Territory of Alberta. If the line be drawn at Medicine Hat, then all the principal towns will, with the railways now projected, be in immediate communication with each other and with Calgary; and the Territory of Alberta, would present a compact whole, harmonious yet diverse, varied in resources yet the several parts supplying what is wanting in each other. We would have the coal mines of the Bow and the Red Deer, the gold of Edmonton, the gold and silver mines of the mountains and the oil fields of the Waterton Lakes in the south and of Athabasca in the north. The Territory—soon to become a province—could boast of the finest agricultural lands, the best summer and winter ranges, the finest product of wheat, barley and oats, the choicest locations for cheese and butter factories, and with all the healthiest climate in America.

The Herald *returned to the scheme of a separate territory of Alberta a few days later. Predicting unanimous support it urged its readers and the community generally to begin practical steps to see the idea accomplished.*

II — 2

'The Question of the Hour': Calgary Herald, October 1, 1890.

. . . On the grounds of economy of time and means, the public convenience and every other consideration in the interests of Alberta, the agitation now renewed should be continued until the work has been accomplished. As soon as the British farmer delegates have left us it will be the duty of our people to take up this question, ventilate it thoroughly and seek the cooperation of all sections of Alberta with a view to pressing for immediate action by the Dominion Government and Parliament. We cannot conceive of any opposition being offered to it within Alberta itself; we cannot believe that anything short of absolute unanimity will exist. It is important, however, to consolidate and utilize this public sentiment and to make this the question of the hour, all other questions being relegated to the rear until this has been satisfactorily disposed of. We shall need an expression of opinion from Town Council and from the citizens en masse, and with the sanction of the citizens a committee of action should be chosen whose duty it should be to promote the movement by every means in their power in conjunction with the other towns of Alberta.

Even as the Herald released the above editorial which expressed its belief in unanimous support for the idea, opposition was being expressed by another regional newspaper.

II—3

'A Very Previous Scheme:' Lethbridge News, October 1, 1890.

The movement on foot for a Territorial division, with headquarters at Calgary, is, we think, a most ridiculous one, and whoever started it is certainly ill-advised. Don't let anyone imagine for a moment that we are jealous of Calgary. On the contrary, when the time comes for a division of the Territories, we would almost promise to support Calgary's claim to be the capital city. But the time has not yet come for any division. Are we not even now striving with the Dominion Government for a recognition of the importance of the Territories as they exist, and having our struggles rewarded by the answer, "not yet awhile." If we would gain Territorial rights to which we claim we are entitled, we must be firm and undivided. Once these powers are obtained, and the Territories have proved too unwieldly for proper handling, it will be plenty of time to demand a division, but it is absurd to suppose that the people will consent to taking chances of losing the relief they are now asking for in order to obtain a new government of the same kind as the present one at Regina. It would be all very fine for Calgary to have public money spent there in erecting Government buildings, etc., but the scheme is too far-fetched to attract support just now. Esop's fable of the dog who dropped his bone in the water in order that he might grasp the shadow, would be suitable reading matter for the promoters of the new idea. Do not be misled by any false feeling of the splendor and grandeur of having a capital within our own Territory, nor yet with the thought that by a division Alberta of itself would be almost a Province. Show your good common sense by opposing the crack-brained scheme, and last but not least (to use the words of the late lamented Shakespeare) 'Don't be a clam.'

II — 4

'Alberta Territory:' Macleod Gazette, October 9, 1890.

The Gazette contends with all the strength of its "decaying powers" and with all force of its "tenderfoot" journalistic ability that the division of the territories as proposed by the Calgary Herald, apart from the numerous advantages set out by that paper, would hasten the coming of those larger powers rather than retard it. We should have a compact territory, whose people would be practically unanimous regarding their wants and requirements. The very agitation which would precede such a division would attract universal attention to the present unsatisfactory state of affairs, and it is nearly an absolute certainty as anything can be in this uncertain world that when the act making this division was passed, acts giving the two great territorial divisions the powers the territory as a whole has failed to obtain, would be passed without opposition. At the present moment the members east of the line drawn north and south through Maple Creek, for instance, could out-vote the members west of that line about two to one. The interests of the eastern portion of the territories are by no means identical with those of the west, and in the event of a clash, Alberta must go to the wall every time. Territorial legislation which may be extremely beneficial for the Assiniboias, might be altogether injurious to Alberta; but Alberta would be made to submit to the injury for the sake of Assiniboia. When it came to a question of the people of the territories voting on the liquor question, it was contended that the matter should be decided by the vote of the whole territories, rather than by each provisional district. That would have meant dictation to Alberta by Assiniboia; and this is only one of the many questions as between the east and west that must come up in the near future. The injury to Alberta as part of the present territories will be still more marked after the control of the funds is granted. Now, then, is the time to strike out for this division of the territories, each part having the powers that the whole has been contending for so long. If we wait until after what will be practically provincial autonomy is granted, it will take ages to move the government in any new direction. It would be well for those whose first impression may be opposition to such a division to carefully consider the matter from every point of view. It is a question calling for grave deliberation, not for spontaneous effusions which show lack of consideration and lamentable in-experience.

While the various newspapers in southern Alberta debated the advantages and disadvantages of division, other groups in Calgary were moving to take the question beyond the editorial pages. On October 21, 1890 a meeting of "leading citizens" discussed the issue and passed various resolutions in its favour. While this meeting cannot be said to be necessarily representative of Calgary views, much less those of Alberta, the presence of a number of political figures does indicate that the idea of a separate Alberta was considered seriously by some. The Mayor of Calgary, J.E. Lafferty, Senator James Lougheed and various city councillors and Members of the Territorial Legislative Assembly gave the resolutions a certain weight.

II — 5

Resolutions of Meeting of October 21, 1890. Cited from Calgary Herald, October 22, 1890.

Moved by J.G. Fitzgerald, seconded by A. Lucas, that it is the opinion of this meeting that we should seek a separate local form of government for Alberta and that portion of the Territories contiguous thereto at the earliest possible date. Carried.

Moved by Mr. H.S. Cayley, seconded by Mr. A. Rowe, that it is the opinion of this meeting that a convention be called to consider what representations should be made to the government on the subject.

Moved by A. Allan, seconded by J.L. Bowen, that the following be a committee to enter into correspondence with other centers of Alberta and Western Assiniboia as to their views on the question of separate government and taking the necessary steps for calling a convention: Messrs Lougheed, George Alexander, A. Lucas, J.G. Fitzgerald, J.E. Lafferty, Jas Bannerman, John Livingston, T.B. Braden, H.S. Cayley, and J. Lineham.

Nothing seems to have come of the resolutions at the October meeting and, after a few more snipes at each other, the various newspapers dropped the subject for the winter. The next June, however, the issue was revived. Once again it was closely tied to the issue of responsible government and the financial grants being fought for by the Territorial government. By this time,

*however, the Calgary Herald decided the two issues could best
be resolved by moving directly to provincial status for Alberta.
For the first time the Herald saw the issue in terms that would
become increasingly common in future years.*

II — 6

Calgary Herald, July 6, 1891.

. . . We have had enough of hybrid systems of government
unknown to the British Constitution. We will be content, after
abandoning the Regina failure, to accept for Alberta nothing
short of the responsibilities and privileges which have fallen to
the Provinces of Canada. The bug-bear of taxation will not
scare the tax-payers of Alberta who very well know that the
absorption of the lands and minerals of Alberta by the Federal
government ensures a very large cash subsidy in lieu thereof
and that the revenues which the Dominion must provide for
local purposes will render local taxation altogether unnecessary. The pretence of the [Manitoba] Free Press that our schools
and roads and bridges must suffer if we have a separate government for Alberta is the veriest flummery. It is put forth by those
who wish to keep things centralized at Regina and by those in
Manitoba who are interested in preventing Alberta from
moving energetically, through a government of her own, in
promoting immigration into this desirable district. It suits the
interests of Regina to cry down the erection of Alberta into a
Province just as it suits the interests of Manitoba to pull on the
same string but in a matter where the interests of Alberta for all
time to come are so seriously affected, Albertans will not go
either to Winnipeg or Regina for advice. Albertans feel
thoroughly competent to manage their own affairs, and they
feel that the time has come to move in that direction. When they
decide that they will govern themselves they mean it. And what
they mean is local government as established in the Eastern
Provinces—nothing more, nothing less. They wish no longer
to be under a liquor law which Parliament has imposed on
them against their will, but which Parliament dare not attempt
to impose on any province of the Dominion. They wish to be
relieved from the blackmail which imposes a special tax of ten
cents on every gallon of "four per cent" beer drunk in Alberta—
a species of blackmail to which no province in the Dominion
would submit for an instant. They wish to be relieved of

government by a governor and a couple of clerks at Regina; for
they feel they are insulted every hour this lasts; and they know
that not a Canadian citizen in the east would submit to such
government for a single moment. When they ask to be relieved
of their disabilities they mean relief in the fullest sense of the
term. They desire to be placed on precisely the same footing as
their fellow-citizens in the provinces in the east. They desire the
same civil rights, the same full control of all local expenditures,
and the same freedom in legislation. Their Bill of Rights is a
simple affair; they ask that a Canadian citizen in Alberta shall
enjoy the same privileges as a Canadian citizen in Ontario, in
New Brunswick, in Manitoba, or in Nova Scotia. The argument
that Albertans are not fit to be entrusted with the governing of
themselves, or that they are less able to bear the responsibilities
than people in other parts of Canada, will not go down here.
There are none in Canada better prepared to assume such
responsibilities or better prepared to legislate for themselves;
and those who assert to the contrary either do not know Alberta
or have sinister motives for wishing to see Alberta tied to the
apron string of Regina and Ottawa.

*The flurry of interest in the idea of provincial status for
Alberta was premature in the early 1890's and by the end of 1891
even the Calgary Herald had turned its attention to other
matters. Through the next few years, as illustrated in Section I,
the main political question was that of responsible government
for the Territories rather than division or provincial status. In
1895, however, the issue reappeared in Calgary and soon spread
to other parts of Alberta. While there would still be a long wait
before realization of the idea, the issue seems to have had more
force in 1895. Certainly it never completely disappeared again
as an issue in Territorial newspapers. In fact, it soon began to
gather political adherents to the cause and would eventually be
adopted as the cause of a number of influential figures in the
Territorial legislature.*

*Interestingly, the reawakening of the theme of provincial
status seem to have come about in a rather indirect way.
Manitoba's demands for better terms caused the editor of the
Calgary Herald, now John J. Young, to remember the crusade
of his predecessor. That was all that was necessary to rekindle
the enthusiasm of several individuals in Calgary for the idea of
a Province of Alberta.*

'Insatiable:' Calgary Herald, January 9, 1895.

So the Province of Manitoba is again sending a delegation to Ottawa to ask for "Better Terms." The horseleach hath two daughters, crying 'give, give'—and so it is with that political Oliver Twist, the prairie province. It has been a succession of 'Better terms.' Those of 1894, in which the Farmers' Union agitation culminated, were supposed to have finally settled its financial arrangements with the Dominion. And, on the whole, Manitoba was very liberally dealt with. There is no legitimate excuse for an attempt to re-open the matter at this juncture. But the Greenway government is getting hard up for political capital, and an agitation on this line is always something to conjure with in a community of such cupidity as Manitoba. . . . The particular bearing of all this on Alberta is that Alberta had better obtain provincial status and endowment before Manitoba succeeds in draining the Dominion treasury dry.

Letter to the editor from James Reilly: Calgary Herald, February 16, 1895.

Towards the end of the month of September 1890, there appeared a leader in The *Herald* that both startled and interested the readers of that paper.

It was from the pen of the late John Livingston, then the editor of that paper, and one of the foremost thinkers and writers in Canada. The article was headed 'The Territorial Autonomy of Alberta' and was one of the most terse and forcible pronunciations in favour of that move that ever appeared from the brain of that great journalist whilst he remained the leading editorial voice in the North West. . . And the question before us now is, how does their reasoning and suggestions apply to our conditions now? At that time a kindred prosperity and hopefulness prevailed both north and south, in our new land of promise, and hundreds came every year to make their homes in our district, where good crops and short winters gave promise of agricultural advancement, comfortable homes sprang up both far and wide, and the increase in value was mutual and concurrent in town and country. And there seemed no call for a change at that time. But what a change has come upon us now! The whole of central and southern Alberta as well as a portion of Western Assiniboia is strangely and unexpectedly paralyzed, and isolated from the rest of the Territories and from the rest of Canada, and in a sense avoided through our great and unlooked for disability a lack of rainfall. Our rich and fertile district rendered suddenly sterile through aridity, our hardy settlers and husbandmen disappointed and for a time embarrassed, our cities and towns correspondingly depressed, property of every kind heretofore appreciable and commanding good prices now reduced to unsaleableness. I think it best that we should realize and measure candidly this widespread dilemma in which we are held together by the cohesion of mutual loss, in order that we may well and unitedly consider the best, as well as the most direct way of obtaining a change. . . . It is a time when all that is suggestive and helpful in our united citizenship should speak out for what is most fit and proper in the present state of our country, its needs, its rights, its possibilities.

It is a time, sir, when the press of Alberta should speak out without ambiguity, speak fearlessly, speak with a comprehensive grasp of the needs of our people, speak out with a purpose of moulding public opinion on the lines of patriotic purpose and action. It is a time when the press of Alberta should pronounce itself in favour of provincial independence for Alberta.

Let the question be fully discussed. I regard some change as being almost a matter of life or death to us, in view of the present state of business. Far removed from Ottawa, the only possible source of political or financial assistance, whence the other Provinces derive their share of Dominion monies by constitutional right, but where the Territories have to appear as an annual mendicant for all we can get, Alberta appealing through her representative finds herself now at the door of an empty treasury (owing to the general depression)—one of 215 applicants, to ask money for irrigation, and immigration: money so sorely needed for direct intercourse with the United States, money to encourage much needed local railways, money to start, encourage and foster our dairy industries is essential and necessary for our provincial advancement and prosperity. Now I appeal to every man enjoying a reasonable share of common sense to decide what chance is given us under present conditions, when every one of the 215 members have behind them a string of wants as long as our own?

Now why continue importuning amidst a swarm of claimants? Why keep boring for oil with a gimlet, when we might draw from the spring supplied from our own provincial credit and independence, and if it is so thought best, then there is no time to lose. A united call should be made to come together and organize for an appeal to this end. The Dominion Government cannot refuse us rights and powers conceded to others less entitled and less needful. Unable to help us in our season of embarrassment, it cannot, dare not, deny us the power to help ourselves . . . Then, I repeat, in the name of all that is expedient and justifiable, let us unite and act at once, and urge it till it is obtained, and with this provincial credit and power I trust a rapid change for the better, that will promote the proserity and happiness of our people.

II — 9

'The Question of the Hour:' Calgary Herald, February 19, 1895.

The three things above all others that are of the most vital importance to Alberta at the present time, and before which all other questions sink into insignificance, are:

PROVINCIAL GOVERNMENT

IMMIGRATION

IRRIGATION

The *Herald* regards these three planks in the Alberta platform as of the very highest and almost equal importance. The success of either will assure the success of the other two. With irrigation placed on a practical footing, immigration will be boomed and Provincial independence hastened. The writer is as yet a comparative stranger in Alberta, but he has watched events here with sufficient care to be convinced that Alberta can never accomplish what she should and could accomplish in regard to both immigration and irrigation until her shackles are thrown off and she is placed in a position to help herself. At present her hands are tied. She cannot send out immigration agents, she cannot advertise herself in the countries from which she seeks population, she cannot charter railways, she is powerless to develop her vast mining wealth, she cannot pledge her credit to bring in capital for the construction of irrigation and other public works. True she has the right to a single representative in the Ottawa legislature and also to a handful in the apology for a legislature at Regina. But against overwhelming numbers and opposing interests the little that they can do is but a drop in the bucket compared with what should be done.

A "Mass Meeting" of Calgary citizens and of political figures from throughout the Territories on March 22, 1895 indicated that the efforts of Reilly and of the Herald were met sympathetically by a number of important local figures. The Mayor of Calgary, Senator James Lougheed and A. L. Sifton, all revealed their sympathy for the idea. Haultain, for his part, experienced at first hand the growing sense of Alberta identity which ran counter to his plans both to concentrate on responsible government within a territorial structure and with his belief that the Territories should remain one political unit, whatever their status.

II — 10

'The Mass Meeting,' Calgary Herald, March 27, 1895.

James Reilly initiated the meeting with a speech in favour of Provincial autonomy for Alberta. He then moved the following resolution which was seconded by Mr. McBride:

That in view of an additional session of the Dominion Parliament being held before dissolution, at which there will be given the opportunity to hear and consider the petition of any portion of the people on any matter whereby their interests may be advanced or facilitated, it is the opinion of this meeting of the citizens of Calgary that a full measure of Provincial Government should be granted to the people of Alberta on the terms and conditions as may be expressed in the address presented to the Parliament of Canada during the coming session for this purpose.

Mr. McBride on seconding the resolution said he was thoroughly in sympathy with it. He thought we had been in leading strings long enough. If the people of Quebec or Nova Scotia knew better what was for our good than we did we had better remain as we were, but if not we had better take steps to have Parliament attend to our needs.

Mr. Murdoch thought this meeting was called to give the visitors from outside points who were present an opportunity of presenting their views.

Mr. Haultain was then called upon and taking the platform wished as a "resident of a small hamlet, etc., etc.," to congratulate the people of Calgary on this meeting. He said he had taken a few notes. Re Provincial Autonomy he did not think the time had come when any portion of the Territories should desire to take upon itself the burdens of Provincial Government. He thought we had been getting along very well as we are. He had urged and had been somewhat instrumental in getting self-government for the territories. Territorial Government was all right in that we got the advantages of self-government without undertaking the larger burdens and responsibilities. He thought we had not yet arrived at the point that we were ready for it; we had progressed too slowly. He said it would open up so many important questions, such as when the whole Territories, with only four representatives and two senators had such little influence in getting what we have got, how would Alberta fare if she went to Ottawa alone to ask these things? Can it be imagined that we can at once obtain them for Alberta when after so many years Manitoba has got so little; our chances of getting them were practically nil. Mr. Reilly had urged as one of the reasons for Provincial Government the power of borrowing money and thus getting into debt, and this was one of the principal reasons he (Mr. Haultain) opposed it. He thought nothing was more dangerous for a new country than getting into debt. He said what we ought to consider was our present institutions and the means of developing them. He said doubtless we were coming to Provincial Autonomy, but we should be improving our present institutions to get ready for it.

Mr. A.L. Sifton was the next speaker, and he began by regretting he had to disagree with all the speakers excepting Mr. McBride. He said he would not like to disparage the members of the Legislative Assembly, for if the people of this country had done what they should have done he would have been a member of that body himself, and he did not believe in disparaging any body of which he had tried hard to be a member. He disagreed with Mr. Haultain for he thought the time had arrived right now when Albertans should put forth every effort to secure a greater amount of self-government than they now enjoy. He said he did not expect to get it this year, nor yet the following year if the people of Alberta did not put forth a much greater effort to secure it. If it was going to take such a long time to secure Provincial Autonomy as Mr. Haultain predicted, it was surely high time that we began. Manitoba with her small handful of people at the time she became a Province, had succeeded well, and although she had representatives in the Dominion Parliament, yet it was only by the Provincial Government taking hold of matters themselves and pushing them vigorously, in spite of their federal representatives and in spite of the Dominion Government that had achieved the success she has. In like manner if Alberta ever got independent railway communication with the outside world it would only be obtained when we were a province to act for ourselves as Manitoba had done. The same was true of imigration, and surely, he said, when our settlers were finding that the land was getting drier year by year and were becoming disheartened and discouraged, it would not do, as the Premier had suggested to sit idly by and let matters take their course, but we must be up and doing to get this matter under proper way. Mr. Haultain had tried to make a bugbear of the expense we would be put to in building our own bridges, looking after our own lunatics and criminals etc. Of course we would, but we would have instead of $30,000 as now, nearly $500,000 to do it with. We certainly did not want the money that had to be expended looking after criminals and lunatics expended in other provinces but we want it done right here in our midst. No doubt, he said, we would not get all we were entitled to from the Government at once, but our representatives would have to work hard for it and the concessions that had been made to Manitoba would be used as a precedent for dealing with the new province. He concluded a powerful and eloquent speech by asserting that Alberta much needed a full measure of Provincial Government and needed it now. He was applauded and cheered most heartily . . .

After repeated calling Mr. Costigan took the platform and carefully reviewed the situation, stating that he had not as yet given much study to this important measure but urged that the matter be not pressed upon the Government at its present session, but rather be left over because he had every confidence in the statesmen of Canada to believe that when they believed it to be in the interests of the whole country to set Alberta aside as a province they would do so. He moved in amendment to Mr. Reilly's motion that the words "at this session" be struck out and the motion as amended carried. Mr. Henry Brown seconded the amendment, which on being put received about half a dozen votes. The original motion was then put and carried with cheers. The meeting then adjourned.

The Committee created at the meeting of March 22, 1895 took a number of steps to promote their ideas. One of these was a widely circulated pamphlet, Provincial Government for Alberta, *which summarized the various arguments in favour of a new Province.*

II — 11

Provincial Government for Alberta. Its Meaning and Necessity (Calgary, 1895).

On the 22nd March, 1895, advantage was taken of the presence in Calgary of a large number of representative men from all parts of Alberta to hold a mass meeting to consider the propriety of taking action to obtain the early constitution of the western portion of the Northwest Territories into a Province, and so secure for its people their full rights as Canadian subjects, a number of which they do not now enjoy. By that meeting the movement was heartily endorsed. The result of the meeting was the formation of a Provisional Committee to take steps towards the organization of a representative League for the advancement of the movement. That Committee has decided that the best way of organizing such a league would be by the calling of a Convention of delegates from all parts of the Territory of Alberta and the westerly districts of the Territories of Saskatchewan and Assiniboia. Such a Convention will shortly be held. In the meantime, that the movement may be well understood and that the delegates to that Convention may be intelligently selected, it has been decided by the Committee to present shortly some of the reasons which have suggested the movement. It is with such object in view that this pamphlet has been prepared and distributed.

The birthright of a British subject is self-government. This principle, hammered out by centuries of conflict in Great Britain, has been extended to every corner of the Empire in a greater or lesser degree. It is based on the common sense notion that every ordinarily reasonable human being knows best what he wants himself, and can best point out the method of attaining it, either by himself or in concert with others in like circumstances.

The British subject who leaves the settled haunts of civilization and goes forth to open up fresh tracts and add new provinces to the Empire, never imagines for a moment that in doing so he is relinquishing one jot or tittle of this right. For a while the necessities of the situation may lead him to acquiesce in a more irresponsible form of government than that to which he has been accustomed, but he regards this state of things as merely temporary, and looks with certainty to the time when every privilege of British citizenship will be handed to him unimpaired.

Such being the unquestioned state of the case, it is proposed in this little pamphlet, firstly, to examine our own position at present in Alberta; secondly, to investigate whether the time has not already arrived for that position to be improved; thirdly, to inquire into the possible benefit which will accrue to the country by such an improvement in our status in the Dominion and Empire, ceded to us by the Central Power.

THE PRESENT POSITION

At present, in common with the rest of the Territories, we are governed by a Lieutenant-Governor who resides nearly 500 miles away, at Regina, and a Legislative Assembly sitting at the same place, to which we furnish a contingent of 10 out of a total of 29 members. The powers of this Assembly are of a very limited nature. They have no authority to legislate for borrowing money on the credit of the Territories, or to regulate any local works and undertaking, or to incorporate any railway, steamboat, canal, transportation, telegraph, irrigation or insurance companies, even for purely Territorial objects within the limits of the Territories. Neither have they any power to make laws with regard to immigration into the Territories. Thus it will readily be seen that they have no real control over the destiny and development of the country. Our representatives have no power to pledge the credit of the Territories in order to raise money for Territorial purposes, and cannot in consequence initiate any large or comprehensive scheme of any kind with a view to the benefit and progress of the country. But it is not only in the meagre power of our Territorial representatives that our inferiority consists. It is not only that as a community we are deprived of the power to help ourselves. As part and parcel of the Dominion of Canada, we do not reap anything like all the benefits our position as such entitles us, nor as long as we remain in our present condition of Territorial infancy have we any chance of doing so. As individuals we contribute, man for man, a fully average share to the customs duties from which the revenue of the Dominion is chiefly derived. But all we received last year for our own use out of the revenue was a paltry $30,000.

This subsidy is given us by the Dominion Government. We have no constitutional claim upon the Federal revenue whatever. The Territorial Legislature has to take whatever sum is doled out to it and be thankful. It has no fixed income of its own and no power to borrow. It is a legal minor. Times may be hard, business paralyzed, the development of the country stagnant, but our local Legislature is powerless to help us. The powers which it should possess are in the hands of the Dominion House, among whose members not ten per cent, either know or care anything about the Northwest. Our mouthpiece in that House is the Minister of the Interior, to whose department we belong along with the lunatics and Indians. And it is not putting the case too strongly to assert that, with one notable exception, the Minister of the Interior, for the past decade, has simply been, so far as the Territories are concerned, the mouthpiece of two or three permanent officials. They are our real rulers. Under the forms of constitutional government, we, freeborn British subjects, have no more to say in the making of the country which we have opened up, and which we are endeavouring under every kind of official discouragement to develop, than the peasants of Russia have to do with the proclamations of the court of St. Petersburg.

PROVINCIAL GOVERNMENT

What is the remedy for these evils? How can we gain our full rights and privileges as Canadians and British subjects? How can we change the present condition of discouragement and stagnation into which we have fallen, to one of renewed energy, hopefulness and prosperity? The constitution of the Dominion points the way and invites us to take it. It provides for the admission of new Provinces into confederation, expressly stating that such admission must be at the request of their inhabitants. It grants the new Provinces the full powers conceded to the old ones, the right to borrow money on their own credit, to initiate undertakings for their own benefit, to charter and subsidize railways within their own limits, to devise and carry out their own plans to attract immigration within their own borders. It leaves the destiny of the new Province to those who have the most thorough knowledge of her requirements and the greatest interest in her development, her own people. We should no longer have to sit helpless with a vast field of fine anthracite coal, the only known field in Canada, the only known field but one in North America, lying undeveloped at our very door for want of proper railway facilities to carry it to the market that is waiting for it in the silver states across the line. We should no longer have to stand by and see our settlers in the semi-arid districts abandoning their farms in despair at a Government that will neither help them to irrigate nor let them help themselves. We could charter and subsidize railways to develop our magnificent mineral resources and to open up fresh tracts to the settler; we could set on foot comprehensive schemes of irrigation in our semi-arid districts; we could start our own government creameries, build the bridges necessary to facilitate the intercourse and commerce of our people, and by the attractions of the area of prosperity and activity which the very inception of these enterprizes would create, induce increased immigration within our limits.

Again, instead of the paltry dole of twenty or thirty thousand dollars conceded to us by the generosity of the Federal Parliament, we, as a Province, would be in receipt of a regular revenue provided for us by the constitution of the Dominion under the enactments of the British North America Act.

This Act provides for fixed subsidies from the Federal to the Provincial Governments, which subsidies fall into four classes: First, those Provinces which are free from debt at the time of incorporation into the Dominion receive a subsidy on capital account. Manitoba receives from the Canadian Government the annual sum of $160,000 on this ground, Secondly, a fixed amount exclusive of the salary of the Lieutenant Governor is yearly paid to each Province for the support of its Government and Legislature. Manitoba receives $50,000 per annum on this account. Thirdly, an annual grant is made to each Province equal to 80 cents per head of the population as shown by the last decennial census until the population amounts to 200,000 souls, at which amount such grant remains thereafter. And it may be noted that the Manitoba Act in estimating the population of that Province at 17,000 souls in 1870 clearly included Indians in the total population entitled to this 80 cents per head. Fourthly, if, as in Manitoba, the vacant lands of the Province at the time of incorporation would remain vested in the Crown, for the use of the Dominion, Alberta would, like that Province, receive an additional subsidy on that account. The total amount of the subsidy to Manitoba this year (1895) figured in its estimates as published in the Free Press of Feb. 14th at $418,267.31, forming by far the largest item among its sources of revenue. Taking these figures as a basis, although both our population and area being at least double that of

Manitoba in 1870, we should in consequence receive more generous treatment in the matter of the first and second class of subsidies, we should be drawing now from the Dominion Government an annual sum of at least $150,000. When we should be receiving this as our right, how much longer do we intend to be humbly thankful for $30,000 as a favour?

These, then, being the obvious advantages which would be the result of our scheme, what are the

OBJECTIONS TO THE SCHEME?

1. The most usual objection to the proposal that the time is ripe to receive Provincial Government which is met with among our own people, is that Provincial Government would mean taxation.

Now, as already has been pointed out, a regular annual subsidy is paid to each Province of the Dominion out of the Federal revenue for the support and maintenance of its Government and Legislature; so that there is no truth in the objection that we should be taxed to keep up a Provincial Government any more than we are at present to support a Territorial one. If, on the other hand, it is meant by this objection that a Provincial Government would have power to levy taxes for other purposes, the answer is obvious. In the first place, it would lie entirely in our own hands whether we used this power or not. Secondly, they would in this respect have no more power than our present Territorial Legislature, to which the North West Act distinctly gives authority to raise money by direct taxation for Territorial purposes. So far, they have not found any occasion to use this power, nor is it likely a Provincial Government would require to do so, since we find, in the third place, that other Provinces manage to make both ends meet without using it. The Manitoba estimates for the current year show a total of receipts from various sources of $1,581,445 but there is not a single item among them derived from direct taxation. If they can get on without taxing their people, under what necessity would a Provincial Legislature in Alberta find itself for resorting to this expedient?

2. It is argued that our present population is too small and that our general standing in the Dominion is too insignificant to warrant the Federal Government acceding to our demand to be raised to the dignity of a Province. We are told that even little Prince Edward Island would laugh at the idea of a Province with only one member in the Dominion House. In the absence

of any fixed rule as to how large a population or how many members of Parliament a Canadian Territory must possess before it can claim a right to become a Province, all that can be done is to follow the invariable constitutional practice of establishing a precedent; and the only precedent for the admission into the Dominion of any community in the least resembling our own is the case of Manitoba, all other Provinces having been Crown colonies previous to incorporation. And the case of Manitoba is fatal to the objection. Her area was smaller than ours, her ascertained resources and prospects of less importance, her population only 17,000—even at the estimate of the Manitoba Act which was 5,000 in excess of the reality—of whom only about 1500 were white, and her first seats in the Dominion House were granted by the very Act, which admitted her to incorporation, no less than four being given to her inconsiderable electorate in order to enable her to take her place in the Dominion with as much dignity as possible. Why should Alberta expect or experience a less generous mode of treatment? One thing is certain. If we are too few in number to become incorporated as a Province, we are too many to continue to exist much longer in this country as a Territory. If our present condition of stagnation and the present Government policy of *laissez faire* is to continue much longer, Alberta is already over populated; and the Ottawa officials, who refuse either to aid any projects tending to develop our latent resources or to give us the power to aid ourselves, had better cease their spasmodic efforts to bring people into it. This "spirited immigration policy", about which we hear so much, without a spirited development policy at the back of it, is worse than useless, it is positively mischievous. It only adds fresh victims to a population that is quite large enough to suffer as it is.

CONCLUSION

If we are tired of this state of things (as who is not?); if we desire to gain the full management of our own affairs, and our full and rightful status as citizens of this Dominion, one thing is certainly necessary. Laying aside narrower aims and aspirations, we must make such an unanimous application to become incorporated as a Province as the Federal authorities can not choose but hear. The voice of our member is only one among 215; but the united demand of our 40,000 citizens, expressed in petitions, mass meetings and conventions, cannot help but be heard. We must take the first step ourselves as one people. And, as we shall only be asking that which on every principle of reason and justice is our own, only one result can follow. The pretensions of Ontario and Quebec to know what we want better than we do ourselves, will speedily collapse before a show of resolute unanimity on our part, and the present attitude will speedily change to one of welcome to the last new Province of the Dominion—youngest in point of date, but designed, perhaps, in course of time to become the greatest and most important of them all.

Not all were as enthusiastic in their support of provincial status for Alberta as was the writer of this pamphlet. The Edmonton *Bulletin, run by Liberal politician Frank Oliver, saw the whole idea initially as a scheme in the interests of Calgary rather than Alberta.*

II — 12

'Hog Like Propensities:' Edmonton Bulletin, April 15, 1895.

We notice that the "hog" like propensities of Calgary are still to the fore and that Jimmy Reilly and a few other political hacks have been airing themselves on provincial autonomy. Not that they think it is necessary for the welfare of the whole of Alberta, but simply the little patch of about one mile by two miles known as the city of Calgary. Calgary to be the capital; Calgary to be the head of half a dozen railways running nowhere of any importance to Alberta; Calgary to be the head of a lot of useless schemes as long as it can get plenty of money to spend in and about it; Calgary to have all the appointments for running the proposed provincial autonomy. Calgary's motto is "The end justifies the means;" but to get down to practical business the following advice is given gratis: 1st, Let Alberta have more representation in the Dominion house; 2nd, Drop all talk of provincial autonomy, and advocate that the government give every farmer living in central and southern Alberta free transport for himself, family and stock to Northern Alberta and also a patent for the same amount of land and pay for whatever improvements he may have in his present abode. In this way the settler will be ahead and the government be in pocket thousands of dollars, and the whole district of Alberta benefited. Five years from now will be plenty of time to talk about "provincial autonomy," and fifty years from now, about irrigating such a vast extent of country in Central and Southern Alberta as is now spoken of.

While the Edmonton Bulletin *initially opposed the* Herald's *push for Provincial autonomy, the very fact that papers and the public in the Edmonton area were beginning to consider the idea indicates that the movement was being taken more seriously in 1895 and 1896 than it had been in 1890. Nor were all in the area opposed to the idea of Alberta as a separate Province.*

II — 13

Edmonton Herald, 'Home Rule for Alberta': Cited in Calgary Herald, November 18, 1895.

The movement in favour of securing the creation of a new province out of the present district of Alberta and part of Western Assiniboia has been carried forward another stage by the Calgary committee, which is composed of solid, steady going business men as far removed from wild enthusiasts or political fadmongers as any body of men that could be possibly imagined . . . They point out that the British North America Act lays down no conditions of population or area to which a district must attain before being admitted to confederation as a province, but that it does require as a necessary preliminary that the people of the district itself shall demand such admission. For the success of the movement it is practically necessary that this demand shall be unanimous, and the Calgary committee wish in consequence to get means to enable them to meet the people of the various towns, villages and settlements in Alberta, explain their views and remove any objections which may be urged against it.

While there are in Edmonton a large number of supporters of the idea of home rule for Alberta, it is quite certain that this place is not taking part in the movement which its importance demands that it should. Instead of ranking, as from our supiness in the matter it is quite certain we must be ranking, in the eyes of the southern public, among those places which require a missionary visit of enlightenment we ought to have a body of our own cooperating with the committee at this very time, and devising a scheme for spreading the agitation through the country immediately around us. An ignorance about the features of the movement and an apathy with regard to it, which is excusable at Duhamel or Josephburg, is unpardonable in a place with the ambitions and prospects of Edmonton.

The movement is on foot. It is no wild visionary scheme, but a perfectly feasible project which can be carried through if the people of Alberta are only alive to their own interests and true to themselves. Are we in this place going to take hold of it, to co-operate on equal terms with Calgary in furthering it, to take our proper place in the front rank of its supporters like men, or are we going to let it alone in sheer indifference, and each in individual seclusion continue the old, old growl against the government for not granting to us as a favor those means for developing the country which a united, determined and energetic demonstration in favour of provincial self-government will place in our own hands, as our undoubted, indisputable right without a by your leave from any official, minister or government whatever. That is the question. The time to answer it is now. The next session of parliament will for obvious reasons present an opportunity for pressing our claims which may not occur again for several years, and if we in Edmonton are to take our proper part in the movement, we must take action now.

A meeting of the Fort Saskatchewan Agricultural Society on January 25, 1896 was one of an increasing number of forums to take up the issue of provincial status for Alberta.

II — 14

Edmonton Bulletin, January 30, 1896.

Mr. F.F. Tims, M.L.A., was called on to give his ideas on it, provincial autonomy, and he did, and read a pamphlet on the subject by the Calgary people, which gives a clear explanation of provincial autonomy. Mr. Frank Marriaggi was also called on and made a good speech on the subject. As this was the first meeting here at which the subject was brought up and explained, everybody took a great interest in it, and on the spot a committee was formed, comprised of F.F. Tims, F. Marriaggi,

J.F. Forbes, J.L. Porte and R. Hardisty to further the object, and work in conjunction with the headquarters of the movement at Calgary.

The formation of committees in central Alberta soon spread. There were, it appeared, several supporters of the principle in Edmonton and area but their involvement brought a demand for an adjustment of the boundaries of the prospective province to include the large area to the north which Edmonton considered a promising hinterland.

II — 15

Alberta's North: Edmonton Bulletin, March 5, 1896.

The committee on provincial autonomy appointed at Saturday's public meeting met on Monday evening in the council chamber to discuss the matter in detail and if possible decide on a plan of action. Mr. McCauley was chairman and S. Chivers Wilson secretary. There were present Messrs. Bown, McDonald, Kirkpatrick, McDougall, Grogan, Emery, Beck, Oliver, Woodworth, Ross, Picard and Bellamy.

Mr. Beck was the first speaker and objected strongly to the limits of the proposed province as laid down in the petition. The following resolution was moved by Mr. Beck, seconded by Mr. McDougall and carried unanimously. "That in the opinion of this committee it is not desirable in the interests of the northern portion of the district of Alberta that the people of the said district should join in the petition now in circulation for the erection of Alberta into a province."

Mr. Woodworth, seconded by Mr. Grogan moved: 'That this committee expresses itself in favor of provincial autonomy for the district now known as Alberta and Athabasca and recommend the immediate formation of these districts into a province, together with such portions of the North-west Territory as lie west of the 107th meridian of longitude and south of the 60th parallel of latitude.' This motion carried unanimously.

II — 16

'Provincial Autonomy': Edmonton Bulletin, March 12, 1896.

A meeting of the committee will be held this evening in C.M. Woodworth's office at eight o'clock to receive the report of the joint committee, and the south Edmonton committee will meet at the same time for the purpose, a telephone communication will be kept up between the committees so that the same resolutions may be arrived at. A letter from the Calgary committee will also be considered this evening. The letter says that the Calgary committee has passed a resolution fully concurring in the boundaries for the proposed province as set forth in the resolution of the Edmonton committee; and recommending that new petition heads giving the boundaries thus suggested be struck off for circulation.

While interest in the proposal was growing in the Edmonton area opposition still existed in the south. Regions south of Calgary expressed little interest in the scheme and the newspapers of towns like Macleod and Lethbridge voiced open hostility. Two factors may have encouraged these newspapers in their course. First, as their editorials reveal, there was a distrust of Calgary's motives. Secondly, this was the area of the North-West where Premier F.W.G. Haultain had his power base. Haultain, as of 1896, opposed both provincial status and separation of Alberta and his well known views may have influenced editors in the region. This suspicion is strengthened by the reversal of position undertaken by the Macleod paper which, in 1890, had been in favour of provincial status (see II-4).

II—17

'Provincial Autonomy:' Macleod Gazette, February 14, 1896.

Let it be understood that the Gazette has no quarrel with the principle of provincial autonomy. It has an abiding faith that in the not distant future Alberta will be a province, and one of the fairest in the Dominion, but that day is not yet. The question has been raised too soon, and the agitation that is now being worked up is so much force badly expended, therefore to a large extent wasted. With a population not one-fifth of Montreal, it is pretended we need a Lieutenant-Governor all to ourselves, a Legislative Assembly to be shared by nobody, a gentleman usher of the Black Rod, and a sergeant-at-arms of our very own, a complete outfit of cabinet ministers and provincial officers, not to speak of parliament buildings, etc. And all this without costing us a cent gentlemen. Who would not throw up his cap and hurrah for Provincial Autonomy. Just look at the advantages. We have not a P.A. pamphlet by us for reference, or even a stray copy of the Herald containing a schedule of the benefits that would at once descend on us, but if memory serves us not amiss, besides the dearly loved right to misgovern ourselves, we are to have immediate railway connection with the south, a network of railways intersecting the country in all directions, an independent immigration department, control of lands, a complete system of irrigation; general activity in all branches of business, and so on, and so on, and so on. Quite incidentally of course, Calgary is to be the capital and being the capital must have parliament buildings. It sounds well, doesn't it?

We would be the last people in the world to oppose the scheme if we could honestly convince ourselves that it was either desirable or necessary at the present time. Careful enquiry, however, among all classes of the people of this part of Alberta, has elicited the fact that there is no widespread dissatisfaction with the existing state of affairs, and no general wish or demand for an independent government. Grievances there are, against both the Dominion and Territorial governments, but people are becoming skeptical about good or bad times being made by Act of Parliament, and as long as they get a fair show, and a chance to work out their own salvation, they prefer to stick to the evils they have rather than trust to those they know not of. We have already more government in Canada to the population than any people on earth, and to have Alberta now erected into a Province, to be followed in a year or two by Assiniboia and Saskatchewan, would bring us in this respect dangerously near to the ridiculous. Another phase of the question is this—are we not wasting our time trying to get what the Dominion government won't give us? If it has taken so many years of agitation to obtain the partial measure of self-government the Territories as a whole now enjoy, how many years will it take to get a complete provincial government for a third or a fourth part of the Territories? Is the part greater than the whole? We in Alberta of course know that it is, but other people are disgustingly hard to convince. On the whole perhaps, life is too short to work out the problem.

British Columbia and Manitoba are pointed out as each having a smaller population than Alberta when they were admitted into Confederation, but neither one of them is exactly a case in point, and even if both were, it would not be a good argument for the perpetuation of a wrong system or course of policy. If a thing is injudicious in itself, it does not make it any more judicious that it has already been twice done. Besides, we doubt very much whether either Manitoba or British Columbia is very much better off by reason of this provincial status. A youngster turned loose at too early an age does not as a rule form the best habits or develop into the best citizen, a town that becomes incorporated too soon, not infrequently has a troublous and expensive time of it, and a district that becomes a province before it has the men or money to support the dignity is apt to have a bitter and costly experience of mis-government and mal-administration before it enters on an assured era of prosperity and stability . . .

It is possible, however, that we are taking this thing too seriously, for after all, the idea of provincial autonomy is rarely heard outside of Calgary, and exists there only on account of two principal reasons. One is that the city has come to a standstill. Farming in its vicinity has not been an unmixed success, no more railroads are being built, English capital is not being lavishly expended as of yore and consequently business is dull and the place wants a fillip. What better scheme therefore than to make it the seat of government, with governor and staff, parliament buildings with a cabinet, and all the paraphernalia appertaining to the functions of law-making and ruling. The idea is excellent—for Calgary. Another reason is that many of the promoters are very worthy gentlemen whose ambition outruns their ability, and who think they see prospects opening for them in Calgary that are denied them in Ottawa and Regina. One would bear a little further inflation and would grace the chair of Lieutenant Governor. Another would attain the very summit of his greatness and become an Honorable before he died, while for ordinary members and officials, the vista is unlimited. While this class exists, and that will be for ever and a day, provincial autonomy will not lack enthusiastic and enterprising advocates, but in the meantime we may be allowed to hope that they will be able to bear up against the disappointment that is surely awaiting them—the indefinite postponement of the accomplishment of their modest designs.

II — 18

Opposition to Autonomy: Lethbridge News, November 18, 1896

The advocates of Provincial Autonomy claim that if the Territories were formed into one or more Provinces the Dominion Government would have to place them on the same financial basis as Manitoba. But it is difficult to see on what this assumption is based. There is no reason why the Territories should not be as equitably treated as Provinces, nor is there any good reason for supposing that if we were formed into a Province we should receive any more generous treatment than we now do. If the people living within the confines of Assiniboia, Alberta and Saskatchewan are entitled to a certain amount annually, they should receive that amount whether these districts are classed as Territories or as a Province . . .

The position which the Northwest Territories occupy under confederation is a unique one. The Provinces of the Dominion have all come into confederation and become part and parcel of the Dominion as Provinces by treaty, and were in a position to negotiate for certain financial grants before consenting to become Provinces of Canada. But the Territories already form part of the Dominion, and when they become Provinces it will not be by treaty or under the auspices of Imperial legislation, but merely by the will of the Parliament of Canada. We shall not be able to negotiate as contracting parties, our position will rather be that of petitioners. It is therefore impossible to judge what our financial position would be under Provincial rule. If the Government of Canada is willing to increase our annual grants, they will as readily do it whilst our present form of administration exists as if we were demanding to be conceded with Provincial autonomy. Outside of this financial question the Territories would probably be wise in waiting until they are much more developed than they are at present before demanding Provincial rule, and if we can succeed in getting our annual grants increased, we will be satisfied to retain our present form of Government for some years to come, and wait until we are considerably stronger before assuming the responsibilities and burdens which Autonomy would entail.

The Alberta movement for provincial status was carried to the Legislative Assembly of the North-West Territories in 1896.

A resolution on the part of Haultain asking for various changes in Territorial status and finances gave R.G. Brett, the member for Banff, an opportunity to push for official recognition of the Alberta autonomy movement's demands. The ensuing debate and the subsequent defeat of Brett's amendment indicates that there were still strong objections both to provincial status in general and to the separation of Alberta in particular.

II — 19

Haultain and Brett on Provincial status in the Legislative Assembly Debate of 1896: Saskatchewan Archives, North-West Territories Legislative Assembly Debates (Scrapbook), 1896-1899, pp. 74-89.

Mr. Brett (Banff): said he agreed the time for presenting the memorial had arrived. The present question was probably the most important the House had before it for consideration. While, however, it was only a temporary measure the memorial asked for, he was one of those who believed the time had come when they should with no uncertain sound tell the Dominion Government or indicate to them in what position they would like the Territories to be placed. He was not going to state that the memorial should indicate that a more radical change than was asked for therein should take place at once. It was a serious thing to too rapidly get to an advanced condition if the conditions of the country would not warrant it; still at the same time it was equally bad that they should linger along and not do that which they considered was for the best advancement of the country. . . .

The time had come when they should tell the Dominion Government in unmistakable terms that at the expiration of this Assembly—two years hence,—they would expect full provincial powers would be given to the Territories, either as a whole or divided. He had stated there were no provincial taxes in Manitoba, nor would it be necessary to have them here. He might be asked,—in what way are you going to raise the revenue to carry on the Government? In the first place they would get a grant of money sufficient for the Government as they do in British Columbia. Then they would have in their power the collection of other taxes, license fees and so forth, as in British Columbia. He would now refer more particularly to Alberta. If provincial government would be a good thing for the whole of the Territories, he claimed it would not be unfair for a portion of the Territories to ask for it. The time had come not only for the Territories as a whole to ask for provincial powers, but it was high time something should be done in the direction of giving to the western portion of the Territories full provincial powers. The conditions of the eastern and the western portions of the Territories were quite different in many respects. In the west there were resources which would greatly assist the country generally if properly developed. They had ranching, grain growing, minerals, coal, industries in coal oil and so on, which under proper conditions would make that portion of the country one of the richest, if not the richest part of the whole of the Territories. With proper railway facilities those coal fields would immediately be got into active operation. That would largely increase the population in those parts. Those people would furnish a local market for those who raised cattle, grain and vegetables to the north of them. They had diversified interests there but that made them stronger because they could deal with each other. The benefits they would obtain from having a provincial form of government would be that they would have the power to do as they thought best for the development of the country. Nearly every member of that Assembly must have a feeling of disappointment with reference to the North-West Territories. They had been standing still—marking time. He did not think the best efforts had been made on their behalf. The powers of the province would make them progress much more rapidly than it had. . . . He hoped the House would amend the terms of the memorial by recommending to the Dominion Government, that at the expiration of that Assembly the time would have arrived when Alberta and Athabasca should be erected into a province. . . .

While Alberta had contributed over three-fourths of the net local revenue, they had received less than one-third in schools and only a trifle over a third of the full amount expended for roads and bridges. That condition of affairs justified him, as one representative of Alberta, to ask that Alberta should be relieved, and placed in a position of collecting its own revenues and doing as it liked. In conclusion the hon. member further argued that Alberta was entitled to provincial status on the ground of excess in increase in population, and also of extent of acreage. He could understand it was not going to be an easy matter to get the sanction of the House. It was not anything the House would voluntarily tender to Alberta. He did not think the Territories were sufficiently tired of Alberta, or sufficiently discontented with the part Alberta played with reference to the contributions to the general fund and so on. He could readily understand, as was always the case in secession, or in one part asking to be relieved from another portion, there would always be some objection taken. But he thought the time would soon come when there would be unanimity of feeling that the course he proposed was the best thing not only for Alberta but also for the several portions of the Territories to be constructed into a Province. (Hear, hear.)

Mr. Haultain: . . . The question so far as the amendment was concerned, so far as any differences of opinion with the memorial was concerned, was a question of what should their institutions be? He went further and said it was a question of what should their institutions be now? and not what they should be at some future date. That involved the question of whether they should have a single province, or whether they should debate the system proposed in the memorial of a gradual development of the present Territorial system until they arrived at such a point that they would be able to slide into confederation almost without knowing it. That question had been complicated by the amendment which meant that Alberta should be established into a province itself. As a member representing an Albertan constituency, he must take exception to the position assumed by the hon. member for Banff undertaking to represent the views of Alberta. He (Mr. Haultain) denied any right on the part of the hon. gentleman to attempt to represent what the opinions of the people of Alberta were except so far as those people were confined to the limits of his own electoral district. He might tell him, and the other hon. gentlemen from Alberta, that he did not believe Alberta wished to be made a province. He did not believe there had been a proper statement of the feeling of Alberta today. He agreed with what the hon. gentleman from Lethbridge (Mr. McGrath) said, that if a poll were taken today in Alberta on the question of whether Alberta should be set aside as a province there would be a very large majority against it in spite of the efforts of the Alberta autonomy movement in Calgary. The movement originated in the town of Calgary in one sense. It was a very praiseworthy movement in so far as it called attention to certain important public matters and gave opportunity to consider the larger question of the form of government in the Territories. But on the other side, if he might judge from the propaganda of the movement, in the shape of pamphlets, and from speeches he had heard from prominent advocates of the movement, after all the movement was largely a very local one. . . . Why, therefore, should the House be asked to spoil a memorial which dealt with their present needs; with their undoubted rights and the righteous demands they wished to make with regard to their immediate surroundings and their everyday institutions? Why should they be called upon to express an opinion with regard to something which was simply anticipatory of a movement which might take place at some future date, as the hon. gentleman put it in his amendment. The hon. gentleman from Banff referred to the present connection of Alberta as a partnership in a firm, and said that member of the firm wished to withdraw. He (Mr. Haultain) did not know exactly what the hon. member meant when he spoke of a partnership existing between what was one single united country, and he believed would remain so. The diversity of interests which existed between various parts of the Territories had been spoken of as giving a good and strong ground for dividing the Territories up. What sort of province did the hon. gentleman wish it to be? Did they want to have one sheep farm, or one wheat field, or one sort of field devoted to some other sort of industry which their own insignificance would allow them to describe? If they wished to have a good strong province, strong in its own resources, they should have a diversity of resources (hear, hear.) Much better than having a comparatively small amount of land devoted to one or two interests would it be if they could have a very large area such as the organized Territories were today with their diversity of interests, but not conflict of interests. They should look forward to having a very much stronger and better province than there would be if they had to be divided up. . . .

He believed that they should have one province, but that they should not have it yet. He believed that they should go on, as they had been going on, with the gradual development of their present institutions, here and there gaining a little more power, here and there extending their jurisdiction, here and there getting more money. These were the practical questions for consideration, and that very discussion showed that they were not prepared to make any definite claim with regard to provincial questions. The very fact that there were three sets of opinions expressed in the House showed they were not prepared to discuss the provincial question with a view to its immediate institution . . . It might be a very good educative movement, and he (Mr. Haultain) certainly would not object to it, but if dreams were to be dreamed, and if visions were to be seen, they had better be dreamed and had better be seen outside of that House, which after all had only to do with practical work. If however they were going to consider the larger subject it should be a little larger than the comparatively small area of Alberta and Saskatchewan, for after all those names were only applied for post office purposes. Their consideration of their needs on that question should be just as broad as the whole of the Territories. And if they were going to dream a dream, the dream he would like to dream would be the dream of one large province with all its varied resources; a dream of one large province with a united population, and not a divided population; and if that dream could come true he believed it would be a much better dream than the dream which was dreamed by the hon. member for Banff. A dream of one large province holding its own confederation, the most powerful province in confederation, would be a much more desirable thing to think about, and to speculate about, than a number of small areas confined in their powers and in their influence. The dream he would like to dream would be the dream of the largest province and the most powerful province in the greatest and most glorious country attached to the mightiest empire the world has ever seen. (Applause.)

The early campaign for provincial autonomy had had as its basis the belief in the beneficial results of a separate Alberta. Division of the North-West Territories was thus integral to that movement. There was, however, no necessary connection between provincial status and the creation of a distinct Province of Alberta. Provincial status could be attained through the creation of one, two or more Provinces and the boundaries of these provinces could be run in various different ways. As the idea of provincial autonomy became more accepted in the Territories other plans began to develop as to how these new Provinces should be delineated. Extension of Manitoba, one large province in the North-West and even annexation to British Columbia were suggested in the process of discussion through the later 1890's. The last of these proposals, annexation to British Columbia, was perhaps the strangest of all and one is tempted to explain it by noting the frustration of the Calgary Herald and, perhaps, by the interest John Young had in mines in British Columbia. Whatever the reason, however, it was soon dropped in the face of ridicule from other editors.

II — 20

'Manitoba Extension:' Edmonton Bulletin, January 18, 1897.

A number of both western and eastern papers are discussing a possible westerly extension of the province of Manitoba. There seems to be a good deal to be said in favor of the idea. The prairie division of Canada extending from the Lake of the Woods to the Rocky Mountains is too large to be formed into only one province; and yet the smaller the number of provinces the greater the economy in government. Although there is too much territory for one province there may not be more than enough for two. As a matter of fact the whole area has been under two local legislatures for the past twenty years, and as far as can be seen there is no particular necessity for a greater number. At the same time the Western or Territorial division is so very much larger than the eastern or provincial division, if a permanent arrangement is to be made nothing would be more natural than that the size of the two permanent divisions should be somewhat similar. The first idea of restricting Manitoba to an area of 100 miles square was abandoned many years ago and her boundaries extended westward. There is therefore nothing new in the idea of their being extended still further west. There is practically no difference of interests between the western part of Manitoba and the eastern part of the Territories. Indeed they are identical in everything except in local legislation. There is no natural division or distinction of any kind between Manitoba and the adjoining portion of the Territories as there is between the western and eastern portion of the Territories. Winnipeg is the natural commercial capital of all the wheat growing area of the plains as far west as Moose Jaw. The fertile eastern and western parts of the Territories are separated from each other by the vast semi-arid grazing region, chiefly covered by the two electoral districts of Medicine Hat and Battleford. This grazing area differs entirely in interests from the eastern wheat growing area; and the far west mixed farming country of Northern Alberta, while it approximates more closely to the conditions of Manitoba is so far detached from it and having its commercial interests tending westward rather than eastward, its local affairs can no doubt be handled to better advantage under a separate legislature. There is no good reason at present apparent why the local control of Central Canada should be divided between more than two legislatures. If there are to be only two their control should be divided as evenly and as much according to natural conditions as possible. This can be done by drawing the dividing line due north and south some distance west of Moose Jaw, which would give the eastern agricultural regions to Manitoba and the western grazing and agricultural area to the new province to be created. Sometime the development of the vast north country might call for further subdivisions, but for present— and for all time as far as East and West are concerned—these would be enough.

II — 21

Annexation to British Columbia: Calgary Herald, November 2, 1896.

The concluding suggestion of an article on Autonomy in these columns on Friday seems to have hit a popular chord. We refer to the proposal that Alberta should ask to be included in the Province of British Columbia. The question is a large one and at first blush somewhat startling, but the public favour with which it has so far been received suggests that it should be given every opportunity for full free discussion and consideration. The benefits Alberta would derive from casting its lot with British Columbia are undoubtedly great. The great bulk of our trade is with British Columbia. Our surplus grain, butter, eggs, poultry and pork all find their way to the growing market beyond the mountains. British Columbia also takes enormous quantities of our beef and mutton. It is our market par excellence. Nor are all the advantages on one side. We buy large quantities of British Columbia fruit and supply her demand for hard coal. But the commercial phase of the question, important though it is, is not the only thing to consider. The union would involve many important issues which only time and discussion would clear up. Three of the greatest of these would be the railway question, the mining question and the land question. Under the union a railway like the Crow's Nest could be chartered by the Province without the difficulties which exist with the present dividing line between us. The minerals of the Rockies would be at once brought into a position for rapid development under the favourable mining laws of British Columbia. A mine in British Columbia is worth something in the eyes of the world. A mine in Alberta, however good the showing, will not be looked at by either the British or

American investor. The question of the ownership of public lands which Alberta would have to offer the new Province is a large one and would require more than the space at our disposal now. The Herald's object in mooting the question of union with British Columbia is the welfare of Alberta and it invites its readers' views on the matter. Be they either for or against they will be equally welcomed.

II — 22

'Desperate:' Macleod Gazette, November 13, 1896.

. . . The Herald has apparently at last recognized the hopelessness of securing home rule, as it is called, for Alberta. Its insanity has not taken much serious hold but that it can see the absurdity of agitating for provincial autonomy, with the great mass of the people opposed to it. Consideration of the larger problem of provincial autonomy for the Territories does not seem to have received its consideration. It has now resuscitated the many years old question of the annexation of Alberta to British Columbia. This fantastic idea was mooted in a recent issue to comments made in the British Columbia press on the proposition. What object is to be gained by annexation to British Columbia has not yet been made apparent. The only results that we can see would be the provincial status, and the reflected notoriety we would gain from the boom in British Columbia mines. The former we can get from Territorial autonomy, and the latter would not put any more money in our pockets than it will if we simply remain as we are, simply the provisional district of Alberta. Politically we might become part of British Columbia—physically we have nothing in common with that province. We are part and parcel of the great agricultural and stock raising country extending from Manitoba to the mountains. We are most favorably situated for supplying the demands of that essentially mining country for food products to feed her toiling thousands, but nature has placed a great barrier between us, and we have quite as much to gain by fighting it out as a very important component of the Territories, as we have by assuming a share of the burdens under which British Columbia is even now staggering.

II — 23

The Regina Leader Comments on Annexation to British Columbia: Regina Leader, December 31, 1896.

The fact that the "Home Rule for Alberta" headline motto of the Calgary Herald was not removed when that paper dropped its "Alberta autonomy" cry and swallowed all the arguments it had gone to pains to advance in its favor, by advocating annexation to British Columbia, must have led the Pacific province people to suspect the *bona fides* of the proposal of matrimony. At any rate British Columbia papers did nothing but laugh at the idea. . . . Apart from the good humored jokes it gave rise to, The Herald's annexation proposal served one good purpose, viz., it showed that even the Herald realizes that the Alberta autonomy fad is dead. And by proposing union with British Columbia, The Herald overturned and buried every argument that had been advanced in favor of erecting Alberta into a separate province, even from the Calgarian viewpoint. The question now is whether The Herald will advance another fad, or turn in and assist in making of the Territories 'the grandest province of the greatest Dominion of the most mighty Empire upon which the sun has ever shone.'

As long as the Legislative Assembly remained largely uninterested or actively opposed to the idea of Provincial status, the movement in that direction remained without official status and without any real power. With the accomplishment of responsible government in 1897, however, various forces worked to alter the attitude of the Assembly and particularly of Premier Haultain, toward the question. First, and probably most important, Haultain and his Executive Council became increasingly concerned about the financial situation of the Territorial government. The 'boom' which marked the years around the turn of the century was welcomed in the West and in Canada as a whole but it also raised very real problems for the Territorial government in terms of provision of services. Haultain had given clear warnings that financial pressures were mounting from 1897 on but the disagreement between the Territorial and federal officials in 1899 over the grants for the coming year seem, more than any other single incident, to have converted a previously opposed Premier to support for Provincial autonomy.

*There was, however, a secondary force involved. The 1898
Territorial election brought one Richard Bedford Bennett to
the Legislature. Bennett had come out in favour of provincial
status during his election campaign and in the Legislature he
continued to push the theme. He also became the focus of
whatever opposition could be said to exist in this non-partisan
legislature. Haultain's recognition of the danger of allowing
his political opponents the exclusive claim to what was
possibly a popular political issue may have contributed to this
change of direction in these years.*

II — 24

**Premier Haultain on the financial limitations of Territorial
Government: Budget Speech of the 1897 Legislature as reported
in the Regina Leader, December 9, 1897.**

We have now a well-defined constitutional position and very
large powers and responsibilities but no fixed or adequate
income. Parliament had continued to manufacture law-making
and administrative machinery without adding the money to
carry it on. . . . The premier went on to say that additional
grants, additional financial recognition, were necessary. He
said that if we could not keep up the development in the
subsidy to keep pace with the development in power, there was
only one alternative. The practical meaning of his statement
was that if the Dominion refused to give the Territories as
favorable financial grants as are given to the provinces, then the
only alternative was for the Territories to take its position as a
province and obtain a proper financial standing.

He made the plain declaration that if due financial recognition is not given, his Government are prepared to take the lead
in a movement for the establishment of the Territories as a
province. Hitherto we had received enough money to meet the
necessary services, and probably, all things considered, were
better off than if there had already been provincial establishment. But we have now reached the jumping off place, and can
go very little farther without becoming a province as far as
regards power, and must have adequate revenues to meet the
enlarging burdens and responsibilities. If the arbitrary amounts
voted by Parliament are to be based not upon present requirements but upon worn-out estimates of earlier requirements,
then he and his Government will go for full provincial
establishment in order to get financial recognition.

II — 25

R.B. Bennett supports provincial status for Alberta: Calgary Herald, September 28, 1898.

There was no disguising the fact that the present time was a most critical period of our history—a time when the people of Alberta must assert themselves. Here in the Territories we have local self government but the growing conditions of the country demanded something more, and what we want is a province. (Cheers). This was the first plank in his platform and one on which he placed the greatest emphasis. We only have to look around and examine the more pressing requirements of the country to see that we have not enough power. For instance we cannot build a railway. We have here a population of 40,000 people and yet Manitoba when she entered confederation had but 16,000 whilst British Columbia at the time she became a province possessed only 10,000 white people. As far therefore as the question of population is concerned the time was clearly come for Alberta and the contiguous territory to be created a province. Further we must not say that it is a merely academic question. Even Premier Haultain who had hitherto avoided any statement on the subject, said in the Assembly during its last session that he was in favor of the Territories becoming a province. There are no insuperable difficulties to overcome, and looking at the situation in the light of history all must acknowledge that the country is ripe for this great change. . . . We should remember that with provincial autonomy Calgary would become the capital. In the east Calgary is always spoken of in terms of praise as an enterprising city with fine buildings and energetic citizens. In every sense of the word we are entitled to become the capital of the Territories—if not the province (Loud Cheers). The citizens of Calgary had built up a town that they were proud of, whereas Regina has practically done nothing. . . .

One man in the House of Commons, even if he be Mr. Oliver, can do little, but if we were a province we could demand such an expenditure [for public works] from the Dominion and if necessary threaten, as Nova Scotia did, secession. This is not a question of party politics and we ought not to make it a party question. Remember, the government will not remove itself the capital from Regina to Calgary for fear of losing their political support from Assiniboia. We must depend on ourselves to bring about this great change.

II — 26

Correspondence Concerning the Federal Grant for the North West Territories during 1899: Unpublished Sessional Paper No. 23 of The North West Territories, 1899.

Haultain to Clifford Sifton, January 14, 1899

The details of the estimates have received careful consideration and are based not only upon present requirements but
actual expenditures during the current year. The estimated
requirements, as will be noted, aggregate $535,000.00, to meet
which revenue can only be looked for from two directions,
namely, the grant to be made by Parliament and the various
local sources which, until the present year, have produced
about $30,000.00 annually. Owing to unusual circumstances, a
large addition was made to the local revenue during the early
part of the present year, which enabled the Territorial Government to meet the demands upon its funds in some measure; but
as this avenue is now closed no such further increased revenue
can be looked for in future. As the requirements of the
Government are in no sense diminished, attention must be
directed to the grant made by Parliament. . . .

The North-West Government has now at its command all
the official machinery necessary to carry on the most intricate
matters of Government. It has undertaken the duties devolving
upon it under its limited powers, and shown a willingness to
assume any other burden which might fall upon it by reason of
any extension of its powers. It only lacks suitable financial and
other arrangements to warrant the successful maintenance of
these burthens. To this end it is proposed for consideration that
a tentative financial agreement be entered into based upon the
terms embodied in The British North America Act and The
Manitoba Act, under which the North-West Government will
be required to undertake all the services which fall upon
Provincial Governments. In this way Parliament would be
relieved from making special provision for particular services
that by reason of their essentially local nature, can be more
readily administered by local authority than that of the
Dominion. Such a proposition implies that as ample powers
will be given to the Legislative Assembly of the Territories as
pertain to the legislatures of any of the Provinces. If reasons
exist why this proposal cannot be agreed to, then the amount
asked for in the accompanying estimates should be appropriated
for the services of the Territories, but the serious consideration

of the Government is urged to the proposal. A favourable acquiescence in its terms need not place the Territories upon any other political footing than they occupy at present, nor need it interfere with the efforts being made to settle the Crown Lands or other matters of Dominion concern. It would, however, follow that several of the Departments at Ottawa would be relieved of much work that at present is done in them but which has no place there.

Unpublished Sessional Paper No. 1 of the North West Territories, 1900

Haultain to Sifton, July 16, 1899

I have the honour to confirm my telegram to you of this date reading as follows:

'Globe of Saturday last reports you to effect that there will be no increase to Territorial grant this year, sincerely hope this is not the case. My official statement of January last and personal representation made since by Ross must have convinced you that present grant is altogether inadequate to meet actual and pressing needs. Large increase of population during last eighteen months has multiplied necessities without increasing income. New settlements must be provided with schools, roads and bridges, besides increasing cost of administration. Need not repeat statement of needs and embarrassments already before you, but simply state we are confronted with impossible conditions unless Federal Government recognizes that its duty does not end when large and dependent settlements are planted in the West.

Sifton to Haultain, August 1, 1899

I have only now been able to take time to answer your letter of the 18th ultimo, and even now have not the time to go into any discussion of the question referred to in your letter. I am afraid that it is quite impossible for me to bring in any further estimate for the Government of the Territories during the present session, and any increase in the subsidy will have to be left over for consideration next year. I quite appreciate the difficulties of your position and would gladly assist you if it were in my power.

Haultain to Sifton, October 19, 1899

I duly received your letter of the first August, stating that it was quite impossible for you to bring down any further estimate for the Government of the Territories during the Session of Parliament then closing and that any increase in the subsidy would have to be left over for consideration next year. The whole tenor of my letter of January 14 last, and telegram of July 18, will convince you that your decision in this matter has been the cause of grave disappointment to myself and my colleagues. We understood that the Federal Government was fully seized of the impracticability of carrying on the Government of the Territories under the conditions imposed upon us. It has, we think, been clearly demonstrated that the increased requirements of the country as represented in our estimates and in my letter of January last accompanying them have been very largely brought about as a result of the activity displayed by the Interior Department in bringing settlers into the Territories in considerable numbers, and placing them in colonies apart from existing settlements, often without any consideration, apparently, of such important matters, (amongst others) as the natural water supply, or the means of communication by roads, bridges or ferries, to say nothing of educational facilities. But no evidence appears that the Government is impressed with the situation.

At the risk of being tedious, and after a full consideration of the whole subject with my colleagues, I must ask your earnest consideration once more of the financial and political position of the Territories as it presents itself. Though Parliament has created a Government for the Territories, with responsibilities to the people of the country as represented in the legislative Assembly, it is continually being forced upon us that the Dominion Government does not consider that fact any warrant for its withdrawal from the paternal attitude adopted in the earlier stages in our history, and then necessarily so. An annual vote (which, under any straining of the word, cannot be called a 'subsidy') is made, as you are aware, to meet the supposed requirements of the Government of the North-West Territories. Twenty per cent. of the amount so voted is retained at Ottawa and administered by officers of the Interior Department, the balance being handed over to the Territorial Government, to be applied to certain definite purposes. These are stated in the words of the vote to be 'Schools, clerical assistance, printing, etc.' The whole of the appropriation is made, and twenty per cent. of it administered, irrespective of the necessities of the country as they have been represented from time to time and in various ways. The appropriation is also made without consideration of the statutory limitations to the powers vested in the Government of the Territories, thus forcibly throwing upon the meagre revenues of the country burdens which they should not be called upon to bear. . . .

The amount of money placed at our disposal—which is all expended with a view to the amelioration of the difficulties met with by the people of the Territories by reason of their surroundings—might have been increased, or such changes have been introduced in the administration of certain matters of Government which would have enabled us to successfully open up other sources of revenue. But nothing is done, though, as we are informed, you quite appreciate the difficulties of our position. Whilst not admitting for one instant that it is the proper view to take of the position, or to intimate that we have even the faintest desire to shirk responsibility in the matter, yet, as it is the view which appears to obtain at Ottawa, I must remind you that these difficulties of ours are also yours. The Federal view-point appears to be governed entirely by that clause in the Act respecting the Department of the Interior which reads—'The Minister of the Interior shall have the control and management of the affairs of the North-West Territories.' We have yet to be informed that anything that has been done in the administration of these Territories by us has not met with your approval, so that the position, as it is forced upon us by the Dominion Government, is one that you must accept some measure of responsibility for. When we meet the Assembly, and have to explain that there are no funds to devote to public works, or that in order to provide for a very small portion of such works as we know to be urgently required, it is necessary to practically wipe out the legislation affecting assistance to education, there can be only one reason to give. We know that our people, in addition to the numerous disabilities created by the nature of their lives, are burdening themselves with public liabilities within their ability to pay equal to those under which the people of any of the Provinces lie, and if it is necessary to increase those liabilities it will be incumbent upon us to make very clear the reason why.

II — 27

James Ross and R.G. Brett on the growing financial problems of the Territories: The 1899 Budget Debate: Regina Leader, May 4, 1899.

Ross: Mr. Ross went on to say that he would now like to make a few observations with regard to the present position of the

Territories and the position he thought we should be in; and he would then have something to say with regard to certain propositions which had been made with regard to the political position of the Territories. The local revenue now amounted to $45,000 or $50,000. It indicated $50,000 at present. The Dominion grant on the same footing as last year would be $282,979. Now there was no question that the amounts were totally inadequate for the service, yet there were other moneys expended by the Dominion Government for purely Territorial purposes. . . . The Government this year had asked for $535,000 from Ottawa and they believed that sum was actually necessary to provide for the needs of the country. Now if it was the case that this sum was needed, was it not very necessary for them to look minutely into the question and see where they would land themselves if they were to enter into confederation on the Manitoba basis? The province of Manitoba was dealt with in the following manner: They received an allowance of $50,000 for the purposes of government; $100,000 on account of lands; and interest on a capital account at the rate of $32 per head on the actual population, or about three and a quarter million dollars. If the Territories were similarly dealt with we would be in this position. We should have a subsidy based on a per capita amount of 80 cents per head . . . that would give us $120,000. Add to that $50,000 for government, the same as Manitoba and we would then have $170,000. Then we would be entitled to a capital account of three and a quarter millions, which at five per cent. would produce $162,500—although it had to be remembered that the Dominion now held the Territories charged with some $3,000,000 on account of capital account expenditures in the Territories. The Province of Manitoba received $100,000 a year in lieu of her lands; but in the Territories we had a little over four and a half times the land of Manitoba—that was in the organised Territories—so that we should be entitled on the same basis as Manitoba to over $400,000 a year in lieu of our lands. This would give us in all $732,500. This then was the position we would be in if we were dealt with on the same basis as Manitoba. We should have a fixed subsidy of $732,500. Was there any member of that House who believed that if we require a grant of $535,000 at the present time for the services we are performing, and if in addition to that we had to perform the services now carried out by the Dominion Government, that such a bargain as this would be a good bargain for all time to come? He did not think so, and he did not think any member of the House thought that the sum

he had mentioned would be a sufficient sum for a fixed subsidy.
. . . He believed, however, and his colleagues believed, that there
was no necessity for the Government to deal in that way, and
this Government had a proposition to make in respect to the
position in which these Territories should be placed. The
leader of the House had looked into the question, and this
Government was prepared to lay down what they believed
would be the proper course to pursue. . . .

In the first place, continued Mr. Ross, the Government
would lay this down as a basis, or starting point, that they
would make the best possible bargain with regard to population. They would get as large an amount as they could for
government. . . . It would be their duty to demand on behalf of
these Territories the whole of the lands of the Territories—
(hear, hear)—that is to demand an account of the whole of the
lands of the Territories including that portion which had gone
from Canada's grasp. It was known that the large grants had
gone out in subsidies and so on, and of these an account must be
given. Something must be given to the Territories in lieu of
those lands which had been alienated by Dominion vote. The
land belongs to the people. It was the only natural revenue
producing asset they have; it is the one asset that grows by the
growth of the population; it is the only asset we can look on to
maintain the equilibrium between revenue and expenditure. If
we have an absolutely fixed subsidy the expenditure is bound to
outgrow the revenue.

. . . . It is our duty as far as we can to educate the people on this
question; and it is the duty of every man in this House, it is the
duty of every good citizen in this country, to stand shoulder to
shoulder at this time to endeavor to force upon the Dominion
of Canada this principle which we believe to be true, that we
have a right to these lands. It is the duty of Grit and Tory, or
Tory and Grit, no matter how you put it, whether he be a
member of this legislature or not—it is the duty of the
Dominion Members of Parliament representing this western
country, that we and they should all stand shoulder to shoulder
on this question—the most important that will be dealt with
during their term in the Parliament of Canada. The question as
to the land regulations, or whether we shall get a bridge at
Edmonton or a post office at Moosomin or some other point,
are in comparison of very little moment to the people of this
country at large, but the question as to what the financial
position of the country will finally be is one of the greatest
moment to the whole of the people of this country. I hope no

question will arise at this time as to whether we are to have one, two or three provinces or whether any part will be given to Manitoba. Let us leave those questions altogether on one side; let us endeavor to force upon the Dominion Government the principle that when the bargain is made it should be made upon the basis of the whole of the lands of these Territories belonging to the Territories, and that a full account should be given of them. . . .

Dr. Brett: . . . Now, when was provincial autonomy going to come? When was the Government going to take action. Were the Government going to come there year after year making nice-sounding speeches to tickle the ears of the members of the public, to buoy their hopes up, and lead them to believe they were going to do something great? Well then the definite policy in 1898 of the Government was provincial autonomy if an increased subsidy could not be secured. But in the elections in the fall what did they find? The proper course of the Government in those elections was to have enunciated and enforced that policy so far as they could. In the western portion of the country where the policy was supposed to suit the people it was their battle cry. They spoke that way at Edmonton and Calgary. What they said at Moosomin and the eastern parts he could not say positively for he was not there to hear them, but he had reason to believe that in that portion of the country the people did not want autonomy because they thought it meant taxation. He did not know how far the Government went in the east to try and educate the people there up to their policy—how far they went in order to induce the people to vote for the men of their choice—but if they did not use every means in their power on that line then they were not acting fairly towards the people of this country. . . .

The hon. gentleman thought that if we could get a million dollars a year in lieu of our public lands we should be in a nice position. We should be getting more than any other Province in the Dominion if this were fulfilled; but he would ask the hon. member—did they take the proposition seriously? Coming from a responsible member and addressed to them as members of that Assembly, did they take it seriously that they were to sit there and wait till the Government could make such an arrangement as that before they could change their political complexion? Did they not take it in the light of mere bombast to attract the attention of those who did not favor the idea of taxation and borrowing money? If the youngest man in the House had to wait for such an arrangement as that to be made with the Dominion Government, he did not venture even to think how old that man would be before the arrangement was made. . . .

Now it would appear that the Government could not put their desire for provincial autonomy too strongly, but with their impracticable ideas he was sure it would be many years before they succeeded—nay, it would be simply impossible for them to get provincial autonomy under the conditions outlined by their friends that afternoon. Were they going to sit down and submit to this? They would, he supposed, have to quietly take their medicine, or if they did not feel inclined to do that, they would have to wait till something turned up to make things happen. But he hoped the hon. gentlemen would take a tumble, as it were, and make things happen themselves, and would present some feasible scheme to which they could ask the support of the House in pressing their claims on the Dominion Government. (Applause).

II — 28

Haultain comes out in favour of provincial status: Yorkton, October 7, 1899: Calgary Weekly Herald, November 2, 1899.

The Territories were a young and growing family and needed education and for this growing population the income was altogether inadequate. It was an unpleasant fact that the most important thing the government had to say to the people of the Territories was that it had got to the end of its tether as far as the financial position was concerned. There were roads and bridges to be built and to be put into proper repair here as they well knew and the same state of affairs prevailed in all parts. There had been an exceptionally rainy season, the rivers had more water than ever known and bridges had been swept away. Roads had been impassable all year and would be more so next year. All the money had been spent and not one-quarter of the work done, so next year things would be much worse, which was a bad outlook for a public man to have to predict. The growth of population from a financial point of view had been embarrassing. . . .

The present institutions were good enough if there was sufficient money to carry them on. Could anyone devise a scheme to raise this money to do the work necessary for next year he would be glad for that person to propose his services to the Territories. The government had come to the point where it was impossible to devise any financial scheme for overcoming the present want of money. The country was unable to stand taxation. The country could not go on year after year and get money from parliament because it had not been got in this 'growing time' in the Territories when $60,000,000 had been voted and none of the extra expenditure had come to the Territories. The federal government knew very well that there was a 'growing time' in the Territories and if ever there was a time when an increase should have been made it was now. The government would have to meet the legislature before parliament met and he did not propose to look for what parliament would give, and the alternative was to undertake those institutions which have associated with them fair and proper financial terms. That was a large jump to take, still he had no hesitation in taking it. They had come to the jumping off point. They would have come to it two years before but for the Yukon venture. Under the present arrangement there was no right to say what amount they would receive. As a province they would have a right to per capita grant and other provincial rights. They had also a right to the lands, minerals and forests in the country, for when the Territories become a province it should become a province under proper terms. He would object to enter into confederation on the same terms as Manitoba, which were perfectly unjust and unreasonable, and when the time came for him to ask them to unite for the purpose of asking for provincial rights, it would be to demand a right to every cent, every stick and every straw which belonged to the Territories, and only on these conditions would he be prepared to say that the time had come to enter into confederation. There was an account between the Territories and Canada as the latter stood in the relation of a trustee to the former. They had heard of eastern people saying: 'We bought you', 'We own the Territories,' 'You have nothing to do with it.' The people who came from other provinces did not lose their rights as Canadians. Our fathers helped to pay what was the purchase price. Canada never bought the Territories. It paid a million and a half dollars for the extinction of a title, but because a trustee paid a bogus claim that was no reason why the Territories should be mulcted for that amount. . . .

There was the question of what kind of a province, one province, two provinces, or three provinces. He had heard it suggested that a large slice of eastern Assiniboia be added to Manitoba and other parts of the Territories be formed into provinces. He believed in one province. It was said that one large province alongside Manitoba would make Manitoba look small and lack symmetry; to be carved up to suit the ideas of symmetry in the minds of cabinet ministers did not suit the west. He was in favor of lines drawn where people had been living under a distinct government and to make a division for any other reason would destroy the equilibrium of their institution and good government, nor was there any line within the Territories where it could be said that one system of government could start and another end, which meant that there should be one seat of government, one civil service and one province. Upon that he proposed to go to the country and maintain the same attitude in the legislature. As yet they had no mandate from the people but it was the duty of the legislature to educate the people on this question of entering confederation. . . . It was the government's duty to consider and discuss interests which affected the Territories, but now it was a duty to investigate and devise upon terms of confederation and then say 'will you send us to power to ask for those terms.' It was the duty of the legislature to prepare the people for this great question and he hoped it would be considered with that absence of party feeling and with that liberality of views which had prevailed and without which no proper, no fair or satisfactory solutions of these questions could be arrived at. (Cheers.)

II — 29

An Alberta paper comments on Haultain's Yorkton speech: The Alberta Tribune, November 4, 1899.

The first key note of the battle for provincial autonomy has been sounded by Premier Haultain at Yorkton and we give an abstract of his speech in another column.

In Alberta we are so far from the seat of government at Regina, it is difficult for us to understand the position of affairs and for that reason a large section of the community have in the past advocated the establishment of a province carved out of the Western half of the Territories with headquarters at Calgary, but if Mr. Haultain more clearly explained the position of Alberta under his proposed provincial scheme the people would be better prepared to consider whether or not it would suit their aspirations.

We have hitherto opposed the scheme of autonomy for the Territories as a whole unless the position and requirements of Alberta are brought to the front, practically giving her the same advantages as if she was a separate province, and as Mr. Haultain represents an Alberta constituency and has had his say at Yorkton from an Assiniboia point of view, we think that Alberta should reserve its judgment on the question until Mr. Haultain has had his further say to an Alberta audience which of course he will meet as soon as the exigencies of public business permits.

When the spring sitting of the Assembly opened in 1900 the Speech from the Throne revealed that the government of the Territories had come to the conclusion that Provincial status was necessary. As Haultain indicated in his speech of May 2, the primary considerations were still financial and the details of the proposal were still to be worked out. Nevertheless, the passage of the Memorial of May 2 marked the first official request of the elected representatives of the Territories for Provincial status. The next step was up to the government of Wilfrid Laurier in Ottawa.

II — 30

Haultain on the Resolution of May 2, 1900: Constitutional and Financial Questions Affecting the North-West Territories. Speech of F.W.G. Haultain in the Legislative Assembly on Wednesday the Second of May, 1900 (Regina, 1900).

Mr. Speaker, in the Speech from the Throne with which this session was opened the following passage occurred. I will not read the whole of it, but only that part which bears more particularly on the resolution now in your hands. It is as follows:

It is gratifying for me to be able to inform you that the Federal government has proposed to Parliament now in session a moderate increase to your annual grant and a large special vote for the purpose of restoring public works destroyed by the floods. In spite of this very substantial increase to the revenue my government can only look upon it as affording a temporary and partial amelioration

of otherwise impossible financial conditions, and will ask
you to take action leading to the earliest practical solution of Territorial financial and administrative problems.

In accordance with the promise practically made to the
House by the government in that portion of the speech, the
resolution which I now have the honour to move, seconded by
Mr. Ross, has been placed on the order paper. I shall not
attempt to occupy very much time in any preliminary remarks
but shall simply say that, in a matter dealing with so many
different points, raising so many different questions, involving
the consideration of so many different topics, each one almost
worthy of a speech in itself, any remarks which I have to make
today must necessarily be very long; so that in anticipation I
will ask the indulgence of the House in that respect. What I am
going to say will not be in itself very original. I am not going to
draw many deductions or indulge in any very long arguments,
but am going to try to introduce to the House the most
important subject we have ever had to deal with and to promote
discussion, not only here but in the country. . . .

Before taking up this part of the resolution I would ask the
House to glance over the recitals which lead up to it. They trace
down the history of the acquisition of this country and the
subsequent dealings with it. They, throughout, suggest a
settled and defined mode of action. They cite the fact that in all
matters pertaining to this country—even to the action of the
Queen herself—everything that is done must be done subject to
the British North America Act. They refer to the undertaking
by the Parliament of Canada to grant political institutions
bearing a close analogy to those enjoyed by the Provinces and
show how that undertaking has been carried out. A consistent
intention and action leading up to the establishment of such
'analogous institutions' can be traced in all the negotiations, in
every public document, in every official statement and every
Act of Parliament, and the underlying principles of the British
North America Act govern in every instance. At this stage, I
suppose, the question might be asked, How long shall this
process of gradual development go on? I have already shown in
what respect the powers we now possess differ from those
enjoyed by the Provinces. The Provincial jurisdiction must be
the limit of our ambition so that there is not much room for
development in that respect, although the few remaining
powers to be acquired are very important ones. We might well
go on developing under the Territorial system for a long time

to come if our revenue would only keep pace with our requirements. But the present financial condition is an impossible one—I mean the condition of being dependent upon the annual vote of Parliament for the larger part of our income. We have already exhausted every means of obtaining any very large increase to that Parliamentary vote. Even were any Parliament so well disposed towards the Territories—and I think all governments are in a way—the conditions surrounding a Parliamentary vote, the conditions which exist at Ottawa, prevent any adequate amount being given to us under our present institutions. I make that statement believing such to be the case. So long as the Territories remain in a dependent condition and receive their financial assistance as a matter of grace rather than the right; so long as the Territories remain in the position of having a large amount of money voted as a grant in addition to a number of other things which the Provinces do for themselves, provided for them every year in the Dominion supply, just for so long will it be impossible for the Territories to secure that suitable financial recognition without which even the present institutions cannot be successfully carried on. We have pretty well passed through the preliminary stages, and we have pretty well come to an end of our usefulness so far as our present condition will permit us. . . . The question is: What shall we do? Shall we simply stand still under the present institutions? My opinion on that question has already been stated. I do not say that we should take the final step at the present moment, but I do ask, Why should we not take it when we have arrived at that point, both financially and constitutionally, when we are unable to make that progress which the country requires? When we have arrived at that point why should we not take the further step? and the further step is to go to the extent of the limits imposed by the British North America Act. . . . My principal argument in favour of the immediate taking up of this question with a view to its discussion and settlement is that we must make progress in this country and without this further step we cannot make progress. Progress is devoutly to be wished and discussion is its instrument. What is the resolution? It recites that Parliament has certain powers. We must always bear in mind that Parliament has the power to form Provinces and the Government of the day may bring down a bill to Parliament forming these Territories, or any portion of them, into a Province, and if that were done, as the Government presumably controls Parliament, that Province, or those Provinces, would be created. We are not in the position of a self governing colony unfortunately; we are not in the position of Prince Edward Island, or of Newfoundland. We are simply the creatures of the Federal Parliament. The Federal Government can bring down a bill to create political institutions in any part of this country without reference to a single individual in it. But we claim to be given an opportunity to discuss and to negotiate, although we have not the right to dictate terms or even to be treated as one party to an arrangement, and we claim to be dealt with in the same way as our fellow citizens in the other parts of the Dominion. The resolution can fairly be said to have left out everything that can be called controversial so far as this House is concerned. There are controversial sides to this question, but in its more important aspects it is not controversial with us. The question, for instance, whether we shall have one, two or more Provinces is a controversial question which it would be perfectly useless for this House to discuss.

Mr. Bennett: Would you not consider it incidentally dealt with in that resolution?

Mr. Haultain: No.

Mr. Bennett: What, not the use of the single word 'Province'— 'shall be established as a Province?'

Mr. Haultain: 'Before any such Province is established?'

Mr. Bennett: Yes, 'before any such Province.'

Mr. Haultain: Any part of the Territories can be established as a Province. I am perfectly willing to make the present resolution quite clear on that point. There is no intention to convey the impression in the smallest degree of any opinion I may have ever held or expressed with regard to this side of the question.

Mr. Bennett: That is the way it is taken.

Mr. Haultain: But that is not the way it is intended, and if it is so taken it is a mistake. . . .

Every Province in the West will be equally interested in what is the basis of settlement of the claims with regard to lands; and so throughout every subject which will form an important matter of enquiry. . . .

The right of administration of the lands has been given to the Dominion and nothing more. They have only been given power to make provision for the administration, peace, order and good government of this country, and there is not a single clause in any of the Acts giving the Dominion the proprietary right in the lands, and there is not a single word conferring anything but a right of administration on the Dominion Parliament. The proprietary right still remains in the Crown, and on the analogy of dealing with the other Provinces, following out the policy of the British North America Act, I think we could establish a very fair claim to be heard with regard to our right to a beneficial interest in the lands of the Territories—that is, the rights of any Province which may hereafter be established in the Territories.

Now the claim to the land being admitted, opens up at once some very large questions. It opens up all the previous dealings with the lands and practically puts the Dominion in the position of trustee for the Province or Provinces which may hereafter be established in the West. I do not propose to go into that branch of the subject, and all I will say with regard to it is that even by the very general way in which I have dealt with it I think I have established that there is ample ground for asking that 'accounts be taken, enquiries be made, and negotiations held.' . . . We will not at this time, I will not at least, anticipate these negotiations. I have simply attempted to indicate in a general way what the subjects for negotiations are. All we have to do at the present time is to convince the people of the Territories that these subjects are important enough to negotiate about and that the time has come, considering the magnitude of the questions involved, for beginning these negotiations. But there must be a certain amount of concession and compromise. We shall never be able to arrive at a reasonable settlement if we sit down and say we demand this or that or the other thing without reference to the actual conditions and to the history of the whole subject. A reasonable time for consideration will be required by both the negotiating parties. The number and the magnitude of the questions involved justify an enquiry, and ample time must be given, and there is not too much time in that period I have mentioned—that is practically the term of the existence of this Legislature. . . . I need hardly dwell again on the necessity for unanimity. If we are not unanimous we are not going to accomplish much. Our individual opinion will not be of much use unless backed up by a very strong public opinion. The duty of every member of this House is to develop that public opinion by discussion and to bring these matters before the people of the country in order to show them that there are large interests at stake, and that they have many claims and rights which it may be they have hitherto not realised, and which can only be established by the fullest enquiry and negotiation. Exaggerated claims may be made, and possibly have been made, but the matters which I have referred to are not matters of fancy or speculation. We have an enormous country with tremendous interests and an almost boundless future. We should not be staggered by the realisation of the splendid heritage which we are entitled to but should rather be uplifted and urged on to try to establish these rights and have these claims satisfactorily adjusted.

II — 31

Memorial from the Legislative Assembly of the North-West Territories to the Dominion Government, May 2, 1900: Sessional Paper No. 1 of the North-West Territories, 1901.

MAY IT PLEASE YOUR EXCELLENCY—

We, Her Majesty's dutiful and loyal subjects, the Legislative Assembly of the North-West Territories of Canada, in Session assembled, humbly approach Your Excellency for the purpose of representing—

That by the British North America Act 1867 it was (amongst other things) enacted that it should be lawful for the Queen, by and with the advice of Her Majesty's Most Honourable Privy Council, on Address from the Houses of the Parliament of Canada, to admit Rupert's Land and the North-Western Territory, or either of them, into the Union on such terms and conditions in each case as should be in the Addresses expressed and as the Queen should think fit to approve subject to the provisions of the said Act;

That by an Address from the Houses of the Parliament of Canada, Her Majesty was prayed to unite Rupert's Land and the North-Western Territory with the Dominion of Canada.

That in order to further the petition of the Parliament of Canada, Her Majesty, under the authority of The Rupert's Land Act 1868, accepted a Surrender from the Governor and Company of Adventurers of England trading into Hudson's Bay of all the lands, territories, rights, privileges, liberties, franchises, powers and authorities whatsoever granted or purported to be granted by certain Letters Patent therein recited to the said company in Rupert's Land;

That in the said Address it was represented to Her Majesty, as a reason for the extension of the Dominion of Canada westward, that the welfare of the population of these Territories would be materially enhanced by the formation therein of political institutions bearing analogy, as far as circumstances will admit, to those which existed in the several Provinces then forming the Dominion;

That the Houses of Parliament of Canada by their said Address expressed to Her Majesty their willingness to assume the duties and obligations of government and legislation as regards these Territories;

That in pursuance and exercise of the powers vested in the Queen by the aforesaid Acts, Her Majesty, by and with the advice of Her Most Honourable Privy Council, ordered and declared that from and after the fifteenth day of July, 1870, Rupert's Land and the North-Western Territory should be admitted into and become part of the Dominion of Canada, and granted power and authority to the Parliament of Canada to legislate for the future welfare and good government of these Territories;

That by The British North America Act 1871 the Parliament of Canada was further given power from time to time to make provision for the administration, peace, order and good government of any Territory not for the time being included in any Province;

That under the several authorities so given the Parliament of Canada has created political institutions in these Territories bearing a close analogy to those which exist in the several Provinces of the Dominion;

That by the Confederation compact the Provinces which formed the Dominion on the fifteenth day of July, 1870, were furnished with the means of carrying on local self-government upon certain well defined bases;

That the Territories being an integral part of the Dominion, and having had imposed upon them the duties and obligations incidental to the political institutions which have been given to them, and which said duties and obligations the Parliament of Canada has declared its willingness to assume, are entitled to such Federal assistance for their maintenance as will bear due proportion and analogy to that given to other portions of the Dominion for similar purposes;

That repeated representations have been made in various ways to the Government of Canada with a view to obtaining just and equitable financial assistance towards providing for the proper and effective administration of local affairs in the Territories and for the public necessities of their rapidly increasing population;

That such representations have been met by intermittent and

insufficient additions to the annual grant, the provision so made by the Parliament of Canada never bearing any adequate proportion to the financial obligations imposed by the enlargement and development of the political institutions created by itself;

That it is desirable that a basis should be established upon which the claims of the Territories to suitable financial recognition may be settled and agreed upon;

That we do therefore most humbly pray that Your Excellency will be graciously pleased to cause the fullest inquiry to be made into the position of the Territories, financial and otherwise, and to cause such action to be taken as will provide for their present and immediate welfare and good government, as well as the due fulfilment of the duties and obligations of government and legislation, assumed, with respect to these Territories, by the Parliament of Canada;

And furthermore that, by The British North America Act 1871, it was (amongst other things) enacted that the Parliament of Canada may from time to time establish new Provinces in any Territories forming for the time being part of the Dominion of Canada but not included in any Province thereof, and may, at the time of such establishment, make provision for the constitution and administration of . . . such Province, we do therefore most humbly pray that Your Excellency will be also graciously pleased to order inquiries to be made and accounts taken with a view to the settlement of the terms and conditions upon which the Territories or any part thereof shall be established as a Province, and that, before any such Province is established, opportunity should be given to the people of the Territories, through their accredited representatives, of considering and discussing such terms and conditions.

All which we humbly pray Your Excellency to take into Your Excellency's most gracious and favourable consideration.

WILLIAM EAKIN,
Speaker of the Legislative Assembly
of the North-West Territories

Early Advocates of Alberta Autonomy

John Livingston
(E. Brown Collection, Provincial Archives of Alberta)

James Reilly
(E. Brown Collection, Provincial Archives of Alberta)

A.L. Sifton
(Provincial Archives of Alberta)

Senator James Lougheed
(Provincial Archives of Alberta)

The Politicians

F.W.G. Haultain c. 1897
(Provincial Archives of Alberta)

Frank Oliver
(E. Brown Collection, Provincial Archives of Alberta)

R.B. Bennett—1901
(H. Pollard Collection, Provincial Archives of Alberta)

A.C. Rutherford
(Provincial Archives of Alberta)

The Provincial Legislature Under Construction
(E. Brown Collection, Provincial Archives of Alberta)

Wilfrid Laurier Speaking at Inaugural Ceremonies, September 1905.
(E. Brown Collection, Provincial Archives of Alberta)

Composite Photograph of Inaugural Ceremonies
(Provincial Archives of Alberta)

The Lieutenant-Governor and First Cabinet of Alberta—1905

W.T.Finlay

Premier
Rutherford

Lt. Gov.
Bulyea

C.W. Cross

W.H. Cushing

L.G. De Veber

(Provincial Archives of Alberta)

Alberta's First Legislature Opens in the Thistle Rink, March 15, 1906

(E. Brown Collection, Provincial Archives of Alberta)

Calgary, 1906

(E. Brown Collection, Provincial Archives of Alberta)

A View of Edmonton and Old Hudson's Bay Fort—1902
(E. Brown Collection, Provincial Archives of Alberta)

Old Fort & New Legislature

(E. Brown Collection, Provincial Archives of Alberta)

Section III
Waiting for an Answer from Ottawa, 1900-1902

The period from May 1900 until 1902 might be characterized as one of optimistic waiting. Action was slow in coming on the Territorial Memorial but every indication out of Ottawa was that the federal government would eventually respond positively. The initial correspondence between Haultain and Clifford Sifton, the Minister of the Interior, was promising and besides the Liberal Party of Laurier was known as a party of provincial rights. When, after many delays, the long awaited meeting between Territorial and Dominion representatives was held in the autumn of 1901, Haultain was optimistic enough to propose a draft bill giving the Territories provincial status.

While awaiting a formal response from the Dominion government, Territorial figures turned their attention to all of those secondary matters which had been carefully avoided in the initial Memorial. The number of Provinces to be created, their shape, the question of Manitoba extension and, of course, the financial terms of provincial status all became lively subjects for discussion over the winter of 1901-1902. The principle of Provincial autonomy, it becomes apparent, was widely accepted but the details of it remained controversial.

The internal Territorial controversy suddenly became secondary when, in the spring of 1902, Clifford Sifton replied to the Territorial proposals with a refusal to grant Provincial status. In the face of resistance from Ottawa to an idea that had not only become popular but, to a large extent, had been assumed to be very near in time, the Territories closed ranks. Haultain used the Territorial election of that year to ask for a mandate for his demand for provincial status and he obtained an overwhelming degree of support. What had previously been a matter of internal debate within the Territories now became a debate between Ottawa and the North-west.

III — 1

Haultain to Sifton, January 30, 1901: Canada Sessional Paper 116a, 1904.

Following up the discussion between you, Mr. Ross and myself, on the subject of the North West Assembly memorial of May 2 last, I now beg, agreeably to your request, to make a further statement in writing.

The memorial while leading to definite constitutional changes, approaches the subject from the financial point of view and points out how, in the opinion of the Legislature, our legislative jurisdiction and administration responsibilities have been enlarged and increased out of all proportion to the means at our disposal. I need not enlarge on this side of the question, as it has already been placed very fully before you in the financial statements furnished to you for the past two years by my colleague Mr. Ross. While financial embarrassments rather than constitutional aspirations have led the North-West Government to discuss the provincial status, I think that sufficient practical reasons can be given for the early establishment of provincial institutions in the West. We have a rapidly growing population, much larger as the census will show, than that of British Columbia ten years ago, and than that of Prince Edward Island today; a population trained to the exercise of powers of self-government falling a little short only of those enjoyed by the Provinces. For nearly thirteen years the North-West Legislative Assembly has been occupied with founding local institutions and a body of laws suitable to the condition and circumstances of the country. Our parliamentary vote is apparently incapable of expansion at all in proportion to the needs of a rapidly developing country and our powers circumscribed as they are by the necessities of our present anomalous constitutional position, fall short just at the point where further progress demands their exercise. The Territories have arrived at a point, where by reason of their population and material development, the larger powers and larger income of a Province become necessary. I have already in former communications pointed out to you how our limited powers are still more limited by the reservation of such subjects as the Land Titles law, the administration of criminal law and the control of the public domain. It is undoubtedly in the interest of any Province or Provinces hereafter to be established, that the important questions surrounding the subject of the public domain should be settled at once, and before any more of the public lands of the Territories are alienated from the Crown.

For these and other reasons which need not be advanced at length, I would ask you to urge the earliest possible action on the part of the Government on the lines suggested and with the object proposed by the Assembly Memorial.

III — 2

Sifton to Haultain, March 21, 1901: Canada Sessional Paper 116a, 1904.

Referring to your communication of January 30, and the conversations which I had with yourself and Mr. Ross in Ottawa, I may say that I realize very fully the difficulties of the position in which the Government and Legislative Assembly of the North-west Territories is placed, and I admit that there is very much in the suggestions which are made in your letter and in the memorial regarding the necessity of a change in the financial and constitutional position of the Territories.

Without at the present moment committing myself to any positive statement I am prepared to say that the time has arrived when the question of organizing the Territories on the provincial basis ought to be the subject of full consideration. It would appear to me that the better way of bringing the matter to a more definite position would be to arrange for a conference upon the subject between the representatives of your Government and a committee of Council representing the Federal Government. I shall be pleased to bring about such arrangements for a conference at any time that is mutually convenient.

III — 3

Walter Scott, Liberal M.P., supports autonomy:
House of Commons Debates, March 25, 1901, 2006, 2012.

Occasionally, in the House—even since this session has opened—there have been remarks dropped which might lead a western member to believe that the opinion is held down here that the western people are very impatient; that they are looking for their wrongs to be righted immediately; that they want things to move a little too fast; but, Sir, in regard to this question the people of the North-west cannot be accused of any undue haste. They have been heretofore working under such a constitution as the Federal parliament thought well to grant. They have now come to a stage when they feel that some additional powers are required and when some different arrangement ought to be made so as to enable them to better carry on the work of local government. The difficulty they labour under is not so much constitutional as it is financial. So far as their constitutional powers are concerned the people feel that they might possibly get along for some time yet without any marked change. But they have come to a point in their history when they feel hampered as regards their finances. . . .

The representatives of the Territories think the time is approaching, and we may conclude from this statement of the Minister of the Interior that the government here are seized of the fact that the time is rapidly approaching when a change must be made in the relations of the North-west legislature to this parliament; and as the census is to be taken this year, the data thus obtained will make it possible to intelligently negotiate, and will bring a favourable time for commencing discussions.

III — 4

The Territorial Treasurer, A.L. Sifton, presents a deficit budget, June 6, 1901: Regina Leader, June 13, 1901.

Sifton: As regarded the revenue it was not necessary to say much as it was not raised by specific taxation. As a rule, therefore, there was not much to say. The bulk of the revenue came from the Dominion Government. There was a specific amount voted. That amount, unfortunately, was not sufficient for the purposes required. But it was practically all they had to depend upon. The revenue from the Dominion Government was practically some $340,000 and various other items brought it up to $413,000. In addition to that there would be paid on 1st January next year $180,000, so that there was in sight for the present House to consider a sum that would approach $600,000. But that was anticipated, so that practically there was a deficit. The Assembly therefore had to consider, and consider seriously, that unless some radical change took place they would not have enough monies for carrying on the work of the country. . . .

What was to be done? It had been shown over and over again that it was impossible to carry on the affairs of the country under the present system of raising revenue. There were no dissenting views on that point. There might be difference of opinion as to what should be the remedy: but he thought that he had shown that the remedy was not to continue the course that had been taken of endeavoring to persuade the Dominion Parliament to increase the grant, and to make the periodical trips that had been made: but that they had now to press upon the Dominion Government the necessity of a radical change. This brought him to the great question that had been before the country more or less for fifteen years, the question of erecting the Territories into a province. He had said for fifteen years because if he remembered rightly it was in 1885 that in Saskatchewan the people were bringing to the notice of the Dominion Government the question of being erected into a province. Later in Alberta the matter became one of importance to the people of that country, and for the same reason that it had now reached an acute stage all over, namely, the necessity of roads and public works. In the eastern portions of the country the same necessity now existed. Any person could discuss how the question could be met. They had it in the power of that House to consider the question, and it would be for the Territorial Government to announce its policy in regard to the matter; but it had nothing to do with the actual legal responsibility. The power was in the hands of the Dominion Parliament and in their hands alone. It was, however, in the hands of the Assembly to look after the interests of the North-West and to endeavor to secure a settlement of the question that would meet the wishes of the people.

III — 5

Calgary Herald comments on A.L. Sifton's budget, Calgary Herald, June 8, 1901.

Mr. Sifton has delivered his budget speech in the Territorial Legislature and from the tenor of his remarks it would appear as if the Territorial government had burned its boats and were advancing at once to the question of provincial establishment.

The estimates show that appropriations have been made for a larger amount of money than is at present available.

Only one construction can be put upon this action of the government, and that is they know that the Federal authorities are now prepared to grant us provincial status. It has virtually committed the Territories to accept provincial establishment within the next three months.

There is a note in Mr. Sifton's speech that rings a little ominous and that is where he speaks of compensation for lands. It is hoped that he means compensation for lands alienated by grants to railways and other Dominion schemes and not for all the lands still vested in the crown. However, judging from present indications time will soon show what is in store for us.

III — 6

The Meeting on the question of Provincial Autonomy takes place, October 27, 1901: Calgary Herald, October 28, 1901.

The conference between the northwest delegates Premier Haultain and the Hon. A.L. Sifton, and the Dominion Government over the status of the Northwest Territories took place yesterday afternoon in the premier's office, and lasted about two hours. There were present the following members of the Dominion cabinet: Sir Wilfred [sic] Laurier, Sir Richard Cartwright, Hon. Clifford Sifton, Hon. W.S. Fielding, Hon. J.I. Tarte, and Hon. R.W. Scott. The whole question was gone into fully.

Premier Haultain was the first speaker to present the case for the Territories. He pointed out that the time had arrived when the Dominion should take up seriously the question of extending to the Territories free provincial powers. This would be the only permanent remedy because as long as the Territories were dependent upon the financial assistance extended to them from Ottawa, which is given now as a matter of grace no matter how well disposed the Dominion government was and he recognized that the Dominion was well disposed. Still, so long as this continued it would be very difficult to secure suitable financial recognition.

He spoke of the people of the west being well prepared for self-government. That was generally recognized. As it was at present the legislature had pretty well exhausted all the powers given to it in an effort to keep up with the growth and development of the country. The foundations for self-government had been laid. He pointed out the position the legislature had taken upon this question and which was embodied in an address to his Excellency the Governor General stating that the time had arrived when provincial autonomy should be extended to the Territories and asking for a conference, which was now being given to permit the whole question being discussed.

While Mr. Haultain's speech was along these lines, he was particularly strong in his argument for the urgent need of an

increase in the financial grant at once so as to permit of the
Territorial Government meeting to some extent the increased
requirements which the country demanded.

Hon. A.L. Sifton strongly supported the view taken by his
colleague.

It was evident from the numerous questions asked by the
members of the Dominion government present, that they were
not only deeply interested in the subject but that they had been
looking into the latest phases of it. The North-West delegates
were ready to answer all the questions put to them, and when
the whole matter had been gone into fully in this way, the
Premier asked the delegation to submit their case in writing
when an answer would be forwarded as soon as the whole
cabinet had time to look into it. He promised the delegates that
their views would receive the most careful consideration. Mr.
Haultain and Mr. A.L. Sifton will prepare the document before
leaving Ottawa and will hand it in to the government. The
delegation appears to be very well satisfied with the result of the
conference, which was of course held behind closed doors.

*The draft bill in the following Memorandum which is to be
found in the Laurier Papers, 208428-208431, has various
comments scribbled on it, presumably by Laurier. Clause 18
has the note 'Reserved for consideration'; Clause 19 has a
comment which looks like the word 'same'; Clause 22, Section
(B) and Clause 23 has the word 'reserved'; Clause 25 is scratched
out.*

III — 7

**Memorandum of F.W.G. Haultain to Wilfrid Laurier with a
proposed draft bill for the establishment of a Province in
the North-West Territories, December 7, 1901:
Canada Sessional Paper 116, 1903.**

The Right Honourable Sir Wilfrid Laurier, G.C.M.G.,
    President of the Council,

In response to the request made by the sub-committee of the
Privy Council, convened to consider the matters referred to in
the Address to His Excellency the Governor General in
Council, presented by the Legislative Assembly of the Territo-

ries, pursuant to resolutions adopted on the 2nd of May, 1900 (a copy of which is attached hereto), I have the honour to submit, on behalf of the Government of the Territories, the following statement of the present position as it appears to us, together with such remarks as seem to be necessary to properly set forth the reasons which led the Assembly to request that enquiries be made and accounts be taken with a view to the establishment of provincial institutions within that portion of the North-west Territories lying between the provinces of Manitoba and British Columbia.

For a number of years back the attention of the Dominion Government has annually been directed to the necessities, financial and otherwise, of the Territories, in the estimates submitted through the Honourable the Minister of the Interior. Occasion has always been taken to set forth, as briefly as possible, but necessarily with some considerable detail, the difficulties met with in the administration of affairs in the Territories. The documents submitted, I understand, were presented to Parliament during its last session, so that their tenor will no doubt be familiar to you, and it will not be required that the matters they dealt with shall be repeated here. Put in the briefest possible form, the position is simply this: The population of the Territories has been and is increasing so rapidly as a result of the efforts put forth by the Immigration Branch of the Interior Department, that the means at the command of the Territorial Government are far from being sufficient to enable it to properly administer the affairs of the country. The increase in the population has increased our work and expenditures by a rate far greater than can be measured by the mere increase in the number of the people. Immigration in other parts of the Dominion has resulted largely in adding only to the population in settlements and towns previously in existence; in the Territories it is not so. New settlers in the North-west seem desirous to pass by the settlements already opened up, and to become pioneers in districts removed as far away as practicable therefrom. The new settlements are too small and the settlers are too widely scattered to bear the burdens which necessarily go with the opening up of a new country, and the fact cannot be disguised that they must be assisted to do so if the people are to become contented and prosperous, or even retained in the country. Bridges or ferries must be provided where it is necessary to cross rivers to reach market points. Where difficulty is met with in procuring an adequate water supply, the government has found it necessary to procure and operate machinery at considerable expense in order to sink public wells, or, as has been found practicable in some districts, to construct reservoirs in valleys or other natural depressions in order to conserve the surface water for the use of stock, and even, in some instances, for domestic purposes. Wherever water courses run in the Territories, the valleys are deep, the banks being often precipitous. These have the effect of rendering the ordinary road allowances, as laid down by the Dominion lands system of survey, impossible. They cannot be travelled and new roadways have to be provided, generally at considerable expense for right of way and construction. These are but a few of the difficulties which the government of the Territories is called upon to find a means of ameliorating. There are others which it would appear to be needless to take up your valuable time by enumerating in detail, as it may be said they are all of the same character, being hindrances and drawbacks to the settlement of the country. In the older settled districts other difficulties arise. Where the people have advanced beyond the pioneer stage they often find themselves handicapped for lack of proper transportation facilities in order to place their produce upon their markets. Roads may be made, but when grain and dairy produce have to be hauled twenty, thirty and at times a greater number of miles in order to reach a market or shipping point, no matter how good the road may be, the return for the farmer's labour and use of his capital will show a tendency to pass the vanishing point.

It is thought that sufficient has been said to indicate to you the position in which the Government of the Territories finds itself. In addition to the work of administration which devolves upon all governments, there is a constant—and hitherto, it must be admitted, lamentably ineffectual—struggle to keep pace with the work, caused by the rapid development of the country by reason of the great increase in the population. It may be thought that the people ought to do this work for themselves, as to them will accrue the benefits, but whilst I am disposed to agree to the general proposition that, under ordinary conditions, the question of the provision of what may be called local public improvements is a matter of purely local and sectional concern, yet I am confident that you will readily recognize that the conditions at present existing in the Territories are far removed from being ordinary. After the subsidence of the first movement of people into the Territories consequent upon the completion of the Canadian Pacific Railway, the influx of population for a number of years did not proceed at the rate so noticeable of late, and no very great difficulties were met with in dealing with the conditions as they then existed. With the means provided in those days, the Government was in an infinitely better position than is the case now, notwithstanding the fact that the grants made by Parliament for government in the Territories have been materially increased upon the representations made to the Dominion Government from time to time. The public necessities are not created so much by the mere fact that thirty, forty or even fifty thousand people may be added to the population in any one year; but rather to the certainty that nearly every small group of new settlers, united by any tie whatever, means practically the opening up of a new settlement. We have no congested communities in the Territories. In some districts the land available for homestead purposes has practically all been taken up, but they are very few in number and extremely limited in area, and there is no evidence of any disposition amongst the people now coming to us to locate in districts already settled. I do not desire to press this point unduly, and I think that it will be made abundantly clear by a brief consideration of the following statement respecting the number of school districts and the annual increase during the past few years:—

From the date of the passage of the School Ordinance in 1884 to the end of 1896, school districts were organized to the number of 436.

At the end of 1897 there were 457—an increase of 21.

At the end of 1898, there were 480—an increase of 23.

At the end of 1899, there were 524—an increase of 44.

At the end of 1900, there were 576—an increase of 52.

At the present time, besides 35 districts in process of erection, there are 649—an increase of 73.

These figures give some idea of the number of new settlements that have been opened up within the past five years, though it is not intended to convey the impression that the school districts represent all the settlements in the country, as there are a number, mostly opened up but recently, where the pressure of the struggle for mere existence has prevented any attempt being made to establish schools, notwithstanding the efforts of the local Government in that direction.

I have spoken of the number of the settlements in the Territories, and, as I have said, these are not only small for the greater part and far removed from the other, but the people themselves are scattered widely.

In very few districts have the people begun to emerge from

what may be referred to as the pioneer form of existence, and the creation of anything but the simplest and most elementary organization amongst them is impracticable. We have, however, succeeded in bringing such organization into existence, notably in our school districts and local improvement districts. Through their means we have been enabled to call upon the people for all that it is possible to expect of them. Further additions to the public taxation might possibly be made, but good and sufficient reasons exist why they should not. In the first place, it would be calculated to militate against the work of the Dominion Government in seeking to induce people from other lands to come and settle down amongst us. After all is done and said, the real and most successful immigration agent is the contented settler, and a heavy rate of taxation, no matter how necessary, is not calculated to satisfy the man who is struggling to make a home in this undeveloped country. Then, again, to require the people of the Territories to carry on the work of opening up and developing the country would not be to treat the early settlers in the North-west in the manner in which the people of the older provinces have been treated. I need hardly remind you that on the completion of the confederation of the Provinces of Upper and Lower Canada, Nova Scotia and New Brunswick, the new Dominion immediately found itself in the possession of a debt amounting to $93,000,000, of which sum only about $17,000,000 could be shown to be represented by assets in any form or at any value whatever. It would be difficult at this date to state with any degree of certainty in what manner and for what purposes the provinces originally forming the confederation had created the debts they transferred to the Dominion, but I can refer you to the statement of Mr. (afterwards Sir) Alexander Galt, the Finance Minister in the last government of the old Province of Canada, made in his speech upon the discussion of the Quebec resolutions. Mr. Galt, in presenting the financial aspect of the Confederation question to the House, said:—

'It is necessary for us to review the liabilities of each province, the reasons why they were incurred, the objects which have been sought. In doing so, the House will not fail to remark that the same policy has animated the legislatures of all the provinces, or perhaps I should speak more exactly in saying those of Canada, New Brunswick and Nova Scotia. The public debt of all these provinces has, with some slight exceptions, been incurred for public improvements, intended to develop the resources of the country, to attract immigration and wealth to their respective shores, to cheapen the means whereby the products of their farms were to be taken to market, and to reduce the cost of freight of articles which enter largely into the consumption of their inhabitants.'

This statement appears to have passed without contradiction, and it may therefore be accepted that some considerable portion of the net debt of Canada on July 1, 1867, amount to $75,728,641, had been created by expenditures for the purposes described by Mr. Galt. This debt is still unpaid, and its cost is borne by every person in Canada who contributes in any form to the revenue of the Dominion, whether he resides within the boundaries of the provinces for whose benefit the money borrowed was expended or elsewhere. These provincial debts, too, it must not be forgotten, represent expenditures made over and above the expenditures rendered possible by the public revenues. You will, I trust, pardon me if I press your attention to the different manner in which the Dominion looks upon the development of the North-west. All our public revenues go to swell the Consolidated Fund of Canada, our public domain is exploited for purely federal purposes, and we are not permitted to draw on the future. Our revenues are rigidly limited, for all practical purposes, by the grants annually made by Parliament for 'Government of the North-west Territories,' and we are not even entrusted with the expenditure of the whole amount of that sum. The grants made have never been considered from the view point of the requirements of the Territories. Carefully and economically prepared estimates of the cost of public require-ments have been annually forwarded to Ottawa, but provision has never yet been made for the actual and crying necessities of the country. Last January we asked for a grant of $600,000, based upon closely considered details. Parliament met the request by appropriating the sum of $357,979 to meet the case. As a result, from one end of the country to the other, complaints are rife as to lack of transportation facilities—roads, bridges, ferries, drains, and other similar necessities—to permit not only old settlers to travel, but to enable new settlers, brought into the country by Dominion officials, to reach the locations to which their attention had been directed and which had been selected for their future homes. Expenditures, and large expenditures, too, are as urgently and imperatively required in the North-west today for 'public improvements,' 'to develop the resources of the country,' 'to attract immigration,' without speaking of 'wealth,' 'to cheapen the means whereby the products of the farm are to be taken to market,' as they ever were in the old Provinces of Canada, Nova Scotia or New Brunswick, and it does not seem at all inappropriate, in view of the circumstances, that Canada should provide the money for those purposes, for it is Canada at large, and not the North-west in particular, that will most benefit by the attraction of desirable immigrants to the country.

One other objection to the introduction of a sufficiently heavy rate of taxation to meet the general public requirements is found in the fact that the cost of a large number of public works we are now constructing should properly be chargeable to capital expenditure. As we have no capital account, having no power or authority to utilize the public credit in any way, we are compelled to devote an unreasonably large part of our limited annual income towards defraying the cost of such works, instead of spreading the expenditure over a term of years.

You will at once perceive that it would be an undoubted hardship upon the people who are now here were they required to tax themselves for the cost of such works. They would not only be compelled to bear the cost of rendering the country habitable for themselves, but at the same time to develop it for the benefit of those who are yet to come, instead of being enabled to place part of the cost upon those who will benefit by the results of the expenditure. Besides, such works not only serve the purpose of providing public conveniences and improvements, but every dollar spent upon them enhances the value of the land held for various corporations by the Dominion Government, and which do little or nothing to assist in the work. This is felt to be a public grievance, but is one which, I am glad to learn, the Government is making an earnest endeavour to remove as far as it is at present practicable.

Our financial difficulties, though the most serious which we have to meet, are not the only ones, nor are they more pressing or important in their bearing than others to which I have the honour to direct your attention. I will be brief in doing so, though I have no desire to minimize their importance. They might, for the purposes of consideration, be divided into two classes, those, namely, which relate to our administrative work and those others which relate to our legislation, but having pointed out that possible distinction, I do not think it will be necessary to deal with the questions involved in detail. The

North-west Territorial Act, by which our constitutional powers
are defined, derives its authority from that section of the British
North America Act, 1871, which gives to the Parliament of
Canada power to make provision for the 'administration,
peace, order and good government' of the Territories. Under
that authority, from time to time, step by step, power by power,
and in keeping with the spirit of the representations made to
her late Majesty by Parliament when the intervention of the
Imperial authorities was sought in order to have Rupert's Land
brought into the Dominion, Parliament has built up in the
Territories 'political institutions bearing analogy, as far as the
circumstances' probably admitted, to those which existed in the
several provinces forming the Dominion in 1867. Section 92 of
the British North America act, 1867, and section 13 of the
North-west Territories Act, as it has been amended from time to
time, run along almost identical lines, but there are omissions
in and additions to the North-west Territories Act which for
many purposes render futile the powers which it professes to
give; I might instance the power given to the Assembly by the
Act to pass Ordinances with respect to 'property and civil
rights.' In the face of the enactment by Parliament of the Land
Titles Act, 1894, it will be realized that with respect to land,
which forms by far the most visible form of 'property in the
North-west,' the Legislative Assembly is powerless. With
respect to the administrative duties created by our territorial
position, I will do no more than refer to the fact that public
necessities and the exigencies of the case have required us to
practically duplicate much of the administrative work now
being carried on for the Territories by the Dominion, and will
refrain from doing more than instancing the work called for in
the administration of justice as a case in point.

The impossibility of continuing the present system upon its
present basis must be self evident. On the one hand, our limitations—rigidly fixed by Parliament in some instances and
equally firmly placed by circumstances in others—preclude
our doing for ourselves the things that ought to be done, and,
on the other hand, Parliament makes no effort to assist us with
even an approximate degree of adequacy. I have spoken of the
work to be done by the Government of the Territories as being
'ours', but I am satisfied that you realise as fully as we do that
the work is only ours to do, as the doing of it and whatever may
be accomplished when it is done will all redound to the credit
and be for the benefit of Canada. We have been moderate in our
requests for means to carry on the work given to us to do, and

the successive annual failures of Parliament to meet the requirements have now brought us face to face with accrued public necessities far and away beyond our means to cope with. The Legislative Assembly has prayed that His Excellency will be pleased to make inquiry into the position of the Territories, and to cause action to be taken to provide for their present and immediate welfare and good government. What can be done? In the first place I have to assure you that the present conditions of the Territorial Treasury demands that a sum of not less than $465,000 be available before the close of the current Dominion fiscal year in order to enable us to even attempt to perform our public duties during the first half of 1902. Towards that sum Parliament has already made an appropriation out of which $178,989.50 will be available and which we may possibly be able to increase by $35,000 from other sources. We thus have a depleted Treasury to meet a deficit which in six months from now will amount to at least $250,000. We can only look to Parliament for this money. It is not possible for us to obtain it here or advisable to make any attempt to do so. The work must go on, and the longer it does so under existing conditions the further behind will we fall. This position is not one upon which either the Government or the Legislative Assembly of the Territories can look with equanimity, and I am convinced that once it is realized by the Dominion Government it will not be permitted to continue. Neglect to furnish prompt relief cannot but have the effect of neutralising the efforts of the Dominion to people the Territories, and it does not seem to us to be probable that Parliament, after making generous provision for carrying on the work of inducing immigration to the Territories, will be niggardly in providing for assisting to retain the people so brought here.

Granting that the foregoing statement has the effect which we earnestly trust it will have, and that we shall receive your assurance that our present financial necessities will be relieved as soon as Parliament can be asked to make the necessary provision therefore, what then? How shall the future requirements be met? From official announcements made on different occasions we are led to the belief that there are good prospects of larger and more extensive movements of people towards the North-west than any yet seen. Will Parliament continue to provide the means for carrying on the work we know to be necessary, making increases in the grants made for the purpose bearing some proportion to the increases in the numbers of the people coming to us, as well as capital to permit development work to be carried on? If so, well and good. The Legislative Assembly has suggested that the time has arrived when some consideration be given to this question, and by its Address before cited has asked that 'inquiries be made and accounts taken with a view to the settlement of the terms and conditions upon which the Territories or any part thereof shall be established as a province.'

This request is made in the belief that such an inquiry will make it clear that the establishment of a province in the Territories upon equitable terms will relieve the Dominion of any necessity for annually considering Territorial questions. It is thought that the time is opportune for looking into this matter. Our official machinery is now upon a working basis, and it does not appear that any disturbance of equilibrium can result from the operation of the increased powers and added duties that will follow the change. The present tentative nature of much of our legislation and some of our public institutions can be amended by the introduction of measures tending to place them upon a permanent footing, which work can be better done in the near future than at a time when the weakness and ineffectiveness of much of our work, due to causes already referred to, have had time to create public dissatisfaction and uneasiness. During the consideration which I have no doubt will be given to this part of the prayer of the Legislative Assembly, there are some matters which, we respectfully submit, should receive most careful and thorough examination. It goes without saying, that the principles of the British North America Act will form the basis of the constitution of any province created. We seek for no advantages over any other province, and we do not anticipate that we will be denied any privilege given elsewhere. After giving some earnest thought to the matter of presenting this part of the subject as desired by the Sub-committee of the Privy Council, I have concluded that I cannot do so in any better manner than by submitting the views of the Executive Council of the Territories in the form of a draft Bill, in which the several points we would like to have brought to an issue are duly set forth, making such comment upon the principles involved as occurs to me in connection with each section or group of sections, and from this point onwards this communication will take the form thus indicated.

(No.   )   BILL.   1901.

An Act to establish and provide for the Government of the

province of   His Majesty, by and with the advice and consent of the Senate and House of Commons of Canada, enacts as follows:—

1. On, from, and after the first day of January, 1903, that portion of the Territory known as Rupert's Land, and the North-western Territory admitted into the Union or Dominion of Canada by Her Majesty Queen Victoria, by and with the advice and consent of Her Majesty's Most Honourable Privy Council by Order bearing date the twenty-third day of June 1870, under the authority of the 146th section of the British North America Act, 1867, described as the provisional districts of Assiniboia, Saskatchewan and Alberta as the said districts are defined by Orders of His Excellency the Governor General of the Dominion of Canada made in Council on the eighth day of May, 1882, and the second day of October, 1895, respectively: and that portion of the provisional district of Athabaska, as the said district is defined by Order of His Excellency the Governor General of the Dominion of Canada made in Council on the eighth day of May, 1882, and the second day of October, 1895, respectively, lying to the south of the fifty-seventh parallel of north latitude, shall be formed into and be a province which shall be one of the provinces of the Dominion of Canada, and which shall be called the province of . . . .

MEMORANDUM

In considering the question of the area to be included in this province it may be claimed that the area proposed is too large for one province. In this connection it should first be noted that the proposed area when compared with several of the other provinces of the Dominion stands as follows:—

	Area.
Quebec	347,000 square miles.
Ontario	220,000 square miles.
British Columbia	383,000 square miles.
Proposed province	404,000 square miles.

From this comparison it will be noted that the proposed province contains an area considerably larger than that contained in either of the three other provinces, mentioned, but it must be remembered that a large portion of the district of Athabaska and of the northern and eastern portion of Saskatchewan proposed to be included in the new province will never, owing to situation or physical features, or both, contain anything more than a very small and scattered population. The area which it is proposed to include in the new province is practically the area administered by the present Territorial Government and the experience of the past few years has indicated that there is no difficulty in properly administering the area from one centre.

The present cost of the government 'machine' in the Territories is proportionately much less than in the older provinces above mentioned and although the full provincial powers will bring with them added duties and necessitate additions to some of the present Territorial departments, these additions can easily be made and the departmental machinery extended to cover these services.

Our present cost of government only amounts to ten per cent of the annual Territorial expenditure, which is much less than the percentage of charge for this service in the older provinces and indicates that the present machinery of government is well suited to the requirements of the country and can be extended much more cheaply and satisfactorily than any new government departments can be organized.

The people in the provisional districts now administered by the Territorial Government, and which it is recommended should form the new province, are well acquainted with and satisfied with the present territorial laws and their administration, and there certainly does not seem anything to gain from a multiplication of governments in the area proposed to be created into a province.

The area in question, of course, contains much diversity of climate, soil, and other physical conditions which render it difficult to legislate in such a manner as to make the laws equally suitable to all portions, but no matter what division of the Territories might be made this condition would still exist and these difficulties have been fully realized and provided for in the existing territorial laws.

2. On and after the said first day of January, 1903, the provisions of the British North America Act, 1867, except those parts thereof which are in terms made or by reasonable intendment may be held to be specially applicable to or to affect only one or more but not the whole of the provinces under the Act composing the Dominion, and except so far as the same may be varied by this Act, shall be applicable to the province of . . . . in the same way and to the same extent as they apply to the several provinces of Canada and as if the province of . . . .

. . . . . . had been one of the provinces originally united by the said Act.

Memo.

This is the provision adopted on the incorporation of each of the provinces since the Union.

3. The said province shall be represented in the Senate of Canada by four members until it shall have, according to decennial census, a population of two hundred and fifty thousand souls, and from thenceforth it shall be represented by five members, and thereafter for each additional increase in population of fifty thousand souls according to decennial census there shall be an increase of one member in its representation until it is represented by twenty members.

Memo.

This provision partially assumes a basis of representation by population which is not the usual basis for an upper chamber, and the basis applied at Confederation, but it was the basis adopted with certain limitations when Manitoba was formed, two members being given for the then population of 17,000, to be increased to three for a population of 50,000, and the ratio for subsequent representation being fixed at 25,000, practically one-half the ratio in the present instance from the commencement. The maximum number is reasonable on the basis of representation fixed by the Confederation Act, by which the country was divided into districts not equal in area or population, but representative of different interests. The prairie portion of the country, consisting of Manitoba and the proposed province, comprises a division of the country as different in conditions and interests from the other portions of the country as the divisions under the Confederation Act, and the representation under this Act and the Manitoba Act would give it the same representation as each of the other divisions; while the limitation of twenty, as compared with Manitoba's four, seems reasonable on comparison of the areas and probable future populations.

4. The said province shall be represented in the first instance in the House of Commons of Canada by ten members, and for that purpose shall be divided by Act of Parliament or by proclamation of the Governor General into ten electoral districts, each of which shall be represented by one member; provided that on the completion of each decennial census hereafter the representation of the said province shall be readjusted

according to the provisions of the Fifty-first Section of the British North America Act, 1867.

Memo.

By the Manitoba Act, passed in 1870, Manitoba was given a representation of four members in a House to be elected in two years. The census taken in the following year showed a population of 18,995, which would have entitled her to one member. In 1881 the population had increased to 62,260, entitling her to three members. British Columbia, admitted in 1871 with a population of 36,247, entitling her to two members, was given six. In 1881 the population was 49,459. The Territories are now entitled, on the basis of redistribution under the British North America Act, 1867, to six members, and the present rate of immigration and the prospects of immediate increase, which are much more promising than in the case of either Manitoba or British Columbia, which were given respectively four and three times the members they were entitled to on the same basis, would seem to indicate that the number of ten or twelve members in a House which is not to be elected for three or four years, errs, if at all, in the direction of being too few, rather than too many. Even at the present moment the immigration for the year just about to close will give an estimated increase of more than 25,000 to the population as shown by the census lately taken.

5. The Executive Council of the province shall be composed of such persons and under such designations as the Lieutenant Governor shall from time to time think fit.

Memo.

This is exactly the same provision as that contained in the Manitoba Act, except as regards the limit in number in the first instance to five, which appears uncalled for.

6. All powers, authorities and functions which under any law or custom were before the coming into force of this Act vested in or exercisable by the Lieutenant Governor of the North-west Territories with the advice, or with the advice and consent, of the Executive Council thereof or in conjunction with that council or with any member or members thereof or by the said Lieutenant Governor individually, shall as far as the same are capable of being exercised after the coming into force of this Act be vested in and shall or may be exercised by the Lieutenant Governor of the province of . . . . with the advice or with the advice and consent of or in conjunction

with the Executive Council or any member or members thereof or by the Lieutenant Governor individually as the case equires subject, nevertheless, to be abolished or altered by the Legislature of the province.

Memo.

The provision of this section is practically the same as that contained in the 65th section of the Confederation Act in relation to Ontario and Quebec, and while there is no similar provision in the case of any of the other provinces then or afterwards admitted, they stand on a different footing inasmuch as all of them, except Manitoba which had had no previous existence, were self governing colonies with Governors directly representing the Crown, whereas the North-west Territories have for years had a Lieutenant Governor exercising certain functions which, as well as the existence and status of such Lieutenant Governor, are purely the creation of a Dominion Act, and the section as proposed would settle any question which might arise with regard to the authority of such Lieutenant Governor of the province in respect to functions exercised by the Lieutenant Governor of the Territories.

7. Unless and until the Executive Government of the provinces otherwise directs the seat of Government of the same shall be at . . . .

(See memo, following Section 8.)

8. There shall be a Legislature for the province consisting of the Lieutenant Governor and of one House styled the Legislative Assembly of . . . .

Memo.

Sections 7 and 8 are the provisions of the British North America Act, Sections 68 and 69, and the Manitoba Act, Sections 8 and 9 on this subject.

The location of the provincial capital is a matter of local concern and can only be finally decided upon after the creation of a province. In the meantime, for practical reasons, the seat of government will remain as it is.

9. The Constitution of the Legislature of the North-west Territories as it exists on the first day of January, 1903, shall subject to the provisions of this Act continue to be the Constitution of the Legislature of the province . . . . until altered under the authority of this Act and the Legislative Assembly of the said Territories existing on the said first day of January, 1903, shall unless sooner dissolved continue as the

Legislative Assembly of the province of . . . ., till
the completion of the period for which it was elected.

Memo.

When the British North America Act, 1867, came into effect,
there were, of course, no legislative assemblies in Ontario and
Quebec, and in Nova Scotia the Assembly was dissolved. In
New Brunswick, however, an Assembly existed and provision
was made by Section 88 of the British North America Act, 1867,
similar to that contained in this section for its continuance.
The Assembly of the Territories occupies the same relation to
the province that the Assembly of the then province of New
Brunswick did to the province under Confederation and it
seems fitting that the same provision should be made.

10. In and for the province the said Legislature may
exclusively make laws in relation to irrigation, and subject to
any right acquired under any Act of the Parliament of Canada
before the first day of January, 1903, the property in and the
right to the use of all the water at any time in any river, stream
watercourse, lake, creek, ravine, canyon, lagoon, swamp,
marsh, or other body of water shall, on, from and after the said
date, belong to and be vested in the province, unless and until
and except only so far as some right of some person therein or to
the use thereof inconsistent with the right of the Crown, and
which is not a public right or a right common to the public, is
established.

Memo.

This section provides that laws relating to irrigation shall be
made exclusively by the province, and transfers title to all water
to the province. It is assumed, in discussing this section, that if
the province be created without special provision for this
matter, that the title to the water in unnavigable streams and
lakes would, under ordinary terms of the British North
America Act, pass to the province, but that the title to navigable
waters would remain in the Government of Canada. This
would make systematic irrigation impossible without joint
legislation.

It has been clearly proved, and admitted by the Dominion
Government, that in a large section of the Territories to be
included in the new province irrigation is a necessity.

This necessity exists in only a portion of the proposed
province and is, therefore, a "local" need, which must be dealt
with in the same way as other "local" needs in other portions of

the proposed province, and under provincial control and administration.

It is admitted by those interested, that the success which has already attended the introduction of irrigation undertakings in the Territories is largely due to the careful government control which has been exercised of the record and use of water rights, and that such control can be best administered from local government sources was recognized some years ago by the Dominion Government, when the delegation of the administration of the North-west Irrigation Act to the Territorial Commissioner of Public Works was made.

If, as has been assumed, the new province will, under the terms of the British North America Act, own the water in unnavigable streams and lakes, the present provisions of the North-west Irrigation Act dealing with the title to such water will, of course, have to be repealed, and unless the provision contained in Section 10 of the proposed Act becomes law, there will at once be a clash between the Dominion Government and the Provincial Government regarding the use of water for irrigation. This difficulty will arise owing to uncertainty as to the streams or other bodies of water which are navigable and must be dealt with by the Dominion, and the other bodies of water which will become the property of the province and can only be dealt with by the province.

In the irrigation States and Territories to the south of the new province one of the greatest drawbacks to irrigation development has resulted from litigation as to the title to water rights, and this difficulty can only be abolished in the new province by continuing the present exact and carefully administered system of government control and record of water rights, and that system cannot be continued if there is any question as to which Government (Dominion or Provincial) is entitled to deal with these water rights.

The difficulty could, of course, be overcome by special provision being made in the Act, reserving the title to all water to the Dominion, but if this were done, the new province would be treated on an entirely different basis from the other provinces of the Dominion, including Manitoba, and would be precluded from dealing with a matter which, as has been stated, is a purely local one, and which experience has proved can best be dealt with by a department in close touch with the people interested.

The provisions of the section are taken from the Federal Irrigation Act of 1895, Section 2, but vesting in the province all water rights.

11. In addition to all other powers the Legislative Assembly

of the province shall have the powers conferred on the Legislative Assembly of the North-west Territories by the nineteenth section of chapter twenty-two of the Acts of the Parliament of Canada passed in the fifty-fourth and fifty-fifth year of the reign of Her Majesty Queen Victoria.

Memo.

The object of this section is to continue in the new province certain powers respecting legislation on the subject of the importation, &c., of intoxicating liquors conferred on the Territories by the North-west Territories Act, and which would not be comprised in the general powers under the British North America Act, 1867.

12. The judges of the courts of the province shall be selected from the bar of the province or from the bar of some other province in which the laws relative to property and civil rights and the procedure of the courts are the same as in the province of . . . .

Memo.

This section contains exactly the same provision as is contained in Section 97 of the British North America Act, 1867, as regards the provinces whose system of law was founded on the English common law.

13. Except as otherwise provided by this Act, all laws in force in the North-west Territories on the first day of January, 1903, and all courts of civil and criminal jurisdiction and all legal commissions, powers and authorities existing therein on the said date shall continue as if this Act had not been passed, subject nevertheless (except with respect to such as are enacted by or exist under Acts of the Parliament of Great Britain or of the Parliament of the United Kingdom of Great Britain and Ireland) to be repealed, abolished or altered by the Parliament of Canada or by the Legislature of the Province according to the authority of the Parliament or of the Legislature under this Act.

(See memo, following Section 14.)

14. All public officers and functionaries, judicial, administrative and ministerial, holding office in the North-west Territories on the first day of January, 1903, shall continue to hold such office in the province of . . . . with the same duties and powers as before until otherwise ordered by the Governor General of Canada or the Lieutenant Governor of the province according to the authority of the Governor General or the Lieutenant Governor under this Act.

Memo.

Sections 13 and 14 contain the necessary provisions for continuing the laws, courts, officers, &c., and are the same as contained in Section 129 of the British North America Act, 1867, here divided into two sections, the words of Section 129 not appearing to be very appropriate as applied to officers.

15. Until altered by the Lieutenant Governor in Council, the Seal of the North-west Territories shall be the Great Seal of the province of . . . .

Memo.

This is a simple provision to prevent the province being without a Seal until one can be provided, and conforms to that of Section 136 of the British North America Act, 1867.

16. The penitentiary situate in the province of Manitoba shall, until the Parliament of Canada otherwise provides, be the penitentiary for the province of . . . .

Memo.

This section contains the penitentiary arrangements at present in force, as was done in the case of the then provinces by the British North America Act, 1867.

17. Nothing in this Act shall in any way prejudice or affect the rights or properties of the Hudson's Bay Company, as contained in the conditions under which that company surrendered Rupert's Land to Her Majesty Queen Victoria, and all rights, privileges and properties conferred on Canada by the said conditions shall, in so far as they relate to matters within the legislative authority of the province, belong to and be vested in the province.

Memo.

Provision for the rights of the Hudson's Bay Company was thought to be necessary in the case of Manitoba (See Manitoba Act, Section 34) and is therefore continued in the present Act. The later provision of the section, though not in the Manitoba Act, seems desirable, particularly in view of the fact that at present the Hudson's Bay Company has denied the right of the Territories to take without compensation lands required for roads through reserves, which right is given to Canada by the conditions of surrender.

18. All lands belonging to the Crown situate in the province of . . . ., other than lands reserved by statute or Order in Council for the use of Indians or for and earned by any

person or corporation, and lands entered for homestead or pre-emption but not granted, and all sums due and payable on the first day of January, 1903, for such lands shall belong to the province.

(See memo. following Section 21.)

19. All mines, minerals, timber and royalties belonging to the Crown situate, being or arising in the Province of . . . ., and all sums due and payable on the first day of January, 1903, for such mines, minerals, timber or royalties shall belong to the province.

(See memo. following Section 21.)

20. The province shall receive and retain all the public property of the North-west Territories not otherwise disposed of in this Act.

(See memo. following Section 21.)

21. All buildings in the North-west Territories belonging to Canada, used or intended for court houses, jails and land titles offices and for residence and offices of the Lieutenant Governor and Government of the North-west Territories, together with all appurtenances connected therewith and all moneys the proceeds from the sale or leasing of school lands in the North-west Territories, and all moneys forming the Assurance Fund under the provisions of the Territories Real Property Act and the Lands Titles Act, 1894, shall be the property of the province of . . . .

Memo.

Sections 18, 19, 20 and 21 deal with the public property within the proposed province, and provide, as far as the circumstances appear to admit, for an arrangement analogous to that which obtains in the several provinces originally forming the Confederation.

The right and title to the public domain is in the Crown, but in the Colonies directly established by Great Britain the beneficiary interest in the revenues arising from the sale or other disposal of the public domain has been surrendered by the Crown for the benefit of the people residing in such Colonies.

The Union Act of 1840 specifically provided that the Territorial and other revenues then at the disposal of the Crown should be placed in future at the disposal of the province of Canada, then being formed. Similar dispositions were made, either by statute or by the exercise of the royal prerogative, in favour of the other Colonies in British North America. The British North America Act continued these arrangements for the benefit of the provinces forming the Confederation, and the sections of the Bill under reference provide for the extension of the principle to the province of which it purports to provide for the formation.

It may be noted that there has been no legislation or exercise of the royal prerogative transferring, to Canada or otherwise, any right to enjoy the beneficiary interest in the Territorial revenues of the North-west Territories. The fifth section of the 'Rupert's Land Act, 1868,' like the Order in Council of June 23, 1870, for which it is the authority, goes no further than to provide that, upon the admission of Rupert's Land into the Dominion, 'it shall be lawful for the Parliament of Canada to make, ordain and establish within the land and territory so admitted all such laws, institutions and ordinances, and to constitute such courts and officers, as may be necessary for the peace, order and good government of Her Majesty's subjects and others therein.' The words of the Order in Council dealing with the admission into the Union of that part of the North-west territories formerly known as the North-western Territory are more sparing as to number but appear to convey a somewhat wider extent of power, as they not only provide for the 'good government' of the Territory, but also its 'future welfare,' at the hands of Canada. With the exception of the grant made to the Hudson's Bay Company by the Imperial Order in Council of June 23, 1870, Section 30 of 'An Act to amend and continue the Act thirty-two and thirty-three Victoria, chapter three, and to establish and provide for the Government of the province of Manitoba,' confirmed by 'The British North America Act, 1871,' appears to be the only authority under which any portion of the rights of the Crown in Rupert's Land or the North-western Territory has ever been alienated. The Act last referred to is this Act under the authority of which the Parliament of Canada has from time to time made 'provision for the administration peace, order and good government,' of the North-west Territories, being a 'territory not for the time being included in any province'; and it is also the Act under which Parliament will provide for the 'constitution and administration of any * * * province' which may be established, 'and for the passing of laws for the peace, order and good government of such province * * * *'

The difference between legislative jurisdiction and proprietory rights was clearly laid down by Lord Herschell in the judgment of the Judicial Committee of the Privy Council in the Fisheries case, but it may be admitted that the necessities of 'administration,' and the duties and obligations of government and legislation as regards these Territories' assumed by Parliament, together with the established Imperial practice in such cases, would probably, though not necessarily, carry with them the privilege of appropriating the territorial and other revenues of the Territories for the maintaining good government and further the ends of legislation. Upon the formation within the Territories of the promised 'Political institutions bearing analogy * * * to those which exist in the several provinces of the Dominion,' it is submitted that whatever interest Canada may have had or exercised in respect of the territorial revenues will devolve upon the province. As Great Britain has divested herself, for the benefit of her colonies, of all her proprietary rights in the public domain within those colonies, so, it is thought, Canada should do with respect to any claim that may be preferred on behalf of the Dominion to the beneficiary interest in the public domain within that part of the Northwest Territories to be included in any province to be established.

It may be that the Government of Canada will admit the principle contended for above on behalf of the people of the North-west Territories who may be included within the limits of any province to be created, but will argue that it will not be in accord with established public policy for the Dominion to divest itself of the ability, largely advertised abroad, to grant lands to actual settlers upon almost nominal conditions. Such appears to have been the view adopted in 1884 by the Government of the day with respect to certain similar representations then made by the province of Manitoba. The validity of the claim was admitted by the agreement to recompense the province for the loss of its public property. It is not deemed necessary, here, at this stage, to discuss any such proposition further than to point out the one fact that, should the Dominion withhold from the province, for the benefit of Canada at large, the right to administer the public domain within its boundaries and to enjoy the revenues therefrom, the addition of each new settler, or—what experience has shown to practically almost amount to the same thing—the opening of each new settlement, will impose a burden and financial strain upon the revenues of the province altogether out of proportion to any revenue derivable on account of such settler or settlement, and one that can only be met by an early appeal to extensive direct taxation. The last issue of the Statistical Year Book gives the following rates of Government expenditure per head in the several provinces—Ontario, $1.74; Quebec, $2.74; Nova Scotia, $2.04; New Brunswick, $2.47; Manitoba, $4.58; British Columbia, $9.88; Prince Edward Island, $2.82. In the year 1900, the expenditure of the Government of the Northwest Territories was limited to $477,374.22 for the simple reason that no more money was available for expenditure. The population of the Territories in May, 1901, is reported to have been in the neighbourhood of 160,000. A simple calculation shows the per capita expenditure, in 1900, to have been about $2.98. Without extravagance and in order to provide for urgent public necessities, the per capita rate of expenditure in the Territories, had the money been available, would have been between $6 and $7. This large rate of public expenditure in the Territories, as compared with the rates of the eastern provinces, is entirely attributable to the extraordinary increase in expenditure due to the energy displayed by the immigration branch of the Interior Department. Whilst such energy is commendable from the view point of Dominion interests, yet its results place a great strain upon the finances of the country, and it is, with all respect, urged that the exploitations of the public domain within the province to be established, in the interests of the Dominion solely and entirely, will place upon the province a burden too onerous to bear, and one which should properly fall where the benefits go.

22. The following amounts shall be allowed and paid by Canada by half-yearly payments in advance as an annual subsidy to the province, that is to say:—

(a) For the support of the Government and Legislature, fifty thousand dollars.

(b) On an estimated population of two hundred and fifty thousand at eighty cents per head, two hundred thousand dollars, subject to be increased as hereinafter mentioned, that is to say:— A census of the province shall be taken in every fifth year, reckoning from the general decennial census of one thousand nine hundred and one; and an approximate estimate of the population shall be made at equal intervals of time between such quinquennial census and such decennial census; and whenever the population by any such census or estimate exceeds two hundred and fifty thousand, which shall be the minimum on which the said allowance shall be calculated, the amount of the said allowance shall be increased in accordance therewith until the population reaches four hundred thousand.

Memo.

Section 22 provides for the payment of an annual subsidy to the new province on the lines of that paid to the provinces under Section 118 of the British North America Act. It may be noted that in the year 1900 the cost of Government and the Legislature in the North-west Territories amounted to $66,311.37, which amount was further supplemented by expenditures made from the Parliamentary vote for Government of the North-west Territories upon matters which, in the provinces, usually devolve upon the provincial revenues, and which principle may be expected to be extended to the province to be formed.

The payment of eighty cents per head upon an estimated population in excess of the present actual population follows the precedent established in the case of British Columbia at the time of its admission into the Union. Ten years after its admission the population of that province had not reached to within ten thousand of the number upon which the subsidy was based. In the case of the North-west Territories, the population is rapidly increasing through immigration. Since the census was taken, in May, it is estimated that more than 25,000 people have come into the Territories, and it is reasonably expected that by the earliest date the province can be established the population will reach the initial figure referred to in the Bill, and that long before 1906 the population will be largely in excess of that upon which payment up to that date will be made.

23. The Province shall be entitled to be paid and to receive from the Government of Canada by half-yearly payments in advance, interest at the rate of five per cent per annum on the excess over the sum of . . . . of a sum to be ascertained by multiplying the population of the province by 32.46, and for the purpose of this section, the population of the province shall, until after the next decennial census, be deemed to be two hundred and fifty thousand. Provided, that immediately after the census of . . . . there shall be a readjustment under this section on the basis of the population as ascertained by such census.

Memo.

This clause provides for the establishment of a capital account between the province and the Dominion upon similar terms to those which have been given to the province of Manitoba, with the exception that the arrangement proposed is not final, the Bill providing for a readjustment on the basis of the population at a future date, when it may be expected that the ratio of increasing will approximate more closely to those in the other provinces than is the case at present.

24. The province shall be entitled to receive by half yearly payments in advance from the Government of Canada interest at five per cent per annum on the sum of one dollar per acre for each acre of land in the province granted by the Dominion otherwise than for homesteads or pre-emptions under the provisions of the Dominion Lands Act or in settlement of half-breed claims.

Memo.

Section 24 would probably be more properly referred to in connection with Sections 18, 19, 20 and 21 of the draft Bill as it deals with the public domain in so far as grants of land in the North-west Territories made for federal purposes are concerned, and seeks to place the indebtedness of Canada, to meet which these lands were given, where it properly belongs, namely, the Dominion at large, and not upon the property of the province. These grants have, in the main, been made in aid of railway construction in the west. Of such grants the following have been made, from Manitoba and the North-west lands, to the companies named:—

	Acres
Alberta Railway and Coal Company	1,114,368
Calgary and Edmonton	2,176,000
Canadian Northern	9,907,200
Canadian Pacific	19,816,010
Great North-west Central	320,000
Manitoba and North-western	2,752,000
Manitoba and South-western	1,396,800
Qu'Appelle, Long Lake and Saskatchewan	1,625,344
Red Deer Valley	352,000

Of these roads only four are entirely within the Territories, those namely,—of the Alberta Railway and Coal Company, the Calgary and Edmonton Railway Company, the Qu'Appelle, Long Lake and Saskatchewan Company, and the Red Deer Valley Company, and the lands granted lie within the area of the proposed province. The other roads named lie either entirely in Manitoba or partly within both the Manitoba and the Territories. With respect to three of these roads, namely, the Great North-west Central, the Manitoba and North-western and the Manitoba and South-western, the following is noted. The whole of the line constructed by the Great North-west Central is entirely within Manitoba. An area of 708,827 acres has been reserved for this grant, of which about 705,000 acres are in the Territories, and from which the bulk of the 320,000 acres earned under the grant will have to be selected, there being only some 5,800 acres of the reserve in Manitoba. An area of Territorial lands, equal to the whole grant to the Manitoba and North-western Company, has been reserved for the purposes of that grant, though less than one-fifth of the road constructed lies in the Territories. The line of the Manitoba and South-western Colonisation Company is entirely within Manitoba, but an area in the Territories of about 681,000 acres has been reserved for the grant on account of this road. Of the grants to the Canadian Pacific Railway Company the balance of that on account of the construction of the main line (18,206,986 acres) is the most important. As has been before stated, only some 2,500,000 acres have been selected outside the Territories, the balance being within the Territories. The Canadian Pacific Railway Company has been granted lands in aid of its Deloraine and Napinka, Glenboro and Souris, Kemnay and Estevan, and Pipestone Branches, amounting in all to 1,609,024 acres. A reserve approximating 1,900,000 acres, in the Battleford district of the North-west Territories of Canada, several hundred miles from the location of these branch railways, has been made for the purposes of these grants, though only about one-half of the Kemnay and Estevan branch is within the Territories, the Pipestone branch has just entered the Territories, the balance of these two roads together with the whole of the other two named being entirely without the Territories in the province of Manitoba.

The case of the Great Northern Railway Company may be mentioned also, as it is extremely probable that a very considerable part of the grants to that company, which aggregate nearly 10,000,000 acres, will when located be taken from territorial lands, though those portions of the company's system for which the grant has been made lies entirely outside of the Territories.

These railways have been aided by the Dominion on the ground that their construction was a benefit to Canada, and the policy followed in Manitoba and the North-west Territories is in remarkable contrast to that adopted by the Dominion in all other parts of Canada. Published Government statistics show that the Dominion Government has granted aid to railways constructed and under construction, up to June 30, 1900, by way of loans and bonuses, a sum of $166,009,303. The people of the Territories, man for man, bear an equal proportion of the cost to the Dominion of such expenditures.

There are some ninety railway enterprises, each wholly within its own province, which have been granted cash subsidies at the charge (it is again repeated) of the people of the Territories, equally with those of other parts of Canada, but in the Territories, railways, constructed as much in the interests of Canada as any one of the ninety referred to above, are subsidized entirely at the cost of the public domain within the province, notwithstanding the fact that some of the roads so subsidized will not benefit the province in any form or shape. The principle being once conceded, it must be admitted that if one is, all railways constructed are for the benefit of Canada whether it be the Canadian Pacific system with its six thousand and odd miles of track or the Phillipsburg Junction road, two-thirds of a mile in length. Canada should therefore bear the cost of the grants made by the Dominion and the Bill seeks to provide an equitable arrangement for transferring the burden of these and other similar grants from the Territories to the Dominion, so that the people of the province will not be dealt with in these respects otherwise than are the people of the provinces of Ontario, Quebec, New Brunswick, Nova Scotia, Prince Edward Island and British Columbia.

In addition to the matters dealt with in the foregoing draft Bill, I have also to direct your attention to, and to press for the removal by ancillary legislation of the exemption from taxation granted to the Canadian Pacific Railway Company under Clause 16 of the Schedule to Chapter 1 of the Dominion Statutes of 1881. The exemption, as is well known, is two-fold. First, that in the words: "The Canadian Pacific Railway, and all stations and station grounds, workshops, buildings, yards and other property, rolling stock and appurtenances required and used for the construction and working thereof, and the capital stock of the Company, shall be forever free from taxation by the Dominion, or by any province to be hereafter established, or by any municipal corporation therein"; and, second, in that part of the clause which reads: "and the lands of the Company in the North-west Territories, until they are either sold or occupied, shall also be free from such taxation for twenty years after the grant thereof from the Crown." The effect of these exemptions is to prohibit any province which may be established, or any municipal corporation therein, from requiring the Canadian Pacific Railway Company to assist in the "administration" of the country of the maintenance of "peace, order and good government" within its bounds with respect to a part of its property forever, and with respect to another part for a limited period of time. This exemption falls hardly upon the people of the North-west Territories in a number of ways. The nature of the land grant to the Company, in that it is spread over the whole country in small blocks of one mile square, alternating with those open for homesteads, causes every dollar spent by a settler in the Improvement of his homestead, where it lies within the districts reserved for the selection of the land granted on account of the construction of the Canadian Pacific Railway, to enhance the value of the lands held for the Company in its neighbourhood. All public expenditures made in such districts for roads, bridges and other works of a similar description improve the value of the lands still held by the company under its main line grant, the company contributing nothing on account of such lands towards the cost of the works by reason of which they are benefited.

An examination of the terms of the grant to the Canadian Pacific Railway Company shows that the exemption will bear with particular stress upon any province established within the area referred to in the draft Bill. The paragraph lettered (a) of Clause 9, in the Schedule to the 1881 Canadian Pacific Railway Act (Chapter 1 of the Statutes of that year) reads:

(a.) The said subsidy in money is hereby divided and appropriated as follows, namely:—

CENTRAL SECTION.

Assumed at 1,350 miles—
1st—900 miles at
$10,000 per mile $9,000,000
2nd—450 miles at
$13,333 per mile 6,000
————————$15,000,000

EASTERN SECTION.

Assumed at 650 miles, subsidy equal to $15,384.61 per mile.

10,000,000
_____
$25,000,000

And the said subsidy in land is hereby divided and appropriated as follows, subject to the reserve hereinafter provided for:—

CENTRAL SECTION.

1st—900 miles at
   12,500 acres per mile 11,250,000
2nd—450 miles at
   16,666.66 acres per mile 7,500,000

_____18,750,000

EASTERN SECTION.

Assumed at 650 miles, subsidy equal to 9,615.35 acres
  per mile 6,250,000

25,000,000

The original land grant of 25,000,000 acres has been reduced
by 6,793,041 acres at a cost to Canada of $10,189,521, thus
leaving the company to receive 18,206,986 acres. In other words,
the amount of that apportionment of the land grant on account
of the construction of the "Eastern Section"—or that part of the
railway between Callander and a point east of Red River to
which the road has been constructed from Selkirk by the
Government, all of which lies in the Province of Ontario—has
been exchanged for cash, at the cost of the people of the Territories equally with those of every other part of Canada. Of the
balance of the land grant, the company has selected some
2,500,000 acres within the province of Manitoba, leaving the
balance to be selected from the lands within the North-west
Territories out of the extensive areas reserved for that purpose.
This particular grant is that made on account of the construction
of the "Central Section" of the railway, namely that from
Selkirk to Kamloops, which has been definitely ascertained to
be a distance of 1,250 miles. This distance is divisible as
follows:—
Manitoba, 220 miles; North-west Territories, 760 miles; British

Columbia, 270 miles. It is, therefore, apparent that a proportionate area, based upon the mileage through the province at the rate granted per mile through the Prairie portion of the Central Section (220 miles at 12,500 acres per mile, being 2,750,000 acres) has not been taken from Manitoba lands, and that in addition to this shortage of 250,000 acres, the whole of the grant earned by construction through British Columbia (at the Mountain rate of 16,666.66 acres per mile) is being made out of the lands of the Territories. Even if, under any process of reasoning, the exemption clause can be justified as regards the construction of the railway through the Territories, it is not thought that the Territories can in equity be required to bear this extra burden on account of the construction of the railway through the province of Manitoba and British Columbia. If they are so required, the people of the Territories, who are individually contributing equally to the cost to Canada of the interest upon the debt created by the payment of the original bonus of $25,000,000, the payment of $10,189,521 for the repurchase of the land grant on account of the Eastern, or Ontario Section of the railway, together with the annual payment of $100,000 to British Columbia for lands conveyed to Canada under the terms of the Imperial Order in Council of May 16, 1871, "to aid in the construction of the railway," will be also liable to bear whatever the exemption from taxation under the Canadian Pacific Railway Act of 1881 may mean. By the terms of that Act the province to be established—or any municipal corporation therein—will be prohibited from taxing the company or its property in any manner or for any reason. Unless invidious comparisons are made between the Canadian Pacific and other railway companies, this will mean the involuntary relinquishment of resources to that avenue of revenue, as no competing company will be liable to expend the necessarily vast sums of money required, unless it has the prospects of obtaining similar exemption from taxation at the hands of the province.

The necessity for this extraordinary burden upon the people of the West is not obvious. Ample evidence exists to show that the railway was not in any sense built for the benefit of the North-west. In 1865, the Honourable George Brown voiced the opinion of the Government of the day, when he stated, in his place in the Parliament of Canada, during the Confederation debates, that "the Confederation is, therefore, clearly committed to the carrying out of both these enterprises," his reference being to the construction of the Intercolonial Railway, and the opening up of the communications with the North-western Territory. "I doubt," he proceeded to say, "if there was a member of the Conference who did not consider that the opening up of the North-west and the improvement of our canal system were not as clearly for the advantage of the Lower Provinces as for the interests of Upper Canada. Indeed, one gentleman held that the Lower Provinces were more interested— they wished to get their products into the West—they wanted a back country as much as we did—they wanted to be the carriers for that great country—and they were, therefore, to say the least, as much interested in these questions as we were." But there is no need to go back beyond the solemn compact entered into between Canada and the Colony of British Columbia in 1871. The Imperial Order in Council of May 16, 1871, respecting the province of British Columbia, sets forth, as one of the terms and conditions upon which that Colony consented to enter the Confederation, the undertaking of the Government of Canada "to secure the commencement, simultaneously within two years from the date of the Union, of the construction of a railway from the Pacific towards the Rocky Mountains, and from such point as may be selected east of the Rocky Mountains towards the Pacific, to connect the seaboard of British Columbia with the railway system of Canada; and further to secure the completion of such railway within ten years from the date of the Union." The preambles to Chapters 71 and 72 of the Dominion Statutes of 1881, all set forth the fact in various ways that (to quote from the last-mentioned Act) "by the terms and conditions of the admission of British Columbia into union with the Dominion of Canada, the Government of the Dominion has assumed the obligation of causing a railway to be constructed connecting the seaboard of British Columbia with the railway system of Canada."

All this being so, it is difficult for the people of the North-west Territories to understand why they should be called upon to assume any other burden than that of contributing proportionately—and no more—with the people of other parts of Canada towards the cost of carrying out the obligations assumed by Canada under the compact with British Columbia. The exemption from taxation granted by the Canadian Pacific Railway Act is undoubtedly such an added burden and an imposition upon the people of the North-west Territories that cannot be justified. For no reason that is conceivable, this exemption bears with greater stress upon the North-west than it does even upon Manitoba. Except those lands selected by the company under its land grant which lie in that part of Manitoba added to the original province after the contract of 1881, none of the property of the company is exempt from taxation in Manitoba. That province today is taxing the company under Chapter 57 of the Provincial Acts of 1890.

In view of the foregoing, it is submitted that Parliament should be asked to take such steps as may appear advisable in order to countervail the operation of the exemption clause of the Canadian Pacific Railway contract within the limits of the province to be created.

In conclusion, I would venture to express the hope that His Excellency's advisers will, at an early date, arrive at a favourable conclusion to their consideration of the subject matters herein set forth.

F.W.G. HAULTAIN.

(No.   )   BILL.   1902.
An Act to establish and provide for the Government of the province of . . . .

His Majesty by and with the advice and consent of the Senate and House of Commons of Canada, enacts as follows:—

1. On, from and after the first day of January, 1903, that portion of the territory known as Rupert's Land, the North-western Territory admitted into the Union or Dominion of Canada by Her Majesty Queen Victoria and by and with the advice and consent of Her Majesty's Most Honourable Privy Council by Order bearing date the twenty-third day of June, 1870, under authority of the 146th Section of the British North America Act, 1867, described as the Provisional Districts of Assiniboia, Saskatchewan and Alberta as the said districts are defined by Orders of His Excellency the Governor General of the Dominion of Canada made in Council on the eighth day of May, 1882, and the second day of October, 1895, respectively; and that portion of the provisional district of Athabaska, as the said district is defined by Order of His Excellency the Governor General of the Dominion of Canada made in Council on the eighth day of May, 1882, and the second day of October, 1895, respectively, lying to the south of the fifty-seventh parallel of north latitude, shall be formed into and be a province which shall be one of the provinces of the Dominion of Canada, and which shall be called the province of . . . .

2. On, from and after the said first day of January, 1903, the provisions of the British North America Act, 1867, except those parts thereof which are in terms made or by reasonable intend-

ment may be held to be specially applicable to or to affect only one or more but not the whole of the provinces under the Act composing the Dominion, and except so far as the same may be varied by this Act, shall be applicable to the province of . . . . in the same way and to the same extent as they apply to the several provinces of Canada and as if the province of . . . . had been one of the provinces originally united by the said Act.

3. The said province shall be represented in the Senate of Canada by four members until it shall have, according to decennial census, a population of two hundred and fifty thousand souls, and from thenceforth it shall be represented therein by five members and thereafter for each additional increase in population of fifty thousand souls, according to decennial census, there shall be an increase of one member in its representation until it is represented by twenty members.

4. The said province shall be represented in the first instance in the House of Commons of Canada by ten members and for that purpose shall be divided by Act of Parliament or by proclamation of the Governor General into ten electoral districts each of which shall be represented by one member; provided that on the completion of each decennial census hereafter the representation of the said province shall be readjusted according to the provisions of the British North America Act, 1867.

5. The Executive Council of the province shall be composed of such persons and under such designations as the Lieutenant Governor shall from time to time think fit.

6. All powers, authorities and functions which under any law or customs which were before the coming into force of this Act vested in or exercisable by the Lieutenant Governor of the North-west Territories with the advice, or with the advice and consent, of the Executive Council thereof or in conjunction with that council or with any member or members thereof or by the said Lieutenant Governor individually shall as far as the same are capable of being exercised after the coming into force of this Act, be vested in and shall or may be exercised by the Lieutenant Governor of the province of . . . . with the advice or with the advice and consent of or in conjunction with the Executive Council or any member or members thereof or by the Lieutenant Governor individually as the case requires, subject nevertheless to be abolished or altered by the Legislature of the province.

7. Unless and until the Executive Government of the

province otherwise directs the seat of Government of the same shall be at . . . .

8. There shall be a legislature for the province consisting of the Lieutenant Governor and of one House styled the Legislative Assembly of . . . .

9. The constitution of the Legislature of the North-west Territories as it exists on the first day of January, 1903, shall, subject to the provisions of this Act, continue to be the constitution of the Legislature of the province of . . . . until altered under the authority of this Act and the Legislative Assembly of the said Territories existing on the said first day of January, 1903, shall, unless sooner dissolved continue as the Legislative Assembly of the province of . . . . until the completion of the period for which it was elected.

10. In and for the province the said legislature may exclusively make laws in relation to irrigation and subject to any rights acquired under any Act of the Parliament of Canada before the first day of January, 1903, the property in and the right to the use of all the water at any time in any river, stream, watercourse, lake, creek, ravine, canyon, lagoon, swamp, marsh or other body of water shall on, from and after the said date belong to and be vested in the province unless and until and except only so far as some right of some person therein or to the use thereof inconsistent with the right of the Crown and which is not a public right or a right common to the public is established.

11. In addition to all other powers the Legislative Assembly of the province shall have the powers conferred on the Legislative Assembly of the North-west Territories by the nineteenth Section of Chapter twenty-two of the Acts of the Parliament of Canada passed in the fifty-fourth and fifty-fifth year of the reign of Her Majesty Queen Victoria.

12. The Judges of the courts of the province shall be selected from the bar of the province or from the bar of some other province in which the laws relative to property and civil rights, and the procedure of the courts are the same as in the province of . . . .

13. Except as otherwise provided by this Act, all laws in force in the North-west Territories on the first day of January, 1903, and all courts of civil and criminal jurisdiction and all legal commissions, powers and authorities existing therein on the said date shall continue as if this Act had not been passed; subject nevertheless (except with respect to such as are enacted by or exist under Acts of the Parliament of Great Britain or of

the Parliament of the United Kingdom of Great Britain and Ireland) to be repealed, abolished or altered by the Parliament of Canada or by the Legislature of the province according to the authority of the Parliament or of the Legislature under this Act.

14. All public officers and functionaries, judicial, administrative and ministerial holding office in the North-west Territories on the first day of January, 1903, shall continue to hold such office in the province of . . . . with the same duties and powers as before until otherwise ordered by the Governor General of Canada or the Lieutenant Governor of the province according to the authority of the Governor General or the Lieutenant Governor under this Act.

15. Until altered by the Lieutenant Governor in Council the Seal of the North-west Territories shall be the Great Seal of the province of . . . .

16. The penitentiary situate in the province of Manitoba shall until the Parliament of Canada otherwise provides, be the penitentiary for the province of . . . .

17. Nothing in this Act shall in any way prejudice or affect the rights or properties of the Hudson's Bay Company as contained in the conditions under which that company surrendered Rupert's Land to Her Majesty Queen Victoria and all rights, privileges and properties conferred on Canada by the said conditions shall in so far as they relate to matters within the legislative authority of the province, belong to and be vested in the province.

18. All lands belonging to the Crown situate in the province of . . . . other than lands reserved by the Statute or Order in Council, for the use of Indians or for and earned by any person or corporation, and lands entered for homestead or pre-emption, but not granted, and all sums due and payable on the first day of January, 1903, for such lands shall belong to the province.

19. All mines, minerals, timber and royalties belonging to the Crown situate, being or arising in the province of . . . . and all sums due and payable on the first day of January, 1903, for such mines, minerals, timber or royalties shall belong to the province.

20. The province shall receive and retain all the public property of the North-west Territories not otherwise disposed of in this Act.

21. All buildings in the North-west Territories belonging to Canada used or intended for court houses, jails, and land titles

offices of the Lieutenant Governor and Government of the North-west Territories, together with all appurtenances connected therewith, and all moneys, the proceeds from the sale or leasing of school lands in the North-west Territories, and all moneys forming the assurance fund under the provisions of the Territorial Real Property Act, and the Land Titles Act, 1894, shall be the property of the province of . . . .

22. The following amounts shall be allowed and paid by Canada by half yearly payment in advance as an annual subsidy to the province, that is to say:—

(a) For the support of the Government and Legislature, fifty thousand dollars.

(b) On an estimated population of two hundred and fifty thousand at eighty cents per head, two hundred thousand dollars, subject to be increased as hereinafter mentioned, that is to say:—A census of the province shall be taken in every fifth year, reckoning from the general decennial census of one thousand nine hundred and one; and an approximate estimate of the population shall be made at equal intervals of the time between such quinquennial census and such decennial census; and whenever the population by any such census or estimate exceeds two hundred and fifty thousand, which shall be the minimum on which the said allowance shall be calculated, the amount of the said allowance shall be increased in accordance therewith until the population reaches four hundred thousand.

23. The province shall be entitled to be paid and to receive from the Government of Canada by half yearly payments in advance, interest at the rate of five per cent per annum on the excess over the sum of . . . ., of a sum to be ascertained by multiplying the population of the province by 32.46 and for the purpose of this Section the population of the province shall until after the next decennial census, be deemed to be two hundred and fifty thousand. Provided, that immediately after the census of . . . . there shall be a readjustment under this Section on the basis of the population as ascertained by such census.

24. The province shall be entitled to receive by half yearly payments in advance from the Government of Canada, interest at five per cent per annum on the sum of one dollar per acre for each acre of land in the province granted by the Dominion, otherwise than for homesteads or pre-emptions under the provisions of the Dominion Lands Act, or in settlement of half breed claims.

*In the initial period after the passage of the Legislative
Assembly Resolution of May 2, 1900, most comments on
provincial status remained concerned with the general principle
or with the question of control of lands. With the meeting in
Ottawa in late 1901, however, and with the growing assumption
that Provincial status was not far away, individuals began to
return to the troublesome question of the number of provinces
and their shape.*

*At this time the issue was still very much an open one. A
group centered in Calgary had, as has been indicated, been
encouraging a separate Province for that district. In the east,
Manitoba looked to the alteration in the Government of the
North-west Territories as an opportunity to adjust its own
boundaries. In addition, other members had other schemes and
other capitals to present to the public. Haultain, of course,
favoured one province and his position as Premier made his
views potentially very powerful.*

III — 8

**F. Villeneuve, M.L.A. for St. Albert, on the number of Provinces.
Legislative Assembly, June 7, 1901: Regina Leader, June 20, 1901.**

The House ought to have an explanation of what was meant
by provincial autonomy,—but the Government submitted no
policy. He feared that Northern Alberta would not be properly
represented by the Government at the conference. (Oh, oh.)
That district was against centralisation and wanted two
provinces, at least. Everything now had to be done by correspondence and on information and advice of men residing
sometimes hundreds of miles from the work to be done. He
could assure the executive that the Opposition would give all
the advice and assistance they could to have the best bargain
possible made. The members of the Government should be
accompanied by the members who represent the North-west
Territories at Ottawa. The Government should appoint to go
with them a member of the Catholic faith, and one whose
language is French. The members for Wolseley and North
Regina had reason to be satisfied with the Government because
their districts were perfect: but Northern Alberta and St. Albert
districts were badly in need of roads and other improvements.

III — 9

**T.O. Davis, Saskatchewan M.P., supports two Provinces:
Macleod Gazette, November 8, 1901.**

[Mr. Davis] is of the opinion—and he states that the people of
his constituency agree with him on this—that the Territories
should be divided into two Provinces by a line running along
the southern boundary of Saskatchewan to British Columbia,
constituting eastern and western Assiniboia and southern
Alberta into one province with a capital at Regina and the
other to consist of Saskatchewan, Northern Alberta, Athabasca
and other unorganized territory with Battleford as capital. If
the population of the northern part of his scheme is not
considered sufficient to form a province, then Mr. Davis is in
favor of leaving it as it is until the country is more thickly
settled and, he says, it is only a matter of a short time until it
will be sufficiently populous, as settlers are going to the Peace
River valley north of Edmonton in great numbers, the country
there having proved to be one of the best wheat raising districts
of the west.

The people of the west are decidedly averse to sharing
provincial responsibilities with Manitoba, Mr. Davis states.
The Territories have no debt; possess what they consider is the
best local improvement system in the world; have no expensive
and cumbersome system of municipal councils, with their
salaried officials to support, and in this desirable condition can
see no object in helping Manitoba out with its provincial
obligation.

III — 10

**The Regina Leader supports one Province: Regina Leader,
November 21, 1901.**

A variety of reasons may be urged against the formation of
the organised Territories into one province. Not many of these
have yet been mentioned. One which has been whispered is that
as one province the North-west would have too much weight in
federal affairs. At best it is a shallow reason, and at any event it
is not one to be urged by any citizen of the Territories. The

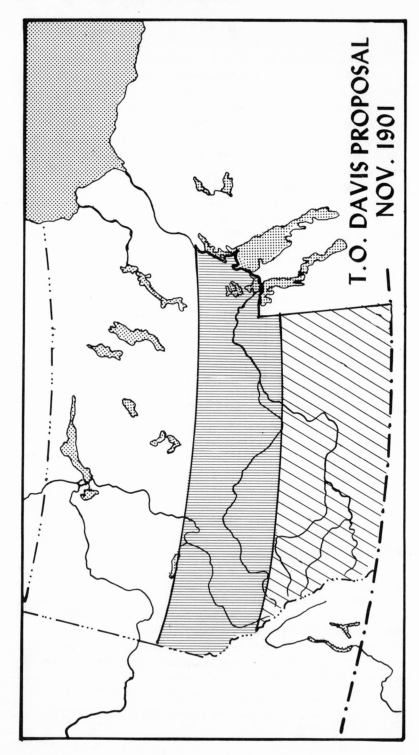

T.O. DAVIS PROPOSAL NOV. 1901

advocates of two provinces rely simply on the bare assertion that the area is too large for one. Too large in what way?—for efficient provincial government, says one two province paper. If the area is too large for efficient government, the reason is good. Indeed it is the only reason of any moment that it is possible to advance. It is not capable of absolute demonstration. It must be viewed in the light of fact and experience.

One fact is that to the present time the area has been under one local government—during a period when means of communication were in the most imperfect stage and when conditions generally made government difficult. This is perhaps the most valuable fact which the earnest student of the provincial question will find available.

Too large in what way? It has not been too large for efficient local government to date. Would two governments in the North-West have given us better schools and more public improvements than we have? No one can say so. Two governors, two legislatures, two sets of ministers, two sets of officials, would have meant practically double the machine expenditure, and just so much less for schools and public works.

Too large for what? For efficient government? The burden of proof rests upon those who declare it. Are the smaller States in the Union better governed than the large ones? The reverse is the fact. Ontario with the largest inhabited area of any existing province is the most efficiently and economically governed Canadian province. It is the only province with no direct taxation and no bonded debt. Let the two-province advocates point to a state or province which has been found by experience too large for efficient government.

The British Isles with more than 40,000,000 of people are under one government which, in addition to the local subjects which are dealt with provincially in Canada, is charged with the national subjects such as are in Canada dealt with by Parliament and a multiplicity of colonial matters and questions of foreign relations affecting every nook and corner of the civilised and uncivilised globe. The work devolving upon the British Legislature is too enormous to permit of efficiency in every branch, but the margin between what it does accomplish and what a legislature of our 'one-province' will ever even in the remotest future be called on to accomplish, is also enormous. This fact tends to show that our area is not too large for efficient government.

The two-province advocates say that while our area is but little larger than Ontario, but little larger than Quebec, and much smaller than British Columbia yet the habitable portion is larger than in those two provinces. The argument then is not that the area is too large but that the population will be too large for efficient government, which is driving directly in the teeth of the modern movement in the science of government and the science of commerce. Today's motto is Concentration. Political economists all agree that New Brunswick, Nova Scotia and P.E.I. would be better with one government than three. The cities of New York and Brooklyn have population twenty times larger than the present Territorial population. Four years ago they had two governments. Today they are under one government. The change was made to bring about efficiency and economy.

Too large in what way? The cry shows that even in the North-west we have people of the 'Little Englander' variety. Would the area of the United State be better governed by two national governments than by one? Is Canada, is Australia, is Germany too large for efficient government?

We have cited and hinted at a few facts from which useful lessons may be drawn. There are many other facts which may be cited. So far we have not discovered a single fact or the record of a single experience tending to show that the North-west area which is now efficiently managed under one legislature can not continue to be efficiently managed without division. The farther we look into the question, the stronger becomes our belief that a mistake will be made if more than one province is carved out of the Territories.

By far the most controversial proposal surrounding the question of provincial boundaries was that proposed by Premier Roblin of Manitoba which would have seen a westward extension of that Province's boundaries. On December 18, 1901 a full debate on the issue took place at Indian Head, N.W.T., between Roblin and Haultain. Roblin's speech was cautious and heavily statistical, pointing to the financial situation of Manitoba rather than making any grandiose promises to those present. Haultain, in his reply, extended his subject to deal not only with the Roblin proposal but with the general question of the shape of any province or provinces carved out of the North-west Territories. It thus presents a clear summary of Haultain's position at this time toward the one province issue.

III — 11

Haultain opposes Manitoba extension and supports the one Province idea, Indian Head, December 18, 1901: from the pamphlet, Full Text of the Indian Head Debate.

We are all glad to have Mr. Roblin present tonight; we are glad to have him here as a friend and as a neighbour, as well as a man occupying a foremost position in our sister province of Manitoba. Mr. Roblin says he has been able to extend his friendships among us. I can assure him, if I do not misjudge the spirit of our people, he may well be able to extend his friendships much further in the West, even if there is a limitation applied to his boundaries. Mr. Roblin says he does not come as an invader; he comes with all the graces, and all the promises of a wooer, although he says he does not offer any allurements. He does his wooing very well, and even if we are obliged to reject him, we will always be willing to be a sister province to him and be perfectly friendly. . . .

The general policy of the government practically involves a discussion of three points: First—Whether it is desirable at all to have provincial institutions? Secondly—If we are to have them, are we to have one, two or more provinces? Thirdly—The subject which Mr. Roblin has discussed tonight—if we are to have provincial institutions is it going to be after a portion of the Territories have been included in Manitoba?

First, let us consider whether it is desirable that any portion of the Territories should be added to Manitoba.

In discussing that question I have to take for granted certain things which I will have to prove later on. I will have to take for granted that provincial institutions are going to be established so far as a certain portion of Eastern Assiniboia is concerned. You will be in a better position as part of a western province, under provincial institutions, than you will be as part of Manitoba under, of course, similar institutions? I want to say at the very beginning that the western province or provinces will have the same sources of income as have been stated by Mr. Roblin that Manitoba possesses. You must not forget that because Manitoba is a province today, and has certain definite sources of income, they would have to be as definite in the case of the new province established here. The argument is not 'will you be better off as a part of Manitoba than you are today under present conditions?' That is not the question at all. The question is, 'Will you be better off as a part of Manitoba than as a part of the new province after the Territories have been erected into a province?' It is part of my argument tonight that you would better off under provincial institutions, but that your position would be far better off as a part of the new province than as a part of Manitoba. . . .

The very condition that we find ourselves in today, that we are hammering at the doors of the government at Ottawa and asking to be admitted as a province, shows that the government of the Territories, and the legislature, at least, are not satisfied with the present conditions. As long as the people are satisfied with their conditions, and doing well, and having their ordinary wants supplied, they do not look for a change. But why is it the people ask for a change today? Simply because they are not satisfied with the present conditions. No man can live in this country without being alive to the unfortunate conditions that exist today. The only remedy is one we must apply ourselves. We are now demanding to be created into a new province that we may apply the remedy. We shall be able to apply the remedy ourselves as a province equally as well as if we go into the province of Manitoba.

In anything I say with regard to Manitoba and its position, I do not wish to be taken as criticizing in an unfriendly way. Manitoba is in a very favorable condition, according to Mr. Roblin; but you must remember it has taken thirty years under provincial institutions to arrive at that point. I do not wish to say a single word which might be taken as aspersing the financial position of that province. It will sufficiently meet the purposes of my argument, and your argument, if we can show that they have a debt for instance. We do not care for what it was incurred; the question after all is—Have they a debt and are you willing to take a share of it? Consequently I do not wish to attack Mr. Roblin's government, or any previous government of Manitoba, or to pry with unfriendly feelings into the affairs of a neighboring province, but simply wish to point out certain facts and let you say whether they are sufficiently enticing to warrant you in joining your fortunes with theirs. . . .

I now come to what I consider the most important part of my statement tonight. Although there may be certain advantages, and although present conditions may prompt some of you to feel like rushing into almost anything to get rid of your disabilities, yet I do not think any of you take the wooing of Mr. Roblin's seriously. The most important part of my statement I still have to make, that is: what is the proposition which I have made to the Dominion government and which I now make to you, and through you to the people of the Territories, with regard to the future of this great western country? There are parts of the Territories where I would be justified in taking up considerable time in arguing that we are not quite as well off as we ought to be. It is only within the last few months, even within your progressive settlements, that you began seriously to believe that you had to have a provincial establishment. I believe that if I had come down here two years ago and made a speech in favour of provincial autonomy, I would have met with a cold reception from many of you.

If you have followed events in the legislature, and the statements made by members of the government of the Territories for the past two years I don't believe you will have any difficulty in anticipating what I am going to say tonight. . . . The Territorial constitution is not sufficient. We have worked under it up to a certain point, and I think we have exhausted our usefulness. The country has arrived at a point where further development is necessary, and that development can only be brought about by the exercise of the larger powers which we do not now possess, and which are possessed by the provinces. . . .

Now the question is: shall we have one province, or two provinces? or will we go into Manitoba, and a province be formed for the west? or will there be two provinces formed running north and south as some gentlemen propose? You have quite a variety to choose from. I have had to express an opinion at Ottawa, and my opinion is in favour of one province.

A voice: You will never have a railway then.

Mr. Haultain: I don't know exactly what the gentleman means by that, but it would strike me that one big province—rich, wealthy and populous—can just as well build up a railway system as a little province that is not so rich, wealthy and populous. And then, you can control such a railway. If you cut this country up into little provinces, you are going to have a Manitoba railway, and an Assiniboia railway, and an Alberta railway, and a Saskatchewan railway. Each province will control the line within that province, and you will have three, or four, or five provincial governments trying to control freight rates, or control little pieces of a great trunk continental railway. You can imagine what a 'fist' they will make of it.

A voice: We are farmers, and the west are ranchers.

Mr. Haultain: That is perfectly true, and for that reason we will have a very much better country. We will have ranches and farms and other things; we do not want a province made up of one big wheat field, or one big cattle ranch and coal mine; we want wheat fields, cattle ranches and coal mines, and every other thing that goes to make up a big, rich country.

Some people urge that one province would be too large. Canada, under the federal system is not too large for one government at Ottawa, dealing with a variety of important subjects. The United States is not too large to be controlled by one central government. In case one province was formed in the west, we should not want to take in a portion of the far north. We do not want a lot of those islands around the Arctic circle, and a great deal of the country further south of that because it would only involve administration without any return. But no matter how much of the north we took in, there would be no population, and consequently no responsibilities or expense resting upon us. The actual area, however, to be administered by the provincial government I have proposed would be something over 400,000 square miles. Now the present area of Quebec is 347,000 square miles—not so much less than an actual area to be administered here. British Columbia has 383,000 square miles, which is still nearer our prospective area. . . .

Then again, diversity of interest is not hostility of interest. There is plenty of room in this country for the rancher and for the farmer to carry on their respective industries successfully without squabbling. We want all those things. We want a big province, and want a lot of industries established in it. Can any gentleman propose a solution which will map out a province which would not have a diversity of interests? The province of Manitoba has diversity of interest in its ranching and farming; Eastern Assiniboia has the same: and in Alberta we are not all ranching; the whole of the north country is a farming district just as you are here. So you cannot cut up the country without having diversity of interest, and that same argument will apply to the smallest province you can suggest, as much as the large one. Then again, we have been for a number of years working together. We have a legislature with representatives from all these different parts. There has been no clashing, and I have never heard of the west or east fighting over things which each thought they should have. If they required different laws, we made one law applicable to the west and one applicable to the east. So that I say, where could we cut our institutions in two? We founded a school system. Why should we cut it in two for the sake of establishing two provinces instead of one? We founded other institutions which are working together. Why should we suddenly cut them in two, simply for purposes we do not understand? Two provinces will only mean duplication of government machinery. You cannot put your hand on any point on the map and say: At this point there should be a change of government, at that point there is such a diversity that harmonious government is impossible; and you cannot say that at any particular point on the map facility for self-government ceases. If you establish two provinces, you would simply double the government, double the legislature, and double every expense as it would be necessary to double all the institutions which we need at the present time. . . .

Are you afraid of the proposal? Are you afraid to be a part of a province exceeding all others in area, in population and in resources? Are you staggered at the realization of your splendid prospects? It does not seem to me to be the occasion for fear or for shrinking but we should rather raise our hearts and brace our energies and resolutely accept the duties and responsibilities which are ours by reason of the splendid destiny which in the order of Divine Providence lies before us.

One of the most revealing comments on the Indian Head debate came from Haultain's home-town paper, the Macleod Gazette. Generally loyal to Haultain this paper was careful not to disagree with him on this occasion but a certain ambiguity is apparent in its attitude toward the one province stand taken by the Premier.

III — 12

The Provincial Question, The Macleod Gazette, January 10, 1902.

We reprint this week that portion of Premier Haultain's Indian Head speech which deals with proposed provincial establishment in the Territories. Mr. Haultain's pronounce-

ment appears to have been very clear and to the point, and
certainly disarms those of his critics who have been accusing
him of self-sufficiency and refusal to take the people of the
Territories into his confidence. . . .

Mr. Haultain, as will be noticed has taken up the question of
diversity of interests, which has been raised as an objection to a
single large province. Opinion, especially in the west, has been
somewhat divided on the question of one or two provinces. It is
beyond doubt a very important question, and one which
should receive the very fullest consideration. While it might be
extremely unwise at present to duplicate provincial machinery
in the Territories by erecting them into two or more provinces,
we must also consider what our future needs might render
necessary. Will a single large province answer our requirements
for all time to come? If the Territories now become a single
large province, can it be so constituted that a division could
afterwards be made without serious complications arising,
should it ever become necessary, as it might? Diversity of
interests is perhaps the strongest argument in favor of the two
provinces idea, provided of course that it is an argument at all.
It ceases to become a factor in the discussion, if it can be shown
that diversity of interests can be harmonized rather than
antagonized by legislation; because it is legislation itself and
alone that renders diversity of interests of any moment to those
concerned. For example legislation which is doubtless of
benefit to the eastern and northern portions of the Territories,
where farming is practically the sole business, or at all events
whatever stock raising is done, is carried on the farm principle,
is considered by those affected a positive injury in those
portions of the Territories where the range cattle and horse
business obtains. Mr. Haultain is right when he states that,
'You cannot cut up any portion of this country into provinces
that will not have diversity of interests.' But we cannot agree
with him that 'diversity is not hostility of interests.' As we said
before, there can be no hostility as between diversified interests,
unless it is created by legislation. It is surely a fact, however,
that legislation can bring about this state of affairs, by the
enactment of a general law which is applicable to one, and
altogether inapplicable to another. After all diversity of
interests becomes hostility of interests when intelligent men
who are engaged in some particular industry decide, upon
their actual experience, that some general law, which may be
beneficial to other interests, is inimical to their business.
Experience, not theory, is surely a fair test. There is a wide

diversity of interest between pure farming and range stock raising as carried on in Southern Alberta, but there can be no hostility unless laws which are applicable only to a farming community are forced upon a ranching community. This is recognized in all legislation. The Dominion government enact separate and distinct legislation for the several industries of the Dominion. A man does not take up a homestead under the same regulations that he acquires coal lands. Coal land regulations do not apply to minerals or petroleum, or grazing lands, etc. Why then should there not be separate legislation as between the farming community and the range cattle raising community. The difficulty could be overcome, apart from distinct legislation, by providing in certain of the ordinances that they should only take effect in specified sections of the Territories by proclamation. If this could be assured and carried out, as we submit it could be, then the chief objection to the single province would be overcome. The comparison of the area of the new province with that of other similarly constituted areas, made by Mr. Haultain, shows that there can be no valid objection to the single province on the score of size. In view, then, of the possibility of harmonizing the varied interests of the Territories by legislation, or by legislation which will be confined to certain portions of the Territories until extended by proclamation, it is probable that a large majority of the people would declare for the single province.

Haultain and other Members of the North-West Assembly had hoped for an answer from the federal government on the question of autonomy by sometime in early 1902. That answer, however, was slow in coming and the Assembly thus had to meet for its spring session before knowing whether the Dominion had agreed to the principal of provincial autonomy and on what terms they would accept it. Nevertheless, when the Assembly opened there was a general optimism that provincial status was only a matter of time, especially given Sifton's earlier communications on the subject. When the reply of the Minister of the Interior finally arrived and was negative it was thus a matter of shock and disappointment to Haultain and those who supported autonomy. In response the earlier debate on the exact shape and number of the Provinces faded in importance compared to the basic principle of the right of the Territories to provincial status.

III — 13

Haultain urges the Dominion Government to Respond to Request for Provincial Status, March 1902: Canada Sessional Paper 116a, 1903.

Haultain to Laurier, March 15, 1902

Legislature opens Thursday. Important that we should know nature of reply to letter of December 7 for reference in speech. Will you kindly have summary wired.

Laurier to Haultain, March 18, 1902

No answer can be sent until return of Minister of Interior, who is absent through illness.

III — 14

Clifford Sifton to Haultain, March 27, 1902: Canada Sessional Paper 116a, 1904.

Absence from Ottawa due to ill-health has prevented me from communicating with you on the subjects discussed by you and your colleagues when here respecting the financial and constitutional status of the North-West Territories. I presume, however, that you would have gathered our views from the expressions of opinion which took place during our interviews, and our conclusions will not therefore, I trust, come in the way of a surprise.

It is the view of the Government that it will not be wise at the present time to pass legislation forming the North-west Territories into a Province or Provinces. Some of the reasons leading to this view may be found in the fact that the population of the Territories is yet sparse; that the rapid increase in population now taking place will in a short time alter the conditions to be dealt with very materially, and that there is a considerable divergence of opinion respecting the question whether there should be one province only, or more than one province. Holding this view, therefore, it will not be necessary for me to discuss the details of the draft bill which you presented as embodying your views.

Respecting the present financial requirements, the question of an increase in your subsidy is now receiving consideration, but the result cannot, as you are aware, be communicated until

the Estimates are brought before Parliament. This I have every
reason to hope will take place soon.

III — 15

Haultain to Sifton, April 2, 1902:
Canada Sessional Paper 116a 1904.

I beg to acknowledge the receipt of your letter of March 27,
conveying the decision of the Government with regard to the
financial and constitutional questions which have been the
subject of discussion during the past year and a half. So far from
your conclusions not coming as a surprise as you suggest, I
must say quite frankly that the decision of the Government has
come not only as a surprise, but as a deep disappointment as
well. In your letter of March 21, 1901, you say:

> 'I may say that I realize very fully the difficulties of the
> position in which the Government and Legislative Assem-
> bly of the North-west Territories is placed, and I admit
> that there is very much in the suggestions which are made
> in your letter and in the memorial regarding the necessity
> of a change in the constitutional and financial position of
> the Territories.
>
> Without at the present moment committing myself to
> any positive statement I am prepared to say that the time
> has arrived when the question of organizing the Territories
> on the Provincial basis ought to be the subject of full
> consideration. It would appear to me that the better way of
> bringing the matter to a more definite position would be
> to arrange for a conference upon the subject between the
> representatives of your Government and a Committee of
> Council representing the Federal Government.'

Again on April 5, 1901, you write:

> 'The latter portion of the Section of Parliament here
> finds all the Members of the Government extremely busy,
> and it would be hopeless to expect from them that mature
> and careful consideration of the various and important
> subjects which will require to be debated and settled in
> connection with the establishment of the Territories as a
> Province or upon the Provincial basis. I think I shall

therefore be compelled to ask you to defer the discussion
until after Parliament has prorogued.'

These opinions and the long delay that followed, in order to
choose a convenient time for that 'mature and careful consideration of the various and important subjects which will require to
be debated and settled in connection with the establishment of
the Territories as a Province or upon a Provincial basis,' led us
to suppose that when the subject was finally taken up it would
be taken up with a view to immediate settlement. The written
statements, which have been made by me, must have proved
conclusively that the necessity for the change was a pressing
one and that we had arrived at a point when our constitutional
and financial position was not adequate to the proper performance of the duties devolving upon us. Recognising this state of
affairs we have gone to the Dominion Government and have
said: 'If you cannot or will not deal with the questions which
have arisen in the Territories give us the powers and the income
which would justly accompany those powers and allow us to
work out our own salvation.' To this you answer: 'That it is the
view of the Government that it will not be wise at the present
time to pass legislation forming the North-west Territories
into a Province or Provinces.' One of the reasons given for this
position is: 'That the population of the Territories is sparse.' I
might point out that we have at least ten times the population
of Manitoba, when it was erected into a Province, and a larger
population than that Province had so lately as 1891; a considerably larger population than the Province of Prince Edward
Island, and with the immigration of the present season a
considerably larger population than the Province of British
Columbia according to the late census.

Another reason advanced is: 'That the rapid increase in
population now taking place will in a short time alter the
conditions to be dealt with very materially.' This rapid increase
in population is one of the principal reasons why we are asking
to be formed into a province, in order that we may be able to
deal with the new conditions that it brings about. The longer it
goes on without the change the more aggravated the present
difficulties will become.

With regard to a divergence of opinion as to one or more
provinces, I might say that that is a difficulty which will always
exist and which any postponement of action will not remove.

I must say also, on behalf of the North-west Government,
that after having been asked to meet a sub-committee of the

Privy Council, and to state our case not only verbally but in writing, it is extremely unsatisfactory that the Government has come to the conclusion: 'That it will not be necessary to discuss the details of the draft bill which embodied our views.' This is a conclusion to the negotiations which have been held which we could hardly have expected considering the importance of the subject discussed and the formal manner in which the discussion has taken place.

We cannot but regret that the Government has not been able to recognise the urgent necessity for the change that has been asked, and can only trust that as you have denied us the opportunity of helping ourselves you will be at least impressed with the necessity and the duty, which is now yours, of meeting the pressing necessities of these rapidly developing territories. While we may, in your opinion without inconvenience, mark time constitutionally, we cannot do without the transportation facilities, the roads, the bridges, the schools and the other improvements which our rapidly growing population imperatively requires, and at once. Whether we are made into a province or not, our financial necessities are just as real, and in conclusion I can only trust that when the question of an increase to our subsidy is receiving consideration, more weight will be given to our representations in that respect than has been given to our requests for constitutional changes.

III — 16

"The Betrayal of the West," Calgary Herald, April 9, 1902.

Clifford Sifton and his friends in the Government have been guilty of a distinct breach of faith with regard to creating the Territories into a province or provinces.

There is not the slightest doubt in the world that Mr. Sifton and his colleagues gave Mr. Haultain the impression that the resolution passed by the Assembly in May, 1900, would receive favorable consideration. For some reason, however, Mr. Sifton has now changed his mind, and has turned down the Territories in a way that is at once humiliating and unjust. . . .

The Territories require provincial establishment and they require it as soon as possible. Development is being retarded from want of local appropriating power, transportation facilities are poor, the roads and bridges in the country are utterly inadequate, and our local Government have to face the

situation with an empty treasury and a limited legislative
power. . . .

The Herald is not prepared to state whether there should be
one, two, or three provinces; that is not the question at all at
stake. The limitation of the boundaries is not nearly so
important as the question of having the administration of our
own affairs in our own hands. There is little doubt that the
Hon. Clifford Sifton in pursuing the course he has in this
matter is consulting the interests of party, and not those of the
country. There is a well defined and strong feeling growing
which is backed up by certain significant facts—that the matter
of provincial status for the Territories, will be held in abeyance
until the general election in Manitoba when Mr. Sifton will
enable Mr. Greenway to appeal to the country with a definite
promise of the extension of Manitoba's boundary westward.

We are not concerned particularly in this part of the country
whether Manitoba's boundary is extended or not, nor do we
care very much whether we have one big province, or two small
ones, but we do know that the requirements of the country
imperatively demand that we be placed in a position to
administer our own affairs. Clifford Sifton and his colleagues
in the Government have again played the role of the political
charlatan, and the Territories have been, and are being
sacrificed for the political exigencies of the most unscrupulous,
immoral and selfish Government that ever held the reins of
power within the bounds of the British Empire.

III — 17

**The North West Territory Assembly replies to Clifford Sifton,
April 16, 1902: Regina Leader, April 17, 1902.**

Moved by Premier Haultain and seconded by G. Bulyea:
Whereas the larger powers and income incidental to the
provincial status are urgently and imperatively required to aid
the development of the Territories and to meet the pressing
necessities of a large and rapidly increasing population. Be it
resolved, that this House regrets that the Federal Government
has decided not to introduce legislation at the present session of
Parliament, with a view to granting provincial institutions to
the Territories.

III — 18

The House of Commons Debates the future of the North-west Territories, April 18, 1902: House of Commons Debates, April 18, 1902, 3064-3114.

Mr. Scott: . . . For a considerable time past the people of the North-west Territories have been looking forward to the formation of that country into a province or provinces. I took occasion during my first session in this House last year to call the attention of parliament at some length to some phases of that matter. I did not deem it necessary then to argue that the time had arrived for granting full provincial powers to the people of the North-west Territories, because some time previous we had had a statement from a member of the government to the effect that it was their intention in the near future to take up that matter and deal with it. I have to express my regret that a decision has been arrived at by the government not to deal with that question this year. I would not go so far as to say that the people of the North-west Territories unanimously regret the decision of the government; there may be a considerable number who hold the view that it is yet too early in their circumstances to grant full provincial powers. But I believe I express the opinion of a very large majority of people when I say that the conditions have now reached a stage when it would be advantageous to those people as well as the entire Dominion, to have this question settled without further loss of time. Some hon. members may be aware of the fact that within the past two weeks the question has been debated in the local legislature at Regina, and by a vote of 23 to 7, I think, in a House of 31 members, it was decided that it was a matter of regret that this question had not been taken up and an endeavour made to settle it this present year.

Frank Oliver (Alberta): . . . It was with some considerable surprise that I saw in the estimates that the amount to be voted for this purpose for the coming year was no larger than the vote for the present year. I am at a loss to understand upon what basis of calculation this sum was arrived at. If it is necessary or desirable to meet the requirements of the public service in any part of the country, account must be taken of the increase of those requirements. Now, this whole country is ringing with a knowledge of the increase of population and therefore increase of requirements in the North-west, and that knowledge has produced no result in the way of meeting the requirements which necessarily arise. . . . The government of the North-west Territories has approached this government repeatedly during past years, and most formally during the past year, asking for a definite financial arrangement based on the terms of confederation, as applied to the different provinces of the Dominion. They are not here from time to time clamouring for unknown and unheard of amounts. They are asking simply that the government or parliament either meet the requirements of the case, as they arise from time to time, or else put the Territories in the same financial position as the various provinces of the Dominion, so that they may enjoy as a right what they now must ask as a favour. I submit that the position is this: This parliament and government are required either to meet the conditions that exist by an adequate vote, or else to put the territories in the position of the various provinces of the Dominion as regards financial arrangements. Either one thing or the other, and the responsibility is upon the House and the government in the matter. . . .

The Minister of the Interior (Clifford Sifton): Respecting what has been said in connection with the conduct of the government upon the application of the territorial government for provincial autonomy, let me say I do not think that in respect to that application, that as yet at least there is any serious, reasonable grievance existing on the part of our territorial friends. The settlement of the constitutional and financial status of that vast territory is surely worth a little consideration. The time to consider the question, even in the opinion of the most urgent friends of provincial autonomy, did not arrive until a year ago. It was not suggested until about a year ago that the subject should be seriously considered, and if hon. gentlemen will remember how long it takes to settle questions of this kind and to settle them satisfactorily, I think they will admit that rash haste with regard to a question of such vast importance—a question which must be satisfactorily settled if settled at all—rash haste would not at all be conducive to a settlement which would be satisfactory in the long run to the people of the territories. I would not feel that I was taking an unreasonable position before this House if I said: That if the people of the North-west Territories get a reasonable and satisfactory settlement, a settlement that the people of Canada and the people of the territories particularly will regard as a good settlement; a fair and reasonable settlement promising permanency; promising lack of agitation, and difficulties, and applications for re-opening of the case in future years—if they get such a settlement within three or four years I should feel very well satisfied indeed, and I should feel that we have accomplished that result in a comparatively short time. In saying that, I am not at this moment indicating any view I have just now as to when this question will be finally and definitely settled. . . .

Therefore, I think we may possibly be able to look forward to a settlement of this constitutional question, at least when it is proposed by the government to this parliament, being carried out without any acrimonious discussions upon a question of that kind which might be a most difficult and unpleasant one to have to decide, if there were any contention upon it.

I gave certain reasons in the brief letter which I wrote to Mr. Haultain as to why the government did not feel disposed to deal with this question at the present time. Now, I have lived a great many years in the western portion of Canada and I think I have some little understanding of our people there. I sympathize with them, but I know that when they get an idea about a thing to be done they generally have an idea that it should be done right off. They are not disposed to allow the march of events to proceed very long without having the final settlement of what they claim ought to be settled. They are not generally desirous to listen to counsel which goes in the direction of delay. My hon. friend from Alberta (Mr. Oliver) has possibly been the clearest exponent of that principle which is generally followed by western people, and he puts it very well. He says: We have asked you for certain things and if you are not prepared to do just exactly what we say, why pay the shot and pay as much as we ask. My hon. friend (Mr. Oliver) forgets that he takes for granted the whole of the discussion and all the points involved in the discussion because he says: We are entitled to what we ask in the first place, and if you do not give us what we ask we are entitled to fix the amount you will give us. I think the House of Commons will hardly admit that that is the case, because we shall have to take the position, however much we sympathize with our friends in the North-west Territories, that there are two parties to the question of their financial status, and two parties to the question how much they ought to have. These questions cannot be settled by a logical proposition such as my hon. friend from Alberta (Mr. Oliver) puts with such clearness. A good deal of thoughtful consideration will have to be given to the details.

. . . The analogy as to the number of people who were in Manitoba when it became a member of the confederation, or as to the number in British Columbia, does not hold at all, because those provinces were brought into confederation by way of a necessity which existed at that time. It was not in the deliberate exercise of the discretion of the parliament of Canada, thinking that it would be an ideal or desirable state of affairs to have 17,000 people constituted into a province, that the province of Manitoba was formed. It was formed because the necessity arose. There were people who demanded local powers, and the peaceful settlement of the country could not have been effected, and that territory could not have been brought under the rule of the Dominion of Canada, without those terms being granted at that time. Hon. gentlemen will remember that there was a rebellion, and it is possible that the trouble arose only on account of the belief that was created by interested persons that the government here did not intend to give them provincial autonomy or to treat them fairly. They had to be treated in that way, because they were insisting that the existing status should be recognized, and it was recognized as a matter of necessity. British Columbia came in as a sovereign colony under a bargain made with the people of Canada, and the people of Canada had no choice in that respect. But that is no reason for saying that when you get 17,000 people in a territory in any part of the Dominion of Canada, you are to form them into a province. That is not justified by common sense or by the precedents cited in favour of it. I think what parliament will be disposed to do will be to treat this question on a fair and liberal basis; but they will desire, when they come to deal with it, to have before them sufficient data to enable them to feel that they are working out a settlement which has in it the element of permanency. And I think parliament would be rather prepared for two or three or four years to vote sums of money, which might be reasonably arrived at as approximately what the territories actually require for their immediate necessities, and let us get more information with regard to what the position will be and what the necessary requirements of the territories will be, so that when we do arrive at a settlement, it shall have some of the elements of finality. At this late hour, I shall not undertake to discuss the various details which will have to be considered in the formation of a province in the North-west. If hon. gentlemen will look through the Bill presented for our consideration by our friends from the territories, they will see at once that there are items in it quite sufficient to make any government take a little time for their consideration. We have in this Bill a provision that all mines, minerals, timber and royalties, belonging to the Crown, situated or arising in the territories, and all sums due and payable on the 1st of January, 1903, for such mines, minerals, timber and royalties shall belong to the province. In addition to other matters relating to the finances, which were supposed to be dealt with somewhat on the line that has been taken in the other provinces, and as to which possibly no serious objection would be taken, there is a provision that the province shall be entitled to receive, by half-yearly payments in advance from the government of Canada, interest at 5 per cent per annum on the sum of one dollar per acre for every acre of land granted by the Dominion otherwise than as homesteads or pre-emption. I see some hon. members smiling, and I think I have convinced the committee that there is sufficient material in that Bill for a year's consideration. When I said that it was desirable that we should take a little time to consider, I do not think I was asking anything unreasonable. I did not discuss with premier Haultain the details of the Bill. I desire to say, in all frankness, to the committee, that I did not think it desirable to discuss the details. I do not think 'it desirable, in a matter of such vast importance to the people of Canada generally and of the territories in particular, to unnecessarily rush the government of Canada into a record on these questions. They are questions upon which a good deal of light may be thrown by further discussions. The circumstances during the last year were not propitious to a complete discussion of the question with the members of the North-west government, and perhaps that is one of the most important features which I ought to bring before the House. . . .

Mr. Borden (Halifax): Would my hon. friend (Hon. Mr. Sifton) be good enough to inform the House what the exact status would be if provincial autonomy were granted. I am not as familiar with the legislation as the hon. gentleman.

The Minister of the Interior: They have responsible government, but the jurisdiction of the government is defined specifically by the Act of this government. There are, as I have said, certain departments in which they have no jurisdiction, one being the police, another the administration of justice and another the registry office. This last is a small matter, as I say, which might be turned over without discussion. We get a little surplus revenue out of the registry offices, but it might readily be admitted that they might have it. These are the three principal subjects with regard to which they have no jurisdiction, which occurred to me at the present moment. . . .

Mr. Scott: Is there really any difference with regard to the police in the state of the territory and the state of the province?

The Minister of the Interior: Speaking from recollection, I think there are only two clauses in the constitution under which the police jurisdiction of the provinces arises. The province has control over municipal institutions, which has been held in some cases, I think, to give a certain amount of police power. In addition the province has power over the administration of justice. That is in reality the clause in the constitution which gives the provinces the power to do and to control police work. The North-west Territories have not the power under the present condition of things, that power being held by the government here.

Mr. Borden (Halifax): This government retains control of mines and land and minerals?

The Minister of the Interior: Of all the Crown lands.

Mr. Borden (Halifax): In that respect the position differs from that of a province.

The Minister of the Interior: From the position of the original provinces. The only two portions of Canada where the Crown lands belong to the Dominion are the province of Manitoba and the North-west Territories, including, of course, the Yukon. The control of the administration of justice and police by the Dominion government brings upon this government very great expense, caused very largely by the present peculiar circumstances of the case. The proportionate expense would be nothing like the same if there was a large population in the territories. The position would be very substantially changed if there was a reasonably large population in that district. On the question of the power to incur indebtedness, I speak with some deference. I do not wish to express the idea that the people of the North-west Territories are not as competent to conduct their own affairs as the people of any other portion of Canada, for I think they are. But it must not be forgotten by a body like the

House of Commons who are responsible for what may happen in the future, that you have there a very sparse population of about two hundred thousand people situated in a vast and very rich territory. If they had the power to mortgage that territory for all time to come, which they would have if they were granted provincial powers, it might be mortgaged for very unwise and very unnecessary purposes. In saying this, I wish to guard against the imputation of saying that the people of the North-west Territories are not as capable of taking care of themselves and doing their own business as any others. But I say it is a fair subject for consideration for this parliament whether the time has come when power should be given to the people of the North-west Territories to incur indebtedness. . . .

Mr. Borden (Halifax): Now with regard to the details of the Bill, with which I am not at all familiar, as I have not had an opportunity of seeing it—I do not think those details have much to do with the question. It is a question which will have to be dealt with by this government, it is a question, of course, which should be dealt with in a manner satisfactory to the territories for the time being. But because the government of the territories submits a Bill which this government does not regard as satisfactory, that of itself is hardly a significant reason for putting off a settlement of this question for four or five years. I would like to say to the Minister of the Interior, that some of the reasons which he has advanced for not dealing with this question at the present time seem to be reasons for never dealing with it. He speaks of the question of population. Now we do not apprehend that population in the North-west Territories is going to stand still after the expiration of four or five years. It will probably continue to increase, at least we hope it will, at the rate of 60,000, 70,000 or 80,000 every year, and that for many years to come. My hon. friend suggests that the question should be put off four or five years, or until the population attains 600,000 or 700,000 people. Well, is there any particular reason why the people of the North-west Territories, when they have attained the number of 200,000 or 300,000, should not be entrusted with the government of their own territory? My hon. friend refers to the fact that they have a very rich country, a country of great resources. Is it not true that we may place the same confidence in the people of that country as we place in the people of other communities in Canada? Is there any special reason to suppose they will unduly mortgage their future? There is not a province in Canada that is not capable at this very moment of abusing its borrowing powers so as to make itself hopelessly bankrupt, not one; and why should it be supposed that these people are any more likely to abuse their borrowing powers than the people of Ontario, Quebec, or the maritime provinces? I am glad to note that my hon. friend regards the school question in that country as satisfactorily settled, and I trust that it is so. With regard to his view that if terms were made with that territory now these gentlemen would come again year by year, I suppose that is more an argument of convenience, from the standpoint of the government than otherwise. It does not seem to possess much value, even from that standpoint, because the people of the North-west Territories are coming every year, as it is now, and if they should continue to come it will occasion no greater inconvenience to the government than it has in years past. . . .

I do not pretend to have given this subject sufficient consideration to make my remarks of any great value. What I have said is merely my impression gathered from what has been placed before the committee tonight so fully and ably by my hon. friends on both sides of the House from the North-west Territories, and from statements which have been made by the hon. Minister of the Interior; but, having regard to the information which I have derived from these hon. gentlemen, it does seem to me that the hon. Minister of the Interior is inclined to unduly postpone the granting of provincial rights to the people of the North-west Territories in stating that it is not a matter which can be properly or reasonably considered until the expiration of four or five years from the present time.

Sifton's rejection of the North-west Territories' demand for provincial status helped prompt a Territorial election call. As Haultain made clear, the major issue in the election was the question of provincial autonomy and support of his administration's approach to the question. Those who acted as the 'opposition' in the Assembly were put in an awkward situation by Haultain's call for support. Most of these opposition members supported provincial autonomy but had to make it clear to the electors that a vote for them was also a vote in favour of autonomy.

III — 19

Haultain to A.C. Rutherford, April 26, 1902:
Rutherford Papers, University of Alberta Archives.

I was glad to hear through your letter of the 23rd April that you are going to contest the Strathcona District and hope you will be successful. A supply of campaign literature will be sent to you within the next few days, and I am going to have some Departmental reports etc., sent up at once. If you want any information at any point during the election write or wire to J.A. Reid, Regina and your needs will be supplied if possible. I am enclosing a copy of my election address which deals as directly as possible with the main issue. The question of one or two Provinces is important but, in my opinion, not vital. I shall be sorry to see this country cut up, but if the people want two provinces and say so at the coming election I suppose we shall have to yield the 1 province idea. My idea is to work for one province until a majority of the people ask for two. Even then it would still be an unsettled question at Ottawa, but I should not feel justified in pressing the one province idea officially if the Legislature was largely in favour of two. Better two provinces at once than any indefinite postponement of the question.

III — 20

Haultain's Election Address to the Electors of the
Macleod District, April 30, 1902: Rutherford Papers.

Gentlemen:— The Legislature having been dissolved and Writs having been issued for the election of Members to serve in the next House, I once more solicit a renewal of the confidence so generously and so often given to me during the past fifteen years.

What my record as your Member in the Legislative Assembly of the Territories during that time has been is well known to you, and were there no other matters of importance to refer to I might allow the question of my re-election to rest entirely upon that record.

It has, however, fallen to my lot to be called not only to represent you in the Legislature but also almost continuously to lead the Government of the Country ever since any measure of responsible government has been granted to these Territories.

Coupled, therefore, with my record as your Member are the broader questions of the policy and administration of the government, upon all of which your judgment will be pronounced. Within the limits of this address it will not be possible to enter at any length into a discussion of these matters, but there are some that I must direct your attention to. I refer particularly to the present financial and constitutional position of the Territories and the influence of the result of the elections upon the future of the country.

At the present time the Government of the Territories is engaged in negotiations with the Dominion Government leading to the establishment of a part of the Territories upon the Provincial basis. Apart from all other considerations, financial necessity has forced this question to the front. A rapidly increasing population has caused the present revenues of the Territories to become totally inadequate to meet the public demands, and in the opinion of the Government the only solution of the difficulties now being met with is to be found in the larger powers and income which go with the Provincial status upon proper terms. Larger powers, it is true, mean larger responsibilities, but these same larger powers will carry with them the ability to discharge any duty that can be placed upon the people of the West.

The Government has presented to the Federal authorities the claims of the people of the Territories in a document which has been published and is being widely distributed. In that document the Territorial Government has expressed its opinion in favour of the organization of one Province only. Action upon the whole question has been postponed by the Dominion Government, principally upon the ground that there is a "divergence of opinion respecting the question whether there should be one Province only or more than one Province"—a question which in the last resort is one for the Dominion Government to settle. The opinion of the Territorial Government is based upon the fact that in the past one Government and one Legislature have found no difficulty in conducting the affairs of the country other than such as arose from the inadequacy of the revenue, and it is not anticipated that any difficulty which cannot be met will arise in the future. There is a widespread and well founded opinion existing throughout Canada against what has been called 'over government' or 'multiplicity of governments,' and there appears to be no substantial reason for the formation of more than one Province in the Territories at the present time. Much less is there any reason for considering that other proposition which has been made on the part of the Province of Manitoba, namely, the division of the people of the Territories by including within the limits of that Province a considerable portion of the present District of Assiniboia, for the whole sentiment of the people concerned is against that proposal. Upon this phase of the question, at least, there is no divergence of opinion. Even should there be any material divergence of opinion in the Territories on the one or more Province question—and there undoubtedly is some—the result of the election can only demonstrate and accentuate the fact. The Territorial Government, however, has indicated to the Federal Government what it believes to be the opinion held by a very large majority of the people of the Territories as promising to be in the best interests of the country as a whole. Whilst this is so, it is at the same time to be clearly understood that though the Government's opinion has been formed after careful consideration of all the facts before it, such is its strong conviction that Provincial establishment upon the general terms proposed is imperatively required, and at the earliest possible date, that it does not consider the question of one or more Provinces to be of paramount importance in view of the magnitude of the other questions involved. These questions deal with the things which the Government on behalf of the people of the Territories has claimed must of right belong to any Province established in the West, and which were practically unanimously approved by the Legislature at its last session. They are, briefly, (1) Equal rights with all the other Provinces of the Dominion and the same financial consideration that has been given to those Provinces, (2) Control of the public domain in the West by the West for the West, (3) Compensation for the alienation of any part of the public domain for purely Federal purposes, and (4) The removal of the unjust and onerous Canadian Pacific Railway exemption from taxation. These are the matters that the Government of the Territories is now fighting for, and those are the matters upon which your judgement is invited in my appeal to you for re-election as your representative in the Legislature. A similar appeal is being made in every constituency in the country by every candidate whose election will give support to the Government at this critical period in the history of the Territories. The issue is plain, and it is for the people of the Territories to decide.

I am, Gentlemen,
Your obedient servant,
F.W.G. HAULTAIN

Some idea of the support for provincial status was given at a public meeting in Calgary during the election campaign. In a scene that was repeated in many constituencies through the North-west, supporters of Haultain and his opponents scrambled to prove to the electorate that they were in favour of provincial status.

III — 21

The Calgary Candidates on Provincial Autonomy, May 13, 1902: Calgary Herald, May 14, 1902.

James Reilly: In May 1900 the Assembly at Regina passed a resolution to the effect that accounts be taken and investigation made with regard to the elevation of the Territories to provincial standing. The resolution also provided that before any such province were established an opportunity be given to the people to discuss the terms. The Dominion government should not therefore be blamed for turning down the Territorial government. They were simply kept to the terms of their own resolution. Now was the time, however, to obtain a mandate from the people. Mr. Reilly then proceeded to pass severe strictures upon the government for precipitating an election. There was no reason he said why the elections should not have been held in October or September. . . .

The speaker referred to the bill of rights presented to the Dominion House by Mr. Haultain as one of the ablest state documents ever prepared in Canada and it marked Mr. Haultain the man who drafted it as one of the ablest men in the country. It stated in a nutshell that the Territories demanded all that the older provinces have. Mr. Reilly then went in detail into the bill of rights submitted by the Territorial government and gave an able exposition of the financial position of the new province or provinces. He closed with a very fine peroration respecting the future of Alberta. His speech was an excellent exposition of the questions at issue. . . .

John J. Young: Ladies and gentlemen, after the charming combination of modesty and fine oratory to which you have just been treated by my venerable friend the 'father of Provincial Autonomy,' it would ill become me to attempt anything of the kind. I make no pretensions to oratory, or to any great political ability. I do not even come before you as a politician. I come before you as a plain, everyday citizen—one of yourselves— who has been singled out by a large number of his fellow citizens as a fit and proper person to represent you in the Assembly. . . .

Some of my friends have sought to know what my attitude toward the government will be if I succeed in being elected. In reply to them I would prefer to let my actions speak for themselves; but I have no hesitation in saying this, that as long as Mr. Haultain's administration continues to work in the interests of the country, I shall give him a free and fair and independent support. I have supported Mr. Haultain ever since he became premier of the Territories. I have supported him because I believe on the whole he is working in the interests of the country. If, in my opinion, he makes mistakes, I shall not hesitate to say so, as I have done in the past; but, on his general policy, and especially upon his attitude in regard to the question of provincial government, Mr. Haultain will have my independent support so long as he sticks to the programme he has outlined, and fights for the rights of the North West against the dilatory opposition of the Federal authorities, headed by the Minister of the Interior (Loud cheers).

In regard to the general question of Provincial Government, most of you know my views, and it is unnecessary for me to go very much into detail. The Calgary Herald was one of the very first papers, if not the first, to advocate this question, and now that the successful achievements of our objects is apparently so close at hand, I think I can be safely depended upon to watch to negotiations, and see that we get the very best possible terms from the reluctant authorities at Ottawa. . . .

In the present state of the country the principal thing in connection with this Provincial Government question is that we should get sufficient money for the needs of the country. If we get the money we can possibly do without provincial autonomy for another year or two.

After discussing the Provincial Government question at further length, Mr. Young said in the short time allotted to him it was impossible to touch on all the questions which he would have liked to discuss. But he mentioned a few of the things which are part of his policy, and which he would endeavor to have carried out, if elected:

1. That Calgary should be the capital of the new province.

2. That when created into a province or provinces, we should have full control over all crown lands, minerals and timber.

Mr. Bennett: . . . He felt that as the country had reached its full age of 21 years, he thought it time that the shackles should be thrown off, and that it should emerge with all the privileges to which it was entitled. . . . It was a fact that the people here had declared that they must have provincial rights. It was felt that posterity should assist in bearing the burden incidental to the opening up and developing of the new country. Debt was not always a great evil. The measure of the greatness of countries was estimated by their power to borrow money. The proud position occupied by Great Britain was due to the borrowing power; this also applied to the United States after the war. It was felt that great arteries of traffic must be built by the generations of today, and that those who came after, and reaped some of the benefits, should also bear some of the burden. The welfare of this country was inevitably bound up in the transportation question. The present railway facilities were utterly inadequate. Last year's grain crop was not yet out of the country, and next year the problem would still be a greater one. In this country we must have the power to incorporate railroads. . . . It was the duty of the people to press forward and to do everything they could to obtain a full measure of responsible government. It was the duty of the people, as they loved their city and their country, to send men to the assembly who would not be put off but who would press for instant action. As Carlyle had said, all revolutions were the result of persistent effort. 'If the movement drags,' said Mr. Bennett, 'be not discouraged; press on, press on, and where your vanguard camped today, your rear guard will camp tomorrow.'

What he had always stood for in the House in 1898, 1899, 1900 and 1901 was the same measure of self-government as the eastern provinces.

'What matter,' said the speaker, 'if it means wiping out of existence the Department of the Interior. That is not our affair. We do not ask it as a favor; we demand it as a right.'

The absence of party lines make an exact tabulation of the election results difficult. Later votes in the Assembly indicate, however, that Haultain had the support of at least 24 of the 34 M.L.A.s. In addition, several of the opponents of Haultain, such as R.B. Bennett, were supporters of the provincial status. The public in the North-west had given the Territorial government a clear mandate to continue to press to Ottawa on the subject of Provincial status.

Section IV
Political Cross-Currents, 1902-1904

After waiting nearly two years for an answer to its initial request, the Territorial government once again found itself forced to wait in the two years following the local elections of 1902. In spite of Haultain's victory in the 1902 election there was, in fact, little that the Territories could do in the face of federal resistance. That resistance continued through to 1904 and thus, in one sense, little or no progress was made on the question of provincial autonomy in spite of continued speeches, editorials and renewed petitions from the new Legislative Assembly.

At the same time, however, these years were ones of intense activity. The refusal of the Liberal government at Ottawa to consider autonomy created new pressures and unleashed a number of political forces at both the federal and Territorial level. Until 1902 the Liberal government had been that government which had, after years of Conservative resistance, granted full responsible government in 1897. The refusal of March 1902, however, raised doubts about that image and new partisan pressures began to be felt. Basic to this growth of partisanship was the response of the Conservative opposition in Ottawa to Sifton's refusal. Robert Borden, as his speech of April 18, 1902 indicated, was relatively unaware of the Territorial Question before that time. Thereafter, however, he became interested in the issue and increasingly vocal in support of provincial autonomy.

The entry of the federal Conservatives on to the scene, in turn, put pressure on the federal Liberals and especially their Members from the North-West Territories, to defend their party in the face of partisan criticisms. This polarization at the federal level also strained the traditional non-partisan approach of Haultain. Haultain was in the somewhat anomalous position of being a Conservative Premier who depended largely on Liberal Support in the Legislature. Both Liberals and Conservatives in the Territories felt the pulls toward the assumption of a position similar to their federal counterparts. It is the evolution of these various complex, on is tempted to say Byzantine, cross-currents, that form the real political activities of Territorial-Dominion relations in these years. The backdrop, however, must not be forgotten for it is vital. Public sentiment in the Territories remained in favour of immediate provincial status and this was confirmed in countless ways at both the official and unofficial levels over the next two years.

IV — 1

Robert Borden Tours the West, Speech in Lethbridge, September 18, 1902: Lethbridge News, September 24, 1902.

I am truly regretful that we have not the opportunity of seeing more of your enterprising and progressive city and of the country which surrounds it. I have heard of the wonderful progress which the country around Lethbridge is making, and which your town is making. I believe that progress will proceed even more rapidly in the future than it has in the past; it is a stable and sound progress you are making, and I may say that I agree that every possible obstacle shall be removed towards the full and complete settlement of this country. . . .

The first question upon which I desire to say a few words is the question of the right of the people of this great Western Territories, to have the same kind of responsible Government which is possessed by the people of the Eastern Provinces and also by the great Province of British Columbia.

Let us see what this question means. At the present time you have responsible government of a sort. You have not the same powers or responsibilities as those which are possessed by the people living to the East and West of you, and the first question which I ask is 'What is the reason (if any) why responsible government in the true and full sense of the term should not be conceded to the people of the Territories, if they believe themselves capable of dealing with their government in the same way as the people in the older provinces?'

Now various objections have been raised. In the first place it has been said that the conditions as to population in this country are not sufficiently stable at the present time. It has been said that we may expect that in this great country, within the next five or six years, there will be a great influx of population, and it is said that the time is not yet ripe for the granting to you of Provincial Autonomy, because the condition of affairs, which will present itself in the next five years, is entirely different from that which we have at present.

My answer was, in the House of Commons, that you cannot expect that the conditions in five or six years in this country will be any more stable than now. Can anyone suppose there will be a cessation in the flow of immigration into this country at the end of that time. You may get half a million, or one million or two million people into these territories in the next five or ten years. Let us suppose you get 500,000 or a million people; are the Territories to stand still after that? Does anyone suppose that the tide of immigration will then cease? I say 'No.' I dismiss that reason, and I say it does not seem to me a sufficient reason why autonomy, in the full sense of the term, should not be granted to the people of these Territories now.

Another reason which is brought forth is this: It is stated that the people of these Territories are at present but a sparse population; that they have a magnificent heritage in this country, and that if they are granted a full measure of Provincial government, which is enjoyed by the other provinces, they might unduly mortgage the future of this country in various ways which have been suggested. For example, by incurring an amount of debt, by improvidently dealing with the public domain or otherwise administering their affairs so that the future of this country would be prejudiced.

The first question is this: 'Is it not possible for the people of any province in Canada at the present time to absolutely ruin their prospects and run it into bankruptcy if they do not possess the due sense of their responsibilities?' I say there is not a province in Canada from which responsible government should not be taken at the present time, if an argument of that kind is to prevail as to you people in the Territories. . . .

I believe if you gentlemen are to be intrusted with the management of your own affairs, that should include all matters which are dealt with by the people of the Eastern Provinces in their own local government. I see no reason why the people of this country should not be intrusted with the control and management of their own public domain. It is said they might improvidently deal with it. Why should they? Are they not the people of all Canadians, upon whom the importance of that particular question has been most fully impressed. I do not fear for any acts which the people of the West may do with regard to their public domain. I do not fear any improvident dealing by them, because I think the people of this country are impressed with the importance of preserving its public domain, and in thinking carefully of any question which affects the alienation of that domain for any purpose other than a public purpose.

IV — 2

**The Calgary Herald attacks the Liberal Party:
Calgary Herald, October 8, 1902.**

The Herald has stated—and quite fearlessly—the proofs being on hand—that the Liberal party has abandoned the idea of provincial government for the North-west Territories and if the country is to get local government, it will only be through the Conservative party. One or two of the Liberal newspapers have now the audacity to attack the assertion made by the Herald, and the position the latter takes. Having no arguments to support their position, these papers say that the statement made by the Herald is a venomous falsehood. It is barely possible that some people may believe the Liberal press, and for that reason, the Herald will put the facts up to date again before the public; and with the latter's verdict the Herald will be quite satisfied.

It is now, of course, well known that Mr. Clifford Sifton is against giving the people provincial government. He has stated so openly in parliament, and he is evidently insisting on the Liberals of the North West abandoning the project and creating at least differences of opinion about the matter, thus making the question impossible.

The Liberals of Alberta, when they met in convention a short time ago, passed resolutions as to their party, covering every possible question except provincial government. On this they were absolutely silent. We are told now that the meeting was called for a special purpose, and the resolutions were incidental. It is more than passing strange that nobody heard of this excuse before, and still more strange that the resolutions contained a full endorsement of Mr. Sifton's conduct in the cabinet, yet he declined to give the people self-government. . . .

Mr. Borden in his speeches in the Territories was very clear on the question that provincial government should be granted, and practically all the Liberal newspapers in the North West, except the Regina Leader, have criticized Mr. Borden's policy.

Now what does all this mean? It can only mean one thing, and that is, that provincial government is not part of the policy of the Liberals.

Borden's tour and the subsequent editorial attacks on the Liberal Party in the Territories led the Liberal faithful to

*defend their party's position in what was becoming an
increasingly partisan issue. The Regina Leader, under influential Liberal M.P. Walter Scott, was one of the first to abandon
the position it had held in favour of Provincial autonomy.
Turning to Haultain's original complaint that the financial
requirements of the Territory forced provincial status, the
Leader argued that a new, and more generous, attitude of the
federal government had made such a complaint obsolete.*

IV — 3

**The Leader says Provincial Status is unnecessary:
Regina Leader, January 6, 1903.**

The Leader is attacked because of our assertion that at this
present moment the North-west settler lacking autonomy is as
well placed as the Manitoban or British Columbian who have for
more than thirty years enjoyed autonomy's advantages. But
those who attack our assertion do not attempt to disprove it.
Such an assertion could not have been truly made in past years,
but it is true today owing to the better understanding of the
North-west which the efforts of our representatives in Parliament have brought about. Last year it could be complained that
our railway needs were neglected, and that we required
autonomy to enable us to charter and aid new roads. Last year it
could be complained that there were trunk roads and big
bridges urgently needed, which we could not construct owing
to lack of borrowing power, and that we required autonomy to
enable us to borrow money for these works. Last year and in
every previous year it could be complained that we lacked
revenue to meet the ordinary needs of local government. These
reasons led to the agitation for autonomy in which agitation
The Leader took more active part than any other Territorial
newspaper. The same reasons do not exist today. In these
several respects until the present time the North-west settler
was not as well placed as the British Columbian or Manitoban,
but we repeat the assertion that today he is not only as well
placed but much better placed than his provincial neighbors on
either side. His railway needs have now been provided for at
Canada's expense. Action has been taken to enable his big
bridges and trunk roads to be constructed on capital account.
And he can no longer complain of serious shortage of ordinary
revenue because Parliament at last has granted practically as

much money as Premier Haultain asked. Every urgent reason which we had a year ago for desiring autonomy is removed for the time being at all events, and today we can congratulate ourselves on the fact that we are upon 'easy street' compared with either British Columbia or Manitoba. . . .

The duty devolves upon those who are trying to make the North-west settler dissatisfied and to make him think he is wronged and robbed by being deprived of autonomy, to come down to facts and show just in what way he is in a worse position today without autonomy than his neighbors in Manitoba and British Columbia who have had autonomy for a generation.

The position of the Leader *taken in early 1903 was followed up by a visit of Clifford Sifton to the capital of the Territorial government in Regina. His speech was equally part of the campaign to blunt the growing criticism of the Liberal Party and, as the following report indicates, was designed to convince the North-west voter that Sifton favoured provincial autonomy and that the only difference was the matter of careful timing in order to assure the best possible terms. Again it was the financial problem that Sifton stressed. However, in his reply to that speech Haultain made two extremely powerful points. First, he noted that the Territorial elections of 1902 had indicated the widespread support for provincial autonomy and second he reflected his own changing view of the situation when he noted that constitutional as well as financial considerations were now considered important reasons for the elevation of the Territories into a province or provinces.*

IV — 4

**Speech of Clifford Sifton in Regina, January 1903:
Regina Leader, January 22, 1903.**

. . . There were some questions of special interest for the people of the west and one of them was the status of the Territories in relation to the Dominion of Canada. Mr. Haultain came to Ottawa a year and a half ago and the subject was discussed between him and his colleagues, and he (Mr. Sifton) and other members of the Government. The result of that discussion was that nothing was done at the time and the matter was debated in the North-West Assembly. He noticed from the discussions in the Territories that an impression had been created that he was hostile to autonomy. It seemed to him that there was a lack of intelligence shown by a portion of the press and by certain persons in striving to put the question fairly before the people of the Territories. He assumed that any person representing the Territories in the Government would not be hostile to their becoming a province. He thought, however, that a very cursory and elementary discussion would show that there were a great many difficulties, a great many important questions, to be dealt with when the subject is before the federal Parliament. It would be unwise for a Minister to attempt to put a measure through before he was satisfied that his colleagues and Parliament were in sympathy with his views and that the proposed arrangements would be satisfactory to the people of the Territories. It was not a very vital point whether the Territories were formed into a province this year or next year; but it was vital as to what the terms were on which the constitution was framed. (Hear, hear.) If in any respect the wants of the North-West should be clipped or its resources seriously impaired by any measure forced through then the North-West might very properly turn round and say 'we were not particular about a year or two; what we were particular about was that the terms should be sound and satisfactory and provide properly for the functions of the Government of the North-West Territories.' . . . He would ask them as he might fairly do, that in regard to a number of matters that were matters for discussion, that they should not form an opinion until they had been fully discussed. He quite understood the rapid growth of the responsibilities of the local Government. He believed that Government would admit so much.

IV — 5

Haultain to Clifford Sifton, January 31, 1903.
Canada Sessional Paper 116b, 1903.

At various times during the past year whilst I was in England one or other of my colleagues in the Territorial government discussed territorial questions with you, on my return I met you in Ottawa with Mr. A.L. Sifton for the same purpose. More recently I had an opportunity of discussing these questions at some length with you in Regina, and I have also read a report of a speech made by you here in which you gave expression to your views upon the same subjects. As parliament will be meeting at an early date, I think it will bring these matters to a definite issue.

I agree to the fullest extent with all that has been—or can be—said respecting the advantage to the Territories to be gained by the introduction into the Dominion government of a gentleman so well versed in all our affairs as is my friend Mr. Ross, to whom, it is generally understood, your references in that connection are made, as your united influence should have a marked and beneficial effect upon the destinies of this part of Canada. I must, however, say that I have heard and read with great concern your opinion to the effect that it is desirable to postpone action upon the memorial of the Legislative Assembly of May 2, 1900, and the claims of the Territories founded thereon. The necessities are so urgent and the movement in favour of provincial institutions is so unanimous, that I should like, if possible, to convey to your mind an adequate apprecia- tion of the significance of the movement, and of the unfortunate effect which its neglect or suppression will have upon the North-west. You are reported in the Regina *Leader* of the twenty-second instant, as having stated in a meeting of your friends here that—

'. . . a very cursory and elementary discussion and consideration of the subject would show that there were a great many difficulties, a great many important questions, to be dealt with when the subject is before the Federal parliament. . . . It was not a very vital point whether the Territories were formed into a province this year or next year; but it was vital as to what the terms were on which the constitution was framed. . . .'

Further on in the report it is stated that you said that you—

'. . . had impressed upon Mr. Haultain that what was of importance was that when the terms were settled they should commend themselves to the great majority of the people, and that the terms should be loyally supported, and not lead to agitation year after year for other terms. . . .'

Whilst what you say requesting terms is very true, I cannot agree with what you are reported as having said respecting the time at which provincial institutions should be introduced into this section of the Dominion. Time—an early time, the earliest time—is of the essence of this contract, and it is our opinion that the best time is the present. Without entering into any further argument on that point here, I must say that it does not seem to me that sufficient justification for postponing the consideration and settlement of the questions involved in the provincial question—which would appear to be the present general attitude of the Federal government—has been established. . . .

It is true that you arranged and brought about a conference between a committee of the Privy Council and members of the Territorial government, but no one can be more familiar than yourself with the reasons which led the Dominion government to adopt the position set forth in your letter of March 27 last. What those reasons were in full does not yet openly appear, and I feel it incumbent upon me to say that, in view of all the conversations and correspondence had upon this subject, in view of the official negotiations held, upon request, as a result of those conversations and that correspondence, and also in view of the circumstances surrounding the whole of the questions involved, I have been forced to the conclusion that those reasons which the Dominion government has not yet seen fit to place before the Territorial government and legislature must have been more cogent than those set forth in your letter of last March. For take these reasons seriatim. First, 'the fact that the population of the Territories is yet sparse.' It is to that fact that we owe in large measure our present financial disabilities. It is to the second reason given, namely, 'the rapid increase in population,' and the consequent and continuous material alteration in our conditions, that our administrative difficulties are due, while that same rapid increase has a very direct influence upon our financial needs, not the least of which is the necessity for some other provision for expenditure upon matters properly chargeable to 'capital' account than by taking the money required from current revenue.

There is nothing new in these statements. They have, supported by details more or less full, been laid before you each successive year since accession to office, as reasons for asking the Federal government to take such measures as are calculated to afford relief from the intolerable position in which we are placed, and it comes as a surprise to us to find the reasons we have advanced to you for so many years in succession to support our claim to fair and just treatment put forward as 'some of the reasons' for the refusal of the Dominion government to even take our claims into consideration.

The last reason advanced in your letter for the government's inaction, that, namely, 'there is a considerable divergence of opinion respecting the question whether there should be one province only or more than one province,' has been very definitely answered by the people of the Territories. With my proposition to the government having been disseminated in every possible way through the length and breadth of the country beforehand, the people of the Territories elected representatives to a new legislature on May 21 last. In my address to my own constituents, which was reproduced, I believe, in every newspaper published in the West, I said:—

"At the present time the government of the Territories is engaged in negotiations with the Dominion government leading to the establishment of a part of the Territories upon the provincial basis. Apart from all other considerations, financial necessity has forced this question to the front. A rapidly increasing population has caused the present revenues of the Territories to become totally inadequate to meet the public demands, and in the opinion of the government the only solution of the difficulties being met with is to be found in the larger powers and income which go with the provincial status upon proper terms. Larger powers, it is true, mean larger responsibilities, but these same larger powers will carry with them the ability to discharge any duty that can be placed upon the people of the west.

The government has presented to the Federal authorities the claims of the people of the Territories in a document which has been published and is being very widely distributed. In that document the Territorial government has expressed its opinion in favour of the organization of one province only. Action upon the whole question has been postponed by the Dominion government, principally upon the ground that there is a 'divergence of opinion respecting the question whether there should be one province only or more than one province'—a question which in the last resort is one for the Dominion government to settle. The opinion of the Territorial government is based upon the fact that in the past one government and one legislature have found no difficulty in conducting the affairs of the country other than such as arose from the inadequacy of the revenue, and it is not anticipated that any difficulty which cannot be met will arise in the future. There is a widespread and well founded opinion existing throughout Canada against what has been called 'over-government,' or 'multiplicity of governments,' and there appears to be no substantial reason for the formation of more than one province in the Territories at the present time. Much less is there any reason for considering that other proposition which has been made on the part of the province of Manitoba, namely, the division of the people of the Territories by including within the limits of that province a considerable portion of the present district of Assiniboia, for the whole sentiment of the people concerned is against the proposal. Upon this phase of the question, at least, there is no divergence of opinion. Even should there be any material divergence of opinion in the Territories on the one or more province question—and there undoubtedly is some—the result of the election can only demonstrate and accentuate the fact. The Territorial government, however, has indicated to the Federal government what it believes to be the opinion held by a very large majority of the people of the Territories as promising to be in the best interests of the country as a whole. Whilst this is so, it is at the same time to be clearly understood that though the government's opinion has been formed after careful consideration of all the facts before it, such is its strong conviction that provincial establishment upon the general terms proposed is imperatively required, and at the earliest possible date, that it does not consider the question of one or more provinces to be of paramount importance in view of the magnitude of the other questions involved. These questions deal with the things which the government on behalf of the people of the Territories has claimed must of right belong to any province established in the west, and which were practically unanimously approved by the legislature at its last session, they are briefly:—

(1) Equal rights with all the other provinces of the Dominion, and the same financial consideration that has been given to those provinces;

(2) Control of the public domain in the west, by the west, and for the west;

(3) Compensation for the alienation of any part of the public domain for purely federal purposes, and

(4) the removal of the unjust and onerous Canadian Pacific Railway exemption from taxation.

These are the matters that the government of the Territories is now fighting for, and these are the matters upon which your judgment is invited in my appeal to you for re-election as your representative in the legislature. A similar appeal is being made in every constituency in the country by every candidate whose election will give support to the government at this critical period in the history of the Territories. The issue is plain, and it is for the people of the Territories to decide."

On the question of the establishment of the provincial institutions in the west, the assembly, in May, 1900, was unanimous, and the result of the elections in May, 1902, demonstrated definitely that the assembly clearly represented public opinion throughout the Territories upon that subject. As I stated in my address, 'the issue is plain;' I do not know how it could have been made plainer. The people have decided, and their decision is found in the fact that not only am I offered the support of a greater proportion of the members of the House than I ever had before, but also that 24 out of the 25 members of the last House who sought re-election (and who all voted 'yea' on the resolution of May 2, 1900) were returned at the top of the polls in their respective districts. I may also say that the result of the election has justified my statement that it could only demonstrate and accentuate the fact that there undoubtedly is some divergence of opinion in the Territories upon the one or more province question. There are probably a few members of the new legislature who support the view of two provinces, but they are not united as to the manner in which the Territories should be divided. Annexation of any part of Manitoba has not a single advocate in the House, while an overwhelming majority of the constituencies has pronounced in favour of one province.

I will go further, and say that the people of the Territories practically unanimously voted for the establishment of the country upon the provincial basis. The manner in which that shall be done is, to again quote from my address, 'a question which in the last resort is one for the Dominion government to settle.' At the request of Sir Wilfrid Laurier, in my letter of December 7, 1901, I placed on record the views of the government of the Territories as to the matters which should receive consideration, and at the same time condensed those views in the form of a draft Bill. Since then, with a full knowledge of the facts, the people of the Territories have elected new representatives, a large majority of whom support and approve of those views. So that I am free to claim—as I do—that the people of the Territories have given their answer to the statement, expressed on behalf of the Dominion government, that they are not united on the question of the provincial establishment. I have admitted that there are divergencies of opinion upon details of the question, as there are upon all questions in which any community is interested, but there is certainly no divergence of opinion upon the question of the establishment of provincial institutions in the Territories upon fair, just and equitable terms, analogous to those upon which the older provinces have been dealt with. We are seeking no favours—we but request that we be fairly dealt with. We have nothing new to lay before the government, nothing but what has already been stated, save only that the conditions are growing more intolerable, the financial stringency is more accentuated, and our constitutional inability to do anything to help ourselves still more marked. We claim—as we have always claimed—that our sparse population, as well as its present rapid increase, are factors in our public life urgently calling for the early attention of parliament, with a view to dealing adequately with our disabilities, and it has already been sufficiently demonstrated that there is no warrant for the belief that the people of the Territories are not sufficiently alive to their own well being as not to be practically a unit upon this question.

In a letter addressed to you on January 30, 1901, I said 'that financial embarrassments rather than constitutional aspirations' led us to request the full provincial powers. I might now say that we are driven by both reasons. Financial necessities have developed constitutional aspirations, but apart from the purely financial aspect of the case we demand that system of government under which we shall have as full opportunities for the exercise of our citizenship as our fellow-citizens in the provinces. The local government and legislature should have full and free scope of action left to them on many subjects which relate to the prosperity and happiness of the country, and the North-west will not be satisfied until this is granted.

This letter will be presented to you by Mr. Bulyea, and I have to earnestly ask that you will be so good as to afford him an opportunity to present to both yourself and Sir Wilfrid Laurier such supplementary remarks as may seem to him to be required to make clear the views of the government upon this—to the Territories—most momentous matter.

In conclusion, I would once more urge upon your consideration the questions involved in the whole subject of the future welfare of the Territories, in the hope that such consideration will result in the introduction of legislation dealing with these matters at the coming session of parliament.

In spite of the increasingly partisan tone of the debate on Provincial autonomy at the Federal level the non-partisan

*coalition under Haultain in the Territories had held into 1903.
Even that was put under severe strain, however, as Territorial
Conservatives sought to follow events through to their logical
conclusion by adopting a partisan stance. In Moose Jaw in
March of 1903 a series of resolutions put those Conservatives on
record both in favour of provincial autonomy and, more
controversially, in favour of running on the party label in the
next Territorial election. Haultain balked at this latter resolution but put himself in a rather ambiguous position when, in
spite of his refusal to accept partisan politics, he did accept the
position of honourary President of the Territorial Conservative
Association.*

IV — 6

**Resolutions Passed at the Territorial Liberal-Conservative
Convention at Moose-Jaw on March 26th, 1903:
Public Archives of Canada, Borden Papers, Vol. 310, p. 182107**

1st. That the Liberal Conservatives of the North-west Territories in convention assembled congratulate Mr. R.L. Borden,
K.C., M.P., upon his rapid promotion to the Leadership of the
Liberal Conservative party of Canada, and upon his able and
effective leadership of the party and congratulate their fellow
Conservatives throughout the Dominion on having secured the
services of a leader whose unequivocal support of the claims of
the people of these Territories to be immediately granted a full
measure of Provincial autonomy including Provincial ownership and control of the public domains, and whose recognition
of the principal of our claims for compensation for lands
alienated has, in an especial manner commended him and that
party to the support and confidence of the people of these
Territories.

2nd. That this Convention is unanimously opposed to the
grant by Parliament of any of the public domain of the North-
west Territories, by way of bonus to Railway or other Corporations, or the alienation of, or the sale of, or the lease of, lands,
except to bonafide settlers. . . .

5th. Whereas the North-west Territories is acutely suffering
at the present time from inadequate transportation facilities,
our farmers, business men, and others losing heavily thereby,
and whereas this state of affairs could easily be remedied by a
policy of energy. Therefore, be it resolved that the Convention

deplores the fact that the Dominion Government has not made any effort to secure the immediate amelioration of the conditions under which we suffer, and we further deplore the fact that the Dominion Government refuses the Territories the right to deal as they deem best with the Railway question—a right possessed by every other Political Division of Canada, further, this Convention declares in favor of the building of a Railway to Hudson's Bay as one means to provide a cheaper and more direct outlet for the products of the Territories and we further demand as a right that the Dominion Government either secure to us immediately the Railway facilities necessary to grant to us the power to secure them for ourselves. . . .

7th. That in furtherance of the objects of this convention be it resolved that Conservative candidates as such be placed in Nomination in every constituency at the next General Election of Members to the Legislative Assembly of the North-west Territories, and kept in the field till the close of the polls.

8th. That in the opinion of this Convention, Provincial Autonomy and the granting of provincial institutions upon the same terms as those enjoyed by the older Provinces of the Dominion—including the ownership of our public lands, our mines and minerals and compensation for lands alienated for Federal purposes—should be immediately granted to the Territories.

As the political situation in the Territories followed a series of twists and turns, one thing remained fairly constant. There was continued strong support for provincial autonomy. Resolutions, editorials and private and public letters must have made it apparent to observers on both sides that provincial autonomy was supported by the majority of people in the Territories. This basic fact could not be ignored by the political players in either party and it gave Haultain a certain strength and manoeuvring room lacking among Territorial Liberals as would soon be revealed.

IV — 7

Resolution Adopted by the Lethbridge Board of Trade at a Meeting held on the eighth day of April, A.D. 1903: Canada Sessional Paper 116, 1903.

Resolved, that this board endorse the stand taken by the

North-west Government in regard to the granting of provincial autonomy to the Territories, and are strongly in favour of such autonomy being granted on the terms formulated and demanded by the Honourable Mr. Haultain, and that copies of this resolution be forwarded to the Honourable the Prime Minister and the Minister of the Interior.

IV — 8

Resolution of the Okotoks Board of Trade, April 18, 1903: Public Archives of Canada, Laurier Papers, enclosure in O.B. Stockford to Laurier, April 18, 1903, 208706.

Whereas the population of the Territories is rapidly increasing;

And whereas this rapid growth has given rise to greatly increased demands for money for public works and for educational purposes, and has also made necessary the granting of larger powers to our Local Legislature, and the bestowment of local responsible government upon the people of the Territories to the extent enjoyed by the Provinces of the Dominion;

And Whereas these ends can only be fully obtained by the establishment of provincial institutions in the Territories;

Therefore Resolved that this Board is of the opinion that the time is ripe for the granting of provincial autonomy to the Territories, and we therefore heartily endorse the request of our Legislative Council and Assembly, that such institutions be given to us, together with all Crown Lands, Minerals, and Timber.

And further Resolved that this Board is of the opinion that one province will better serve the interests of the people of the Territories at large than will the establishment of more than one.

And we would respectfully urge our Federal Government to give this matter their serious consideration as soon as possible.

IV — 9

'Home Rule for Ireland but not for the Territories,' Calgary Herald, April 14, 1903.

Parliament at Ottawa, by a very large majority, passed

resolutions last week in favor of granting home rule to Ireland. The resolution was introduced by the Hon. John Costigan and the reports of the debate indicate that fervent speeches and eloquent pleas were made in favor of relief for Ireland.

Sir Wilfrid, it appears, made one of his usual careful speeches and extended a serious appeal to England now 'to trust the people of Ireland, give her home rule and allow her to manage her own affairs.'

This almost seems a travesty. Here we are in the North West making appeal after appeal for provincial or self government and Ottawa not only turns a deaf ear but is even unwilling to discuss the question with us. Though time and zeal can be found for Ireland, both hands being extended to help her, nothing of the kind for the good Canadians of the North West. Hon. Clifford Sifton has said in effect that we are unfit to govern ourselves and has passed word to his colleagues, and this has been accepted at Ottawa by the government.

IV — 10

A.E. Forget to the Secretary of State, April 24, 1903: Canada Sessional Paper 116, 1903.

I have the honour to forward herewith for transmission to His Excellency the Governor General the inclosed address from the Legislative Assembly of the North-west Territories upon the present constitutional and financial condition of the North-west Territories.

May It Please Your Excellency:

We, His Majesty's dutiful and loyal subjects, the Legislative Assembly of the North-west Territories of Canada, in session assembled, humbly approach Your Excellency for the purposes of representing:—

That by an Address dated the second day of May, in the year one thousand nine hundred, a copy of which is attached hereto, the Legislative Assembly pointed out that repeated representations had been made, in various ways, to the Government of Canada with a view to obtaining just and equitable assistance towards providing for the proper and effective administration of affairs in these Territories and for the public necessities of their rapidly increasing population, and that such representations had been met by intermittent and insufficient additions to the annual grant, the provision so made by the Parliament of

Canada never bearing any adequate proportion to the financial obligations imposed by the enlargement and development of the political institutions created by itself;

That by the said Address the Legislative Assembly humbly prayed that Your Excellency would be graciously pleased to cause an inquiry to be made into the position of the Territories, financial and otherwise, and to cause such action to be taken as would provide for their present and immediate welfare and good government, as well as the due fulfilment of the duties and obligations of government and legislation assumed with respect to these Territories by the Parliament of Canada, and it was furthermore humbly prayed that Your Excellency would also be graciously pleased to order inquiries to be made and accounts taken with a view to the settlement of the terms and conditions upon which the Territories, or any part thereof, should be established as a province;

That since the passing of the said Address, further representations have been made in various ways to Your Excellency's Government with regard to the financial and constitutional position of the Territories;

That during the past three years the immediate necessities of the Territories have been vastly increased by a remarkable immigration movement, which is still going on;

That no adequate response has been made to the repeated requests for the financial assistance necessary for 'the proper and effective administration of the affairs of these Territories and for the public necessities of their rapidly increasing population';

That the Legislative Assembly, representing as it does the unanimous opinion of the people of the Territories, believes that nothing short of that system of government enjoyed by our fellow-citizens in the provinces will afford a solution of the legislative and financial difficulties which confront it;

Therefore, we do humbly pray that Your Excellency will cause such action to be taken as will provide for the present and immediate financial necessities of the Territories, and will further provide for the establishment of provincial institutions in the Territories upon fair and just terms analogous to those upon which the old provinces have been dealt with;

All which we humbly pray Your Excellency to take into Your Excellency's gracious and favourable consideration.

A.B. GILLIS,
Speaker of the
Legislative Assembly of the
North-west Territories.

The major test of Haultain's non-partisan, or perhaps by now bi-partisan, coalition, took place in the spring of 1903. Haultain's association with the Moose Jaw resolutions and the growing political partisanship present in Territorial debates had put the Liberal members of the coalition under pressure. In the meantime the Liberal government of Laurier continued to seek to ease the political pressure on the party by enlarging the financial grant to the Territories. Unfortunately for the plans of Laurier and Sifton, their proposal to give the Territories a loan on the capital account and their attempt to bill the Territorial government for two bridges raised new controversy. While Liberal M.L.A.'s petitioned Laurier for a generous grant, Haultain was in the process of refusing the terms of that grant. As the following documents indicate, the end result was to force the Liberal Members of the Territorial Assembly to face a question they would rather have avoided. Did they support the Haultain government in a direct disagreement with a Liberal government in Ottawa or were they willing to risk handing the government over to Haultain with the very likely consequence of a Conservative Territorial government? At stake was not only the Territorial legislature but the political complexion of the future provinces and their federal M.P.'s. In the end a short term split with the federal Liberal party seemed preferable to possible disaster at the polls. George Bulyea and a number of other prominent Liberals backed Haultain and thereby preserved the coalition.

IV — 11

Haultain to Laurier, April 15, 1903: Canada Sessional Papers 116b, 1903.

Shortly before Mr. Sifton left for England he wrote me a note saying that the sub-committee of Council, appointed to deal with North-west affairs, had had a final meeting, and that I should hear from Mr. Fielding what the government intended to do.

When in Ottawa I pointed out to Mr. Sifton and to the sub-committee of Council that it was important that we should be made aware of the intentions of the government at as early a date as possible. The North-west legislature will meet on

Thursday, as the session could not be postponed any longer, owing to the statutory necessity for meeting within one year of last session. We have not, as yet, heard from Mr. Fielding, and we shall be obliged to meet our legislature on Thursday next without having any idea at all as to the amount of money which will be available for legislative appropriation this year. May I ask you to see that we are informed as soon as possible of the result of our interview with you.

I am inclosing a copy of a letter, addressed to Mr. Sifton, for the information of the government, to which I referred in my interview with the sub-committee, and which, no doubt, you have already seen. It deals exclusively with the question of provincial institutions in the Territories; and I would again, on behalf of my colleagues, earnestly ask your consideration of our request.

I would also, in Mr. Sifton's absence, ask for your particular attention to our request for a vote supplementary to the vote for the current year. Whatever amount the government may decide to give us for the year beginning on the 1st July next, it will be quite inadequate for the purposes of the year for which it is voted, and will leave us, so far as the conditions of last year and the necessities for the first six months of this year, in a very awkward position. As I pointed out to the sub-committee, we were obliged last year, not only on account of the unexpectedly large increase in our population, but also on account of floods and other untoward conditions, to undertake the large amount of work—imperatively necessary at the time—on the credit of the small amount of money payable to us in the beginning of January, for the first six months of this year. Nothing but the most urgent necessity, I admit, could have justified this expenditure, but we are quite confident that the conditions of the past season were an absolute justification of our action.

These circumstances constitute the ground for our request, not only for a large increase to our grant for the coming Dominion fiscal year, but for a substantial supplementary vote to meet the actual necessities of the present moment.

To sum up, I beg to ask for an early reply to our request: First, for the granting of provincial institutions to the Territories; secondly, for a vote supplementary to the North-west grant for the current year; and thirdly, for a largely increased vote for the year 1903-1904.

IV — 12

W.S. Fielding, Dominion Minister of Finance, to Haultain, April 16, 1903: Canada Sessional Paper 116a, 1904.

Government will place in supplementary estimates for coming year two hundred and fifty thousand dollars to cover over-expenditure of the Territories, and also recommend to Parliament an advance on capital account up to $500,000 from time to time for approved public works. The two bridges which have been specially arranged for to be charged to the capital advance. It will be better that all bridges in the Territories be left to the Territorial Government. Please treat this as confidential for a day or two until I can arrange to have it dealt with by Order in Council.

IV — 13

Haultain to Fielding, April 20, 1903: Canada Sessional Paper 116a, 1904.

I have to apologise for the delay which has arisen, but which has been unavoidable, in confirming my telegram of the seventeenth instant reading:

> Supplementary vote quite satisfactory if made supplementary to current year. Other propositions absolutely unsatisfactory in method and amount. Conditions here require large increase to annual grant for coming Dominion fiscal year apart from question of capital advance, for which we have made no request. In case capital advance is made unrestricted disposal by local legislature must be allowed and we should strongly protest against any part of cost of replacing Macleod and Lethbridge bridges, both Federal undertakings, being charged. Writing.

The above telegram was sent in reply to your message of the previous day which it would seem well to quote in full as received here.

> Government will place in supplementary estimates for coming year two hundred and fifty thousand dollars to cover the over-expenditure of the Territories and also

recommend to Parliament an advance on capital account up to five hundred thousand dollars from time to time for approved public works. The two bridges which have been specially arranged for to be charged to the capital advance. It will be better that all bridges in Territories be left to the Territorial government. Please treat this as confidential for a few days until I can arrange to have it dealt with by Order in Council.

It is with much satisfaction that I note that the Government has so far appreciated the position of affairs in the Territories as to approve, in the most practical manner possible, of our methods of administration by providing for the expenditure we found it necessary to incur in the public interest during the year 1902. It would appear, however, to have escaped your observation that the placing of the appropriation to cover our expenditures of last year in the supplementary estimates for the *coming* Dominion fiscal year will have the effect of keeping the money from the Territorial revenue until after the first day of July next. All the representations we have made—both written and oral—have been to the effect that the supplementary appropriation is desired to the *current* fiscal year's appropriations, so that the money may be rendered available at the earliest possible moment. To do otherwise can only embarrass us still further, and I would submit that with a prospective surplus of thirteen million dollars, to a very large extent due to the present flourishing condition of these Territories, the Dominion will not be put to any very serious inconvenience by granting us the money it has been agreed to give us during the month of May instead of July. I trust that upon further consideration of the subject you will see your way clear to recommending the Government to grant our request that the $250,000 referred to in your telegram be provided for through the supplementary estimates for 1902-3.

Your telegram makes no mention whatever of any proposal to increase our grant for the coming fiscal year. I take it that the suggested advance on capital account has no connection whatever with that subject. In discussing the various phases of the question of Territorial finances, it has been found necessary at times to point out that our limited and inadequate revenues were more restricted, and rendered only more inadequate, by the necessity for making expenditures out of current income which in themselves were more properly chargeable to a capital account. That is to say, we have occasionally found it necessary to incur heavy expenditures for the construction of bridges the cost of which has been a heavy drain upon our revenues, and which should have been spread over a series of years instead of being provided for out of the revenue of one year, to the exclusion of other and equally important works. But we have never asked for the establishment of a capital account, and we do not wish for the establishment of such an account until a more satisfactory subsidy or annual grant is provided. We would even prefer, if possible, to postpone all discussion of the question until the details of the financial position of the Territories under the Provincial status are settled. Whilst the Dominion retains to itself the control and beneficiary interest in our revenue producing property it seems but fair to us that the Dominion should provide all needed funds for the proper carrying on of our business. Further, we cannot assent to any proposition that our expenditures shall be subject to approval at Ottawa. The Legislative Assembly of the Territories has for a number of years been providing for the administration of public affairs in the Territories. What has been done in that regard has met with the approval of the people of the Territories, and this government cannot consent, at this date, to any such proposal as that made in your telegram. In one sense, I quite agree with you that 'it will be better that all bridges in Territories be left to the Territorial Government,' but that proposition must be coupled with another, namely that adequate financial provision therefor be made by Parliament. The Dominion Government in the first place built the two bridges at Macleod and Lethbridge without reference to the Government of the Territories. It was possible that at the time they were built it was not practicable to do so, but the fact remains that, in pursuance of its general public works policy, the Dominion Government built the two bridges in question and has undertaken to replace them. Under existing conditions, which the Dominion Government does not appear to wish to remedy, we are content to leave that matter as it stands at present.

With respect to the general question of the establishment of a capital account, as I have already stated, we have never asked for such a grant and are not disposed to accept it coupled with the conditions laid down. Even if those conditions are waived we could not agree to the proposal whilst what we consider our just claims to fair treatment from the financial point of view are deliberately set aside and not met. For instance, representations were made on December 17 and January 9 last by Mr. A.L.

Sifton, the then Territorial Treasurer, that it was necessary that Parliament should be asked to provide for the expenditure of the sum of $880,000 during the year 1903, upon the services devolving upon the Government of the Territories. On February 21, whilst in Ottawa and at the request of Sir Wilfrid Laurier, I submitted a carefully detailed statement of our affairs, showing the nature of the requirements of the country, and pointing out particularly that the public necessities were to a very large extent due to the rapid influx of population, a cause entirely beyond our control but which, to some extent, may be attributed to the Dominion Government's efforts to direct immigration to the West. I also pointed out that between December and February conditions had so far changed that the amount asked for in December would be entirely insufficient to provide for necessary expenditures in new and unforeseen directions. In December, we asked that Parliament should provide $880,000 for our use during 1903. As a reply to that request, the Government proposes to vote $457,979. This is the same amount as was voted last year and which fell short of the smallest possible expenditure we could make by $250,000. Climatic conditions created a general and urgent necessity for replacing a large number of bridges that had been carried away by floods, but that necessity only made it impossible for us to consider other public undertakings of comparatively less urgency, but which are all calling for attention this year. If we were $250,000 short last year, what we will be this year with increased demands and necessities in every direction, I can safely leave you to form your own estimate.

Without going over the ground again I would here simply say that if we have found the necessity for making capital expenditures out of an annual income a particularly onerous burden, the difficulties of our financial position will be rendered only the greater by the strong temptation to draw upon a capital account, should such an account be established, for expenditures that should, under every rule of legitimate finance, be provided for only out of annual income, but which condition of affairs would be forced upon us by the manner in which the Dominion government fulfils its self-imposed duty of providing for the peace, order and good government of these territories.

I trust that the further consideration of this whole subject, promised in your telegram of this date, will result in some more definite recognition of our necessities than has hitherto been evidenced. The one, and the best solution of all these difficulties has, on several occasions of late, been suggested to the Dominion government, and it seems to me that I might well close this communication by an expression of the opinion that just so long as the provincial status is withheld from the territories will it be necessary for the government of the territories to direct attention with increasing force and emphasis to the present unsatisfactory manner of making financial provision for the public requirements of the country.

IV — 14

A.C. Rutherford to Laurier, May 22, 1903: Laurier Papers, Reel 1165.

Previous to the adjournment of the Assembly of the North-West Territories it was suggested that each of the Liberal members should address a communication to you with regard to the desirability that your government should give an increased grant to the Government of the Territories this year.

Owing to the large influx of population and other causes heretofore pointed out to your Government by the Territorial Government the present Dominion grant is entirely insufficient to meet the ordinary requirements of the North West.

The Liberal party has now a grand opportunity of strengthening themselves in the North West. The only effective argument of the Conservative party in the West will be taken from them, if your government will only meet the financial necessities of the North West government generously.

May I take the liberty of informing you that I am a member of the Assembly for the Strathcona Electoral District and a supporter of the Liberal party.

IV — 15

Laurier to Rutherford, May 28, 1903: Rutherford Papers.

I have the honour to acknowledge the receipt of your favour of the 22nd instant. We had made very liberal offers to the Government of the Territories, and we are prepared to implement them. I am sorry to say that the answer we have received from Mr. Haultain is not what we should have expected. We thought that they would be gladly accepted, and we hope that when they are communicated to the Legislative Assembly, they will be found more than satisfactory by the friends of the Liberal party in that body.

IV — 16

Fielding to Haultain, June 6, 1903: Canada Sessional Paper 116a, 1904.

Referring to previous communications we do not understand your reference to certain bridges as federal undertakings. Highway bridges of a similar character in all the provinces are provincial undertakings, and there does not appear to be any reason why, in the case of the North-west, they should not be treated as other public works coming under the authority of the local government. Our view is that we should provide a liberal allowance for the North-west Government and leave you to deal with the management of all such roads and bridges as in the case of the provinces fall under local control.

As to the capital account, we have no disposition to impose unnecessary restrictions. In the case of provincial governments desiring advances from their capital account, the applications are subject to the approval of the Governor in Council. We do not anticipate any difficulty on this score, but we see no reason why the rule which exists as respects all the provinces should not apply also to the capital account of the North-west Territories. . . .

IV — 17

Haultain to Fielding, June 15, 1903: Canada Sessional Paper 116a, 1904.

I have the honour to acknowledge the receipt of your telegram of the sixth instant an earlier acknowledgement of which has been postponed in the expectation of receiving some written confirmation of it.

With regards to the proposed provision for the Government of the North-west Territories, I would say that the supplementary vote of $250,000 for over expenditure will be a very welcome addition to the slender resources of the Territories. The addition of $250,000 to the amount provided in the main estimates, while helpful so far as it goes, falls far short of the amount requested by us and shown to be absolutely necessary in the various statements already submitted.

My reference to the Macleod and Lethbridge bridges as 'federal undertakings,' was based on the fact that the structures they are intended to replace were built by the Federal Government and that the Federal Government had already undertaken to pay for them under the arrangements referred to in your telegram of April 16. I might further say that highway bridges of a similar character have not always been dealt with as provincial undertakings.

A reference to the Dominion Appropriation Acts for the seven years from 1896 to 1902 (both inclusive) and the estimates for 1903-4 will show votes aggregating $716,000 for roads and bridges, most of which might equally appropriately be designated 'provincial undertakings.' I would also urge that the Territories are entitled to some expenditure for works of urgent necessity as a small offset to the large expenditure made in the provinces for 'public works.'

I would further respectfully submit that the argument of 'provincial undertakings' does not apply to the Territories. I need hardly remind you that the Territories are not a province and that they do not enjoy the revenues or powers of a province, and further that it is the opinion of the government and legislature of the Territories that the 'liberal allowance' you provide is not liberal enough to establish an analogy. We are not only ready but anxious to assume responsibility for all provincial undertakings, and with that end in view have been pressing for the granting of provincial institutions to the Territories.

With regard to the question of an advance on capital account I can only refer to my letter of April 20, and the position therein taken up. An advance on capital account is nothing more or less than a loan upon which eventually we should have to pay 5 per cent per annum. We feel indisposed to consider an invitation to borrow money as a satisfactory settlement of our request for the necessary amounts to carry on the affairs of this country. At all events the proposition to give us an advance on capital account of $250,000, already debited with $84,000 for the bridges mentioned above, is one which we cannot entertain. We cannot reasonably object to the requirement of the consent of the Governor in Council to any broad scheme of expenditure under this heading, but to be obliged to ask such consent to every detail would be as burdensome as it would be unnecessary. After all, the money would be advanced to the people of the

Territories and its proper expenditure might safely be entrusted to their responsible government and legislature.

In conclusion, may I ask for a reconsideration of your decision to charge the two bridges in question to any advance which may be agreed upon, and also to give me some more definite information with regard to the mode of advance, the date upon which interest would begin to run and the information required for obtaining the consent of the Governor in Council.

IV — 18

George Bulyea to Laurier, June 16, 1903:
Canada Sessional Paper 116a, 1903.

You will please excuse the liberty I take in addressing you, if it is a liberty to lay before you facts that I consider will be of material influence on the welfare of the Liberal party in the North-west Territories.

You are, of course, cognizant of all the representations that the Territorial Government have made in reference to increase of the financial assistance that is voted to us from time to time, and the arguments that have been advanced why a material increase is absolutely necessary, if the alternative of provincial autonomy were not granted to us. I have had considerable correspondence with the Federal members representing the Territories, who were kind enough to apprize me of the general representations they had made to your Government, and I advised them that I consider that if such were adopted it would reasonably satisfy the general public in the Territories, and would put your candidates and your supporters in the coming election in a position in which they could fight with zeal and, I am pleased to say, with every prospect of success.

The supplementary grant, and the addition to the main vote, while not as much as we asked for, will be of very material assistance to me in the work of my Department as Commissioner of Public Works. The capital advance tendered is also needed for the construction of the large and permanent structures that must be completed to meet the requirements of the large influx of settlers into the country.

I regret to say, however, that not only as a member of the Territorial Government, but as a citizen of the North-west Territories, I must dissent most strongly from the proposition to charge up against this vote the large expenditure of $84,000 which is purely and simply for the reconstruction of two federal public works, viz:—the bridges over the Old Man's and Belly rivers, erected by the late Conservative government.

During the floods of last year these two bridges were washed out, and your government, through its officers, agreed to have them replaced by permanent structures. Your officers in the Territories reported on the necessity of such reconstruction, took charge of the old bridges, and sold the old material. Later, through the late Commissioner of Public Works, the Hon. A.L. Sifton, the matter was taken up with the Federal Public Works Department, and as we have a fairly large staff of competent bridgemen, and have been very successful in the construction of bridges of a less size than these, it was arranged that the Territorial Government should proceed with the construction of the bridges, and that they would be recouped for such expenditure to the amount of $55,000 in the case of the bridge over the Belly river at Lethbridge, and $29,000 in the case of the bridge over the Old Man's river at Macleod.

For your information I attach a copy of extract from the report of the Committee of the Honourable the Privy Council, approved by His Excellency on February 6, 1903.

On the authority of this Order in Council my department proceeded with the work. Considerable preliminary work has already been done in making the necessary approaches to the bridges, tenders have been called both for the material and the concrete piers, and for the steel super-structure, and I maintain that the Federal Government cannot, in honour, recede from the position that they have taken as shown by this Order in Council, even if there were no political reasons for carrying out their definite agreement in this matter.

Official correspondence from this government will no doubt be laid before you in due course, protesting against the suggested charges, and while the matter is, in a sense, sub judice, we cannot of course proceed to use the suggested advance on our capital account.

I trust, therefore, that you will see the necessity of meeting the reasonable views not only of the North-west Government but of your friends who are members of the Territorial Assembly, and who uphold unanimously our government in claiming that the territories are entitled to have these Federal structures replaced at the general expense of the Dominion of Canada.

The undersigned members of the Legislative Assembly strongly approve of the tenor of the above letter:—

GEORGE W. BROWN.	P. TALBOT.
L. GEO. DE VEBER.	B. PRINCE.
J.W. WOOLF.	R.A. WALLACE.
W.J. FINLEY	J.A. SIMPSON.
C.A. FISHER.	A.S. ROSENROLL.
A.D. MCINTYRE.	THOS. MACNUTT.
CHARLES FISHER.	ALEX. C. RUTHERFORD.

IV — 19

Haultain to Laurier, June 2, 1903: Laurier Papers, 208538.

I have the honour on behalf of the North-west Government to again ask for a reply to the requests set out in my letter to you of the 15th April last. Acknowledging the letter on the 20th April you say "As Mr. Fielding has communicated with you already by wire on the subject therein mentioned, I do not suppose that it requires any further reply." Mr. Fielding's telegram of the 16th April was a confidential and informal proposition and only dealt with the financial position. On the 17th April I telegraphed Mr. Fielding our objections to his proposition, and informed him that I was writing on the subject. On the 20th April Mr. Fielding telegraphed "Will await your letter before taking further action." My letter to Mr. Fielding was dated the 20th April. On the 25th April the territorial legislature adjourned for six weeks to await the decision of the Federal Government with regard to the North-west Grant, and up to the present time no further communication on the subject has been received by us. In further reference to your letter of the 20th April I beg to point out that Mr. Fielding's telegram does not deal with the most important part of my letter of the 16th April, namely our request for Provincial Institutions, and I would most respectfully urge that our representations on this important question merit some further reply than can be gathered by implication from the fact that Mr. Fielding does not refer to them.

IV — 20

Laurier to Haultain, June 8, 1903: Laurier Papers, 208541-2.

I have the honour to acknowledge the receipt of your letter of the 2nd instant. The Minister of Finance has by this time communicated with you respecting the financial grant to be given to the North-west legislature.

With regard to your further request that legislation be introduced this session conferring on the Territories full provincial organization, I have had the honour to discuss the matter with the members of the House of Commons from the Territories. I have asked them to consider whether it would be advisable to have such legislation introduced this year. We are, as you know, introducing a Redistribution measure at the present session, and we are giving the Territories a much larger representation in the House of Commons of ten members. Were they to be admitted at once as a province they would be entitled to only six members. It would be a question of extreme difficulty and complications to give to the Territories at the same time all the advantages of full provincial organization, without the corresponding disadvantages.

IV — 21

Haultain to Laurier, June 15, 1903: Memorial of the Legislative Assembly of the North-West Territories to His Excellency the Governor General in Council, of May 2, 1900 . . . and all Correspondence relating thereto. (Printed by Order of the Legislative Assembly).

SIR,—I have the honour to acknowledge receipt of your letter of the Eighth instant relating to the question of Provincial Institutions in the Territories, and to express regret on the part of the North-west Government that that question has again been put on one side for a reason which seems quite foreign to the subject.

With all deference to the opinion expressed by you, I cannot see that the representation proposed to be given to the Territories under the Redistribution Bill could be in any way affected by the passing of concurrent legislation granting the Provincial status to the Territories.

The provisions of the B.N.A. Act relating to representation would not, I submit, apply to a Province which, at the earliest, could only come to existence at the same time as the Redistribution Bill became law. Even if legislation creating a Province were introduced at the present session of Parliament, the actual coming into existence of the Province would necessarily be

postponed for some months to enable Territorial affairs to be
wound up, and thus any question with regard to representation
and the effect of the B.N.A. Act would be removed. I might also
remind you that upon the admission of British Columbia into
the Confederation and upon the creation of the Province of
Manitoba larger representation was given than these two
Provinces were respectively entitled to under the B.N.A. Act.

You say that you have discussed the question of Provincial
organization with the Members of the House of Commons
from the Territories and have asked them to consider whether it
would be advisable to have such legislation introduced this
year. Your letter does not make clear what the opinion of those
gentlemen is, but I feel justified in asserting that that opinion
was not in accord with the wishes of the people they represent
unless it supported the claims made by us which are unanimously endorsed by the North-west Legislature, and were
practically unanimously endorsed by the people of the North-
west Territories at the General Elections in May, 1902. The
question of larger representation in the Federal Parliament is
without doubt an important one, but the infinitely more
urgent question of Provincial organisation should not be
subordinated to it. The two questions are quite separate and
independent, and cannot, I think I have shown, affect one
another. Under any circumstances, however, the obtaining of
Provincial powers is in our opinion of much greater importance
to the people of the Territories than additional representation
in a Parliament whose failure to fulfil the duties and obligations it has assumed with regard to the North-west is one of our
strongest reasons for demanding Home Rule.

IV — 22

Clifford Sifton to William Fielding, August 20, 1903:
Public Archives of Canada, Clifford Sifton Papers,
Vol. 252, pp. 707-709.

Arrangements have been made which will be of the utmost
importance a little later on under which the North-west
Government, which has been somewhat antagonistic during
the last six months, will probably smooth things out a little,
even if they do not go as far as we wish. My policy will be during
the present Session not to antagonize them or take an attitude of
opposition. What I would like you to say is that the Govern-

ment recognizes the difficulties of Territorial Government and the large claims that have been made upon them for services of all kinds, and that we have authorized the large additional grants of the present Session in view of the necessities so arising.

Then I would like you to make the following statement in substance on the subject of Provincial Autonomy;—that the Government have no desire or disposition to put off for any length of time the settlement of the question of Provincial Autonomy for the North-west Territories; that the rapid settlement now going on and the considerable increase in population which has already taken place have created a necessity for dealing with the subject with very little delay. So soon as the preliminary difficulties such as the tax exemption question which is now before the Courts are out of the way the Government will be prepared to deal with the question.

You will observe that the purpose of having the matter stated in the above way is to make it so that the opponents cannot take the ground that we were opposed to granting Autonomy or wish to put it off indefinitely.

By the autumn of 1903 the two parties and the Territorial and Dominion governments had become fixed in their position. The Conservative Party continued to push for Territorial autonomy and, it should be noted, with terms which would have turned the lands over to the new Provinces. The Liberal government of Laurier continued to resist while attempting to smooth over difficulties. In this they were supported by the Liberal M.P.'s from the Territories who, as a result, came under constant criticism from Conservative newspapers and Haultain. Continued petitions and angry editorials, however, had little effect. The next move was up to the federal government for as Haultain said in June of 1904 everything had been done by the Territories that could be done.

IV — 23

Haultain speaks to a Conservative rally in Calgary, October 7, 1903: Calgary Herald, October 8, 1903.

Mr. Haultain said he was not in the habit of dragging federal politics into local matters. He did not believe that his position as leader of a non-political government debarred him holding his opinions or expressing them. . . .

The premier declared that for two years the government had been united that provincial institutions were necessary. He then told of the dealings between the North-west government and the federal government on the autonomy question, scoring Sir Wilfrid Laurier very hard. The responsibility of this whole question rested with the Dominion government, as the matter had been put off by the government as they claimed there was a divergence of opinion. However, the government had hustled the G[rand] T[runk] P[acific] bill along although there had been objection to it from several points.

Frank Oliver's recent deliverance at Ottawa for the North-west to wait until there were more people and better arrangements could be made for provincial autonomy, was scored. The speaker believed almost everybody was unanimously in favor of provincial autonomy.

The North-west claimed the same rights to her lands as the people of the other provinces. The Dominion government had already taken away almost 40,000,000 acres with which to help Dominion or provincial roads. The last proposition to take thirty or forty millions of acres to build a road from Moncton to Winnipeg and to the mountains, was too much. The claim for these lands was before the government in a formal way now, but he believed that in the light of the conditions of today it was a crime for the government to give these lands away to benefit the east at the cost of the west. Ontario would not do it nor [sic] British Columbia would not submit to such a thing about its lands.

Premier Haultain dealing with the question of representation said he had sent a memorandum to Sir Wilfrid Laurier asking 18 members, to which the North-west was entitled, instead of ten members.

In closing the premier said that the people had two parties to choose between. The Liberal party with its many abandoned policies and broken promises and the Conservative party which had been consistent and kept any promises made. 'If you have any regard to public morality or consistency you will have no alternative,' said the speaker, 'but turn the Liberals out of power.'

IV — 24

Robert Borden moves that the Territories be granted Provincial Autonomy, October 13, 1903: House of Commons Debates, October 13, 1903. 13882-3.

By humble addresses of the legislative assembly of the North-west Territories of Canada to His Excellency the Governor General, in the year 1900 and again in the year 1903, the said legislative assembly did humbly represent and pray (inter alia) to His Excellency as follows:—

'14. Therefore, be it resolved, that an humble address to His Excellency the Governor General be adopted by this House praying him that he will be pleased to cause the fullest inquiry to be made into the position of the territories, financial and otherwise, and to cause such action to be taken as will provide for their present and immediate welfare and good government, as well as the due fulfillment of the duties and obligations, of government and legislation assumed, with respect to these territories, by the parliament of Canada.

15. And be it further resolved, that, whereas by the British North America Act, 1871, it was (amongst other things) enacted that the parliament of Canada may from time to time establish new provinces. . . . His Excellency be also prayed to order inquiries to be made and accounts taken with a view to the settlement of the terms and conditions upon which the territories or any part thereof shall be established as a province, and that before any such province is established opportunity should be given to the people of the territories through their accredited representatives of considering and discussing such terms and conditions.'

That under the provision of the British North America Act and amending Acts the people of the several provinces of Canada enjoy large powers of local self-government committed to and exercised by the executive and the legislature of each province.

That the time has arrived when the same powers of local self-government should be granted to the people of the North-west Territories of Canada and to this end the said representations and prayer contained in the said humble addresses should be taken into immediate consideration and acted upon forthwith.

Borden's motion was defeated in a party vote of 63 to 29. All the Territorial Members of Parliament present in the House voted against the motion.

IV — 25

A.E. Forget to the Secretary of State, November 21, 1903: Territorial Sessional Paper No. 9, 1904.

SIR,—I have the honour to enclose, herewith, for submission to His Excellency the Governor General-in-Council, the following original document, viz.,—

An humble petition of the Legislative Assembly of the Territories, to His Excellency in Council, adopted on the 20th day of November, 1903, reaffirming the statements, and renewing the prayers contained in its addresses, dated respectively the Second day of May, 1900, and the Twenty-fourth day of April, 1903,—and praying that the same be taken into His Excellency's most gracious, favourable and early consideration.

The two addresses, above referred to, were transmitted by the undersigned, to your Department, the first under cover of despatch dated the 20th July, 1900, and the second under cover of despatch dated the 24th April, 1903.

MAY IT PLEASE YOUR EXCELLENCY—

We, His Majesty's dutiful and loyal subjects, the Legislative Assembly of the North-west Territories, in Session assembled, humbly approach Your Excellency for the purpose of representing—

That this House does most respectfully and earnestly reaffirm the statements and renew the prayers contained in its Addresses to Your Excellency, dated on the Second day of May, 1900, and the Twenty-fourth day of April, 1903.

All of which we humbly pray Your Excellency to take into Your Excellency's most gracious, favourable and early consideration.

A.B. GILLIS,
Speaker of the Legislative Assembly
of the North-west Territories.

IV — 26

'Territorial Autonomy,' The Macleod Gazette,
November 27, 1903.

'That an humble address be adopted by this House to his
Excellency the Governor-General-in-Council for the purpose
of representing that this House does most respectfully and
earnestly reaffirm the statements and renew the prayers contained in its address to His Excellency, dated on the second day
of May, 1900, and the twenty-fourth day of April, 1903, and
humbly praying that His Excellency will be pleased to grant
favourable and immediate consideration.'

Such was the resolution passed by the Territorial Legislature
last week, and mark this, passed unanimously. There were only
two absentees from the full strength of the House, thus the
resolution is the congested opinion of the Territorial people. It
of course refers to the request for provincial autonomy made by
the same body in the early part of the year. . . .

We, who live in this country know, have known for some
considerable time, that we must be allowed to manage our own
affairs or we cannot keep up our end in the way we ought to, in
the way in fact that we have to. That was one of the reasons why
Mr. Haultain and those representing his policy received the
overwhelming support of the electorate in the Territorial
elections a little more than a year ago. That, in fact, was the
main reason of such a result, for it was precisely upon this
question of Provincial autonomy that Mr. Haultain made his
appeal to the people and staked the existence of his government.
The results proved, there is absolutely no way of getting round
the fact, that the people of this country *DO* want a provincial
establishment, and that Mr. Haultain in pressing his demands
has practically the solid support of the whole country. What
effect has this upon the Liberal government in Ottawa? Sir
Wilfrid Laurier with a courteous wave of his hand (always
courteous) and a bland expansive smile refers the matter to Mr.
Sifton. That gentleman hasn't much time for such petty local
matters, but he has consulted Mr. Walter Scott, M.P. for
Western Assiniboia, and Mr. T. Davis, M.P. for Saskatchewan,
and Mr. Frank Oliver, M.P. for Alberta, and a few more of the
Independent, save the mark, members from the West, and they
assure him that all this rumpus about the people wanting

Territorial autonomy is absurd, and in any event he (Mr. Sifton) has need for a few more million acres of North-West lands, in fact for all there are left, and until he gets through with them, why the Territories can whistle for their autonomy. . . .

And Mr. Frank Oliver, M.P., the shining gentleman who was going to place the North-west before everything and who was sent to Ottawa with the assistance of more than one good Conservative vote (votes by the way which neither he nor his successor will ever get again) has reached the conclusion that the Territories are making money hand over fist by not being allowed provincial rights. 'Just hold on,' he says, 'what's your hurry; you've only got a population of 300,000 at present, wait until you've 300,000,000 and then think of what a magnificent per capita grant you'll get, and besides, how the dickens are we going to build the Grand Trunk Pacific which you know is going to be such a boon and a blessing to you Northwesterners, if we can't sell your millions of acres of lands, why the thing's absurd. What do you want provincial autonomy for anyway? You're not fit to run yourselves, let alone your country. Well: and what if I did want provincial autonomy myself. That was years ago, and—er—I wasn't an independent member from the West in those days.'

These, of course, are not Mr. Oliver's words but they amount to the same thing.

To cut a long story short, it seems we can make up our minds to one thing and that is that the Liberal government has definitely decided to keep these Territories tied to its apron strings until further orders. Its reasons for this must be apparent to any reasonable man. It wants our lands, it wants our forests, our minerals and our coal, and last but not least, the patronage that is part and parcel of this country. Compare this with the policy of the Conservative party. Why provincial autonomy for the North-west is one of the planks of their platforms. Can any North-wester hesitate as to how he shall lean? Surely no one of any independence can. We are entitled to run our own affairs and we are eminently capable of doing it, and it is up to all of us throughout the length and breadth of this North-west to bring home to the Liberal party the fact that their greediness has obscured their political perspicuity and that the North-west goose has laid all the golden eggs she intends to, or very nearly so. . . .

IV — 27

**'The Stigma of Inferiority,' Edmonton Journal,
December 2, 1903.**

Provincial organization means increased provincial responsibility, states the present Dominion member for Alberta, and
he would have the citizens of the North-west remain in leading
strings until the parties at Ottawa are prepared to grant the
Territories such sufficiently generous financial arrangements
that as previous they may not go into debt or sell lands. Unless
the citizens of the North-west demand that justice be done them
now, they will be compelled year after year to go begging to the
Ottawa Government for loans on capital account to carry out
improvements that are absolutely necessary for the development
of the country—and why, it may be asked, should we beg and
borrow of those who owe us—who are in duty bound to give us
control of the estate which we inherit when we come of age.
Politically speaking, surely we are of age—are old enough to
demand that what is ours be given to us to use and to enjoy.

Sorry indeed is the spectacle of the bearded man who begs a
remittance of his father, and sorrier still the spectacle of the
father who declares that his bearded son is not of age and refuses
to give him control of the estate left him by his grand-parent
and who having unfairly alienated part of his son's estate
calmly proposes to dispose of the remainder and put the
proceeds into his own pocket. Figuratively speaking that is the
political spectacle which Mr. Oliver appears to want to keep on
exhibition indefinitely. Our political grand-parent, the Imperial
Government, has made our political parent, the Dominion
Government, trustee of our estate to administer in trust for us
and to deliver to us when we come of age.

Nobody proposes, nobody has ever proposed, that we should
change our present political status for a worse one. That would
not be 'Provincial Autonomy!' What is proposed is that we
shall be political remittance men no longer—That we shall be
admitted to the full status of Canadian citizenship. The stigma
of political inferiority has been attached to us too long.

IV — 28

**The Liberals and Autonomy, Edmonton Journal,
January 20, 1904.**

. . . This self-congratulating government have treated the

elected representatives of the great North-west with the utmost contempt, refused their requests for necessary means to build up the province, disregarded opinion of its legislative assembly, and egotistically, (we will not use a stronger word) presumed to use the whip hard over some 350,000 people inhabiting this part of Canada.

The Federal government refuses the draft bill submitted to it, by the vote of the elected representatives solely because Sir Wilfred [sic] Laurier and his colleagues do not consider it expedient at the present time to grant provincial autonomy to these territories. Let our readers note specially the decision arrived at; the actual words are 'it will not be wise.' Decidedly not! emphatically not! The test of wisdom in the opinion of some individuals is self interest; The Laurier government, and Mr. Sifton especially, have amply proved the wisdom of their decision; for if the government were to surrender control of these Territories what power would it possess to fill up the lucrative offices held by their nominees for the last half decade? where else would lands be available for financing their pet schemes of railroads, canals, and every other desirable undertaking in which their friends and supporters might be involved? The country is not yet very populous! It's nobody's business to interfere! Its legislative assembly may deliberate and forward resolutions, but their decisions are valueless, and the numbers returned to the Federal parliament are of no importance individually, and numerically not worthy of consideration. If we permit these people in the North-west to get any more power over their own property, they will be increasing their population too rapidly, and will prove too energetic; for they are the men who had the strength of will to open up this almost unknown Territory, and the advancement already made proves their capacity for self government. . . .

Why should a country containing such a large population be held in leading strings by one or two men, even if they be Sir Wilfred [sic] Laurier and Mr. Sifton, Liberals and Conservatives alike voted in the legislative assembly for provincial autonomy. Mr. Oliver in the Federal house opposed the collective decision of this assembly, for some reason which is unknown to anyone but himself. These are facts for every elector to consider. The electors of the North-west remember that when casting their votes, they are not voting for a party or an individual, but for political freedom, for the power of governing themselves, of controlling their own finances, their own lands, and their own interests.

IV — 29

'The Old Old Story,' Calgary Herald, March 21, 1904.

The conduct of the administration at Ottawa is quite sufficient to raise another rebellion in the North-west Territories. This time, however, it will not be carried on by a few poorly organized half breeds, but by the stalwart and honest inhabitants of the country, incensed at the way they have been and are being treated.

The latest thing to dangle before the people is the report for last year of the department of the Interior, which administers our lands and retains the proceeds. In this report it is stated with a flourish of trumpets that during the year the proceeds of sales and other revenues from Dominion lands reached in the gross the very large sum of $2,418,351.84. This of course includes Manitoba and probably British Columbia, but as everyone knows, the revenue from lands in these two provinces forms a very small portion of the above total. In the number of statements in the report it is difficult to ascertain what were the expenses. It is, however, stated 'that the total average cost, including expenditure in caring for and location settlers in the whole of Canada, was $5.02 per head.' and that the 'total number of immigrants reported to have declared their intention of settling in all Canada was 128,364.'

Assuming these figures are correct, and adding a reasonable sum, if not already included in the per capita cost, for departmental expenses at Ottawa, there would appear to have gone last year into the Dominion cash box over a million dollars, as a low estimate, the proceeds of revenue from lands in the Territories. Premier Haultain asked for $250,000 and Hon. Mr. Sifton and his friends refused it, but cooly asked him to take it as an advance.

A more exasperating situation can hardly be imagined. The North-west government demanded a reasonable sum to assist in the development of the Territories, in improving our roads and in building bridges to facilitate communications between settlers and their means of reaching the market place. The Dominion having over a million dollars of our money in its hands declined to give one cent and this is the way we are treated.

The other provinces in the Dominion administer their lands and sell them, using the proceeds for the benefit of the people of their respective provinces, yet the North-west people are not only denied this, but branded as people incapable of governing themselves. This is the way the Liberal party treats us.

IV — 30

Haultain to Laurier, May 19, 1904: Territorial Sessional Paper No. 9, 1904.

SIR,—In the course of the correspondence which I had with you last year on the subject of the creation of a Province in the Territories, you informed me that on account of the delay in the formation of a Province the Territories were enabled to secure larger representation in the House of Commons. While not agreeing with the arguments which you advanced on this question, but still believing that the most important question for the Territories is the obtaining of full Provincial powers, I would like to point out to you that if the larger representation in the Commons is to be regarded as a set-off to our demand for Provincial powers we have not received that representation under the new Redistribution Act to which we are entitled. Your letter pointed out that by the postponement of the Provincial question you were able to deal with the question of Territorial representation apart from the terms of The British North America Act, which in the event of the establishment of the Province would apply. I would therefore call your attention to the fact that according to the figures given by the Department of the Interior our population at present is about 450,000, and that on the present basis of representation we are entitled to eighteen members instead of the ten given us under the Redistribution Act. This representation of ten, which is at the present time far below what we are actually entitled to on population, will, long before the first Parliament elected under the new Act has come to an end, be still more inadequate. I would therefore ask you to consider the question of amending the Redistribution Act before the next General Elections, and of granting to the Territories at least the representation which they are actually entitled to at the present time, if not a representation based upon a reasonable expectation of increased population between now and next Dominion census. If we were a Province at the present time we would be entitled to the representation which I am asking for.

IV — 31

Haultain to Laurier, June 1, 1904: Canada Sessional Paper 53, 1905.

SIR,—On several occasions since the Second Day of May, 1900, I have had the honour to direct the attention of the Dominion Government, both through yourself and the Minister of the Interior, to the Memorial of the Legislative Assembly of the Territories, adopted on that date, asking that preliminary steps should be taken towards the creation of Provincial Institutions in that portion of the Dominion. You will, I have no doubt, recall the conference held in the fall of 1901 by a sub-committee of the Privy Council, of which you were a member, with my then colleague, Mr. A.L. Sifton, and myself on behalf of the Territorial Government; and you will also be familiar with the extended statement setting forth our views and crystallising them, as it were, in the form of a draft Bill, submitted by myself on December 7, 1901, at your request. I presume you are also acquainted with the nature of the communication sent to me by the Hon. the Minister of the Interior in March, 1902, in which it was intimated that the conditions with respect to population and alleged divergence of opinion in the Territories upon details of the question were sufficient reasons, in the opinion of the Dominion Government, for not discussing our representations. As the correspondence has been laid before Parliament I assume that you are aware in January, 1903, I addressed a communication to the Hon. Mr. Sifton in which I took occasion to point out that in May, 1902, I submitted the issue to the people of the Territories, with the result that, without exception, every member of the Legislative Assembly supports the contentions of this Government upon the question of the urgency of carrying on the negotiations and taking accounts looking toward the establishment of the Territories upon the Provincial basis, no matter what their views upon other subjects may be. This statement is based, amongst other reasons, upon the fact that even as late as the Twentieth day of November last the members of the Assembly unanimously adopted a resolution to present an humble Address to His Excellency the Governor in Council reaffirming the statements and renewing the prayers upon the subject of the Provincial establishment contained in their Addresses to His Excellency, of the Second day of May, 1900, and the Twenty-fourth day of April, 1903.

To all these addresses and supplementary correspondence the only replies we have been favoured with from the Dominion Government have been the letter, referred to above, from the Hon. the Minister of the Interior, dated on March 27, 1902, and another from yourself dated on June 8, 1903. I deem it necessary in this connection to impress this fact upon you, namely, that the Members of the Legislative Assembly are closely in touch with the people of this country, and they, one and all, have repeatedly expressed opinions entirely contrary to those which have apparently determined your action on this question. Further—and I make this statement advisedly—of the 35 members of the Assembly one-half are well known to be in active sympathy with yourself and your Government, and these gentlemen are in full accord with the other members of the House upon this subject. I might also refer to the fact that some, at least, of the political conventions at present being held in the Territories for the selection of candidates representing your party, and which are being largely guided by members of our Legislature, are adopting resolutions calling upon your Government to take up the question of our Provincial establishment and carry it to a satisfactory conclusion. I think it becoming to mention these matters at this time, as it seems to me that they are in themselves evidence that the advice tendered to you by some of your supporters in Parliament from the Territories has not been in accord with the desires of the people as they are giving expression to them.

I need not urge you to deal with this matter upon other grounds for I have already done so as fully as I am able to do, and it only remains for me, on behalf of the Government of the Territories, to give point to the representations of the Legislative Assembly by demanding with all respect, that your Government will take up the negotiations at the point where they were carried to by my letter of December 7, 1901, and continue them until the matters involved are settled. In doing so I have to say that we request that, at the earliest possible date after the conclusion of the negotiation and settlement of the accounts between the Dominion and the Territories, legislation be introduced into Parliament organising upon the Provincial basis that portion of the North-west Territories lying between the western boundary of Manitoba and the eastern slope of the Rocky Mountains, and extending northward from the International boundary and the Northern boundary of Manitoba as far into the district of Athabasca as may be decided upon. We further ask that, whatever else it includes, the legislation introduced shall contain provision for—

(1) The application of The British North America Act as far as possible to the area dealt with;

(2) Adequate representation in both Houses of Parliament, bearing in mind the difference in the ratio of increase in the population in the Territories from that of the longer settled parts of the Dominion;

(3) Government, Legislature, and the administration of Justice;

(4) The preservation of vested rights;

(5) The transfer of the public domain with all Territorial rights and the beneficial interest therein involved;

(6) A subsidy based as nearly as may be upon those given to the Provinces;

(7) Remuneration for that part of the public domain alienated by the Dominion for purely Federal purposes; and

(8) The placing of the burden of the Canadian Pacific exemption upon the Dominion, where it properly belongs.

In conclusion, I beg to be permitted to state that all these matters have been repeatedly brought to the notice of your Government, and I trust they will now receive some consideration at your hands.

IV — 32

Haultain interviewed on the chances for autonomy:
Calgary Herald, June 18, 1904.

Winnipeg, June 18.—Premier Haultain was here yesterday en route home after two months spent at Ottawa. 'I have been nearly two months in the east on Territorial business, the two chief matters of interest being autonomy and appropriations for the Regina government,' he said.

'Will the Territories get autonomy soon?' he was asked.

'I do not believe we will get self government during this session of parliament. The government, I believe, can put any issue through the house now if it wishes, but I feel that autonomy will not be given us just now.'

'Outside of parliamentary circles however, the feeling for autonomy for the Territories is strengthening steadily. The business men and people generally are coming to an appreciation of our right to autonomy as they learn more about the West, the vast expansion of business out here and the rapid peopling and settlement of the country.'

'Does your government contemplate any radical action, any more than you have already carried out in order to aid the question of autonomy?'

'Well, really, I don't see what more we can do. We have already petitioned through our legislature-four times to the Dominion parliament for a petition from the people of the Territories. Of course every day that passes brings added strength to this issue, even among ourselves in the Territories.'

Haultain's comment that 'every day that passes brings added strength to the issue' was a perceptive one. The Laurier govern-ment could not continue to ignore the sentiment that had developed in the Territories without risking political disaster. By 1904 the Laurier government had been in office for eight years and various tactical reasons made an appeal to the electorate desirable late in that year. However, to have gone to the public of the North West while opposing provincial autonomy would have been to risk the seats at stake there. Moreover, there were now ten federal seats in the region and it was thus perhaps inevitable that as the federal election approached, the Laurier government ceded the principle of provincial autonomy. The period of political manoeuvring had not ended but the period of waiting for a decision had.

IV — 33

Walter Scott to Clifford Sifton, September 1, 1904:
Provincial Archives of Saskatchewan (Saskatoon), Walter Scott Papers, #4632.

The North-west Assembly has been called to meet 22nd Sept. You will remember that I suggested that an official reply should be sent to Haultain's former letter to Sir Wilfrid and that it should contain the definite statement that your Govern-ment is prepared to enter immediately into the taking of accounts and negotiations asked for by the North-west Govt. with the purpose of arriving at the terms upon which the Territories will be admitted into Confederation as a province or provinces.

In view of the early meeting of the Assembly Bulyea considers it highly important that such letter shall be forwarded to them as soon as possible. He thinks that such a statement from the Ottawa Government, together with the generous amount of grant voted at the recent session, will put things into such position as will enable the session here to be carried through without the threatened split, and considering everything I think this is a consummation devoutly to be wished.

IV — 34

Laurier to Haultain, September 30, 1904: Canada Sessional Paper 53, 1905.

DEAR SIR,—My attention has been called to the fact that there has been no reply sent to your letters of the 19th May and June 1, respectively. In regard to the subject raised in the letter of May 19, permit me to say that I do not think that I, upon any occasion, indicated an opinion that larger representation in the House of Commons was to be regarded as a set off to the demands of the North-west Territories for provincial powers. I merely pointed out that the action of my Government in declining to introduce legislation to constitute the North-west Territories into a province at a time when your Government requested it had resulted in an increased number of representatives being granted to the North-west Territories in the House of Commons. Had the request for provincial autonomy been granted when it was made, the representation would necessarily have been governed by the British North America Act, and you would now be entitled to six members, which number could not have been increased until the decennial readjustment of representation. By reason of the fact that the North-west Territories still remain without provincial autonomy we have been able to deal more liberally in that respect. It was not suggested that the Territories were entitled to call for an annual readjustment of their representation on the basis of population, nor do I think that any precedent can be found in constitutional practice for such a suggestion. The number of members granted in the last Redistribution Act was based upon a somewhat liberal computation of the population as presumed to exist at the time when the Act was introduced. The question as to what should be the representation of the Territories when they are constituted as a province or provinces is one which will call for renewed consideration when the question of provincial autonomy is dealt with.

In reference to your letter of the 1st of June, I do not think I need discuss at length the representations which it contains, further than to intimate my opinion that circumstances have justified the wisdom of the course adopted by the Government in declining to deal finally two years ago with the many important questions involved in the admission of the North-west Territories into confederation as a province or provinces. Rapid development has taken place in the North-west Territories during the intervening period, and I am inclined to the view that all those who will be called upon to give consideration to the subject will be in a position to deal with it in the near future with the advantage of fuller and more comprehensive information than could possibly have been available two years ago.

You will have learned prior to the receipt of this letter that Parliament has been dissolved. The new House of Commons will contain not four but ten representatives of the North-west Territories, who, coming fresh from the people, will be entitled to speak with confidence as to the views and requirements of those whom they represent. Should my Government be sustained, we will be prepared immediately after the election to enter upon negotiations for the purpose of arriving at a settlement of the various questions involved in the granting of provincial autonomy, with a view to dealing with the question at the next session of Parliament.

IV — 35

Haultain to Laurier, October 5, 1904: Canada Sessional Paper 53, 1905.

I have the honour to acknowledge receipt of your letter of the 30th ultimo, in which you inform me that your attention has been called to the fact that there had been no reply sent to my letters of May 19 and June 1, that Parliament had been dissolved, and that if your Government is sustained you will be prepared, immediately after the election, to enter upon negotiations for the purpose of arriving at a settlement of the various questions involved in the granting of provincial autonomy with a view to dealing with the question at the next session of Parliament.

Section V
The Controversy Over the Terms, 1904-1905

The months from October 1904 through to July of 1905 were by far the most significant and the most complex in the formation of the Province of Alberta. A federal election campaign, the drafting of the bills, the resignation of a senior Minister, the longest parliamentary debate in Canadian history all took place in this period. Laurier's acceptance of the principle of provincial autonomy transformed and enlarged the political controversy surrounding the question of the future of the West. Easterners became passionately involved in the issue, though often not in the way the West would have liked, and Westerners took their campaign east. In the end, it is tempting to conclude, nobody was completely satisfied. Practically all the major figures, Laurier, Haultain, Sifton—were forced to accept positions and solutions they would have preferred to avoid. In the end, nevertheless, the Provinces of Alberta and Saskatchewan were created.

Laurier's promise of September 1904 was, as many in the West, pointed out, rather vague in details and in the federal election of that year many Conservatives, including Haultain, warned the Territories of the political nature of the promise. Such warnings, however, did not have a great deal of effect. In the nation as a whole the Laurier government easily won re-election and even in a North-west that had some reason to be suspicious the Liberals won seven of the ten seats at stake. The Liberal victory was followed, as Laurier had promised, with movement toward provincial status. By the end of the year procedures were underway to create new provinces in the North-West and a Territorial delegation was once again in Ottawa to discuss the question with their Federal counterparts.

V — 1

'Political Trickery,' Calgary Herald, October 10, 1904.

The letter sent Mr. Haultain by Sir Wilfrid Laurier within the past few days, is a most palpable political trick. For the past four years the Legislative Assembly of these Territories has at each recurring session dealt with the rights of the Territories to provincial autonomy, and many resolutions and memorials have been forwarded to Ottawa. . . .

To these important communications addressed by the Premier of the Territories to the Premier of the Dominion not even the courtesy of an acknowledgement is vouchsafed until the Dominion elections are called, when Sir Wilfrid Laurier writes saying that his 'attention has been called' to the fact that no reply has been sent.

It is quite easy to understand where the letter or telegram 'calling his attention' came from. The pure political trickery of the transaction is also apparent. The Liberal party in the West realized fully that the failure on the part of the Dominion Government to pay any attention to the question which had repeatedly been brought to their notice by the Legislative Assembly as the vital issue in the West was going to have a marked effect on the Dominion campaign, and at this late hour 'called attention' to the necessity for at least an acknowledgement of the important communications relating thereto. . . .

On a previous occasion when political exigencies required some attention being given to the demands of the people of the West, the Liberal Government invited the Legislative Assembly to send delegates to Ottawa to consider this matter.

The delegates went but, the moment the political situation cleared, the Ottawa government contented themselves with sending a curt letter through the Minister of the Interior saying they were not ready to deal with the matter.

The present action on the part of Sir Wilfrid Laurier has too much of the appearance of a second 'gold brick' transaction to be swallowed by the people of the West. It certainly does not display any of the earmarks of statesmanship with which his followers are ever ready to credit Sir Wilfrid Laurier.

V — 2

Haultain supports Conservative candidates in the 1904 election: Edmonton Journal, October 14, 1904.

Premier Haultain, in speaking to the *Telegram*, said that Sir Wilfrid's letter made autonomy more of an issue than ever, and made one more reason why Conservative candidates should be elected. Incidentally, it cut the ground from under the feet of the Liberal candidates.

On the one hand, he said, we have the definite distinct policy of the Conservative party, declared by Mr. Borden, who urges the immediate granting of full provincial rights. On the other, we have the tardy, indefinite, avowedly accidental remark made by Sir Wilfrid on the eve of an election. He only promises to open negotiations. Negotiations were opened long ago—and then stopped.

Sir Wilfrid, however, says that he expects the Territorial members to go to Ottawa and tell them there what the people here want. The Liberal members have been taking a position which is not what the people here want, and to send them would be to mislead the parliament at Ottawa. In this connection Mr. Haultain said:

'Sir Wilfrid's letter completely satisfies his government and his Western supporters, all of whom, for the past year and a half and up to the very last moment, have been practically arguing against the immediate necessity for autonomy and declaring that, so far as the pending Dominion elections are concerned, it is a dead issue.

Sir Wilfrid's letter intimates that he expects the ten Territorial members of parliament to go to Ottawa fully informed on the views of their constituents upon this question.'

V — 3

'Terms of Autonomy,' The Calgary Herald, November 29, 1904.

The Dominion government has notified Premier Haultain that the cabinet will be prepared to begin negotiations looking to the ultimate and early establishment of provincial establishment the first week in January. A delegation is invited to visit Ottawa at the time for the purpose of arranging details.

This is glad news to the people of the west. Because of the failure in the past to obtain home rule for the Territories there was a serious disposition to question the good faith of ante-election pledges. Now that the practical details are to be disposed of, there is satisfaction throughout the country between Manitoba and the mountains.

Now the chief concern of the people is the terms of admission—the public lands. No question is settled until settled right. Therefore the citizens of the Territories will be satisfied with nothing less than the assumption that the resources of the country belong to the new province. If this broad aspect of the subject appeals to the Dominion authorities as strongly as to the west, the minor details will not prove obstacles to an early agreement.

The school question, the division of the Territories into one or more provinces or the slicing off of the eastern section and attaching it to Manitoba will all follow as a matter of ordinary details.

It is therefore a matter of first concern that the delegates at the conference representing the Territories have this point established in the primary stage of negotiations.

V — 4

Calgary Herald Returns to the Two Province Position, December 1, 1904.

The local Liberal organ displays some surprise over the position of the Herald in favor of two provinces being carved out of the Territories. The paper mentions the editorial reference of the Herald as if it were something new.

As a matter of fact the Herald has steadily advocated the organization of two provinces. Ten years ago the management thought events forecasted the necessity for this division of the North-west. Frequently since then the present management has constantly emphasized this view. In the light of developments the Herald's idea appears to have been vindicated.

Two provinces today are absolutely imperative. That the division will be by a north and south line rather than an east and west may be expected because it has been the policy in the past to give each province a slice of the boundary line.

If the east and west line were drawn it would leave a province to the north with no direct outlet. This, however, cannot be regarded as a matter of as much [sic] serious consequences as the necessity to make a division that will put those sections of identical interests together.

For instance, there is a vast region lying west of Swift Current and east of the mountains where the agricultural conditions are similar, for five hundred miles north of the state line. It would seem to be the rational thing to keep this section in one provincial division. Even with these two divisions there will remain two provinces of greater extent than even Ontario, and, in addition, all of the western provinces will be capable of settlement, whereas much of Ontario is barren.

These considerations will probably dictate the policy that will determine the fate of these Territories. It is quite likely that the government will consult some of the pioneers of the west— men of progress and thought in the west on the utility of the geographical lines before a fixed policy is outlined.

V — 5

The Medicine Hat News Comments on the Various Possible Provincial Alignments: Cited in Edmonton Journal, December 6, 1904.

The arrangements under which provincial autonomy will be granted are what most interests Westerners. It is a question of terms. We don't think the West would consider for one moment the portioning off of a piece of the Northwest to Manitoba which has been intimated in the Globe and in the Winnipeg Telegram. This is one feature of the business on which the Westerners should stand pat. In the West we do not know our own minds on the question of one or more provinces. Premier Haultain's idea of one large province comprising the districts of Assiniboia, Saskatchewan and Alberta does not meet with favor at Prince Albert or Edmonton where they desire separate provinces and separate capitals. It looks as if a great deal of district selfishness would enter into the question and possibly balk the granting of autonomy. As was quite proper when Mr. Haultain made his former representations to Ottawa, he went to the extreme limit of asking for everything which he considered due to the West. Probably the Dominion Government will not see eye to eye with him in all the details. Probably they will have something different to suggest. At any rate, the people of the West look with interest to the conference and hope that the outcome will be satisfactory to us for it is true that our whole future more or less depends upon the terms upon which we enter confederation as a province.

V — 6

Haultain and Bulyea Reach Ottawa to Discuss Terms: Calgary Herald, January 11, 1905.

Ottawa, Jan. 11,—Premier Haultain and Hon. Mr. Bulyea of the Territorial Government are here discussing with Sir Wilfrid Laurier the question of autonomy for the North-west Territories. They began their conference with the First Minister on Tuesday. Mr. Bulyea, who is the Commissioner of Public Works for the Territories, said this evening: 'Our proposition is before the Government, and has been for some time. We ask for the creation of the Territories into a Province, and a subsidy of 90 cents per head of the population, the same as the other provinces. We also desire to secure Dominion lands, so that we may be able to augment our revenue. Any arrangement which might now be made would not, of course, be permanent. Our present population is about 400,000. Five years from now it may be double that number, when a readjustment would be necessary, or great injustice would result. We have no school question on our hands, and do not expect any. Protestant and Catholic teachers qualify before they teach in the public or separate schools. In some instances where the ladies of religious orders desire to give instruction, they have qualified at the normal school. We desire a much larger revenue than we are now in receipt of , and it should be given without delay. The country is vast in extent, and the people are passing in. To meet the necessities of the settlers, roads and bridges, and other works, need to be constructed. If Government should decide there must be two Provinces, that is their affair, but as I have already said, we are asking for one. I should be sorry to see the North-west Mounted Police go when provincial autonomy is granted. They are a federal force, maintained by the Dominion, but their presence would still be necessary for the enforcement of law and order, and the prevention of crime. . . .'

Bulyea's comment that there was no school question referred to one of the most sensitive questions facing the Laurier government in creating the new Provinces. In 1875 the Dominion government had created a dual school system in the North-west. Gradually, thereafter, the Territorial governments had tended to work toward a common 'national' school system. Separate schools had not been abolished but they were subject to a high degree of government control and the feeling was general both in the West and the East that, if left on their own, the new Provinces would eventually unify the school system totally. Laurier was under great pressure to ensure not only that this would not happen but also to strengthen the separate school structure in existence in the West. It is unlikely that Bulyea was aware that even as he spoke Laurier and his Minister of Justice, Charles Fitzpatrick, were in discussion with papal delegate Archbishop Sbaretti and had pledged themselves to a series of education clauses that would, in fact, make the school question a very real problem indeed.

V — 7

The Toronto News on Autonomy and Schools: Cited in Calgary Herald, May 20, 1903.

Why are the Territories so persistently kept in leading strings? The apprehension of trouble over language and education is the main reason. Manitoba has a provincial autonomy, and she swept away the French language and the separate schools. In the Territories both are presented by virtue of Dominion enactment. The law legalizes the use of French in the Legislature and courts, and directs that the records and journals of the Assembly all be printed in both languages. The fate of this provision under autonomy may be guessed from the fact that it is already virtually a dead letter. It has been quietly disregarded, and French is heard neither in law courts nor in the Assembly. The official papers are printed in English only. As for schools, the North-west Territories Act of 1886 provides that the school established by the majority of rate-payers in a district shall be styled the public school, and that the minority may establish a school which, whether Protestant or Catholic, shall be the separate school. The majority of the public schools are Protestant, but the Protestant separate schools are not denominational, and are subject to exactly the same regulations as the public schools. The Roman Catholics are represented in the educational Council. The school ordinances provide for the teaching of a primary course in French. This so far has proved a workable arrangement. But in what spirit will the West meet a demand for a guarantee or a compact such as that which renders separate schools obligatory in Ontario. That is the difficulty ahead.

V — 8

Archbishop Sbaretti to Laurier, March 1, 1904: Laurier Papers, 82981.

Yesterday the Hon. Mr. R.W. Scott Secretary of State came to see me and declared that you, as Chief of the Government and the Liberal Party, had promised that in the event of the erection of the North-west Territories into Provinces a Clause in the Constitutional Act of these Provinces would be inserted, guaranteeing the Catholics the system of separate Schools. I have given to this very important question my most serious and earnest consideration, in order to defend with all the zeal and energy the sacred rights of Catholics to have their own separate schools, as I am bound, following the dictates of my conscience, to do for all Catholics, whose sacred rights are entrusted to me, as the representative of the Holy See, in this country.

Now as I have to report to my superiors in Rome about the prospects of solution of this question, it would be certainly gratifying if the declarations made and the assurances given by the Hon. Secretary of State would be communicated in a document signed by you as Chief of the Government and Leader of the Liberal Party, for the purpose that I might communicate it to Rome, and so allay any uneasiness that may be felt about this matter.

V — 9

Laurier to Sbaretti, March 7, 1904: Laurier Papers, 82982.

For the reasons which I have already explained I again beg to express my regrets that I could not ere this, answer your letter of the 1st instant.

The views which I hold as to the status which ought to be extended to the minority in the North-west Territories in matters of education, when those territories at a very early date, are admitted into the Confederation with the full rights of a province, cannot be a matter of doubt; they are based upon the letter and the spirit of the constitution under which the Canadian Confederation was brought into existence.

The Constitution provides in explicit and positive terms, that in any province where a system of separate schools exists, the Legislature shall not have the power to do anything which may prejudicially affect those schools. This disposition is embodied in section 93 of the Act. The effect of this section was to guarantee to the minority an absolute right to the separate schools which were in existence at the time Confederation was established, and to take away from the legislature the power to abolish those schools, or even to, in any way, impair their efficiency.

The reasons which induced the framers of the Act of Confederation to introduce this safeguard on behalf of the minority in every province where a system of separate schools existed, apply with equal force for the benefit of the minority in any new province that may be formed, if therein the minority is similarly situated.

Such is the condition of the minority of the North-west Territories. When these Territories in 1875 were organized and endowed with the first rudiments of a civilized administration, the system of separate schools existing in some of the other provinces, was therein introduced by positive enactment of the law. The system has grown up, keeping pace with the development of the territories. Hundreds of schools have been established under that system by the new settlers who professed the religious faith of the minority. These new fellow citizens have the same right to the guarantee of their schools under the constitution, as the inhabitants of the older provinces where the same system existed, when Confederation was created.

My opinion is very clear, that when the territories are admitted as a province, the minority should not be placed in a worse condition than it is today; that its schools ought to receive the same degree of protection as is granted to the minority in Ontario and Quebec where separate schools existed at the first establishment of Confederation, and that the act of admission of the territories into confederation should especially provide that the system of separate schools now in existence shall be secured and beyond the power of the provincial legislature as provided by section 93 of the Constitution, either to abolish or even prejudicially affect such schools.

V — 10

Sbaretti to Laurier, December 30, 1904: Laurier Papers, 93069.

I would be very grateful to you, if the Draft of the Bill for the admission of the Territories as a Province of the Dominion, would be given me at least by the 1st of January, as it is your expectation expressed in your kind letter of the 24th inst. But in any case, I would be very much obliged to you, if you could send me at once the special clause formulated concerning education, especially the right of the minority to separate schools.

V — 11

Laurier to Sbaretti, December 31, 1904: Laurier Papers, 93070.

I have the honour to acknowledge the receipt of your favour

of yesterday. I am sorry to have to inform you that the Department of Justice have not yet fully settled the dispositions about Education in the North-west Bill. Dr. Fitzpatrick tells me that he hopes to have it ready at a very early day and I shall then make it my duty to call on Your Excellency or to ask Mr. Fitzpatrick to do so.

V — 12

Sbaretti to Laurier, February 11, 1905: Laurier Papers, 94671.

I have given consideration to the draft of the section regarding separate schools, which you kindly handed me yesterday and which it is proposed to insert in the Constitutional Act of the new Province or Provinces to be erected in the North-west Territories. I am glad to say that we have succeeded in agreeing upon a clause directed to preserve the rights of the minority. I have no doubt that those rights will always be safeguarded.

In the weeks when the Autonomy bills were being drafted one of the most important figures involved in the question was absent from Ottawa. Clifford Sifton was unwell and had been resting in the United States throughout much of this crucial period. Laurier was, however, in regular correspondence with his Minister of the Interior and, as the following letters indicate, relied on him for advice on most matters. There was, of course, one major exception. Laurier was probably well aware that Sifton would have disagreed with the proposals that were taking shape for the future of education in the North-west. The vagueness of Laurier on the schools question differs sharply from the close and detailed consultation on questions of land. If Laurier hoped that by leaving Sifton uninformed as to the direction of the Schools clause, he could avoid trouble then he made a serious mistake.

The nature of Laurier's consultation with Sifton, Walter Scott, and James Ross on the one hand and with Sbaretti and Fitzpatrick on the other raise an interesting question. Just how relevant were the discussions between the Territorial delegation and the Dominion Government? No completely accurate answer can be given to this, of course, but given Haultain's later reaction the impression is left that, as the Premier of the Territories had warned years before, the federal government could do what it wanted in the matter of Provincial status. It was not a discussion between equals and, in fact, one wonders how much of a meaningful discussion it was at all.

V — 13

Clifford Sifton to Laurier, January 22, 1905: Laurier Papers, 93969-73.

I received your letter today and was glad to know that everything is going so well, also that you are making such rapid progress with the North-west bills.

As to the public land [word illegible] do not yield. The proposition to give them the grazing lands originally came from some remarks of my own but I think it is unpracticable. It would be found absolutely impossible to say what were and what were not to be regarded as grazing lands. As to the other lands, giving them to the Provinces would be ruinous to our settlement policy and would be disastrous to the whole Dominion. The mere report that our lands had been handed over and that there might be a change in the policy of administering them would cost us tens of thousands of settlers in the next two years to say nothing of the more distant future. The continued progress of Canada for the next five years depends almost entirely on the flow of immigration.

As to names my idea is that Alberta must be retained for the Western Province. As to the Eastern Province I prefer Assiniboia but if Saskatchewan is thought better I do not think it matters much, both are names identified with the history of the territories.

As to irrigation—I had made up my mind to recommend that the power be retained by the Dominion. It is in many ways undesirable to do so but the balance of desirability seems in favor of retaining the powers at Ottawa. In regard to every stream of importance inter-provincial questions will arise and in regard to some, international questions will arise. The idea of Bulyea and Haultain that theoretical objections will disappear in practice is not borne out by experience; experience generally demonstrates that not only objections that are foreseen but many others arise in working out such problems. By retaining the plenary power at Ottawa you [word illegible] the fact that a central body which for its own interest is bound to try to do justice to all parties will be able to adjust difficulties as they arise. In the case of the Provinces there would be no way of dissolving a deadlock should one arise.

You do not say anything about the school question and I assume that you have not as yet discovered any serious difficulty in dealing with it.

V — 14

Laurier to Sifton, January 26, 1905: Laurier Papers, 93974-6.

I received your letter in answer to mine, yesterday. I now see my way clear to the two points as to which I wanted your advice: the grazing lands and irrigation. I will have the bill drafted so as to leave the control of irrigation in our hands, and treat the grazing lands as all others.

Yesterday afternoon, I had an interview with Ross and Walter Scott, on the subject of lands. Ross gave me some opinions which I asked him to put in writing for communication with you. I enclose his letter just received. The first part refers to the grazing lands, and can be dismissed without observation. The second part refers to lands generally and it expresses a new idea which, I must admit, has struck me favourably.

The difficulty that we have at present in arranging the financial terms, is as to the amount which we must provide for the maintenance of the new Provincial Governments. At present we pay to the Province of Ontario, eighty cents per head of population, based on the census of 1861, which was about 1,300,000 souls. We pay about the same thing to the Province of Quebec. I enclose a statement as to the amounts paid to the different Provinces for their annual subsidies. All the Provinces, with the exception of Manitoba, have retained their lands and they have found in them a valuable source of assets. You know better than anybody, how Manitoba has always felt aggrieved at not having had the disposal of her own lands. The compensation that has been given to the Province, from time to time, in the way of better terms, has not completely removed the grievance. The opinion of Ross is that we should hold all lands as a trust, keeping the administration in our own hands and handing over the proceeds annually to the Province. He attaches a great importance to this view, politically. It would give to our friends the satisfaction which the people of Manitoba never had and it would sufficiently safeguard our interests, in the view of immigration. We might, perhaps, put some charge upon the trust so created. As I told you above, I am favourably disposed towards that view, but I will be guided altogether by your own judgement. Think of it and let me know at your earliest convenience. We will not make as rapid headway as I thought when I wrote you last. We are now stuck upon this question and I will not dispose of it until I hear from you.

There also remains the school question which I am slowly working out. I am satisfied with the progress which we have made on it, though everybody dreads it.

V — 15

Sifton to Laurier, February 1, 1905: Laurier Papers, 94354-61.

I am here to meet Mrs. Sifton who arrives tomorrow and I am improving the time by answering your letter. I received it yesterday morning but delayed replying in order to see if a little further reflection would alter my opinion. Further reflection however has confirmed it.

The point you ask my opinion on is as to the creating of a trust as suggested by Ross. I am entirely against it. My reasons are—

1st. It involves setting up a fiction in place of a fact. i.e. it involves an admission that the new Provinces were or ought to be constitutionally owners of the land. This is wholly untrue. The original provinces owned the crown lands. The Dominion owns these lands & decides now to erect provinces—It is for the Dom. to say upon what terms. You may give or withhold what you *now* own, you may give or withhold money but to crystallize an assumption that the Provinces are owners & entitled to the rights of a *cestui qui trust* is to set up an elaborate & untenable fiction.

2nd. If you admit a trust you can never refuse the Provinces *all* the rights of a *cestui qui trust* i.e. the right to demand an account of everything from the beginning. You may seek to limit the admission now but the future will see the limitations broken down—You will lay the foundation for a pereanial [sic] agitation in these new provinces for *more*.

3rd. You cannot if you seek to make up an account now tell what to charge against the new provinces in the land account— Every item will be a subject of dispute and interminable argument.

4th. Just as soon as the Provinces get strong enough they will demand Readjustment of the account & get it.

I think the facts should be taken as they are—we should say to the Provinces [,] You have no lands & we cannot give them but we shall provide a liberal revenue in lieu of it.

1. The allowance for the government is fixed [.]

2. The per capita grant will increase with the population—I think it should be adjusted every 2½ years as was done with Manitoba.

3. I think the Debt. capital $32 per head should be based on 250,000 for each province and as a special consideration provision should be made for readjusting it on the increased population once at the end of five years & once at the end of ten years—This will be a great & valuable concession.

I think they should each have about $200,000 in lieu of lands per annum and I think they should each have about $50,000 per annum as compensation for assuming the administration of justice in the northern & unoccupied territory.

The addition of the northern territory to Manitoba should also be considered—& if it is done Manitoba should get about $50,000 a year to pay for cost of administration. Possibly however you wish to defer this. I still hold strongly to the opinion that all the northern territories should be annexed to the provinces lying to the south of them.

V — 16

'Control of Crown Lands,' Edmonton Journal, February 7, 1905.

Opinion in Edmonton has never been decidedly expressed for one or two provinces and there is no justification for the accusation made by western towns with other interests to serve that district selfishness with an eye to the capital location is the prime consideration that is moving the citizens of this city and of Northern Alberta to favor a longitudinal division of the North-west Territories and the erection of separate provincial governments. Our citizens know that the location of the capital could be of immense value in giving prestige to the city, but it is a poor honor to be the capital of a province without that natural wealth and extent which would promise a thriving vigorous self-governing community in the immediate future. If Edmonton is favorable to a division of the Territories it is so because there lies to the north of Alberta and Saskatchewan, territory of a vast extent, of magnificent possibilities, and of greatest resources, a country which can only be properly developed under the direction of the more settled districts to the south. Form one province comprising the districts of Assiniboia, Saskatchewan and Alberta and the whole country north is left to be opened up under federal direction. What this means is in evidence every day in the North-west, where settlement has been retarded by the indifference of the federal authorities. With what energy and success colonization effort will be carried on by the people whose burdens are to be made easy by the development of the wealth of the new regions under their control is seen in the case of Ontario. The wealth of new Ontario is staving off the day of direct taxation in Ontario and the forest and mineral resources of new Ontario would never have contributed to the prosperity of Old Ontario had this region been under federal control. The inclusion of Athabasca in the scheme of a self-governing province is vital to the prosperity of what is now styled the North-west. But the addition of this territory would create a provincial area out of all proportion to any of the existing ones. With the inclusion of the district of Athabasca there will certainly arise the necessity of a division of the North-west, and on the broad ground of the future prosperity and progressive government of the newly formed provincial divisions, the citizens of Northern Alberta favor two separate provinces.

V — 17

'Meddling with the West,' Calgary Herald, February 9, 1905.

Some of the Ontario newspapers are determined to thrust on the west a controversy of a more or less bitter character on the excuse that the public school system of the new provinces is threatened with destruction. Here is a sample of one 'telegram' from Calgary published in a Toronto paper, with a big display of black type, under a scare head entitled "Furious Turmoil Prophesied":

'Calgary, N.W.T. Jan. 31—(Special) It is firmly believed by politicians and citizens who know whereof they speak, that the Northwest Territories are on the eve of a furious turmoil. Should the autonomy legislation reaffirm the clause in the Northwest Territories Act guaranteeing separate schools to the minority, the turmoil will be precipitated, and the fiery cross will be carried through the length and breadth of the territories. The school question is the great issue in the territories. Men born and bred in old Ontario have taken up their abode here. They have brought Ontario ideas and ideals with them. The separate school question is to them like a red flag to an infuriated bullock. The bullock is easily enraged. Will the red flag drop.'

Well, isn't that the limit! Just what reason a sane person would have for talking about 'furious turmoil in the west' is not clear to us. 'The fiery cross' may be carried through the length and the breadth of the hair trigger brains of some eastern enthusiasts but that the virile, fair-minded people of the west can be dragged into such a controversy, or stampeded by the shout of people two thousand miles removed from Alberta, who are absolutely uninformed as to what are the true conditions existing here, is entirely unlikely.

On February 21 the long awaited Autonomy bills were presented to the House of Commons. This marked the beginning of a growing crisis in the government that would lead to Sifton's resignation and to Laurier's retreat on the education clauses. In this atmosphere attention in Parliament and in much of the eastern Canadian press focussed on the question of separate schools. As the following documents indicate, however, in the West there was much less concern with schools and much more with the land clauses and the boundaries of the new Provinces. The schools question was primarily an eastern controversy and only gradually would westerners pick up on a theme that many felt to be ridiculously overblown by the Ontario press while the real issues were being ignored.

V — 18

Laurier introduces the Alberta Bill, February 21, 1905: House of Commons Debates, February 21, 1905, 1421-1467.

Rt. Hon. Sir WILFRID LAURIER (Prime Minister) moved for leave to introduce Bill (No. 69) to establish and provide for the government of the province of Alberta. He said: Mr. Speaker, the Bill which I have now the honour to present is for the admission of another member into the Canadian family of provinces. As the house, no doubt, has noticed, this Bill is to be followed immediately by another for the same purpose, in relation to the province of Saskatchewan. These two Bills are intimately connected; they form part of the same subject; and, by your leave, Sir, the explanations which I shall have the honour to give to the House, will apply to both. They will apply likewise to the resolutions which will be introduced as the basis for the financial clauses of these Bills.

It has been observed on the floor of this House, as well as outside of this house, that as the nineteenth century had been the century of the United States, so the twentieth century would be the century of Canada. This opinion has not been deemed extravagant. On this continent and across the waters, it has been accepted as the statement of a truth, beyond controversy. The wonderful development of the United States during the space of scarcely more than one hundred years may well be an incitement to our efforts and our ambition. Yet to the emulation of such an example there may well be some exception taken; for if it be true that settlement of the western portion of the America union has been marked by almost phenomenal rapidity, it is also true that every other consideration seems to have been sacrificed to this one consideration of rapid growth. Little attention was given, up to the last few years, to the materials which were introduced into the republic; little regard was paid among the new settlers to the observance of the law; and it is not a slander upon our neighbours—for, indeed, the fact is admitted in their current literature—that frontier civilization was with them a byword for lawlessness. We have proceeded upon different methods. We have been satisfied with slower progress. Our institutions in our own North-west have been developed by gradual stages, so as to ensure at all times among these new communities law and order, and the restraints and safe-guards of the highest civilization.

The time has arrived when we are all agreed, I believe, nay, I feel sure, upon both sides of the House, that another step, and the last, can now be taken to complete the passage of the North-west Territories from what was once necessary tutelage, into the fulness of the rights which, under our constitution, appertain to provinces. . . .

When we came to consider the problem before us it became very soon apparent to me, at all events, that there were others; that the others were of comparatively minor importance, but that there were four which I was sure the parliament of Canada and the Canadian people at large might be expected to take a deep interest in. The first was: How many provinces should be admitted into the confederation coming from the North-west Territories—one, or two, or more? The next question was: in whom should be vested the ownership of the public lands? The third question was: What should be the financial terms to be granted to these new provinces? And the fourth and not the least important by any means was the question of the school system which would be introduced—not introduced because it was introduced long ago, but should be continued in the Territories.

Now, Sir, I will proceed to examine one after the other, all these questions. The first, as I have just said is: How many provinces should be admitted into the confederation? . . .

When we were first approached on this subject, it was proposed to us that we should make a province extending from the American boundary up to the 57th parallel, that is to say, somewhat to the south of the provisional boundary between the provisional districts of Mackenzie and Athabaska, but we thought it preferable to take in the whole district of Athabaska. The reason for this is, that although Athabaska is not considered to be a fertile country, and the eastern portion of it is barren, the western portion, the valley of the Peace river, is equal to the valley of Saskatchewan and settlement there is already proceeding rapidly. There are today on the Peace river two grist mills, provided absolutely from wheat grown in the Peace river valley, and therefore we have decided to include within the new provinces the provisional district of Athabaska. The area of these two provinces together will be about 550,345 square miles. This is, in our estimation, altogether too large an area to be made into one single province according to the size of the other provinces, the largest of which is British Columbia, and the next largest Quebec, British Columbia with an area of 372,000 square miles and Quebec with an area of 351,000 square miles. By dividing it into two you have two provinces of 275,000 square miles in round numbers, each about the size of the province of Ontario. If any of the members of the House will care to look at the map, they will see that we have put the provisional boundary on the fourth meridian and according to our present information, this will give about the same area and also the same population to the two provinces. It is estimated that the population today in these two provinces is about 500,000 souls. We have no accurate data, but we can proceed pretty confidently upon this information. The census of 1901 gave to these North-west Territories a population of a little over 100,000 souls. Since that time, during the seasons of 1901, 1902, 1903 and 1904, the population, by immigration alone, has increased by over 100,000 a year, so that today we feel we are on pretty safe ground when we say that there is in those two provinces a total population of 500,000 souls, and we calculate that this population is about equally divided between the two provinces, giving a population of 250,000 to each. . . .

The new provinces shall, as a matter of course, be represented on the floor of this House, and, until another election takes place, they shall continue to be represented as they are today. There will be in each province a legislative assembly, of which it is proposed that the number of members shall be twenty-five.

A question which has given some difficulty to the members of the committee who had the preparation of this Bill, has been the selection of the capitals of the respective provinces. As to the capital of the province of Saskatchewan, the difficulty is easily solved, it will be, as it is at present, Regina. But as to the capital of Alberta, the selection was not so easy. There were three claimants for it—Calgary, Red Deer and Edmonton, each of which had a good claim. We have decided that we would not make any final selection, leaving the final selection to the province itself. In the meantime, if you look at the map, you will see that Edmonton seems to be the most central point, and therefore we propose to make Edmonton the capital for the present.

Beyond this, I have only to say that it is the intention to have this Bill come into force on July 1 next.

The point being settled as to the number of provinces to be admitted into confederation, the next question is that regarding the public lands. In whom should the ownership of the lands be vested? Should they belong to the provinces or to the Dominion? A strong plea was presented to us on behalf of the provinces. It was represented that as a matter of law and equity, the public lands in these two provinces should belong to their governments. This plea was no doubt suggested by the fact that at the time of confederation, all the parties to the original contract, that is to say, the provinces of Nova Scotia, New Brunswick, Ontario and Quebec, each retained her own lands; and when at a later day the province of British Columbia was admitted to the Dominion, she also retained her lands. But, Sir, the cases are not at all parallel. When the provinces which I have named came into confederation, they were already sovereignties. I use that term, because barring their dependence as colonies they were sovereignties in the sense of having the management of their own affairs. Each had a department of government called the Crown Lands Department, which was entrusted with the power of dealing with those lands, either for revenue or for settlement.

But the case of these new provinces is not at all similar. They never had the ownership of the lands. Those lands were bought by the Dominion government, and they have remained ever since the property of the Dominion government and have been administered by the Dominion government. Therefore I say the two cases are not in any way parallel; they are indeed absolutely different. When the provinces which I have named came into confederation they retained the ownership of their lands; but when the two new provinces came into the Dominion, it cannot be said that they can retain the ownership of their lands, as they never had the ownership.

Therefore, the proposition that in equity and justice these lands belong to the provinces is not tenable. But for my part I would not care, in a question of this importance, to rest the case on a mere abstract proposition. We must view it from the grounds of policy; and from the highest grounds of policy, I think it is advisable that the ownership of these lands should continue to be vested in the Dominion government. . . .

Now I come to the financial terms which should be given to the new provinces. Our constitution, which is to be found in the British North America Act, contains a very remarkable provision. It contains the provision that out of the Federal treasury there shall be paid to the provinces a large amount of money in the shape of subsidies to assist them in carrying on their business. This, I say, is a very extraordinary provision. It is, I believe, unique. At all events, so far as my information goes, I do not know that any similar provision is to be found in the constitution of any other federal government. It is a sound principle of finance, and a still sounder principle of government, that those who have the duty of expending the revenue of a country should also be saddled with the responsibility of levying and providing it. That principle has been departed from in our case, and no doubt was departed from with some object. What can have been the reasons which induced the fathers of confederation in 1867 to depart from so obvious a principle of finance and government? The reasons are simply these. Confederation was the result of several compromises. It would have been impossible to establish it if there had not been a policy of give and take adopted among all the constituent bodies. And I am quite sure, I am speaking absolute historical truth when I say that neither Nova Scotia, New Brunswick, Ontario nor Quebec would ever have consented to part with their revenues, to give up their powers of taxation in customs and excise, if they had not been promised that out of the federal revenues they would be allowed a certain sum every year to defray the expense of their own local governments and administrations. This is the reason why this provision is to be found in the British North America Act. It is there. I do not think it is sound, but though in my judgment unsound, it is the duty of everybody in this House and in this country to take confederation as we find it, with its good points and its blemishes, and carry it to the end of the principle upon which it was established. Therefore upon this point I believe it is the duty of the Canadian parliament to continue that policy in this instance and make a liberal provision for these two new provinces which we are about to admit into the Canadian family. . . .

Now, this Act is not to come into force until the 1st of July, and we estimate that by the 1st of July the population will have increased to 500,000 souls. This is the basis of our calculation. Now, I said a moment ago, and the House seemed to agree with me, that as we retain the lands in our own hands, it is natural and to be expected that government and parliament would be liberal in their allowance to the new provinces for compensation in that respect. Manitoba, which has an area of 73,000 square miles, received as compensation for her lands some fifteen or twenty years ago an annual grant of $100,000. Apart from that, Manitoba has received the swamp lands. The swamp lands are perhaps the most valuable lands in the province of Manitoba. They require some preliminary work for drainage, but when drained there are no better lands in the whole province. When the late government gave to the province of Manitoba the swamp lands, they made her a valuable gift, and it has proved to her a most important asset. But the North-west Territories have no swamp lands, we could not do for them what the government did for the province of Manitoba. We have, therefore, made the following arrangement, which we commend to the favourable consideration of the House:

As the public lands in the said provinces are to remain the property of Canada, there shall be paid by Canada to the said provinces annually by way of compensation therefor a sum based upon the estimated value of such lands, (namely, $37,500.00); the same being assumed to be of an area of 25,000,000 acres and to be of the value of $1.50 per acre, and upon the population of the said provinces as from time to time ascertained by the quinquennial census thereof, such sum to be arrived at as follows:—

The population of the said provinces being assumed to be at

present 250,000, the sum payable until such population reaches 400,000 is to be one per cent on such estimated value, or $375,000.

Thereafter until such population reaches 800,000, the sum payable is to be one and one-half per cent on such estimated value, or $562,500.

Thereafter until such population reaches 1,200,000, the sum payable is to be two per cent on such estimated value, or $750,000.

And thereafter such payment is to be three per cent on such estimated value, or $1,132,500.

In additional compensation for such lands, there shall be paid by Canada to such province annually for five years from the time this Act comes into force to provide for the construction of necessary public buildings, $62,500.

Let me now recapitulate to see the minimum each province is to receive. At present, this year, the province is to receive for civil government $50,000; for capitation allowance, $200,000, which is going to increase until the population has reached 800,000 souls. It will receive for debt allowance $405,375, and this year it will receive also for land compensation $375,000; total, $1,030,375, to which sum must be added, for five years, $62,500, in order to allow the province to provide for her buildings and public works generally.

This is the minimum which will be paid to the province. The only thing new in these arrangements is in respect to the lands. The maximum which will be paid to the province at any time when the population shall have reached 1,200,000 souls is $1,125,000; that is to say, we pay to each of these provinces the maximum sum of $1,125,000 as compensation for the lands which we retain in our possession. I submit to the House that this is a very fair, a very moderate and very equitable adjustment indeed; at all events, I so present it to the House, and I think it will be so regarded. . . .

I now come to the question of education, and this question is perhaps under existing circumstances the most important of all that we have to deal with. There are evidences not a few coming to us from all directions, that the old passions which such a subject has always aroused are not, unfortunately, buried; indeed, already, before the policy of the government has been known, before the subject is fairly before the people, the government has been warned as to its duty in this matter, and not only warned but threatened as well. The government has been warned, threatened from both sides of this question, from those who believe in separate schools and from those who oppose separate schools. These violent appeals are not a surprise to me, at all events, nor do I believe they are a surprise to anybody. We have known by the experience of the past, within the short life of this confederation, that public opinion is always inflammable whenever questions arise which ever so remotely touch upon the religious convictions of the people. It behooves us therefore all the more at this solemn moment to approach this subject with care, with calmness and delibera- tion and with the firm purpose of dealing with it not only in accordance with the inherent principles of abstract justice, but in accordance with the spirit—the Canadian spirit of tolerance and charity, this Canadian spirit of tolerance and charity of which confederation is the essence and of which in practice it ought to be the expression and embodiment. . . .

Let me recall to the House the Quebec resolutions which were adopted and which were the basis and the charter under which the Canadian parliament now lives and the Canadian nation has been formed. Section 93 of the Quebec resolutions states as follows, and I pray you, Sir, mark the language:—

The local legislatures shall have power to make laws respecting the following subjects:—

1. Direct taxation, and in New Brunswick the imposition of duties on the export of timber, logs, masts, spars, deals and sawn lumber; and in Nova Scotia, of coals and other minerals.

2. Borrowing money on the credit of the province.

3. The establishment and tenure of local offices, and the appointment and payment of local officers.

4. Agriculture.

5. Immigration.

6. Education; saving the rights and privileges which the Protestant or Catholic minority in both Canadas may possess as to their denominational schools at the time when the union goes into operation.

Again I say, mark the language. The legislatures of Nova Scotia, New Brunswick, Quebec and Ontario were given the power to make laws for the following purposes:

Direct taxation.

Borrowing money.

The establishment and tenure of local office.

Agriculture and colonization.

Upon all these subjects their powers are unlimited and they can do as they please, without any check, except their responsibility to the people of their respective provinces. Then on the subject of education the legislatures of Nova Scotia and New Brunswick can do as they please and are not responsible to any one except to the people. But when we come to the provinces of Ontario and Quebec, we find that the powers of these two provinces are limited as regards education. Neither the legislature of Ontario nor that of Quebec was given power to pass any law which might prejudicially affect the rights of the minority in either province. So long as this constitution endures the schools of the minority in Quebec and Ontario must likewise endure. Yet, remarkable as is this enactment, it is perhaps still more remarkable, if we remember that one of the men who assented to this limitation to the power of the province of Ontario was Mr. George Brown himself—Mr. George Brown who said again and again that he was opposed to separate schools, who had carried on a crusade of years against separate schools in his province. If you look only at the surface of things, without trying to find the inspiration, it is indeed remarkable that Mr. Brown, who, with Sir John Macdonald was the central figure, agreed that the powers of the legislature of his own province should be limited in that respect. We need not marvel if Mr. Brown was attacked and assailed for the action he then took. He was assailed perhaps by some of his own disciples whom he had taught to object to separate schools as strongly as he did himself. Mr. Brown defended his course in the confederation debate, or rather he explained his policy, because he was under no necessity to defend his course; and I beg on this occasion to commend his language to those who today have forgotten confederation, when he came to discuss the 43rd resolution. He spoke as follows:—

> The people of Upper Canada will have another legislation for their local matters and will no longer have to betake themselves to Quebec for leave to open a road, to select a county town, or appoint a coroner. But I am told that to this general principle of placing all local matters under local control, an exception has been made in regard to the common schools. (Hear, hear.)
> The clause complained of is as follows:—
> 6. Education, saving the rights and privileges which the Protestant or Catholic minority in both Canadas may possess as to their denominational schools at the time when the union goes into operation.

Now, continued Mr. Brown:—

I need hardly remind the House that I have always opposed and continue to oppose the system of sectarian education, so far as the public chest is concerned. I have never had any hesitation on that point, I have never been able to see why all the people in the province, to whatever sect they may belong, should not send their children to the same schools to receive the ordinary branches of instruction. I regard the parent and the pastor as the best religious instructors—and so long as the religious faith of the children is not interfered with, and ample opportunity afforded to the clergy to give religious instruction to the children of their flocks, I cannot see any sound objection to mixed schools. But while in the conference and elsewhere I have always maintained this view, and always given my vote against sectarian public schools, I am bound to admit, as I have always admitted, that the sectarian system carried to the limited extent it has yet been in Upper Canada, and confined as it chiefly is to cities and towns, has not been a very great practical injury. The real cause of a line [sic] was that the admission of the sectarian principle was there, and that at any moment it might be extended to such a degree as to split up our school system altogether. There are about a hundred separate schools in Upper Canada, out of some 4,000, and all Roman Catholic. But if the Roman Catholics are entitled to separate schools and to go on extending their operations, so are the members of the Church of England, the Presbyterians, the Methodists, and all other sects. No candid Roman Catholic will deny this for a moment; and there lays the great danger to our educational fabric, lest the separate system might gradually extend itself until the whole country was studded with nurseries of sectarianism, most hurtful to the best interests of the province and entailling an enormous expense to sustain the host of teachers that so prodigal a system of public instruction must inevitably entail. Now, it is known to every hon. member of the House that an Act was passed in 1863 as a final settlement of this sectarian controversy. I was not in Quebec at the time, but if I had been here, I would have voted against that Bill because it extended the facilities for establishing separate schools. It had, however, this good feature, that it was accepted by the Roman Catholic

authorities and carried to parliament as a final compromise
of the question in Upper Canada. When, therefore, it was
proposed that a provision should be inserted in the
confederation scheme to bind that contract of 1863 and
declare it a final settlement, so that we should not be compelled, as we have been since 1849, to stand constantly on
our arms, awaiting fresh attacks upon our common school
system, the proposition seemed to me one that was not
rashly to be rejected. (Hear, hear.) I admit that, from my
point of view, this is a blot on the scheme before the
House; it is confessedly, one of the concessions from our
side that had to be made to secure this great measure of
reform. But assuredly, I, for one, have not the slightest
hesitation in accepting it as a necessary condition of the
scheme of union, and doubly acceptable must it be in the
eyes of hon. gentlemen opposite, who were the authors of
the Bill of 1863. (Cheers.) But it was urged that though this
arrangement might perhaps be fair as regards Upper
Canada, it was not so as regards Lower Canada, for there
were matters of which the British population have long
complained, and some amendments to the existing School
Act were required to secure them equal justice. Well, when
this point was raised, gentlemen of all parties in Lower
Canada at once expressed themselves prepared to treat it in
a frank and conciliatory manner, with a view to removing
an injustice that might be shown to exist; and on this
understanding the educational clause was adopted by the
conference. . . .

Let us pause a moment to consider this language. Mr. Brown
did not believe in separate schools. He had struggled all his life
against that system. But a great object had to be achieved, a
noble conception had to be realized, an inspiring idea had to be
made a fact, and in order to reach that supreme goal, differences
of opinion had to be reconciled, fears and apprehensions had to
be removed, misgivings had to be alleviated, and above all the
rights of conscience, the tender rights of conscience, had to be
placed in as firm a position of security as they previously
enjoyed, so that no one could object, and all, without regard to
origin or creed, could give a cheerful and enthusiastic support
to the new constitution.

Sir, Mr. Brown told his friends that he did not believe in
separate schools; but there were fellow-citizens of his in
Ontario and in Quebec who believed in separate schools, and,

in order to remove their objections and win their co-operation in the scheme which was the great work of his life, he agreed to make the sacrifice of his own convictions. In order to achieve the great object he had at heart, he agreed to fasten upon his own province a system in which he did not believe, but in which others did believe. Sir, for more than twenty years Mr. Brown has been in his grave; but his memory is not dead. And if his teachings and his spirit be still alive, it is surely in the hearts of that staunch yeomanry of Ontario who gave him such constant support during the years of his political struggles. They followed him devotedly in his crusade against separate schools. They followed him even more devotedly, when he asked them to accept separate schools, to sacrifice their own opinions, and his own, upon the altar of the new country which it was his ambition to establish on this portion of the North American continent. If it were my privilege that my poor words might reach that staunch yeomanry of Ontario, I would remind them that the work of confederation is not yet finished; I would tell them that we are now engaged in advancing it; and I would ask them whether we are now to reverse our course, or whether we are not to continue to work it out to completion on the lines laid down by the great leader himself.

Now, Sir, such was the condition of things at the time of confederation. But I shall be told that this exception applied to Ontario and Quebec alone, and not to the other provinces. Sir, that is true. Amongst the four provinces then united, Ontario and Quebec alone had a system of separate schools. But I reminded the House a moment ago that it was not the intention of the fathers of confederation, it was not the intention of Sir John Macdonald or Mr. Brown to limit confederation to the narrow bounds it had in 1867. They had made provision in the very instrument of confederation, to extend it over the northern part of the continent; they had made provision to take in British Columbia, Newfoundland and Prince Edward Island; they had made provision to take in also the North-west Territories, which were then uninhabited, but which now have a teeming population and are at our doors asking admission. It is reasonable to suppose, if the Confederation Act recognizes that other provinces were to come into confederation similarly situated to Ontario and Quebec, that the same privileges should not be given to the minority as were given to the minority in Ontario and Quebec? What would have been the value of the invitation to enter confederation. If the provinces invited to enter, had been told that the security to the minority given to Ontario and

Quebec was a privilege which they need not expect from us? Section 43 of the Quebec resolutions has become section 93 of the British North America Act, and is no longer confined to Quebec and Ontario. . . .

So, Sir, now whenever a province comes here knocking at this door, asking to be admitted into confederation, if in that province there exists a system of separate schools, the British North America Act has provided that the same guarantee we give to the minority in Quebec and Ontario shall also be given to the minority in that province. Shortly after confederation had been established, that is, in the year 1870, the parliament of Canada had an opportunity of applying the doctrine contained in the British North America Act in the creation of the province of Manitoba. Until its admission into the Dominion, Manitoba had no regular government. It had been loosely administered by the Hudson Bay Company. There had been some schools in it, maintained by such authority as there was. There had been separate schools maintained by Roman Catholic missionaries. It was the intention of parliament to give the minority the system that they had before confederation; and, so marked was their intention, that instead of accepting without qualification the words of section 93 of the British North America Act, 'right or privilege with respect to denominational schools which any class of persons have by law in the province at the union,' they made it read 'by law or practice in the province at the union.' It turned out, as determined by judicial authority, that the province of Manitoba, when it entered confederation, had no system of schools either by law or practice. It followed, as a consequence, that the power of the province of Manitoba with regard to the subject of education was as complete as that of the province of Nova Scotia or the province of New Brunswick. This is a principle which was not understood at the time by hon. gentlemen opposite when they were on this side of the House. There was the fact, the positive fact—the power of the province of Manitoba with regard to education was as unshackled as that of New Brunswick and Nova Scotia. In 1875, as I stated a moment ago, Mr. Mackenzie introduced an Act for the government of the North-west Territories, and in this Act the parliament of Canada, which, at that time, had among its members some of the ablest men who ever sat in a Canadian parliament—Sir John Macdonald, Mr. Mackenzie, Mr. Blake, Sir Charles Tupper and a score of others—unanimously, deliberately and with their eyes open, introduced into the North-west Territories the system of separate schools. And not only that, but the parliament of Canada, four times successively —in 1880, in 1885, in 1886 and in 1898—deliberately and with their eyes open, ratified the system of separate schools in the Territories. . . .

In everything that I have said I have refrained from saying a single word upon the abstract principle of separate schools. I approach the question upon another and broader ground, I approach the question not from the view of separate schools, but I approach it upon the higher ground of Canadian duty and Canadian patriotism. Having obtained the consent of the minority to this form of government, having obtained the consent to the giving up of their valued privileges, and their position of strength are we to tell them, now that confederation is established, that the principle upon which they consented to this arrangement, is to be laid aside and that we are to ride roughshod over them? I do not think that is a proposition which will be maintained in this House, nor do I believe it is the intention of the House. I offer at this moment no opinion at all upon separate schools as an abstract proposition, but I have no hesitation in saying that if I were to speak my mind upon separate schools, I would say that I never could understand what objection there could be to a system of schools wherein, after secular matters have been attended to, the tenets of the religion of Christ, even with the divisions which exist among His followers, are allowed to be taught. We live in a country wherein the seven provinces that constitute our nation, either by will or by the tolerance of the people, in every school, Christian morals and Christian dogmas are taught to the youth of the country. . . .

I thank heaven that we are living in a country where the young children of the land are taught Christian morals and Christian dogmas. Either the American system is right or the Canadian system is right. For my part I say this and I say it without hesitation. Time will show that we are in the right and in this instance as in many other, I have an abiding faith in the institutions of my own country.

V — 19

Robert Borden comments on the Alberta Bill, February 21, 1905: House of Commons Debates, February 21, 1905, 1462-1463.

Now, I do not propose to discuss the provisions of this Bill in

detail today. Let me say, however, that I regret very much that
the government have not seen fit to give to the people of the new
provinces that control over the lands of the North-west
Territories which is enjoyed by all the other provinces of
Canada. That is a subject which will bear fuller discussion later
on, and I do not propose to weary the House with any extended
remarks respecting it this afternoon. The only thing which
could be called an argument made by the right hon. gentleman
against that proposition was this: he said it might interfere
with the operation of the policy of the government with respect
to immigration. So far as the rest of his argument is concerned,
it would have justified the retention by the Imperial government up to the present time of every acre of Crown lands in
Canada; and I was somewhat astonished to hear from the right
hon. gentleman, the advocate, in the past at least, of responsible government, the defender of the liberties of the people on
some occasions, according to his own view at least, I was
astonished to hear from him the views he put forth this afternoon as to the rights of the people of the North-west Territories
in respect of these lands. He knows something of the history of
this question. We remember that there were statesmen in Great
Britain not many years ago who thought that the public lands
not only of Canada but of all the dependencies of the empire
should be retained under the control of the home government,
and administered not so much for the benefit of the dependency
in which they were situate as for the benefit of the whole empire
at large. But it was soon found, when it was attempted to put
that view in practice, that it was absolutely impracticable—that
to the people living in and developing any dependency must be
entrusted, and might be safely entrusted, the entire control of
the public lands within the dependency. The right hon. gentleman spoke of immigration. Does he not know that there is a
new Quebec and a new Ontario? Does he not know that a tide of
immigration may be expected to flow, and indeed, I suppose it
is now flowing into these portions of eastern Canada? Will he
venture to any that there has been any obstacle placed against
the immigration policy of the government by the governments
which administer these provinces? Is that the ground the right
hon. gentleman takes? Does he speak from experience, or does
he speak from mere surmise? I venture to think that he spoke
only from surmise this afternoon, and that if he had looked at
this question in the light of experience, in the light of what is
happening today in Quebec and Ontario, he might very well
have modified the provisions of this Bill, and might very well

have entrusted to the people of the North-west Territories exactly the same control over their lands as is enjoyed by the people of the other provinces. I venture to say further that if he was not willing to trust the people, in this regard—if he regarded them as possibly, improvident, as was suggested by the Minister of the Interior last session or the session before—if he feared the result, he might at least have given them the control of the public lands within their respective provinces, subject to some such restriction as that which he has proposed in regard to education. If the principle is good in the one case, I do not see why it should not work out fairly well in the other case.

There are other features of the Bill which will undoubtedly invite discussion. The subject which the right hon. gentleman mentioned last, on which he spoke with great eloquence, and in a spirit of forbearance and moderation, will undoubtedly invite discussion. I do not propose to discuss it this afternoon. There is just one thing, however, that I would like to say about it, and that is that I understand that up to the present time there has been really no school question, to use the common expression, in the North-west Territories of Canada; and I sincerely trust that on both sides of the House we will not seek to make this a political question in any sense.

Some hon. MEMBERS. Hear, hear.

Mr. R.L. BORDEN. But at the same time let us beware lest any action of ours may create in the North-west of Canada for all time to come that question which happily has been entirely absent there in the past. . . .

V — 20

School Clause No. 8: House of Commons Debates, February 21, 1905, 1852-53.

16. The provisions of section 93 of the British North America Act, 1867, shall apply to the said provinces as if, at the date upon which this Act comes into force, the territory comprised therein were already a province, the expression 'the union' in the said section being taken to mean the said date.

2. Subject to the provisions of the said section 93, and in continuance of the principles heretofore sanctioned under the North-west Territories Act, it is enacted that the legislature of the said province shall pass all necessary laws in respect of

education, and that it shall therein always be provided (a) that a majority of the ratepayers of any district or portion whatever name it is known may establish such schools therein as they think fit, and make the necessary assessments and collection of rates therefor, and (b) that the minority of the ratepayers therein whether Protestant or Roman Catholic, may establish separate schools therein, and make the necessary assessments and collection of rates therefor, and (c) that in such case the ratepayers establishing such Protestant or Roman Catholic separate schools shall be liable only to assessment of such rates as they impose upon themselves with respect thereto.

3. In the appropriation of public moneys by the legislature in aid of education, and in the distribution of any moneys paid to the government of the said province arising from the school fund established by the Dominion Lands Act, there shall be no discrimination between the public schools and the separate schools, and such moneys shall be applied to the support of public and separate schools in equitable shares or proportion.

V — 21

'The New Provinces,' Calgary Herald, February 23, 1905.

The people of the Territories will hail with delight the fact that they are to receive at last some measure of self government, though the terms and conditions as announced will create great disappointment in any event as regards the boundaries, and the retaining of the public lands by the Dominion.

The areas of the two provinces will be nearly alike. Alberta will have about 250,000 square miles and Saskatchewan 258,000. The dividing line along the fourth meridian is wrong, placed there evidently in an arbitrary manner without regard to the physical features of the country or its agricultural and grazing qualities. The line should have been further east, so as to take in all the grazing land south of the South Saskatchewan even if north of that river it had swerved westward. . . .

In Alberta we are given the administration of all the Peace River region, and the area known as the Mackenzie basin. Of the whole area thus given to Alberta almost one-third of it will be of doubtful value, certainly for many years to come, while the cost of the administration of the northern part will be very expensive.

As to the lands the Dominion proposes to retain them, but

the people of the Territories will never consent to this. All the other provinces (except Manitoba) have received theirs, and there is no reason why there should be any distinction between the new provinces and the old. Sir Wilfrid Laurier and the Hon. Mr. Sifton think we are not able to administer them, and cannot be trusted. We must own and control the lands within our boundaries, and have the benefit of the revenues. We must lodge our protest now, and fight to the end.

The financial part is not clear in the absence of further particulars. We are to receive $50,000 annually for the civil government, and a per capita allowance of 80 cents per head up to a population of 400,000. As to the debt allowance this does not seem clear and as the details are not given in the dispatches sufficiently, we will return to the subject later.

The land allowance of $375,000 the people will never accept. All the other provinces above-mentioned have their lands, and with the area in Alberta we should realize much more than proposed. Apparently we are getting no compensation for the land given to railways. British Columbia received $100,000 a year for the small quantities of land that were taken in that province for a subsidy on account of the construction of the C.P.R., and we should have some compensation.

There are other questions which we will discuss later on.

The bill creating the provinces will go into effect on the 1st July next. Elections will take place for 25 members in each of the new legislatures. The people will have a chance to speak, and we will have an organized body to protest, and subsequently fight for our rights.

V — 22

Haultain comments on the Autonomy Bill. Toronto Globe, February 25, 1905.

Ottawa, Feb. 24.—The second reading of the North-west autonomy bill will be moved in about two weeks time. Several details in the measure bearing on what might be termed matters of internal economy have to be settled, and Premier Haultain is in consultation with the Minister of Justice regarding them. He will remain in Ottawa until the bills pass Parliament. Premier Haultain is not pleased with some of the features of the bills. To the Globe correspondent this afternoon he stated that he was still convinced it would have been better to have had only one Province instead of two.

'I do not believe,' he said, 'that the division of the Territories into two Provinces will arouse very much controversy. Nevertheless, the more I have considered the question, especially in the light of the conference we have just had, the more I am persuaded of the desirability of there being only one Province, and that there was no necessity for creating two. The division is purely arbitrary; there is no point in the country where there is a natural division. . . .'

'What is your opinion of the terms which have been granted the new Provinces?'

'Of course I stand absolutely on the claim of the Province to have the public domain. The question has been dealt with largely as a matter of expediency and policy, without any regard to any question of right. We advanced our claim as a matter of right. I do not think Manitoba is a desirable example to quote because Manitoba is the exception in the whole scheme of confederation. Manitoba's case was dealt with at a time when the conditions were not present which exist today. There was nobody to speak for the people, and possibly the policy may have been wise at the time. . . . I say, we consider we are entitled as a right. There is also the complication that arises when very large areas of country are controlled by an outside authority. On the other hand, I must admit that a substantial net income under this proposition, increasing with our population, may be a very great advantage.'

'What is your opinion about the financial aid to be set apart for the Provinces?'

'Generally speaking, the financial terms are reasonably generous, looking at the matter from all sides. We do not get as much as we asked for, and I did not ask for anything I did not believe we were entitled to. The Provinces will be very well off to start with. There will be no need to resort to any more taxation. . . .'

'What have you to say in regard to the manner in which the educational system is to be dealt with?'

'Of course I am a great believer in the principle that it is better to leave education, which, after all, is a purely domestic question, to the uncontrolled jurisdiction of the Provinces; from the Provincial point of view as being their right, from the Federal point of view as preventing any chance of a purely domestic question being dragged into the Federal arena. Why should the people, say, of Prince Edward Island, for example, be set by the ears because there happened to be trouble on the Pacific slope? I need not elaborate that point, because we have been through the experience once, in the Manitoba School case.

I take exception to Sir Wilfrid Laurier's argument in regard to constitutional guarantees. At the time to which he refers the Dominion Parliament was the only body exercising a Government jurisdiction over the Territories, and they had to make provision for everything. . . . But to say that because the Dominion Parliament passed an act with regard to the educational or any other matter in 1875 it stands forever, that it be imposed upon the Province and perpetuated, is a position which if applied with equal fairness to anything else they did it is very rapidly brought to the reductio ad absurdum.'

V — 23

Clifford Sifton to J.W. Dafoe, editor of the Manitoba Free Press, February 25, 1905: Sifton Papers, Vol. 263, 209-212.

I am sending you a telegram today regarding the position of matters in connection with the North West Bill. I had considered everything before I went away and had put in shape for my colleagues a memorandum recommending the method in which the various questions should be dealt with.

These recommendations have been substantially followed except that the Chief has been led into making what I conceive to be a serious mistake in allowing the compensation for land to be based upon a fixed acreage, the amount of which appears in the Bill. In my judgement the amount, while it is not objectionable, should have been fixed arbitrarily without any reference to the acreage which may prove an admission that will cause serious embarrassment in the future. Everyone sees the mistakes now, but it may possibly be too late to change it.

Respecting the school matter, what I agreed to was that the present system of separate schools in the North-west Territories should be perpetuated. In my judgement the present system is substantially unobjectionable. That is to say, while theoretically there is some objection to it in practice the objection is of no real or substantial moment, and from every standpoint I regard it as most desirable that the question should be settled by simply adopting the principles of the system as it exists now.

Walter Scott was of the same opinion, and in discussing the matter a year ago we practically agreed upon this. As I understand it the North-west members are unanimously of the same opinion, that is to say, they are willing to be bound by this conclusion.

As the clause in the Bill is drawn, however, it seems to go further and it seems to be vague. I do not myself with all my experience in consuming and arguing clauses of this kind profess to know what it means, and the fact that it was drawn by Fitzpatrick does not add anything to my confidence that the draftsman had in mind the same intention that we had. I do not accuse him of intentionally deceiving anyone, but he makes no secret of the fact that he is desirous of meeting the views of the Church.

There are two points that seem to me to be of central difficulty in the present draft. First it does not seem to me at all clear that the central authority will have the power to regulate the separate school, prescribe text books and qualifications of teachers, and these powers are admitted by everyone to be essential. Laurier does not dispute this.

Another and serious difficulty is as to the last clause which provides for a sharing up of the proceeds of public school lands. This question was never discussed before, it has never been discussed at all between myself and any other Member of the Government, and the contents of the clause as it stands now in the Bill are altogether new to me. I have not had time to form an opinion upon it, but with the proviso that I am only writing in a tentative way and that my opinion may change I am disposed to be very much opposed to it, at least in its present form.

I am just sending you this letter as an advance bulletin so that you will know what is going on. I have not discussed the matter with Sir Wilfrid at all further than that he called me into his room yesterday and spoke at some length of the difficulties which he had had. He did not ask me my opinion or what my views were. Sir Wilfrid's proceeding in matters of this kind is always to assume that everyone agrees with him until they insist upon quarreling. He finds this much the easiest way of getting on. He will not seek for an opportunity of allowing me to raise a dispute about it, but I shall of course be compelled to bring the subject up very soon. I will have another talk with the Western Members on Monday or Tuesday.

V — 24

Sifton to Laurier, February 26, 1905: Sifton Papers, Vol. 263, 213-215.

Since seeing you on Friday I have given my best consideration to the proposed educational clause of the North West Acts and have arrived at certain conclusions of which I think I should advise you at the earliest possible moment.

I cannot support the proposed clause regarding the division of the proceeds of school lands or any similar clause. The school lands endowment of the Territories will amount to some millions of acres—the proceeds will be many millions of dollars. The proposition made would constitute a most colossal endowment of sectarian education from public property. I am wholly and unalterably opposed to any such measure.

As to the other branch of the subject, the very furthest that I can go is to support a guarantee of the continuance of the separate school privileges which the people of the North-west possess now, making it perfectly and unmistakably clear that the Legislature has power to regulate and control all the schools in any manner necessary in its judgment to secure efficiency.

The form of the clause as drawn seems to me to be ambiguous. I do not feel at all confident that I or in fact anyone else can be certain what it means, but I am quite satisfied that it does not safeguard the right of the legislature to fully regulate and control all the schools.

I need not say that for me to support a proposition for permanent establishment of separate schools even in the above modified form involves a very great sacrifice of my own personal views. Nothing would induce me to go so far except my conviction that at the present critical moment everyone should do his utmost to assist in arriving at a compromise which will prevent the splitting of parties upon religious lines.

Under any circumstances it seems clear to me that I must retire from the Government. That goes as a matter of course if you proceed with the educational clause as it is. Should it be modified so that I can support it I should still be open to the charge which I do not see how I could meet that I had altered my very well known views and given my support to the measure for the sake of remaining in office.

I need not say how deeply I regret being compelled to come to the conclusion which I have outlined. You will, I am sure, absolve me in advance of any lack of desire to promote harmony.

V — 25

Sifton to Laurier, February 27, 1905: Sifton Papers, Vol. 263, 227.

After giving my best consideration to the matters which we discussed last evening I have arrived at the conclusion that it is impossible for me to continue in office under present circumstances and that it is better for all concerned that I should act at once. I therefore beg to tender my resignation as a member of the Government. I trust that the unhappy necessity which has risen will not in the least impair the friendship with which you have been kind enough to honor me.

V — 26

Sifton explains his resignation to the House, March 1, 1905: House of Commons Debates, March 1, 1905, 1851-1853.

When it was determined that during this session of parliament legislation should be introduced creating new provinces out of a portion of the North-west Territories, I felt called upon in view of the history of the education question in Canada, to give very serious consideration to the position which I should take with regard to the legislative power to be conferred upon the provinces in regard to the subject of education. It was necessary that conferences should take place with members of parliament representing the North-west Territories and with the representatives of the Territorial government, upon the subject of education and other subjects involved in the Bill. These conferences were unavoidably postponed until after the beginning of the new year, by reason of the absence of the Prime Minister, who, after the general election, was compelled to take a short rest, and was therefore absent from the country. Shortly before the time fixed for holding these conferences I was compelled by my own state of health to leave Ottawa, and was therefore unable to be present at the discussions which took place. Before leaving I discussed with the Prime Minister most of the subjects that necessarily required to be dealt with in the Bill which was to be introduced, and so far as I was able to do so at that time, I communicated my views to him upon the various subjects. I may say that when I went away I did not anticipate that it would be considered necessary to introduce the Bill for creating the new provinces, before I returned. As members of the House are aware, I returned to the capital on Thursday afternoon. I immediately took occasion to read carefully the speech which the right hon. the Prime Minister (Sir Wilfrid Laurier) had delivered in introducing the Bill. I regretted that in the right hon. gentleman's address I found some principles enunciated with which I am unable to agree. On Friday, the next day after I returned, at the earliest possible moment, I procured a copy of the educational clause of the Bill which my leader had introduced. . . .

Between Friday, when I procured a copy of the clause, and Monday morning I gave the subject my best consideration, and I had the privilege in the meantime of having an interview with the Prime Minister on the subject. As the result of such consideration I determined that I could not endorse or support the principle of the educational clause. Under these circumstances, Mr. Speaker, my duty became perfectly clear, and on Monday morning I wrote to the Prime Minister tendering my resignation as a member of the cabinet. Subsequently, I expressed the desire that my resignation should be acted upon at once and to that wish the Prime Minister has now assented.

In conclusion, Mr. Speaker, not intending and not considering it proper at this time to enter into a discussion of the merits of the matter which has caused the difference between myself and my leader, I have only to add my regret that circumstances have compelled the severance of my official relations with my leader and with my colleagues with whom my relations have always been of the most harmonious and pleasant character, and with whom upon other questions I am in entire accord. The circumstances, however, in my judgment, make my duty perfectly clear, and it does not seem possible for me to properly consider anything except the principles which are involved.

V — 27

An Eastern Newspaper correspondent comments on the Reaction to the Education Clauses in the West: John Ewan to Laurier, March 1, 1905, Laurier Papers, 208833-5.

Mr. Sifton's resignation has suggested to me the idea of writing to you again. Sometimes a looker on sees more than those who are playing the game. The result of my enquiries for the Globe at the various centres of population is that the school question really excites but a languid interest here. I can quite

believe that if we hunted up all the fiery Methodist or Presbyterian clergy that strong expressions of opinion might be
obtained, but the average Western man is not much worked up
about it. Regina is calm and contented because it has been made
the capital. Edmonton ditto for a similar reason. The only discontented spot is Calgary and I think it would become calm if it
was made perfectly clear that the 25 members who will
eventually decide where the capital shall be would be elected on
a square rep. by pop. basis. I see that provision is made for
taking a census in 1906. If it were provided that a population
census should be taken before the constituencies were apportioned and that they would be apportioned on that basis public
opinion would be greatly calmed in Calgary and no valid
objection could be taken to that course here [Edmonton] and all
efforts to lead them on an agitation against the schools would
be futile I think.

There can be no question that the agitation elsewhere will
not be serious unless it is backed up by an outcry from the
people of the new Province. Were there a serious agitation here
it would add tremendously to the strength of the agitation in
Ontario.

V — 28

'Without Alberta's Consent,' Calgary Herald, March 2, 1905.

Rival gangs of politicians are shouting themselves hoarse in
Ontario over the educational affairs of Alberta. While each
cries: 'Hands off the west,' they urge, with singular unanimity
that the views of their particular crowd should be enforced on
the new province.

A mild mannered man remarked in Ontario last week, after
he had witnessed two meetings of equal violence where the
views expressed were exactly opposite:

'I wonder if it ever occurred to the people of the east that the
people of the west may have some opinions to offer on this
school question before it is definitely settled?'

The west has not spoken on the subject of separate schools.
Not one single utterance from a public man of the west has thus
far been made on this subject, yet, in spite of the complacency of
the very people who are most concerned, Ontario is being
inflamed by orators who display amazing zeal in the affairs of
the country 2,000 miles removed.

It is just possible that Alberta would be more thankful to these enthusiasts if they would urge more even-handed justice for the west in the way of distribution of the natural resources of the country, a more equitable boundary division, capital location, and other features of substantial value to the new provinces.

Ontario speakers marvel that the west is not awakened to the importance of the school question. In truth the west is alert to everything that tends to upbuild the country, but the people are too intelligent to grasp at the shadow and ignore the substance. Just now the people of Alberta at least are more interested in the other phases of the autonomy bill than education. That fact can scarcely be disputed.

V — 29

The Reverend G.E. Lloyd to Laurier, March 2, 1905:
Laurier Papers, 208880.

Finding the proposition to make the 4th Meridian line the dividing line between the two N.W. provinces was taking definite form I wrote to Mr. Haultain and also to the Minister of the Interior pointing out that the maps issued by the Dept. of Interior last year are wrong and that the 4th meridian line would divide our town in two. This would be a very serious matter for us practically ruining our new town just as it has begun to grow.

Might not the line between the Battle and Saskatchewan Rivers be along the 23rd Township line West of 3rd Meridian and so put the whole colony into the Western provinces as Edmonton is our natural centre.

V — 30

R.G. Matthews, Secretary-Treasurer of the Western
Stock Growers Association to Laurier, May 13, 1905:
Laurier Papers, 208718.

I have the honor to state that at the annual meeting of the Association held on 11th inst. the following resolution was adopted,—'That in the opinion of this meeting it would be advisable from a Stockman's point of view to extend the

Eastern boundary of the proposed Province of Alberta as far as the 107th Parallel of West longitude, as far north as the present Northern boundary of Assiniboia.'

V — 31

The Macleod Gazette Complains of the Land Clauses in the Autonomy Bills, March 3, 1905.

Autonomy without the control of Crown Lands is not full autonomy. It is not autonomy consistent with that possessed by all the older Provinces of Canada. It is not right as a matter of public policy and there are no considerations of expediency to justify it. The two new Provinces should be given control of the public lands within their boundaries.

Will the people of these provinces quietly submit to terms which deprive them of the administration of their Crown lands? Have we not as much right to these lands as to the rest of the provinces to theirs? Are we going to accept the sum of $400,000 per annum in lieu of the thousands of acres of land within the limits of our broad domain? Shall we meekly admit the insinuation that we are not capable of administering our own affairs?

The bill provides for our becoming provinces and at the same time withholds from us the very essentials of success by retaining the lands, minerals etc., while other provinces control theirs, forcing us to the conclusion that government considers us incapable of conducting the affairs of state.

The Dominion Parliament can do as its majority decides but if the people make their wishes known emphatically, it is hardly probable that Parliament will go against the expressed wishes of the people. Much depends on our actions in this matter and if we sit down and make no effort to have these matters adjusted more satisfactorily we must be content with what the government sees fit to give us. If on the other hand we make a determined stand for our rights, there is every chance that much for which we are contending may be granted us. . . .

It is up to the people to accept the bill as it now stands or make a determined effort at once. If you are satisfied with the present bill all right but if not get to work without delay and see what can be accomplished by vigorous and concentrated efforts.

V — 32

Haultain to Laurier, March 11, 1905: Laurier Papers, 95679-95691.

Sir,—The somewhat hurried termination of the Conference to which you were good enough to invite representatives of the North-west Government, and the introduction of the Alberta and Saskatchewan Bills, call for a final statement on the subject. In this statement I shall confine my remarks to some of the more important provisions of the Bills, leaving a number of minor matters requiring consideration to less formal mention.

The first question which suggests itself is the question of the necessity for the creation of two Provinces instead of one. After a careful consideration I am more convinced than ever that there is no necessity for dividing the country into two Provinces with the consequent duplication of machinery and institutions. The Provincial machinery is elaborate and expensive, and is more suitable to large areas and large populations. The new Territories have for a number of years been under one Government and Legislature, performing most of the duties and exercising many of the more important powers of Provincial Governments and Legislatures. There has never been any suggestion that the Territorial machinery was in any way inadequate for the purposes for which it was created. Our laws and institutions are admittedly efficient and satisfactory. Under them the people of the Territories have acquired a political individuality and identity as distinct as that of the people of any Province. Up to the thirtieth of June next this will continue to be the case, and there does not seem to be any reason based on necessity or convenience why on the first day of July they should be suddenly divided in two, separated by a purely arbitrary line and obliged to do with two sets of machinery and institutions what they to a great extent have been doing quite satisfactorily and efficiently with one. I must, however, frankly state that this opinion is by no means unanimously shared in the Territories and that the proposed action of the Government will not call forth much hostile criticism.

I must also state my opinion that the dividing line between the two Provinces should have been placed at least seventy-five miles farther east.

I must take strong exception to the way in which the subject of education has been treated both in the conferences and the Bills. I must remind you of the fact that your proposition was not laid before my colleague or myself until noon of the day upon which you introduced the Bills. Up to that time the question had not received any attention beyond a casual reference to it on the previous Friday, and I certainly believed that we should have an opportunity of discussing your proposals before 12 o'clock on the day the Bills received their first reading. No such opportunity, however, was afforded, as unfortunately you were not able to be present at the session when this section was submitted, neither was Sir William Mulock. I feel sure that you will acquit me of any feeling in the matter other than that such an important subject should have been fully discussed before any definite conclusion was arrived at by the Government and before the Bills dealing with it were laid before Parliament.

With regard to the question of education generally, you are no doubt aware that the position taken by us was that the Provinces should be left to deal with the subject exclusively subject to the provisions of The British North America Act, thus putting them on the same footing in this regard as all the other Provinces in the Dominion except Ontario and Quebec. I submit that Parliament is bound by the provisions of The British North America Act, 1867, in passing legislation of this kind. The power of the King in Council, exercising in effect the legislative functions of the Parliament of the United Kingdom under the authority of section 146 of The British North America Act, 1867, is restricted by the words "subject to the provisions of this Act." This restriction must equally apply to Parliament exercising the powers conferred on it by The British North America Act, 1871, which, by section 3 of The British North America Act, 1886, must be "construed together" with The British North America Act, 1867. If the King in Council is bound by the provisions of the Act in admitting an independent and consenting Colony into the Union it can hardly be contended that Parliament has the power to create an unwilling, inferior and imperfect organization. As was pointed out in June, 1869, by the Honourable Edward Blake in the House of Commons in the discussion upon a proposal to rearrange the terms of Confederation with respect to Nova Scotia: "It is perfectly clear, on great and obvious principles, that the basis of Union settled by The British North America Act is not capable of alteration "by Parliament." If the Provincial jurisdiction can be invaded by positive Federal legislation such as is proposed in this case, what limit is there to the exercise of such a power? Similar restrictions might be imposed with respect to any or all of the matters in relation to which, under The British North America Act, 1867, the Provincial Legislature possess exclusive power.

The only jurisdiction possessed by Parliament in this respect is the remedial jurisdiction conferred by sub-section 4 of section 93 of The British North America Act, 1867. The proposed attempt to legislate in advance on this subject is beyond the power of Parliament and is an unwarrantable and unconstitutional anticipation of the remedial jurisdiction. It has, further, the effect of petrifying the positive law of the Province with regard to a subject coming within its exclusive jurisdiction and necessitating requests for Imperial legislation whenever the rapidly changing conditions of a new country may require them. On the fifteenth of July, 1870, the North-west Territories were "admitted into the Union," in the express terms of section 146 of The British North America Act, 1867. To speak of the Provinces of Alberta and Saskatchewan being "admitted into the Union" on the first July, 1905, is an improper and indefensible use of the expression. The territory included within the boundaries of these proposed Provinces was "admitted into the Union" on July 15, 1870, and immediately upon the creation of these Provinces the provisions of section 93 of The British North America Act, 1867, become, as a matter of indefeasible right, a part of their Constitution. On the creation of the Provinces the term "Provinces" in that section interprets itself and the term "Union" bears the unmistakable meaning which is given to it with regard to the area included in the Provinces by the actual language of section 146.

The first sub-section of section 16 of the Bills is drawn in direct contradiction of this principle. It is an attempt to create a Province retroactively. It declares Territorial school laws passed under the restriction imposed by The North-west Territories Act to be provincial school laws. It clothes laws imposed by the Federal Parliament with all the attributes of laws voluntarily made by a free Province. It ignores Territorial limitations and conditions. It denies facts and abolishes time. It declares what was not to have been, and seeks to perpetuate as existing what never was nor is.

I therefore most respectfully demand on behalf of the Territories that the same terms, and no others, imposed by the Queen in Council on the admission of Prince Edward Island and British Columbia be prescribed in this instance. The draft Bill I submitted more than three years ago contains the clause which will be found in the Orders in Council admitting those

Provinces. To impose more or to prescribe less would, I submit, be equally contrary to the law and constitution. The clause referred to is as follows:

"On, from and after the said first day of January, 1903, the provisions of The British North America Act, 1867, except those parts thereof which are in terms made or by reasonable intendment may be held to be specially applicable or to affect only one or more, but not the whole of the Provinces under that Act composing the Dominion, and except so far as the same may be varied by this Act, shall be applicable to the Province of . . . . in the same way and to the same extent as they apply to the several Provinces of Canada and as if the Province of . . . . had been one of the Provinces originally united by the said Act."

The fact that since the acquisition of the North-west Territories Parliament has passed certain laws affecting those Territories does not involve the principle that those laws must be perpetuated in the Constitution of the proposed Provinces. In this respect laws relating to education do not differ from laws relating to any other subject. To state that the law passed in 1875 with regard to education must forever limit the power of the Province with regard to a very important Provincial right involves the theory that Parliament might practically take away all the jurisdiction of a Province and leave it shorn of every power which it is supposed to possess under the Constitution.

I wish to lay great stress on the fact that this is a purely constitutional question and is not concerned in any sense with the discussion of the relative merits of any system of education. The question is one of Provincial rights. It is not a question of the rights of a religious minority which must be properly and may be safely left to the Provincial Legislatures to deal with subject to the general constitutional provisions in that regard. It is the question of the right of a minority of Canadians in the wider arena of the Dominion to the same rights, and the same privileges, the same powers and the same constitution as are enjoyed by the rest of their fellow citizens and which they claim to be their inalienable possession under the one and only Canadian charter, The British North America Act.

The first observation I have to make upon sub-section 3 of section 16 is that it is a direct interference by Parliament with the right of the Province to do as seems to it best with its own.

I would next call attention to the fact that the sub-section appears in effect to repeal sub-section 3 of section 25 of The

Dominion Lands Act, which provides that certain revenues arising from the School Lands Fund "shall be paid annually to the Government of the Province or Territory within which such lands are situated, towards the support of *Public Schools* therein, and the money so paid shall be distributed for that purpose by the Government of such Province or Territory in such manner as it deems expedient."

This clause surely creates as inviolable a right in the solemn form of a trust as it is claimed is created by the adoption of section 14 of The North-west Territories Act which deals with the question of education. Its language is definite and unmistakable. I gather from the history of this section that Parliament defined and limited the scope of the section from time to time, always making it more definite and more restricted.

In 1872, when The Dominion Land Act was first enacted, section 2 of the Act provided that it was "expedient to make provision in aid of education" and set aside certain lands for that purpose without prescribing any particular course of procedure in connection therewith.

When the act was consolidated in 1879 the clause providing for the Trust fund was first enacted. It read as follows:

"Section 23 (3) Provided also that all moneys from time to time realized from the sale of school lands shall be invested in Dominion securities, and the interest arising therefrom, after deducting the cost of management, shall be paid annually to the Government of the Province or Territory within which such lands are situated towards the support of Public Schools therein—the moneys so paid to be distributed with such view by the Government of such Province or Territory in such manner as may be deemed most expedient."

In the next consolidation of the Act, that of 1883, this section was again amended to read as follows, the words added to the former section being italicised:

"Section 20 (4), subsection 4. Provided also that all money from time to time realized from the sale of school lands shall be invested in Dominion securities *to form a school fund* and the interest arising therefrom, after deducting the cost of management, shall be paid annually to the Government of the Province or Territory within which such lands are situated towards the support of Public Schools therein and the money so paid to be distributed *for that purpose* by the Government of such Province or Territory in such manner as may *by it* be deemed most expedient."

The change made, especially the introduction of the words

"by it" show that Parliament was evidently anxious to make it perfectly plain that the expenditure of the money resulting from this fund shall be left entirely in the discretion of the Province. The broad general term "education," after being carried through the Consolidations of 1879 and 1883, was left out in the revision of 1886, and there is no warrant for assuming that the words "Public Schools" in the Act as it at present stands mean or include any other schools.

I therefore wish to express my most emphatic objection to the legislation in regard to this subject. I recognize no power in Parliament to make laws for the new Provinces in contravention of the letter and spirit of The British North America Act. Further I recognize neither right nor justice in the attempt to dictate to the Provinces of Alberta and Saskatchewan the manner in which they shall conduct their own business. I very sincerely regret that it is necessary to give this turn to this discussion. I trust you will believe it is in no sense from any desire of my own to introduce an inharmonious note into these comments. The new Provinces have their own future to work out and I deplore the possibility that they may commence their careers torn with dissension upon such subjects as these. It seems to me that a great deal of this trouble might have been avoided had we been afforded an opportunity of discussing these proposals, and I feel that I must place on record the fact that we are not responsible for the situation.

Sections 19 and 20 provide that the public domain in each Province shall be administered by the Government of Canada for the purposes of Canada, an annual grant being made based upon certain varying rates of interest upon the capitalization of 25,000,000 acres of land at $1.50 per acre. Here again I have to express my dissent from the action taken. By analogy and by the acknowledgement of the principle of compensation contained in section 19 we claim that the Provinces are entitled to be recognized as the beneficial owners of the Crown Domain, and as such that their right to administer their own property for themselves is one that should not be taken away without their consent. As to whether or not the terms offered are fair or suffi-ciently large I am not in a position to judge having no material at hand to enable an estimate to be formed. I have one fact in mind in this connection and it is contained in the statement of the Honorable Clifford Sifton speaking as Minister of the Interior when he said that in one portion of the West alone the construction of the Grand Trunk Pacific Railway would make some 50,000,000 acres of land available for settlers, the value of which was not less than $3.00 an acre, in which manner he pointed out that the whole cost of the construction of the Road might be provided for. This was only in one portion of the country. But I am not unwilling to admit that an immediate income, increasing with population and certain in amount, may in the long run prove quite as satisfactory as any probable net income, resulting from local administration of the public domain.

I think a clerical error has been made by not inserting after the word "census" in the 9th line of the section the words "or estimate." I refer to the estimate between each census contemplated by section 17.

There are also errors in the computation of the amounts payable under the last section of the first subsection and under the second subsection. In these cases the first amount should be $1,125,000.00 and the second should be $93,750.00.

The matter of irrigation so closely related to the land question, in my opinion stands on a different footing and I can see no reason why the section in my draft Bill transferring the jurisdiction with regard to irrigation to the Province should not have been adopted by you. Irrigation is a "local" need in every sense of the word, and will be confined to one portion of the Territories, and peculiarly therefore falls within local jurisdiction. The desirability and convenience of local administration in this regard has been already admitted by Parliament by a delegation of the administration of the North-west Irrigation Act to the Territorial Commissioner of Public Works. The retaining of the jurisdiction in this case by the Federal Government is a serious evasion of the Provincial jurisdiction in matters of property and civil rights and is bound to create both inconvenience and friction.

The Bill does not contain any provision with regard to the selection of Judges for the Provincial Courts. My draft Bill contained the following clause which is identical in principle with the clause on the same subject in The British North America Act:

"The Judges of the Courts of the Province shall be selected from the bar of the Province or from the bar of some other Province in which the laws relative to property and civil rights and the procedure of the Courts are the same as in the Province of—"

As the conference has come to an end and the Government has expressed its own opinion publicly in the form of Bills, the whole of this matter now has become a subject for public discussion and I propose to make this letter public at the very earliest opportunity and not treat it as an official communication only to be made public in the ordinary way.

In concluding this letter I beg to express on behalf of the North-west Government our high appreciation of the attentive and courteous consideration extended to us by yourself and the other members of the Sub-Committee of Council throughout the whole conference.

Faced with a divided caucus and with the possibility of further resignations Laurier decided to rewrite the contentious education clauses to meet some of the objections of Sifton and others. The close involvement of the ex-Minister of the Interior in the redrafting of the bill was in sharp contrast to his role in the first bill.

The presentation of a modified bill by Laurier on March 22 did not end the controversy. Many charged that the revised terms were simply token compromises and that nothing had really been changed. It should be noted, however, that two of the major figures in the controversy, Sbaretti and Sifton, felt the changes to be substantial. Laurier had retreated to a compromise position and in spite of the continued torrent of words on the issue, was now in a better position to resist the pressures coming from all sides.

V — 33

Sifton to Dafoe, March 11, 1905: Sifton Papers, Vol. 263, 660-3.

I think we have practically agreed upon a settlement of the School clauses of the North West Act. The draft may now, I think, be said to be finally agreed to but it is understood that it is not to be given out to anybody. The reason for this is that if it were given out it would be attributed to some particular persons and probably attacked on that account. As at present arranged it will be placed upon the order paper towards the end of next week and the Bill will probably be taken up the following week. The final draft has followed the suggestion contained in your telegram of yesterday, that is to say it applied the British North America Act, Section 93, to the new provinces, but a new subsection is drawn and enacted in the place of sub-section 1 of section 93. This new subsection follows the first subsection as shown in the draft sent to you except that Chapter 31 of the North West Ordinances is not mentioned. Chapter 31 provides for the distribution of the Legislative Grant and instead of confirming it we added a short provision to the effect that in distributing monies appropriated by the legislature for the aid of schools organized under the School Ordinance there shall be no discrimination against any particular class of schools. Then a Section is added to make Subsections 3 and 4 applicable by the necessary verbal changes. I think we have got it into the best possible form. It has been given a very large amount of consideration and discussion. The point to be made in discussing it with our friends is to show that the Church is absolutely eliminated. There is no possibility of the Church getting its finger on the schools known as "separate schools" under the present North West Ordinances, and the result is that they are shut out forever unless they can get the people of the North-west Territories to give them something more, which I apprehend is putting it upon very safe ground.

I have had to make a very determined fight about the School Lands Fund. This is in reality where the conflict was hottest. They did not expect to get much more in the way of separate schools than they have now but they expected to get a declaration in the Constitution which could not be repealed, and which would be an inducement to the Catholic people to organize as many separate schools as possible.

With these explanations I think you will be able to understand the matter fully. Let me now say that nothing published must indicate that you have any knowledge of the contents of the Provision agreed upon until it is given out here. It is of the utmost importance that the Methodist, Presbyterian and Baptist clergymen in Winnipeg should be got to see the desirability of supporting this Provision before it is announced, and I would therefore like that you should either yourself or through someone else have them interviewed confidentially and fully informed as to what is under consideration. On the merits there is no objection to this proposal at all as you know. The only difficulty that we shall be in will be that some people will not be able to get themselves away from the blind adherence to catch words such as "provincial rights" and "separate schools", that is to say they will not take the trouble to analyse the proposition but will oppose it on theory. If, however, the clergy of Winnipeg support it I am not afraid of anything else. When the proposal is published from here it will of course be very desirable to get *as many as possible* of them to express themselves for publication.

V — 34

Sbaretti to Laurier, March 13, 1905: Laurier Papers, 35718-95720.

First by the Hon. R.W. Scott, the Secretary of State, in person, and afterwards by you in your letter of March 7th 1904, confirmed by another on the 12th of the same month, I was solemnly promised that the right of the minority to separate schools in the North-west Territories would be guaranteed in the Constitution of the Provinces to be erected therein, *as in the Provinces of Ontario and Quebec.*

In the elections of last November on the strength of your promise, I exercised my influence with the Prelates and Catholics of this country that no excitement or agitation would be created on the question of schools in the North-west Territories, and in a letter to the Honorable Secretary of State on October 13th, I promised that the same question would not be discussed in the Catholic papers. And my efforts were successful, as you are well aware.

I am extremely sorry to say that the clause read to me last evening does not fulfil the promised security. Neither the money of the Province which might be granted in aid of education, or that of the Trust Fund are legally guaranteed, for although it is said, as far as I can remember, that in the distribution of moneys there shall be no discrimination against any class of schools, you well know that the Government cannot distribute any money for any other purpose than that for which it is appropriated by legislative authority, but the School Trust Fund is already appropriated for the support of public schools and there is nothing in this new clause to prevent the Provincial Legislature from refusing to appropriate for separate schools. Under this respect the other clause formulated by Mr. Sifton that you presented to me on the 5th instant is less objectionable, as it specifically gives this right under the terms of Chapter 31 of the Ordinances respecting the Legislative grant.

Moreover in the present clause the very existence of separate schools is not legally secure against an act of a hostile legislature.

Therefore the clause you suggest is very weak and insecure. If in the first subsection, which is the same as that in the clause formulated by Mr. Sifton and presented to me on March 5th, you would say instead of 'under the terms of Chapters 29 and 30 under the North-west Territories Act and the term of Chapters

29, 30 and 31 etc.,' it would be less objectionable.

As to the other subsections, after one or two readings I cannot remember them well; it is impossible to judge them without a careful study. I beg of you therefore to reconsider this matter and not to force upon us the conscientious necessity of taking open opposition to a clause unacceptable to us and detrimental to our present rights.

V — 35

Peter Talbot to A.C. Rutherford, March 21, 1905:
Rutherford Papers.

Last night the Govt. handed in the Autonomy bill. I have not had time to study it but I think it is fairly satisfactory. It merely continues the present N.W. Ordinances 29 and 30. This matter has shaken the Liberal party to its very foundations. But I suppose that was necessary to prove to Quebec that that Province was not the whole of Canada.

I think Oliver wired the new clause to the Bulletin and you will see it before you get this letter.

V — 36

Laurier Amends the Schools Clause, March 22, 1905:
House of Commons Debates, March 22, 1905, 2915-2929.

Sir Wilfrid Laurier: . . . In the course of the years I have been in this House, many have been the occasions in which parliament has had to face and to solve the questions, simple enough in themselves, but complicated and rendered difficult by sudden outbursts of passion. And here again I may repeat what I had the opportunity of saying some few days ago, that in using this word 'passion,' I do not want to convey any offensive sense. I recognize, we all recognize, that passions are very often the outgrowth of noble sentiment; but let this sentiment be ever so meritorious, if it goes beyond a certain line, it may become blind, unthinking, unreasoning passion. In 1875 on the New Brunswick school question, in 1889 on the Jesuit Estates questions, in 1896 on the Manitoba school question, several parts of the country—now one part, now another—were roused to a high pitch of excitement. . . .

I stand again, as I believe, upon the rock of the constitution of Canada when I say that this parliament should, according to that constitution, give to the minority in the new provinces the same rights and privileges that are given to the minorities in the new provinces of Quebec and Ontario. . . .

Now, Sir, a word as to the changes we have made in that clause. I stated the other day that we proposed to make a change and we have given notice of an amendment which we intend to move to clause 16. What is the reason of this change? It is a fair question to ask and a question to be answered. Sir, we have taken the ground on more than one occasion, we again take this ground and it is the ground upon which we stand in dealing with the present case, that wherever a system of separate schools exists that system comes into force and is constitutionally entitled to the guarantees which are embodied in section 93 of the British North America Act. Be that system much, be it little, whatever it is, it is entitled to those guarantees. That is the position we take, and when we introduced section 16, as it is in the Bill, we had no other intention than to give to the minority the rights and privileges to which they are entitled under the law which they have today.

But, Sir, it has been objected to us that the language used in section 16 was too broad, too vague, and that if it were adopted, it would create trouble and confusion instead of certainty as to the rights of the minority. . . .

We therefore thought it was preferable to have the law made absolutely certain and in order to do that we have incorporated the ordinances under which the law as it is today has been established. It may be disappointing to some, but we believe that on the whole it is preferable to have a clear understanding on this subject so that the minority shall have the privilege of exercising control over their schools as they have today, and so that the law shall be absolutely clear and pronounced as to what is intended by the parliament of Canada if it passes this legislation. That is the reason why we have done this. The law of the Territories on this question is established in three ordinances, chapter 29 of 1901, chapter 30 of 1901, and chapter 31 of 1901. Chapter 20 organized a system of schools and this organization retained to the minority the privileges which they have of separate schools. Chapter 30 regulates the power of assessments over the municipalities for contributions to education and chapter 31 regulates the aid and contributions to be made to the different schools conforming to the law. We have introduced into the amendment chapter 20 and chapter 30; we have not introduced chapter 31 which regulates the aid and grants to be given to schools because we have thought it preferable simply to lay down the principle, putting no burden upon the Territories, not saying how they are to dispose of their money, not telling them what they shall do but simply stating that when schools conform to the law, whether they are separate schools or public schools, all shall be treated equally and there shall be no discrimination between them. That is the reason of the legislation I have introduced.

V — 37

Robert Borden on Second Reading of the Autonomy Bill, March 22, 1905: House of Commons Debates, March 22, 1905, 2963-2980.

Mr. R.L. Borden: . . . I am opposed to the substituted section because it is not different in principle from that for which it is substituted; and indeed it is difficult to understand why there have been three weeks of negotiation, why there have been three weeks of turmoil, why this measure has been postponed from the 21st of February up to the present time, simply for the purpose of bringing down to parliament as a substitute that which is to all intents and purposes, in principle and for the most part in detail, exactly the same as the original section. Is this the result of the efforts of the ex-Minister of the Interior? Is it for this that he resigned office? Is it to accomplish this that he laid down the seals of office and placed himself before the people of this country as the champion of provincial liberties? Is this the result of the unceasing and untiring efforts of the seven hon. gentlemen from the North-west Territories who sit on the side of the House? Sir, the mountains have been in labour, and a ridiculous mouse has been brought forth. What does section 16 as proposed to be amended accomplish? It stereotypes for ever the ordinances and laws of the North-west Territories in a portion of the country where extraordinary progress and development must be expected. I venture to think that an Act of this kind will be productive of more harm in that portion of the country than anywhere else in Canada, because it is into the North-west that our immigration will largely flow, and it is there that we must expect development and progress to a very unusual degree in the immediate future. . . .

Mr. Speaker, education was assigned to the provinces. Let

any necessary agitation in respect to education, in respect to the rights and powers of legislature with regard to education, be confined to provincial limits. That is the true solution of the question. Let the Dominion interfere and the agitation will be widespread. My proposition is to let the people settle the question for themselves, and the agitation if any—and I do not believe there will be any considerable agitation—will be confined within narrow limits, and, in the end, will be settled by some reasonable compromise, because, after all, we can always safely trust to the good sense of the people in this regard. As I said before, I firmly believe that if this question had been left to the people of the new provinces, they would have dealt, and they will deal, fairly with the minority. But we must not oppress or coerce any part of the people to provide safeguards that have not a warrant in the constitution.

V — 38

Clifford Sifton on the Second Reading of the Autonomy Bill, March 24, 1905: House of Commons Debates, March 24, 1905, 3092-3121.

Hon. Clifford Sifton: . . . I gave my advice to the best of my ability. And I may say, so far as that is concerned, that in the main, other than as refers to the question of education, and although there are some variations of detail—in the main, I say, and substantially, the Bill I recommended to my late colleagues is the Bill which has been introduced. There are some matters of detail respecting which difficulties arose, and different decisions were arrived at in the course of the discussions which took place with the representatives of the North-west Territories. These were inevitable. But, substantially the provisions of the Bill are in accordance with the views I had formed in the course of my administration of that country.

So far as the question of the number of provinces is concerned, I formed the opinion which, I think, will be shared by almost every person on careful investigation of the case, that it was not desirable that this vast territory should be formed into one province. Certainly it was not desirable to carry out the old idea which prevailed that there were to be four provinces. I think the best opinion of the House will be met by the decision which the government has reached, that the medium course should be taken, and, that instead of one or four, we should have two provinces. Not only is the question of area to be considered as was shown by the Prime Minister in his remarks in introducing the Bill, but you must consider also the even more important question of population. The population of this one province, if this territory were made into one province, would eventually have such a preponderance as compared with the other provinces that it could not be said to be wise to make such an arrangement. These provinces are composed of territories which, almost acre for acre, is arable land and capable of sustaining population. No other provinces in the Dominion can be similarly described. And to make one province of that particular territory whose capacity for sustaining population is, on the average, so much greater than that of any other province in the Dominion, giving it ultimately so much greater population than the other provinces, would certainly and obviously be unwise. Other considerations supported the same conclusion. The western and eastern portions of this territory lend themselves to different industrial conditions. Great grazing areas exist in the west such as are not found in the east. Mining possibilities in a large scale are to be found in the western part of the territory, and in the north, towards Edmonton, we have what is known as a mixed-farming district. Different classes of local legislation will be needed, and different conditions must be recognized in the two portions of the territory. Everybody who knows the conditions of that territory will be satisfied that the best results will result from having two local governments and two legislatures. Each of these legislatures and each of these administrations will have ample scope for all the energy it may see fit to display in the development of the resources of the great territory which is committed to its charge. And this parliament may be satisfied, I think, that that arrangement which is suggested will give the surest guarantee that the future development of these territories will be best facilitated.

While on the question of boundaries, I may say, having reference for a moment, to a statement made by Mr. Haultain in an open letter addressed to the Prime Minister, that I also suggested, and it was my idea, that the dividing line between the two new provinces should be about sixty miles further east than that which is provided for by the Bill. It was in the discussions which took place with the government that the present arrangement was arrived at. I have not heard the reasons which have led to this conclusion but I have no doubt that the conclusion thus arrived at after careful consideration, will be found upon the whole to be that which is supported by the best reasons. This in any event is a small difference of detail.

But there is one other point I will suggest, perhaps more for the future consideration of the House than for present consideration, that there should be some different principle adopted. I see no reason why these provinces should not extend to the northern boundary of the mainland of Canada. The experience which I have had in the Department of the Interior has led me irresistibly to the conclusion that just so soon as it is possible to do so, the federal government should divest itself of the local administration of distant territory; and therefore I see no reason why, in so far as the administration of these North-west Territories come within the scope of provincial legislation, that their administration should not be carried on by the local legislatures that we are to establish. That however is not an insuperable objection. The Territories of course still remain the property of Canada, and if it be thought wise at a future date they can be added to the provinces which we are now forming.

Upon the question of the lands which has been discussed at some length, I have very clear and positive opinions. I regard the question of a successful settlement policy—and my opinion is not changed by the fact that this policy may now require to be carried on under somebody else's supervision—I regard the question of a successful settlement policy in Canada as perhaps one of the most important, if not the most important of all subjects with which we have to deal. For the last two or three years especially, we have seen the effect of the small beginnings of success of the policy of settling vacant lands of the west upon the general prosperity of Canada, and I think every serious minded man will admit that under no possible circumstances would this parliament be justified in taking any step which would imperil in the slightest degree the success of the immigration policy which we have been carrying on, and which the government proposed to carry on in the future. That is a thing which demands the most careful thought and consideration at the hands of this parliament. It was suggested by the leader of the opposition, and has been suggested by others who take the opposite view, that the handing over of the public lands of the Territories to the provincial government would not seriously interfere with the conduct of immigration. Well, Mr. Speaker, I have had on my shoulders the duty of carrying on a policy of immigration, and of harmonizing the operations of the lands department of the government and of the immigration department for the last eight years, and it taxes the efforts of the department to the utmost, when both the land department and the immigration branch are in the same hands and under the same control, to avoid the difficulties which constantly present themselves in the administration of this work. It would be difficult satisfactorily to carry on that work even if we had the land department in another branch of the same government; it would be embarrassing and difficult to an extent that few men appreciate who have not had the duty of actually carrying on this business. But if you hand over the land to three provincial governments—because you would have to treat Manitoba in the same way as you are treating the Territories—if you hand over the land to three separate provincial governments, each with its own ideas of policy, each with its own Minister of Crown Lands, and if the federal government has to deal with three provincial governments, every man who knows anything about doing business between governments must know that it would be absolutely impossible that satisfactory results could be achieved. It is not necessary to suggest that they would be improvident, that they do not know how to carry on business as well as we do. The people of the west are just as capable as the people in any other part of the Dominion; they are extremely capable, and when they achieve provincial status, if these lands were handed over to them, they would do precisely what people in the other provinces do, they would administer these lands just as they saw fit and in accordance with their own ideas of policy. The result would be that you would have three governments to deal with, each with its own idea of policy, each with its Minister of Crown Lands, and possibly no two of them with the same ideas as to the policy that should be carried out in respect to this subject. It might be, Mr. Speaker, and probably would be, that instead of administering these lands for the purpose of settlement they would administer them for the purpose of revenue, and I do not know that we could blame them very much if they did so. But if they did that, the result would be that the settlement policy of the country would stop. . . .

As to the financial provisions, Mr. Speaker, I think they are generous and liberal, but I do not think they are too generous or too liberal. We expect that these great provinces will play a great part in the history of Canada, and it is creditable to us that on both sides there has come nothing but approval of the liberal and generous treatment accorded by the government to these new provinces upon the inception of their provincial career. Let me say, however, Mr. Speaker, not wishing to say anything ungracious or to throw a note of discord into the discussion of this subject, that there is one suggestion which I desire to make to the right hon. gentleman who leads the government, and it is this: I find in this clause of the Bill relating to the compensation for lands that such compensation is based upon an estimated acreage and upon a price, and the price put upon that estimated acreage is, I think, $1.50 an acre. I have no fault to find with the amount which has been decided upon, and which the government proposes to give. I think it is reasonable and liberal, I think it is generous, and I am quite prepared to agree with it. But I submit that the amount should be fixed arbitrarily, it should not be fixed by a reference to the number of millions of acres of land, nor the price per acre. The moment I laid my eyes upon that clause I felt it was a mistake, and I felt that just as soon as it was published the representatives of the Territories would say: You have by this clause admitted that we are entitled to the beneficial ownership of these lands, you have admitted that we are the owners of these lands in fact, beneficially at least if not in law, by the very fact that you are basing the compensation you give us upon the acreage of the provinces. And so within a few days after the Bill was published and before parliament gave assent to it, our good friend Mr. Haultain seized upon this phase of the Bill to present an objection to the right hon. gentleman, who leads the government. He immediately took the ground which it must be admitted he could take with some degree of force, that by that provision we admitted, impliedly at least, the right of the Territories to claim that they are the beneficial owners of the land. . . .

As I explained a few days ago, the terms of the educational clause of this Bill which was introduced into the House and some of the remarks made by my right hon. friend the leader of the government were the cause of my resigning from the government as a protest against the terms of that clause and the principle to which it was designated to give effect. I have nothing to add to that statement now except to say that while my action was in no sense or nature due to experiencing any feeling of personal pique, yet I did feel, in addition to what I said upon a former occasion, that the right hon. gentleman had not been well advised in bringing this clause to the House of Commons and presenting it to the House without giving me an opportunity of expressing such views as I might desire to offer on the subject. I say I have nothing now to add to what has been said upon that subject and I merely desire, with the indulgence of the House, to proceed to the discussion of the sections we have before us—the original section and the amended section— and to give the reasons which have guided me in coming to the conclusion at which I have arrived as to the support of this Bill or otherwise. I am in a somewhat peculiar position, Mr. Speaker, finding as I do that I agree much more with the statements of my hon. friend the leader of the opposition (Mr. R.L. Borden) than with the statements and arguments of my right hon. friend the leader of the government who is my party leader and who was my leader in the government for so many years. Nevertheless, the conclusion at which I arrived will probably not be the same as that of the hon. leader of the opposition. In the first place let me say that I think he was wrong in his view— and I agree with my hon. friend the Minister of Finance (Mr. Fielding) in this—that when we are about the consider the legislation which will bring a certain state of affairs into existence in the North-west Territories, we should shut our eyes absolutely and entirely to the examination of the actual educational effect of the proposal before us. It seems to me that almost everybody will agree with my hon. friend the Minister of Finance that the man in the street, hearing the hon. gentleman who leads the opposition say that he stands by the constitution, and hearing the right hon. gentleman who leads the government say that upon the rock of the constitution he stands, and seeing these two gentlemen both standing on the rock of the constitution but coming to diametrically opposite conclusions will be likely to say: I cannot hope to understand the law or the constitution, but I do want to know what kind of schools they are going to have in the North-west Territories. Therefore, I desire to address a few words to the House. . . .

We are face to face with two propositions. We have the principle of the British North America Act to apply. The leader of the government and myself can agree that we ought to apply the principle of section 93 of the British North America Act, but as to the particular way in which we are to apply that principle we do not agree. But we ought to apply the principle, and when we come to the question: how are we to apply it, we come up against two separate and distinct and irreconcilable propositions. From my standpoint I say: inasmuch as the North-west Territories are not a constitutionally free community; inasmuch as the ordinances passed are ordinances passed under a special and limited power; therefore when they come into the family of provinces we ought not to apply to them the principle of observing the status quo, because the status quo was not brought about by their own unlimited powers. There is also the view that is presented to us by our friends led by the right hon. the Prime Minister, and held by many other gentlemen here. They say—it was well stated by the Minister of Finance—they say: you constituted that territory 35 years ago; 30 years ago you established separate schools you said when you were doing it that you intended it to be permanent; those who made speeches when the Bill was presented to parliament, said we bring this Bill to parliament because we want the people of the North-west Territories to know what kind of institutions they are going to have and among others they are going to have separate schools. Half a million people have gone into the North-west Territories knowing what the laws were. Although I am not absolutely convinced by the argument made by these gentlemen, yet I know that out of that population of half a million there are 125,000 Roman Catholics, and I further know that many of these people actually went to the educational department at Regina by their authorized representatives and got copies of these school ordinances so that they might know whether they would be allowed to have separate schools before they came into the North-west Territories. Therefore, our friends say: here is a state of affairs existing for thirty years, carried on under your direction, creating vested rights in 125,000 people who have gone there upon the strength of your guarantee. And so, with some degree of plausibility they argue: you are far more bound to maintain that state of affairs than if it had been created by the provinces, because you are responsible for it yourselves. Here we have two separate and irreconcilable propositions. If I talked for ever I do not think I would convince the gentlemen who do not think as I do upon this subject. I do not think I could convince them that we should leave the legislature of the North-west absolutely free in this matter—although I am for my part convinced after the history of the question in the province of Manitoba, and from the knowledge I have of what public men in the Territories think on this whole question from beginning to end—I am firmly convinced that it would be better for the Roman Catholic people of the North-west Territories if the legislature were left absolutely free. But, I shall never convince the gentlemen who do not think so; I shall never get them to think as I do on the question, because if I talked for a hundred years their views would be just the same as they are today.

I am very much inclined to think, Mr. Speaker, that they will not be able to convince me. I do not think they would be able to convince me that it would not be better that the legislature of the North-west Territories should be free. Now, what are we going to do? We are face to face with an absolutely irreconcilable state of affairs. My hon. friend the Minister of Finance put it very well the other evening. He said: What are you going to do? what are you going to decide? The King's government must be carried on: the business of the country must be carried on; and there is only one or two ways in which this question can be decided. The Protestant people of Canada can say to the Roman Catholic people: You cannot convince us, we cannot convince you, but there are more of us than there are you, and we are going to vote you down. I put aside a proposition of that kind. There is no man in this government who would contemplate attempting to carry out a proposition of that kind if he had the power. Least of all would my hon. friend who leads the opposition desire to see a proposition of that kind carried out, no matter what his views on the merits of the question might be. Then, what are you going to do? What is the position of affairs going to be? You cannot make a political religious issue of these questions either for the members of this House or for the inhabitants of the Dominion of Canada; and even if you did—as my hon. friend the Minister of Finance very well said: if those who thought in this House as I do combined with me and if the result of their efforts were to drive the right hon. gentleman (the Prime Minister) from office on this question, all that my hon. friend the Minister of Finance said the other night, and much more, would be true. No greater political misfortune could happen to hon. gentlemen opposite than that they should be called upon to take office under such circumstances. Suppose it happened. Every man who knows the political history of Canada knows that we might fight about this question year in and year out for years, the political and financial progress of the country might be paralyzed, the business of the country would be blocked by the condition of affairs, and after it was all done, we should be simply where we had started, and the people would have to come together on this question and compromise their differences.

What I desire to say, Mr. Speaker, in conclusion, is that I have very strong views on this question. I have not concealed those views from the members of the House. There is a certain distance that I am prepared to go in the way of compromise; I have so expressed myself to my right hon. friend the Prime Minister. To the extent which is embodied in the proposition before this House I am willing to go. I am willing to go that far because I believe that the essential principles of a first-class, thoroughly national school system are not impaired, and the taint of what I call ecclesiasticism in schools, and which in my judgement always produces inefficiency, will not be found in the school system of the North-west under this legislation, unless the people of the North-west choose to have it, in which case it is their business and not ours. I may say, Mr. Speaker, that I have found a very great deal of difficulty in deciding upon my course on this question. When I saw the Bills that had been introduced, I at once came to the conclusion that I could not decide upon my course while remaining a member of the government, in the enjoyment of office and the emoluments of office. I came to the conclusion that, whatever anybody else might do, my course was perfectly clear; I should, when this question came up, be in a position to speak with a freedom with which a member of the government could not speak, and I should be called upon to decide to what extent and how far I would be prepared to compromise opinions which I had publicly expressed, and opinions which I still hold in order not to destroy the government of the country. That question which comes to every man in public life sooner or later, comes today to a good many men in this House of Commons. The question is how far a man is justified in compromising his opinion for the purpose of preventing a political crisis. That is a question which nearly every man in this House has had to decide before; but perhaps no person has had to decide it under quite as remarkable circumstances as the present. For myself, as to the political effect upon myself, I care not for that. I have relieved myself, I think, of the imputation that the course I have taken has been influenced by considerations of office or the considerations of my party remaining in office; and therefore I have to say, having given the subject the best consideration that I am capable of giving it, and having given it that consideration not only from the standpoint of the position of affairs in this parliament but from the standpoint of the position of affairs in the North-west Territories in time to come, that I can, though not with very much enthusiasm, and with some degree of reluctance give my support to the Bill.

V — 39

Frank Oliver on the Second Reading of the Autonomy Bill, March 24, 1905: House of Commons Debates, March 24, 1905, 3152-3169.

Mr. Frank Oliver: . . . Now, there is no one so blind as he who will not see; and the gentleman who can see no difference between the provisions of clause 16 as originally introduced and the provisions as they now stand for the approval of the House, is certainly very blind; I won't say that it is because he does not want to see, very probably it is because he cannot see. The difference between these two provisions, as I understand them is radical. I do not say that it was intentional. We have had enough disputations in regard to constitutional points in this House during this debate to leave us all with the full knowledge that there may be honest differences of opinion with regard to all these points. To my mind the difference is very important. As stated by the ex-Minister of the Interior here today—and I speak as one who knows something of this matter, as one who has had experience in regard to school legislation, as one of those members of the North-west Assembly who made the change in the North-west school law between what it was before 1891 and what it is today—I say the difference, as I understand it, is a difference between clerical control of schools and national control of schools. If that is not a sufficient difference, then I do not understand what we are disputing about. I think it is a radical difference. It is what threw this country into a turmoil in 1896 and caused a change of government at that time. It is the reason why those gentlemen are sitting on that side of the House instead of on this side. . . .

As to the ownership of the lands; it has been urged that these lands are the property of the province, should remain the property of the province and should be administered by the province for the benefit of the revenue of the province. It matters not to me what the legal rights of the province or the Dominion respectively are in that case. The lands belong to Canada whether administered by the province or by the Dominion; the settlement of these lands is for the benefit of all Canada. Whatever method of administration will give us the best results in the way of the settlement of these lands is the policy that is best not only for the Dominion but for the province. As a representative of the west, I believe the idea of using the lands of the west as a source of provincial revenue would be a very great detriment to these new provinces and to the country at large. I am aware that the provinces must have revenue, and failing any other source I would say: Certainly we must have revenue from the lands. But if we can get adequate revenue from other sources than the lands, then we certainly do not want the lands used as a source of revenue. I can easily understand that with a change of policy on the part of the federal government, a change of policy back to what it was say twenty years ago, when it was believed to be the proper policy to take everything that could be taken out of the land in the way of cash payment; then possibly it would be better that the lands should be in the hands of the province rather than in the hands of the Dominion. But, so long as we have a land policy the basic idea of which is the land for the settler, it is certainly better for us and for the Dominion that the lands should be administered by the federal authorities. One hon. gentleman said, that the lands could be better administered by the province than by the Dominion because the people of the province were closer on the ground, and the interests of the province he said, were just the same as the interests of the Dominion. I beg to differ; their interests are not the same. The interest of a province in the land is in the revenue it can derive from the sale of the lands; the interest of the Dominion in the lands is in the revenue that it can derive from the settler who makes that land productive. This Dominion of Canada can makes millions out of the lands of the North-west, and never sell an acre; it has made millions out of these lands without selling an acre. The increase in our customs returns, the increase in our trade and commerce, the increase in our manufactures is to a very large extent due to the increase in settlement on the free lands of the North-west Territories. The prosperity this Dominion is enjoying today is to a very large extent due to the fact that the lands of the North-west Territories have been given away and that people have taken them. I say that the interest of the Dominion is to secure the settlement of the lands, and whether with a price or without a price makes little or no difference. It is worth the while of the Dominion to spend hundreds of thousands of dollars in promoting immigration to that country and to spend thousands and thousands of dollars in surveying and administering these lands, and then to give them away. But the province is not in that position. The province derives no revenue from the customs duties or from the wealth which the settler creates. Every settler who goes on land in the North-west Territories is a bill of expense to the provincial government. That settler requires a road made, he requires a school supported, he requires the advantages of municipal organization, and these have to be provided for him out of the funds of the provincial government, so that as a matter of fact the tendency of the provincial government is to get such money as it can out of the land and to prevent settlement from spreading any further than can be helped. On the other hand, the interest of the Dominion is to get the settlers on the land, to scatter them far and wide so long as they are good settlers and they get good land. That is the position as it strikes us in the North-west, and when we have secured a financial arrangement with the Dominion government that gives us adequate consideration for our lands—I mean to say, gives us an adequate revenue as compared with the other provinces at any rate; gives us a revenue that instead of decreasing will increase as our needs increase; gives us a revenue that is proportionate not only to our population as it will be but to the area over which that population will spread— when we have secured an arrangement such as that, we have secured a very satisfactory arrangement; at least as satisfactory as we can expect to secure. . . .

In regard to the other provisions of this Bill I do not think anything need be said. We have received in the past at the hands of this government very fair consideration. We have received representation in this House and in the upper chamber. We have received reasonable financial consideration, increasing as our needs increased, although possibly not fully up to the mark of our requirements. And now, that it has seemed good to the government of the day and to, I think, the large majority of the people of the country to erect these Territories into provinces, it is certainly something of which we may very well be proud that we enter confederation upon such favorable terms. We only regret that this particular subject should have been the occasion of such a great amount of what I may be justified in calling malicious misrepresentation for the purpose of making party capital. We had hoped that our entrance into confederation as full fledged provinces would be under altogether auspicious circumstances. With this exception they are altogether auspicious and perhaps when we have threshed out this question in parliament we will all understand each other better, we will all know where we severally stand on this important question and perhaps it will be the last we will hear in Canada of this much vexed school question.

V — 40

Henri Bourassa on the Second Reading of the Autonomy Bill, March 28, 1905: House of Commons Debates, March 28, 1905, 3252-3284.

Mr. Henri Bourassa: . . . What has become of the religious liberty, of the liberty of teaching of the Catholic population of the North-west? It has been abolished in Manitoba, against all pledges, against all words of honour; and the author of that legislation can gain applause in this House by saying: 'If I have a title to the approval and support of the people of Canada, it is because I have gone back upon the pledges given in the name of the Queen of England to a law-abiding and peaceful population.' This, Mr. Speaker, is what we have come to. And now we are called upon to bow to this storm of feeling that has been aroused and to allow a still greater invasion of the rights of the people of that territory. It is time to face the storm. The powers that have raised that storm do not deserve that we should acknowledge their sovereignty. The principle of provincial rights is against them. The constitution is against them. The law is against them. Past pledges are against them. I will go further and say that a religious principle is at stake in this matter. . . .

We have frequently been told: Why can't you trust the majority of the people of the North-west? Well, Sir, here again I must speak frankly; and I say: No, we cannot. Suppose we could trust the people who are living there now; is there a man in this House childish enough to say that the condition of things which exists now is sure to exist in the North-west fifty years hence? What will be the population up there? Who knows what feelings will dominate the majority there? Who knows but that the great majority of the people there will be settlers coming from a land where the idea, not only of non-sectarian schools but of Godless schools, now prevails, and to my mind, to the great detriment of the future of the republic? Who can tell what the future will be? But confining myself entirely to a survey of past events, I say now that we cannot trust the present majority of the people of the North-west to stand for right and justice. Their record is before us. . . .

The French Canadian's heart is generous, his heart is grateful and he will never forget what you have done. But on the other hand—and in this I am not uttering any threat—I regret every time I go back to my province to find developing

the feeling that Canada is not Canada for all Canadians. We are
sometimes in Quebec accused of being provincialists. We are
not provincialists by nature. We have stood for the defence of
the whole soil of Canada and have contributed our share for the
benefit of the whole of Canada. But after such examples as we
have had in New Brunswick, in Manitoba, and the North-west
Territories, after such attempts as were made in Ontario itself
where we were preserved only because there was a text of law,
we are bound to come to the conclusion that Quebec is our only
country because we have no liberty elsewhere. I do not say that
we are treated as slaves; but we are proud enough and I contend
that we have rendered service enough to claim at the hands of
the majority of this country not only such treatment as you
would grant to a good natured inferior being, but such treatment as I think we, as your brethren, are entitled to receive at
your hands. If you do that, if you are just and just without
quibbling, just and just without trying to take with one hand
what you give with the other, I say: Trust the French Canadian
in the west or in the east, trust the French Canadian anywhere
in Canada; he will be true to you, true to the British Crown, if
you do not expel from his mind the belief that Canada is a free
country and that the British Crown is in this country the
protector of equal justice and equal law.

V — 41

Anonymous to Laurier, April 5, 1905: Laurier Papers, 96320.

From those that want wat our forefathers gave us we say very
little but we are cut to the hearts thanking for the cut of that day
go as he will be look for like yourself and the rest of the
members that give any more separate schools in Canada you are
not in a Roman Country and will not rule us a one it is men like
you and your friends that have put Russia ware she is to day.

> From those that mean
> to some thanking that
> will open up wat that
> son of a Bitch of a
> day go is look for
> not a L.O.L.
> But a Bomb Maker. . . .

Sifton's resignation had left a major portfolio vacant in the

Laurier government. When the Autonomy bills had been modified many expected Sifton to return to the cabinet. He had no intention of doing so, however, and the position was thus left open for some other Western Canadian Member of Parliament. Walter Scott's name was often mentioned in party circles but in the end Laurier chose Frank Oliver. The presence of an Alberta M.P., and an Edmonton one, in the cabinet in the next months was to have an important influence on the shaping of provincial politics as the region took on its new constitutional form.

V — 42

Frank Oliver's newspaper Comments on
Frank Oliver's Appointment as Minister of the Interior,
Edmonton Bulletin, April 10, 1905.

Early on Saturday afternoon the appointment of the member for Edmonton to fill the vacancy in the Dominion Cabinet was placarded at the Bulletin office, and soon became the centre of attraction for men of all political stripe and the general topic of discussion on the streets. The news may be fairly said to have come as a genuine surprise to the public generally, and to many well-informed in political matters.

Since the announcement of Mr. Sifton's acceptance of the revised school clauses the impression has been general that he might again enter the Cabinet and resume the duties of the portfolio of the Interior. Reports have been freely circulating throughout the West for many days to the effect that Walter Scott, M.P. for Regina, was the probable successor to Mr. Sifton in the event of his not returning to office. The appointment of Mr. Oliver was thus announced without any preparatory prognostication.

The news was not the less pleasing to Edmonton people because it was unexpected. The supporters of the sitting member were naturally and unanimously jubilant, but the gratification was by no means confined to them and may in fairness be said to have been shared by men of all classes and parties. The old-timers were pleased that one of their number had climbed to the upper rounds [sic] of the ladder and the citizens generally, disregarding party affiliation rejoiced at the distinction which had been conferred on the city and district by the selection of Edmonton's member for the Cabinet position, the duties and policy of which bear most directly and powerfully on the future of the Western country. It was and is felt to be a fitting thing and one for congratulations that the first Minister of the Federal Government for the Territories should be the representative of the Edmonton constituency.

Conservatives joined with Liberals in recognizing the honor done our city and many prominent members of the party intimated that they did not consider it probable that Mr. Oliver would be opposed in seeking re-election.

Throughout the spring of 1905 Alberta newspapers and organizations continued to protest the clauses of the Autonomy bills. By this time the schools issue had been picked up in the West but it remained but one of a number of issues of concern to those who disliked the bills. Initially it looked as if the protests would have little influence. Haultain's long letter of March 11, previously listed, had not caused Laurier to alter the bills nor had the numerous letters of protest of which a few are included in the following documents. Laurier, it appeared, felt he could ignore the West as long as he could hold his party's strength in the east.

Growing recognition of this fact in the West gave great importance to two bye-elections being held in Ontario in June. If the Conservative Party could take these previously Liberal seats then the Laurier government might withdraw the 'coercion bills.' If, on the other hand, the Liberals held on to their seats then it would be a clear sign that the party had weathered the storm caused by Sifton's resignation. Thus in late May and early June North-west politicians trooped into the affected constituencies on behalf of both the Liberals and Conservatives. R.B. Bennett, F.W.G. Haultain, Frank Oliver, Walter Scott, Peter Talbot and others made the contest, as the Edmonton Journal said, practically a Western one.

V — 43

Resolution of the Trades and Labor Council of Calgary, April 6, 1905: Calgary Herald, April 7, 1905.

Resolved:—That this meeting of the Trades and Labor Council of Calgary, representing the labor interests of Calgary and district, is opposed to the school clauses in the Autonomy bill introduced on February 21st, being of the opinion that this question should be left to the legislative assembly of the province to be determined according to local institutions.

Further that it is opposed to the retention of lands by the Dominion government, as it is convinced that the lands should be the property of the province, because:

(1) Under present conditions the expenses of realizing a debtor's estate who owns land under the Dominion government in many instances are so great as to cause hardships to creditors.

(2) That in a few years time the subsidy in place of these lands will prove inadequate to pay interest on the money that will have to be expended in the making and maintaining of roads.

(3) The mining, timber and water rights and the power of granting leases which would be lost to the provinces if the lands are retained by the Dominion government would prove valuable assets on which to raise money for all purposes for the development of the provinces.

Further that this Council is in favor of only one province being created, to be called and known as the province of Alberta.

V — 44

An Edmontonian Gives His views on Autonomy to the Toronto News: Reprinted in Edmonton Journal, April 12, 1905.

Dr. H.L. McInnis of Edmonton is in Toronto for a few days. He has been a resident of the North-west for fifteen years, has travelled over the Territories in all directions and is well and wisely known as one who has had much to do with the development of the Western country. Interviewed by the News regarding the Autonomy Bill the Doctor said:

'There are at least four aspects of the question now before the House at Ottawa any one of which ought to defeat the bill and every one of which will raise such a storm in the West that the questions will never be settled until the new Provinces get full Provincial autonomy on the same basis as the older Provinces. In the East I find that almost the only question discussed by the people and the press is the Separate School matter. Now, the land question, the mineral question and others are every one fully as important as the school problem to the development of the West. Take for instance the land question. We in the West would be perfectly satisfied if the Dominion Government kept control of the lands that are open for homesteading and colonization purposes, although the revenue accruing from the sale of such lands should certainly accrue to the Western Provinces themselves. But when it comes to the Dominion Government controlling the timber and the minerals that are on these lands, we think and feel that we ought to have the same privileges as the other Provinces and have complete control of our timber, our minerals, and all the natural wealth of the Provinces, as they will in a very few years become a fruitful source of revenue. At present the timber is being sold by tenders opened at Ottawa and is nearly always purchased by Ottawa persons and other eastern speculators. The amount of timber land which is now held by eastern speculators amounts to many thousand miles. What we in the west want is that the money that is paid for those lands should go to the Provinces, so that the Provinces themselves should benefit by such sales of timber land.

With reference to the minerals of the West—take coal for instance—the Government is selling the coal land at so much per acre, and collecting a royalty of ten or twenty cents a ton. The great increase in the population of the West, which is constantly going on, will soon augment the demand for coal, and at ten and twenty cents a ton, in a few years the Dominion Government will receive more from this source alone than the grant proposed in the Autonomy Bill now before the House.

In the year 1903 the amount of money received by the North-west Territories from the Dominion Government was less by many thousands of dollars than the revenues which the Dominion Government derived from the Territories. The revenue originating in the natural wealth of the Western country should go to the benefit of the Western country itself and not the whole Dominion.

How about the school question? Well, as laid down in the Autonomy Bills the educational clauses are primarily and radically wrong. The only class who really wants Separate Schools is less than one half of the Roman Catholic population. There has been a great deal of misrepresentation on this matter. The other varieties of Catholicism represented, that is the Greek Catholic, the Polish Catholic and all the sub-divisions of the sect who have come from Central Europe, are all strongly in favor of the National School as are also the larger proportion of the Roman Catholics themselves, and they claim that it was represented to them that the National School was in existence in this country and that it was one of the inducements which led them to come to Canada. The movement or what little agitation there is in the West for Separate Schools is solely in the hands of the Oblate Fathers, who have a thorough organization, and who control the Church in that country.

The people of the West will never rest until they get Provincial Autonomy on the same terms as the older Provinces. We want control of our own timber, of our own minerals, of our own lands and, especially, of our own schools. And let me tell you the West will not forget. And if the attempt is made to force the proposed measures on us we will carry the question to the Privy Council in England before we rest.

V — 45

'Autonomy that Insults the West,' Calgary Herald, April 26, 1905.

Sir Wilfrid kept the Territories struggling for years before he would seriously consider the autonomy question. Being forced to grant a measure of home rule, he goes into committee of the whole with Mgr. Sbarretti [sic], and offers the country the most sinister piece of legislation that political intrigue ever produced.

Deprived of the right to adopt an education system of their own choosing, all natural resources administered from Ottawa, the immense coal royalties preserved as a Dominion asset, the control of the irrigation system of the West maintained as a party privilege to be farmed out to Liberal supporters, and many private awards made to strong partisan friends in different parts of the Territories, Sir Wilfrid audaciously extends the naked counterfeit to the west as the substance of provincial rights.

Could anything be more mendacious?

Was there ever a more hateful exhibition of the leader of a great party in the closing days of his splendid career, lending himself to such a policy of coercion?

The new provinces can have little patience with the policy that seeks to denude them of tremendous natural resources, and infinitely less with the idea that proposes to deprive the people of the right to frame their educational system. . . .

It is idle to talk of harmony when everything indicates an unalterable determination to coerce the west.

If Sir Wilfrid is so confident the west is satisfied with his policy, dare he submit the autonomy bills in a plebiscite to the people so much concerned?

This would disabuse his mind on that score if the Premier really imagines that his policy resembles a popular measure today.

By the use of the barest party intrigue, and the tremendous power at his disposal, Sir Wilfrid is in a fair way to force his bills on the country but the dissensions in his own party ought to warn him of the storm he is stirring up. Mgr. Sbarretti [sic] may have his ear, but the popular discontent threatens to reach such proportions as to engage his attention, in spite of his apparent surrender to the ecclesiastical forces.

V — 46

'Ontario Must Speak!' Calgary Herald, May 16, 1905.

Apparently the sentiment of Ontario on the autonomy bills will be registered officially within a few weeks, as two parliamentary vacancies exist. London and North Oxford will perhaps have a chance to speak very shortly. The appointment of Mr. Hyman as minister of public works forces an appeal to at least one constituency. Ordinarily the government should have no difficulty in securing support in either of these constituencies. Just at the present a pretty fight is promised. Sir Wilfrid apparently thinks Ontario does not seriously resent the imposition of separate schools on the Territories. It is possible the result of these elections will prove a shock that may cause him to hesitate in his determination to coerce the west.

With these two vacancies no further attempt should be made to force the measures through Parliament. In fact, with due regard for traditions and fair play, an appeal to the country should be made before the policy of coercion is carried much further. This would be just and worthy of a great party.

What has Sir Wilfrid to fear? Certainly his majority is sufficient. He has behind him the influence of the most colossal private syndicate of railroad promoters the world has ever witnessed. The premier enjoys the confidence and active assistance of the Church, which enables him to count on 'solid Quebec' regardless of all other considerations.

Therefore it would appear on the surface that the government has nothing to lose and something to gain by an appeal to the country. The reputation for fair play to be earned by submitting so momentous a question to the people would warrant such a decisive move. The pull of disaster may be discerned by Sir Wilfrid, however, in such an appeal. Perhaps he realizes that many of his followers might be deprived of their seats by those who refuse to place party above principle—by those who know coercion when they see it and resent the present conspiracy by which the west is threatened.

In any event, one or two constituencies may speak with sufficient emphasis as to cause Sir Wilfrid to give a greater measure of justice to the new provinces. If enough Ontario Liberals demand the abandonment of the coercion policy some good may result.

V — 47

R.B. Bennett campaigns in the Ontario bye-elections, Speech in London, Ontario, May 30, 1905: Toronto Telegram, May 31, 1905.

London, May 30—Let it be known abroad and all about that the west does care.

In the cherished dream that the west was indifferent and apathetic to its educational liberties, coercion organs and orators have sought to lull the people to sleep and have made bold to tell Ontario to mind her own business.

Flashing with the vigor of a vigorous west, R.B. Bennett, M.P.P. of Calgary, tonight refuted this charge before a large meeting of London electors. . . .

'The liberties and possibilities of that west,' he affirmed with upraised hands 'are being menaced by the legislation now before parliament.'

Grasping some of the enthusiasm of the speaker, the audience saw the point and applauded vigorously. Mr. Bennett's next step was to show that the west had never been free, Liberal orators and Charles Hyman to the contrary notwithstanding. He traced the gradual growth of governmental institutions in the Territories explaining that they were accorded powers little by little. In 1875 they received the ordinances but in these ordinances was included a restriction in the matter of education, Separate Schools being insisted upon.

'If any one states,' he went on, referring to recent statements by one Charles Hyman, 'that we have the right to do as we please, he states what is false. I ask you, are you a free man if your hands are tied behind you? We never had the privilege to make laws as we like as to education, and we ask—that is all. . . .'

'Were there any protests from the west?' he asked having shown that the rights of the west were shackled. 'Ah yes, and by none other than Frank Oliver, now Minister of the Interior.' From the records of the Territorial Assembly of 1888 he read a resolution moved by Frank Oliver to memorialize the Federal Parliament to sweep away every feature regarding Separate Schools. 'He thinks it is the greatest thing in the world now.'

'He is Minister of the Interior, and that makes the difference.'

Coming back to the question of protests a little later he said the men at Ottawa little knew the ferment they were causing in the west.

Walter Scott, the Regina member, has said the west does not care. 'Ask him,' suggested Mr. Bennett, 'about the telegrams he received. Why is he not Minister of the Interior? Because the west cares.

The utterance of Rev. Dr. McQueen, in Hon. Frank Oliver's church, the resolutions of all sorts of bodies at Calgary, Medicine Hat, Indian Head and Regina and other places all showed the west cares.

'Rev. Dr. Carman preached in Regina,' he went on, 'and the people cheered when he said Hands off the west. Does the west care? Ah, yes the west cares, but Canada cares more, for the future of Canada is as we treat the west.'

Mr. Bennett scored when he declared that when the west became a province it should become a province with provincial powers and not be made a vassal. Such had been the declaration of Laurier, Davies, Mills and Thompson in days gone by. Prince Edward Island and British Columbia had full rights and that is all the new provinces ask.

'The west will not stand coercion,' he averred with an enthusiasm which indicated some of the energy of the west. 'We will take the question to the courts and to the Imperial Parliament, if necessary. Once upon a time Mr. Laurier declared that if he had been a half-breed on the banks of the Saskatchewan he would have shouldered his musket. That was over land trouble. If Mr. Laurier was justified in shouldering his musket then, surely, we have a right to take all the cannon we can get now.' (Applause)

'By the hopes, the ambitions and the aspirations of your sons, and as you believe in the west, I appeal to you,' he said. 'You can trust the men of the west. They are broad-minded and tolerant, because they breathe the same air as you breathe. I ask you in the name of a free west, a west opposed to coercion as you are opposed to coercion, I ask you to go to the polls and strike a blow for freedom and for freedom's cause forever.'

V — 48

Haultain Speaks in the Bye-elections, London, June 6, 1905: Toronto Telegram, June 7, 1905.

. . . By flashing the X-rays of merciless fact, Mr. Haultain exposed to the light of day the slender reed upon which many a Liberal conscience has been leaning in these troublous times. It was the reed of the national school of fallacy. On every Liberal platform it has been stated that the school system in use in the North-west is excellent, almost ideal. This established, it is triumphantly ordained that the bill practically amended the objectionable clause, 'but continues the present excellent system which is national with the exception of a half hour's religious instruction after 3:30.' Premier Haultain has been at the head of the educational system for 14 years, and he should know. He was pleased to think the system was excellent, 'but,' he added, drawing the line sharp and clear, 'I do not admit that this development is due to the exceptional part of the system that provides for Separate schools.'

In the school law, he made it clear there were two points. One was the federal clause imposing Separate schools. The other was the enactments of the Territories imposing all the good features. 'What are they perpetuating' he asked further. 'Are they perpetuating the good features. There is nothing about that in the bill. It speaks only to the right of the minorities. They are perpetuating Separate schools and that only, and they are representing that all the good features are being perpetuated.'

The audience saw the point and applauded, in the light of this truth, speeches of Ministers were made to look rather strange.

Mr. Hyman had spoken of 're-enacting the present excellent law.'

Mr. Mulock pictured the beauties of the system, and exclaimed 'Why under heaven should we repeal the act?'

Mr. Fielding nobly refused to wipe out a 'system which had the endorsement of thirty years.'

'One would think,' commented Mr. Haultain with a thrust that counted, 'that the great system was in danger and the

Government was rushing to the rescue. It is almost too absurd to discuss. We can look after all the excellent features. The bill doesn't perpetuate these. It perpetuates that which Fielding, Sifton, Walter Scott, Mulock and others say is bad—Separate schools.'

By showing that the original and amended clauses were identical in effect, Mr. Haultain introduced the grave danger which the passing of the bill carries. This was another important phase of his speech in which was revealed a little inside history. . . .

'I have had,' he testified, 'demands every year from the Bishops to restore the things taken away under the regulations, or have been told they were ultra vires.'

It was not unnatural to suppose that, once this law was passed, there would be a request from the Roman Catholics for remedial legislation, and after his struggle to pass the bill Sir Wilfrid could not refuse it.

With quiet dignity Mr. Haultain related the slight which had been put on the west when its Premier had been ignored in the negotiation of the school clauses. Incidentally he used the Sbarretti incident to point out the moral and adorn the tale. He told first of the long years of complete dependence on the Federal power, which had imposed the shackle of Separate schools without any consent of the people. . . .

'Never will there be peace as long as there is coercion,' opined Mr. Haultain. 'This fight is yours as well as ours.' They would never accept the interpretation of the Dominion Government on the clauses. He thanked the people of the east for their interest, and declared it was a fight on behalf of 500,000 Canadians who now filled the west, and who merely asked the right to what other provinces have.

V — 49

**The Calgary Herald comments on the bye-elections,
June 12, 1905.**

The men of Oxford and of London deliver their verdict on the autonomy bills tomorrow. That the government realizes the peril in which its plans are placed by the opportunity afforded these sturdy English-speaking people of Ontario, is emphasized by the number of cabinet officers sent into those ridings to satisfy the people that the west is not being dealt with unfairly. Mr. Oliver and his compatriots realize that it is not Messrs. Gozqyue, Psuogsye, Czsgopeze, et. al., of the European colonists of the Edmonton district they are encountering in Ontario, but independent, liberal-minded people, who know how to think for themselves and resent coercion in every form.

If the coercion tactics are defeated it will be a signal victory for the west, since the returns of each riding last year showed a substantial government majority. If a well oiled party machine and the offer of generous party patronage will help the government secure an approving vote, the coercionists have a fair chance to win. In any event, a few more hours will tell the story.

V — 50

Peter Talbot to A.C. Rutherford, June 14, 1905:
Rutherford Papers.

Got back this morning from N. Oxford. Had a hard fight but the Victory repaid all the trouble. I spoke at nine meetings. All the Lib. members who were there did nobly. We could not get the opposition to attend the meetings at all. The more I study this question the more clearly I see we are right.

The people of Oxford at first thought we had the wrong end of the argument and the Comm. there did not wish us to attend the Cons. meetings. After they heard our case clearly put they took heart and then our men were sent to nearly all their meetings. A tremendous lot of educating was necessary but we did it well. I am delighted with the results in both Constituencies. We have almost as large a majority in N. Oxford as the Lib. candidate had at the last local election. It is not fair to compare this election with Sutherland. A large section of the people in N. Oxford were what is known as Sutherland Liberals. They voted for him because he was Jim Sutherland and not because he was a Grit. We got the normal Grit majority, and we are delighted. I think the result will prevent the spread of that confounded race and religion cry. . . .

V — 51

'The Bye-Elections,' The Edmonton Journal, June 14, 1905.

Keen interest was taken in the progress and outcome of the

London and North Oxford bye-elections by the citizens of Edmonton. The contest was almost a Western contest in the view of very many of our citizens, and although it was scarcely expected that the Liberal candidates, with the whole force of the Government's influence behind them would be defeated, it was the hope amongst those who are most concerned with the defence of principles than the success of a party, that the Government would be administered such a rebuke by the electors of North Oxford at least, that Sir Wilfrid would pause before he forced the coercive educational clauses through Parliament by the support of a partisan majority. The Liberal majority in North Oxford has, the despatches state, been cut down, but the Liberal candidate is safely returned, and it is not to be expected that Sir Wilfrid will turn from his set purpose to perpetuate a system of Separate Schools in the West. London has yielded to the glamour of having as its representative the head of one of the chief spending departments of the Cabinet; the successful appeal to self-interest has won the day, and again, as in the case of Edmonton, Sir Wilfrid can point to the re-election of a Minister as an endorsation of his coercive Autonomy measures by an intelligent electorate. It was, perhaps, too much to expect that principles would dominate over self-interest and hidebound partyism even in constituencies so long schooled in Liberal professions of defence of provincial rights. The Liberals leaders of the day have sadly fallen away from those grand professions of other days, but it would take almost a revolution to convince the vast majority of the Ontario Liberal rank and file of this defection and as man are slow to turn from their idols, so they have voted again for party in the vain delusion that the Liberalism of today represents the Liberal principles of yesterday.

But the battle for national schools has not been decided with the Government's success in these bye-elections. The enactment of Clause Sixteen will bring coercion home to the West, to the people directly concerned. . . . Western public opinion, with the evil effect of Clause Sixteen on the national life becoming evry day more apparent, will yet express itself in a sweeping condemnation of Sir Wilfrid Laurier's mistaken policy. The fight carried to the provincial arena will be a bitter one. For this, the Western electors of the future can thank Sir Wilfrid and his band of self-seeking, place-loving politicians. . . .

The Liberal victories in the Ontario bye-elections served as a fairly clear indication to all parties that the autonomy bills were unlikely to be withdrawn or significantly modified. Thus, after months of controversy these bills were signed into law on July 20, 1905. The delays in their passage meant that the inauguration of the province had to be set back from July 1, 1905 to September of that year.

V — 52

The Alberta Act, 1905: Statutes of Canada, 1905, chapter 3.

An Act to establish and provide for the Government of the Province of Alberta.

[Assented to 20th July, 1905.]
Whereas in and by *The British North America Act*, 1871, being chapter 28 of the Acts of the Parliament of the United Kingdom passed in the session thereof held in the 34th and 35th years of the reign of Her late Majesty Queen Victoria, it is enacted that the Parliament of Canada may from time to time establish new provinces in any territories forming for the time being part of the Dominion of Canada, but not included in any province thereof, and may, at the time of such establishment, make provision for the constitution and administration of any such province, and for the passing of laws for the peace, order and good government of such province, and for its representation in the said Parliament of Canada;

And whereas it is expedient to establish as a province the territory hereinafter described, and to make provision for the government thereof and the representation thereof in the Parliament of Canada: Therefore His Majesty, by and with the advice and consent of the Senate and House of Commons of Canada, enacts as follows:—

1. This Act may be cited as *The Alberta Act*.

2. The territory comprised within the following boundaries, that is to say,—commencing at the intersection of the International boundary dividing Canada from the United States of America by the fourth meridian in the system of Dominion land surveys; thence westerly along the said international boundary to the eastern boundary of the Province of British Columbia; thence northerly along the said eastern boundary of the province of British Columbia to the north-east corner of the said province; thence easterly along the parallel of the sixtieth

degree of north latitude to the fourth meridian in the system of Dominion lands surveys as the same may be hereafter defined in accordance with the said system; thence southerly along the said fourth meridian to the point of commencement,—is hereby established as a province of the Dominion of Canada, to be called and known as the province of Alberta.

3. The provisions of *The British North America Acts,* 1867 to 1886, shall apply to the province of Alberta in the same way and to the like extent as they apply to the province heretofore comprised in the Dominion, as if the said province of Alberta had been one of the provinces originally united, except in so far as varied by this Act and except such provisions as are in terms made, or by reasonable intendment, may be held to be specially applicable to or only to affect one or more and not the whole of the said provinces.

4. The said province shall be represented in the Senate of Canada by four members: Provided that such representation may, after the completion of the next decennial census, be from time to time increased to six by the Parliament of Canada.

5. The said province and the province of Saskatchewan shall, until the termination of the Parliament of Canada existing at the time of the first readjustment hereinafter provided for, continue to be represented in the House of Commons as provided by chapter 60 of the statutes of 1903, each of the electoral districts defined in that part of the schedule to the said Act which relates to the North-west Territories, whether such district is wholly in one of the said provinces, or partly in one and partly in the other of them, being represented by one member.

6. Upon the completion of the next quinquennial census for the said province, the representation thereof shall forthwith be readjusted by the Parliament of Canada in such manner that there shall be assigned to the said province such a number of members as will bear the same proportion to the number of its population ascertained at such quinquennial census as the number sixty-five bears to the number of the population of Quebec as ascertained at the then last decennial census; and in the computation of the number of members for the said province a fractional part not exceeding one-half of the whole number requisite for entitling the province to a member shall be disregarded, and a fractional part exceeding one-half of that number shall be deemed equivalent to the whole number, and such readjustment shall take effect upon the termination of the Parliament then existing.

(2.) The representation of the said province shall thereafter be readjusted from time to time according to the provisions of section 51 of *The British North America Act*, 1867.

7. Until the Parliament of Canada otherwise provides, the qualifications of voters for the election of members of the House of Commons and the proceedings at and in connection with elections of such members shall, *mutatis mutandis*, be those prescribed by law at the time this Act comes into force with respect to such elections in the North-west Territories.

8. The Executive Council of the said province shall be composed of such persons, under such designations, as the Lieutenant Governor from time to time thinks fit.

9. Unless and until the Lieutenant Governor in Council of the said province otherwise directs, by proclamation under the Great Seal, the seat of government of the said province shall be at Edmonton.

10. All powers, authorities and functions which under any law were before the coming into force of this Act vested in or exercisable by the Lieutenant Governor of the North-west Territories, with the advice, or with the advice and consent, of the Executive Council thereof, or in conjunction with that Council or with any member or members thereof, or by the said Lieutenant Governor individually, shall, so far as they are capable of being exercised after the coming into force of this Act in relation to the government of the said province, be vested in and shall or may be exercised by the Lieutenant Governor of the said province, with the advice or with the advice and consent of, or in conjunction with, the Executive Council of the said province or any member or members thereof, or by the Lieutenant Governor individually, as the case requires, subject nevertheless to be abolished or altered by the Legislature of the said Province.

11. The Lieutenant Governor in Council shall, as soon as may be after this Act comes into force, adopt and provide a Great Seal of the said province, and may, from time to time, change such seal.

12. There shall be a Legislature for the said province consisting of the Lieutenant Governor and one House to be styled the Legislative Assembly of Alberta.

13. Until the said Legislature otherwise provides, the Legislative Assembly shall be composed of twenty-five members, to be elected to represent the electoral divisions defined in the schedule to this Act.

14. Until the said Legislature otherwise determines, all the

provisions of the law with regard to the constitution of the Legislative Assembly of the North-west Territories and the elections of members thereof shall apply, *mutatis mutandis,* to the Legislative Assembly of the said province and the elections of members thereof respectively.

15. The writs for the election of the members of the first Legislative Assembly of the said province shall be issued by the Lieutenant Governor and made returnable within six months after this Act comes into force.

16. All laws and all orders and regulations made thereunder, so far as they are not inconsistent with anything contained in this Act, or as to which this Act contains no provision intended as a substitute therefor, and all courts of civil and criminal jurisdiction, and all commissions, powers, authorities and functions, and all officers and functionaries, judicial, administrative and ministerial, existing immediately before the coming into force of this Act in the territory hereby established as the province of Alberta, shall continue in the said province as if this Act and *The Saskatchewan Act* had not been passed; subject, nevertheless, except with respect to such as are enacted by or existing under Acts of the Parliament of Great Britain, or of the Parliament of the United Kingdom of Great Britain and Ireland, to be repealed, abolished or altered by the Parliament of Canada, or by the Legislature of the said province, according to the authority of the Parliament, or of the said Legislature: Provided that all powers, authorities and functions which under any aw, order or regulation were, before the coming into force of this Act, vested in or exercisable by any public officer or functionary of the North-west Territories shall be vested in and exercisable in and for the said province by like public officers and functionaries of the said province when appointed by competent authority.

(2.) The Legislature of the province may, for all purposes affecting or extending to the said provinces, abolish the Supreme Court of the North-west Territories, and the offices, both judicial and ministerial, thereof, and the jurisdiction, powers and authority belonging or incident to the said court: Provided that, if, upon such abolition, the Legislature constitutes a superior court of criminal jurisdiction, the procedure in criminal matters then obtaining in respect of the Supreme Court of the North-west Territories shall, until otherwise provided by competent authority, continue to apply to such superior court, and that the Governor in Council may at any time and from time to time declare all or any part of such precedure to be inapplicable to such superior court.

(3.) All societies or associations incorporated by or under the authority of the Legislature of the North-Territories existing at the time of the coming into force of this Act which included within their objects the regulation of the practice of or the right to practice any profession or trade in the North-west Territories, such as the legal or the medical profession, dentistry, pharmaceutical chemistry and the like, shall continue, subject, however, to be dissolved and abolished by order of the Governor in Council, and each of such societies shall have power to arrange for and effect the payment of its debts and liabilities, and the division, disposition or transfer of its property.

(4.) Every joint-stock company lawfully incorporated by or under the authority of any ordinance of the North-west Territories shall be subject to the legislative authority of the province of Alberta if—

(a) the head office or the registered office of such company is at the time of the coming into force of this Act situate in the province of Alberta; and

(b) the powers and objects of such company are such as might be conferred by the Legislature of the said province and not expressly authorized to be executed in any part of the North-west Territories beyond the limits of the said province.

17. Section 93 of *The British North America Act,* 1867, shall apply to the said province, with the substitution for paragraph (1) of the said section 93, of the following paragraph:—

"(1.) Nothing in any such law shall prejudicially affect any right or privilege with respect to separate schools which any class of persons have at the date of the passing of this Act, under the terms of chapters 29 and 30 of the Ordinances of the North-west Territories, passed in the year 1901, or with respect to religious instruction in any public or separate school as provided for in the said ordinances."

(2.) In the appropriation by the Legislature or distribution by the Government of the Province of any moneys for the support of schools organized and carried on in accordance with the said chapter 29 or any Act passed in amendment thereof, or in substitution therefor, there shall be no discrimination against schools of any class described in the said chapter 29.

(3.) Where the expression "by law" is employed in paragraph 3 of the said section 93, it shall be held to mean the law as set out in the said chapters 29 and 30, and where the expression "at the Union" is employed, in the said paragraph 3, it shall be held to mean the date at which this Act comes into force.

18. The following amounts shall be allowed as an annual subsidy to the province of Alberta and shall be paid by the

Government of Canada, by half-yearly instalments in advance, to the said province, that is to say:—

(a) for the support of the Government and Legislature, fifty thousand dollars;

(b) on an estimated population of two hundred and fifty thousand, at eighty cents per head, two hundred thousand dollars, subject to be increased as hereinafter mentioned, that is to say:—a census of the said province shall be taken in every fifth year, reckoning from the general census of one thousand nine hundred and one, and an appropriate estimate of the population shall be made at equal intervals of time between each quinquennial and decennial census and whenever the population, by any such census or estimate, exceeds two hundred and fifty thousand, which shall be the minimum on which the said allowance shall be calculated, the amount of the said allowance shall be increased accordingly, and so on until the population has reached eight hundred thousand souls.

19. Inasmuch as the said province is not in debt, it shall be entitled to be paid and to receive from the Government of Canada, by half-yearly payments in advance, an annual sum of four hundred and five thousand three hundred and seventy-five dollars, being the equivalent of interest at the rate of five per cent per annum on the sum of eight million one hundred and seven thousand five hundred dollars.

20. Inasmuch as the said province will not have the public land as a source of revenue, there shall be paid by Canada to the province by half-yearly payments, in advance, an annual sum based upon the population of the province as from time to time ascertained by the quinquennial census thereof, as follows:—

The population of the said province being assumed to be at present two hundred and fifty thousand, the sum payable until such population reaches four hundred thousand, shall be three hundred and seventy-five thousand dollars;

Thereafter, until such population reaches eight hundred thousand, the sum payable shall be five hundred and sixty-two thousand five hundred dollars;

And thereafter the sum payable shall be one million one hundred and twenty-five thousand dollars.

(2.) As an additional allowance in lieu of public lands, there shall be paid by Canada to the province annually by half-yearly payments, in advance, for five years from the time this Act comes into force, to provide for the construction of necessary public buildings, the sum of ninety-three thousand seven hundred and fifty dollars.

21. All Crown lands, mines and minerals and royalties incident thereto, and the interest of the Crown in the waters within the province under *The North-west Irrigation Act,* 1893, shall continue to be vested in the Crown and administered by the Government of Canada for the purposes of Canada, subject to the provisions of any Act of the Parliament of Canada with respect to road allowances and roads or trails in force immediately before the coming into force of this Act, which shall apply to the said province with the substitution therein of the said province for the North-west Territories.

22. All properties and assets of the North-west Territories shall be divided equally between the said province and the province of Saskatchewan, and the two provinces shall be jointly and equally responsible for all debts and liabilities of the North-west Territories: Provided that, if any difference arises as to the division and adjustment of such properties, assets, debts and liabilities, such difference shall be referred to the arbitrament of three arbitrators, one of whom shall be chosen by the Lieutenant Governor in Council of each province, and the third by the governor in Council. The selection of such arbitrators shall not be made until the Legislatures of the proivnces have met, and the arbitrator chosen by Canada shall not be resident of either province.

23. Nothing in this Act shall in any way prejudice or affect the rights or properties of the Hudson's Bay Company as contained in the conditions under which that company surrendered Rupert's Land to the Crown.

24. The powers hereby granted to the said province shall be exercised subject to the provisions of section 16 of the contract set forth in the schedule to chapter 1 of the statutes of 1881, being an Act respecting the Canadian Pacific Railway Company.

25. This Act shall come into force on the first day of September, one thousand nine hundred and five.

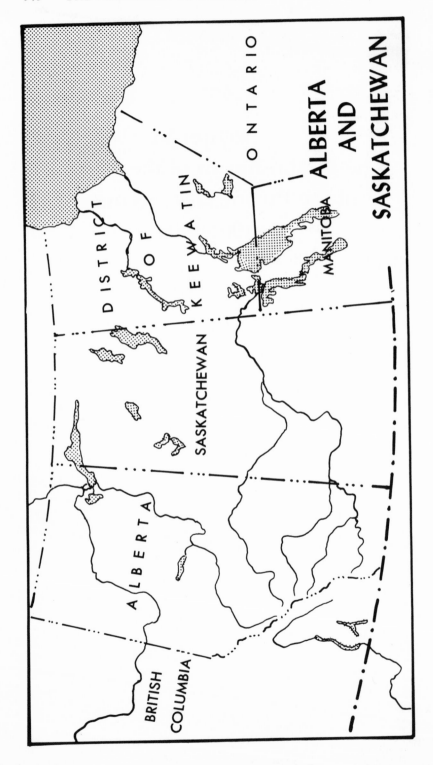

ALBERTA
AND
SASKATCHEWAN

ONTARIO

MANITOBA

DISTRICT

OF

KEEWATIN

SASKATCHEWAN

ALBERTA

BRITISH
COLUMBIA

Section VI
The Establishment of the Apparatus of the Provincial Government, 1904-1906.

*While politicians at the national level were concerned
mainly with the schools clauses and other major sections of the
Alberta bill many in the West found the local aspects of the
formation of a new province to be of equal interest. One of the
most absorbing of these local questions concerned the site of
the capital for the Province of Alberta. The prestige, business
and government activity which would accrue to a capital made
the decision an important one to the municipalities involved.*

*Several centres in Alberta made a bid to become the capital
but, from the beginning, the real contest was between the two
largest cities, Calgary and Edmonton. Calgary had an advantage in that it could boast the greatest population and a long
standing claim to be the capital. It also had a great liability,
however, in that it had elected Conservatives in the 1904 federal
election. Edmonton may have been smaller but it was represented federally by two powerful and persuasive Liberal
politicians, Frank Oliver and, from Strathcona, Peter Talbot.
Their influence was sufficient to ensure that Edmonton was
named provisional capital with the permanent site to be chosen
by the first Alberta legislature.*

VI — 1

**The Herald predicts Calgary will become capital,
Calgary Herald, January 20, 1905.**

The telegraphic reports from Ottawa indicate that negotiations are proceeding very favourably in reference to autonomy.
Many points have been mutually agreed to and evidently little
time will be lost in working out the details.

There is much of significance in the report from authentic
sources that two provinces are to be organized along north and
south lines. This can be regarded as excellent news for Calgary.
If there is such a division of the Territories Calgary can scarcely
be side-tracked in the contest for capital honors. Such a line
would pass somewhere near Swift Current or Moose Jaw,
leaving Regina and Prince Albert as the centres of population
in the east and Calgary and Edmonton as the two cities of the
western province.

With such an arrangement Calgary will be the natural
geographical centre and very likely to be selected as the capital.
Yesterday the western representatives were in caucus and there
seems to be little difference of opinion among them as to the
economy of the proposition.

VI — 2

The Journal Predicts that Edmonton will become the capital.
Edmonton Journal, January 21, 1905.

It has been pretty clearly shown by recent despatches that the intention was to divide the North-west into two provinces, and to the citizens of Edmonton it is very important that we should obtain a commanding position suitable to that to which our geographical situation would appear to entitle us. The recent railway arrangements by which the Canadian Northern and the Grand Trunk Pacific have entered into arrangements with the city to establish their workshops and chief divisional points at Edmonton, should materially influence the government in deciding to make our city the capital of the province of Alberta.

... Coming to the Territories, Regina will be the capital of a province extending north to the 60th parallel, whilst Edmonton should in like manner from its central position and the convenience of its railway system, equally with its great and unsurpassed agricultural prospects, become the capital of a province to include the provincial district of Alberta; thus the Mackenzie district would be entirely north of 60 longitude and would probably include a part of Keewatin, extending to the Hudson's Bay itself.

At the hour of going to press the Journal learns that it is generally understood in the cabinet circles that Regina and Edmonton have been decided on as the capitals of the two new North-west Provinces.

VI — 3

C. Peterson, Secretary of the Calgary Board of Trade, to Laurier,
February 2, 1905: Laurier Papers, 208759-61.

Apparently the time is fast approaching when autonomy will be granted the Territories on the basis of two provinces. This will ultimately necessitate the selection of a capital for Alberta, the Western Province. It is expected that the Dominion Parliament in the Provincial Bill will name a place as provisional capital and that the permanent capital will be finally fixed when the first local legislature meets and funds are asked for public buildings. Whether the capital is located in Northern Alberta, in Central Alberta or Southern Alberta is a matter of very considerable interest to the people of the West. In order that this question may be settled strictly on its merits, and that the wishes of the majority of the voters in Alberta may not be defeated, a large delegation, elected at a mass meeting held in this City last night, has just left Calgary for Ottawa with a view to impressing on the authorities the importance of not naming in the Bill any point as provisional capital that aspires to become the permanent seat of Government, but to appoint as provisional capital a town such as Banff, which would not be a competitor for capital honours.

If either Calgary, Edmonton, or any other competing point become the temporary capital, chances are that the pressure brought to bear on the members of the first Legislature coupled with the moral advantage of possession, would exert so strong an influence that the capital would practically be anchored there. Such a course would be neither just nor desirable and the City of Calgary desires no such advantage, nor do we believe any other Western town does.

In urging upon the Government to name a neutral point as provisional capital, the citizens of Calgary feel that they are making a fair and reasonable request and I am now directed to invite your co-operation in the matter. No objection can apparently be taken to the Dominion Government refraining from casting the weight of its influence with any particular City or Town. The matter is essentially one for the people themselves to pronounce upon.

Another matter the delegation above referred to are instructed to impress upon the Government is that the distribution of electoral districts for the first provincial election be made scrupulously on a basis of actual population in order that full voting power may be accorded each section of the new province. An enormous development has taken place in Southern and Central Alberta since the last census and it is very important that complete allowance should be made in this respect. The people of Calgary frankly admit that Calgary is in the field for capital honours, and that we propose to fairly contest the point against all comers. We are, however, satisfied to rest our case on its merits provided a fair field and no favours are accorded. Should the people's representatives in the first legislature decide against Calgary's claims for preferences and the decision is an unbiased one, we will endeavour to bear our disappointment as gracefully as possible.

VI — 4

John Moore to Laurier, February 3, 1905:
Laurier Papers, 208766.

By wire I learn that a deputation from *Red Deer* (Alberta), which is my present home, will seek an audience from your Govt. to lay before you the reasons why this attractive and *centrally-situated* town should be selected as the capital of that Western Province.

Nature has provided a site there for a beautiful city on a splendid river; and already it is a town of many handsome homes with the modern conveniences of electric light and power, telephones, water works, good drainage and being the geographical *centre* is the most convenient for all concerned.

Meanwhile, dear Sir Wilfrid please give it a place in your warm consideration and believe me. . . .

VI — 5

Edmonton Sends a Delegation to Ottawa, Edmonton Journal, February 4, 1905.

There was a largely attended meeting of the citizens of Edmonton held in the council chamber yesterday afternoon to consider the autonomy and capital question. Mayor Mackenzie presided. President J.H. Morris, of the Board of Trade, presented a recommendation from the board of trade that there be an increase in the number of delegates to be sent to Ottawa to look after Edmonton's interests in the autonomy settlement. On motion of J.H. Morris, seconded by Jas. MacDonald, the meeting unanimously approved of adding to the deputation.

At a subsequent meeting of the city council acting on the recommendation of the public meeting, it was decided to send as Edmonton's deputation Mayor Mackenzie, President Morris of the Board of Trade, and C.W. Cross of the law firm of Short, Cross, Bigger and Ewing. . . .

VI — 6

Talbot to Rutherford, February 16, 1905: Rutherford Papers, 2/3/7/2-28.

Things are getting hot. The delegates from Calgary, Red Deer and Edmonton are all here and have been heard. I have just returned with Red Deer contingent from an interview with Sir Wilfrid. Moore put up a pretty strong argument for his town. It turns out that the actual vote south of the Red Deer River at the last election was over 1000 more than north of that river. Of course that takes in Medicine Hat and also part of the Battleford Dis. west of the 4th Mer., so I fear we may lose. We will do what we can. I will fight to the finish on having temporary capital at Edmonton or Strathcona. I fear Bulyea and Scott are in league with Haultain. J.A. Reid was the one who prepared figures on of late election. Neither Oliver or I have been able to detect any material errors yet. We have a meeting of N.W. members with Haultain and Bulyea this P.M. I expect a big fight. I may fall in the fray. Red Deer and south will put the knife into me when they get a chance but I will try to stay with the parts of my constituency that gave me a big majority. We will do the best we can in the matter of redistribution but I have [?] fears.

VI — 7

C.W. Fisher, M.L.A. for Banff, supports his home town. Letter to Haultain reported in Calgary Herald, February 23, 1905.

As you are now gone to Ottawa to confer with the federal government upon the question of the establishment of provincial autonomy, one of the matters which will be discussed at this conference will be, I have no doubt, the location of the seat of government for the new province.

A number of suggestions have already been made from various quarters upon this point, but I desire to press upon your attention the advantages of one town which has not yet received the consideration from the public generally which it deserves. I refer to Banff.

It will be admitted by every one that no more beautiful site could be chosen for the provincial capital. Banff is already known to travellers all over the world as one of the great sights of the continent. From a business point of view therefore I believe it would be a great advantage to the new province to be able to refer to Banff as its seat of government.

Again, the new capital will necessarily be the educational centre of the new province and in this respect also there could I think be not better spot than Banff. The educational value of the neighbouring mountains, both from the aesthetic and utilitarian point of view cannot be over estimated. The student of natural science would find a wealth of raw material right at his door, while the beauty of the scenery would assist very materially in the moral education and true culture of the youth of the western province.

Then again, although the times are peaceful and Canada desires peace we ought to consider the possibility of war. If such an unhappy event should occur what spot in the west could be so easily defended?

A capital on the prairie would always be exposed to the danger of easy capture, while Banff could in a few weeks be turned into an impregnable fortress. Our provincial capitals are nearly all much exposed in this respect and the opportunity of establishing the next one in a perfectly secure position should not be neglected.

It may be said that Banff is not centrally situated, but I fail to see how this can be considered a serious objection. The present Territorial capital is as much to one side as Banff is and no objection has ever been raised to Regina on this ground. In fact, if we look at the capital cities of the world we shall see that nearly all of them are at one side of their respective countries and I have never heard that much if any inconvenience resulted.

For all these reasons I would seriously urge the selection of Banff as our capital. The place has advantages of many kinds which no other town can claim and I believe that if the capital were placed there the wisdom of the choice would be more and more apparent as time passed on. I therefore trust you will consider the representations I have made and bring the advantages of Banff clearly and strongly before whatever authority may finally have the deciding voice upon this important question.

VI — 8

'Political Reprisals,' The Calgary Herald, February 21, 1905.

The provisional capital of the western province will be located at Edmonton. . . . The north country supported the government in the recent election. The southern half of Alberta was equally loyal in favor of the opposition.

That the one was thus rewarded and the other punished by the Dominion for the public expression of political preferment cannot be doubted. In fact official circles in Ottawa boasted that 'Tory Calgary' had no right to expect any consideration at the hands of the Liberal government.

Under the cloak of political expediency every rule of fair play and representative government has been violated. Under the system of government that obtains in the British Empire the officials at Ottawa are supposed to represent the whole Dominion, not those sections which cast their votes for the government favorites.

This may be the political game, but it is a poor standard upon which to build a nation. It displays a narrow view of the great west that is intolerable to the broad spirit on which the hopes of this part of the Dominion rest.

The Calgary representatives have been met openly with the suggestion at Ottawa: 'Had Calgary sent a Liberal to Parliament, things might have been different.' This is atrocious. Followed to its legitimate conclusion, it makes support of the government a virtue, and support of the Opposition a crime.

Could anything be more repugnant to the best sentiment of fair-minded Canadians? It puts party before public and politics above the people.

From the first Calgary has only asked that to which she was entitled by every consideration of right—fair play. She never sought to have the provisional capital located at Calgary, nor necessarily in the Calgary sphere of influence, but only urged that it not be placed at Edmonton or any other point that was an active candidate for permanent political honors. . . .

But the fight has just commenced. Edmonton has won the temporary capital because her people honestly preferred to cast their votes for the government candidates.

Calgary has lost because the people of the south honestly exercised the same British privilege.

No question is settled until it is settled right. If Edmonton had secured this honor by reason of geographical location, centre of population, or considerations of commercial and industrial importance, she would deserve the praise of the whole country. As it is, the least said by Edmonton interests as to the methods utilized to take the provisional capital north, the better it will be for the men who dictated the policy of political reprisals.

It now behooves Calgary to lay out an elaborate plan of campaign that will present the subject on its merits to the people. Calgary has nothing to fear from a fair fight, but everything to apprehend from the intrigue directed by the Ottawa element that seeks to dominate western affairs.

VI — 9

'Edmonton Attacked,' Edmonton Bulletin, March 2, 1905.

From the attitude previously assumed by the press of that city, it was not to be supposed that the announcement that Edmonton had been selected as the temporary capital of the province of Alberta would be received by the Calgary papers with satisfaction nor with equanimity. Few passions are more desperate or vociferous than baffled greed and to expect that the organs which had devoted themselves solely to the business of preventing Edmonton being made the temporary capital would accept defeat either in silence or good nature and settle themselves to reasonable and legitimate effort to win out in the finals for the permanent location was to expect the hopeless.

But while the right or duty of the Calgary press to advance the claims of that city have not been questioned it might have been expected that the contest would be conducted with some regard for those laws of fairness and truthfulness which are the admitted bounds to all reasonable discussion. If such expectations existed they have been steadily dissipated by the course pursued.

The Bulletin has no desire nor intention to emulate the mud-slinging propensities of the contemporaries in question but neither has it any intention of permitting a campaign of misrepresentation and falsehood to be waged against this city with impunity. Such campaign has been begun by the Calgary press and pursued to the present with a vigor and persistence worthy of a better cause. The effort has not been to prove the suitable location of Calgary but to attack the location, present and prospective, of Edmonton. Realizing the danger of an appeal to fact or argument the ordinary weapons of controversy have been discarded for the bludgeon of falsehood. No statement has appeared too misleading and no forecast too reckless to be used in this savage warfare. A fair sample of the editorial perversion to which these journals have been driven for ammunition with which not to defend Calgary but to attack Edmonton, occurred in the Herald on Friday. In the course of a long article of the same quality appear these paragraphs:

'From every direction members of the Legislature must travel all the way across the new province to reach the provisional capital, and in nearly every instance these members must pass through Calgary.'

It is evident from the map that not one of the representatives to the first legislature will travel more than half way across the new province and that if a fair distribution of seats be made not more than one quarter or at most one third of the delegates will see Calgary en route.

VI — 10

'A Plea for Vegreville,' Fred Lawrence to the Editor of the Edmonton Bulletin, Edmonton Bulletin, March 8, 1905.

Having read with intense interest the almost acrimonious discussion in the Calgary and Edmonton papers concerning their respective rights to the new capital, I beg leave to state herein, my honest impression on so vital a subject. Though both towns have many good points in their favor, yet I think the liberal-minded and unbiassed public will endorse my arguments as to why the new provincial capital should not be located at Calgary but either at Edmonton or our own growing burg of Vegreville.

The first point I shall urge in her favor is that of population. By the census of 1899 there was not a living being on the present site, whereas by the last official statistics, the population comprised some 78 souls. If she has made such tremendous and gigantic strides during the last decade and a half who may not venture to prognosticate what good things are in store for her?

Probably a stronger point in her favor is her most admirable location, situated as it is, on the C.N.R. projected from Battleford and almost touching the G.T.P. Communication with the Dominion capital would thus be much more expeditious than were the new capital at Calgary. Being in almost easterly direction from Edmonton, Vegreville is situated in 53 degrees 23 min. north latitude. It is therefore as far south as Dublin in Ireland, Liverpool and York in England, or Hamburg in Germany, farther south than any port in Scotland, Denmark, Sweden or Iceland and several miles farther south than Hammerfest in Norway. If such cities as these can turn out to be such flourishing metropolitan centres, what may we not expect from Vegreville, situated in the same latitude?

As for the people, we may intimate that we have an admirable class of citizens who for being frugal, industrious and law-abiding, stand peerless. One policeman, without subordinates, is deemed altogether adequate protection to life and property. Can this same comparison stand in considering our sister city Calgary? This is a purely rhetorical question Mr. Editor. . . .

Treating of sanitary conditions, we can assure the public that the water supply is pure and wholesome. The air is pure, clear and asceptic, containing a large part of ozone—the natural air purifier. As to the soil in reference to its influence on health, it is only necessary to say that it does not breed the miasma of malaria, which is the cause of ague in its many forms nor owing to the altitude and low mean temperature, can malaria ever exist. The climate is not only invigorating to adults, whether in full health or otherwise, but seems to have a special influence in developing strong and healthy children. No better climate for children than that of northern Alberta is to be found in America. Sufferers from consumption, asthma, chest and throat infections, rheumatism, ague and many other diseases are always greatly benefitted and frequently cured by a residence here. We are much more remote from the mountains than either Calgary or Edmonton and hence less liable to fall under the influence of chinooks which this season has conclusively proved to be more disadvantageous to man's convenience than otherwise.

Such is the fertility of our soil and the exuberance of the vegetation, that the C.N.R. commission has seen fit to plant their own town almost on the site of our rapidly growing burg.

Situated as we are in the centre of the great Vermillion River Valley, made famous by reason of its rich alluvial deposits, is it any wonder that our citizens and surrounding countrymen should lay claim to the position of provisional capital in preference to our rival city Calgary?

The newspaper debate continued in desultory fashion through the spring of 1905 as to the relative merits of Edmonton and Calgary as a site for the permanent capital. In fact, however, the debates were of little significance at this stage. The federal government had announced that the choice of a permanent location would be left to the yet to be created provincial government. Until such a government was formed there was thus little that could be altered in terms of the capital question.

Of course there was more at stake than the site of a capital in the political questions of these months. The political future of the Provinces was a complex and highly partisan question. The non-partisan government which had characterized the Territorial era seemed unlikely to survive into the new era and this raised all sorts of possibilities for those with an eye to the future of their own parties. Given the history of Territorial controversy with a Dominion Liberal government it might have been expected that the Conservative Party would have an advantage in the new Province of Alberta. This was especially true given Haultain's growing identification with that party and the high esteem for him in the West. In fact, however, Haultain had left himself extremely vulnerable when he chose to confront the Liberal government on a partisan rather than a regional basis. Laurier's Liberals, after all, had powerful weapons of patronage and a strong political organization in Alberta under the guiding hand of Frank Oliver. Also, and perhaps most important, they had the power to appoint the Lieutenant-Governor and hence the power to ensure that the first administration of the new Province would be Liberal. The location of the provisional capital was, it turned out, simply an early indication of the movement of the Liberal Party to assure that they would have a powerful presence in the new Province.

VI — 11

'For Independence in Local Politics,' Calgary Herald, March 2, 1905.

The Herald today declares itself emphatically against the formation of political party lines in the provincial legislature of Alberta, and equally emphatically in favor of an absolutely non-partisan Government.

The Herald takes this step after serious deliberation, believing that such a course is in the best and truest interests of the people. It believes, too, that a non-partisan policy will most effectually solve the serious problems which the province of Alberta will have to face immediately upon its entrance into the sisterhood of Confederation, and will most solidly lay the foundation of stable, beneficient and constitutional government.

Standing as we are on the threshold of full provincial status, we can see no present justification for the adoption of Grit and Tory lines, but many reasons against it. The present is pre-eminently the time for all true citizens to stand together as Albertans. Our people are about to come into their own and there is neither reason nor necessity for political bickerings which can only result in retarding the development of the province. Let our new government be conducted as a strictly business administration. Let our people remember that they are first and above all Western Canadians, and they will seek their guiding star in the peace, progress, harmony and prosperity of the fairest province in the Dominion.

For its own part, in the approaching provincial campaign, the Herald will know no party lines. It will recognize neither Grit nor Tory. It will fight only for the fair province of Alberta—'first, last and all the time.'

VI — 12

Peter Talbot to A.C. Rutherford, March 14, 1905:
Rutherford Papers.

Yours of 9th inst. to hand. So far I can make nothing out of Oliver. He has told me that he would not take the premiership of Alberta. I have represented to him that such a step on his part is the surest way to get capital at Edmonton.

I am not sure but we will be in for a coalition. It seems to me that if Haultain remains in Alberta it would be difficult to get rid of him. His stand however, not only at late elections but even now is going to make it hard for Laurier to call on him to form a Govt. in Alberta. H[aultain] is certainly in league with the Cons. here to embarrass the Govt.

If J.J. Young is now in favor of non-party lines it is with the view of getting a Cons. at head of the big spending Dept. and paving the way to fix things solidly for the Cons. I have no faith in that man.

I would advise you not to commit yourself for the present. . . .

VI — 13

George Bulyea to Laurier, April 4, 1905:
Laurier Papers, 96275-6.

In accordance with promise I have, I think, sized up the situation as far as the people in the Territories are concerned, and I am satisfied that my view of the situation was absolutely correct. While naturally some of our people feel a little restive and anxious about the result in the Territories, I have not yet met any Liberal or any man who supported your candidates in the last Dominion election who will withhold his support in future for anything that has developed so far on the Autonomy question either as regards Schools or Lands. I have made it a point to make enquiries from everyone whom I have met and their version is the same, so that I think we can assure you of the same loyal support in the Territories in the future as has been in the past.

A few hot-heads attempted to hold a meeting here last night and I thought it would be just as well for our people to keep away from that meeting and let them take what action they saw fit, the result is that of the crowd who went there, more from curiousity than anything else, after a resolution had been suggested and put to the meeting, moved an amendment that the meeting adjourn sine die, which was carried by a very large majority. As far as I can hear there were not over 30 or 40 people in the whole meeting who voted against the adjournment, and the significant part of it is that a large per-centage of the people present were Conservatives.

I think I can assure you that should you find it necessary to open a constituency in the Territories for the election of a successor to Mr. Sifton you would either get an acclamation or an increased majority for any man you might select.

On the way up I met the Rev. Dr. Carmichael, who is super-intendent of the Presbyterian Churches for the West, and he expressed himself as quite satisfied with the action of the Government in reference to the Schools, and I think when the people of Ontario and the Clergymen of the different Denominations begin to realize that they were agitating under a misapprehension they will be perfectly satisfied.

One of the more controversial actions of the Laurier government in the movement toward provincial institutions was the

*drawing of electoral divisions which seemed to favour the area
north of Red Deer at the expense of Southern Alberta. Given
that the site of the permanent capital would probably be
decided on geographical rather than party lines it was a 'gerrymander' of some concern to those in the south, both Liberal
and Conservative.*

VI — 14

C.A. Stuart to Rutherford, May 1, 1905:
Rutherford Papers 2/3/7/2-27.

Since returning to Calgary I have had much conversation
with our friends in this City in regard to the questions discussed
at our recent meeting in Edmonton. While there is a strong
determination here to fight on party lines only I find that the
capital question is, as is natural, occupying a good deal of their
thoughts. The Liberals of the City met Oliver privately when
here and urged strongly upon him the necessity from the stand
point of the party interests in this neighborhood, of having the
constituencies fixed by a commission—or some authority not
the government. They pressed the point very urgently upon
him that if the government should do the dividing themselves
then no matter how fair in fact it might be the people of this city
and district would be bound to think that, having been done
practically by Mr. Oliver, it was unfair and fixed for the
purpose of increasing Edmonton's chances to be the capital.
The government turned down one very fair proposition of the
Calgary people as to the provisional capital and if there is any
belief in further favor in the question I maintain it will, I
believe from what even our strong Liberal friends are saying,
simply put the Liberal party out of business in this district for
all time to come. This is the view I take of it myself. If the
government can avoid even the suspicion of favor by naming a
non-political commission we would have a good chance of
redeeming this riding both in Dominion and local politics. On
the other hand if the Northern Liberals with their 2000
majorities cannot afford to join in our representations to Oliver
to have a commission appointed so as to help the party in the
south then all we can conclude down here is that with our
northern friends city comes before party. You must not then be
surprised if you find city coming before party among the
Calgary Liberals. . . .

VI — 15

The Herald comments on the Gerrymander:
Climax of Unfair Tactics, Calgary Herald, May 8, 1905.

Not satisfied with depriving the new provinces of their great natural resources, not content to trust the people of the west with the organization of an educational policy, the government has finally thrust upon the country constituencies design[ed] to further perpetuate this outrage. The crowning infamy of the men who have carried on this nefarious deal, under the pretext of conferring autonomy, was announced Saturday when the schedule for the division of the Alberta constituencies was completed.

To the discriminating elements of both parties this sequel of the Ottawa intrigue is no surprise. It had been forecasted very early in the negotiations, when Bishop Legal hurried to Ottawa to support the position Mgr. Sbarretti and other ecclesiastical authorities assumed toward the west. Apparently it was the determination of Sir Wilfrid and the forces at his command to do a brazen injustice to the whole of central and southern Alberta in order to carry out his compact with church dignitaries. To this end it was necessary, not only to retain control over the natural resources of the new provinces, but to divide the school system and place the seat of government in the extreme north, the centre of the anti-Protestant sphere of influence. . . .

The part Frank Oliver is playing is perfectly clear. Without his cooperation Sir Wilfrid and Mgr. Sbarretti would have encountered serious obstacles. As it is the honest indignation of the people of the west against this violation of every rule of British fair play may be sufficiently powerful to interfere with the plans of the conspirators.

Months ago it was commonly said that Messrs. Oliver and Talbot had received a map of Alberta with the request of Sir Wilfrid to indicate the boundaries of the constituencies. Many Liberals raised their voices against this palpable injustice. Many leading men of the party expressed the hope that a judicial commission would arrange the boundaries if the Liberal organization expected to exercise any influence over the province of Alberta in later years.

When Frank Oliver was in Calgary he was charged with this unscrupulous deal by several prominent Liberals, and his defence was weak. In fact he trimmed with some display of feeling and left the impression by implication, that he would throw his influence in favor of a judicial commission.

Is there a reasonable man in the Dominion who believes he did?

Is it any injustice to the new Minister of the Interior to assume that he was prominently identified with this treacherous affair?

VI — 16

C.J. Stewart and C.A. Stuart to Laurier, May 10, 1905: Laurier Papers, 209704.

Great indignation among Liberals not only in Calgary City but in surrounding districts over proposed constituencies and ask reference to independent commission. The division is grossly unfair to the country south of Red Deer and cannot be defended. We warn the Government that unless changed, long continued soreness and ill feeling between north and south will be endangered and party interests in this region totally destroyed.

VI — 17

Talbot to Rutherford, May 19, 1905: Rutherford Papers.

We are having a tangle here over the distribution Schedule of the Autonomy bill. The Calgary Libs. are putting up a big kick. I spent all forenoon today with Sir Wilfrid convincing him that the distribution was a fair and just one. He showed me a statement made by Dr. Stuart of Calgary which would indicate that Calgary was the center of population, etc, etc, etc. It was the most absurd statement I ever saw. Our friends in Calgary are no good. The Schedule will come up for discussion in a few days. The Cons. will fight it to the finish. It is possible they will obstruct proceedings for months. Calgary and the C.P.R. are backing them up. Sir Wilfrid thinks that when the facts that I placed before him are put before the house even the Tories may be convinced. He is of the opinion that when our case is put before the country it would do no harm to have it settled by a Comm. of Judges. To this I don't think Oliver will agree. So we may have trouble yet. . . . I suppose you are in touch with all the Lib. candidates. You will find lots of trouble but I think you are the man to smooth matters out.

The party that gained the powers and privileges of office at the time Alberta was constituted a province would have an inevitable advantage in fighting the first election in that new Province. That party, in turn, would be selected by the Lieu-tenant-Governor. It is thus not surprising that Laurier turned to an able and well known Liberal politician, George Bulyea, as the first Lieutenant-Governor. As Laurier's correspondence with Bulyea indicates, political considerations were very much on both minds in this crucial period.

VI — 18

Laurier to Bulyea, July 25, 1905: Laurier Papers, 100389-91.

The time is fast approaching, when the organisation of the two new provinces must be seriously considered, and as the time is thus coming nearer and nearer to unavoidable action, I every day feel more keenly the difficulties of the task.

At the outset, I had indulged the hope of an easy solution, a solution which then seemed so natural as not even to suggest the possibility of another and different one.

When you and Haultain came to Ottawa, in the early part of January last, I thought, and indeed every one thought, that as soon as the two provinces came into existence, the then existing government of the Territories would naturally become the government of Saskatchewan.

The attitude of Haultain has made this, in my judgement, an impossibility. When in the early part of the struggle which followed the introduction of the bills, Haultain went out of his way, to openly take side with the opposition, I am free to admit that I was keenly disappointed but even then I did not come to the conclusion that the breach was irreparable. When however he threw himself into the contests of London and North Oxford and especially when he announced his intention of carrying on the provincial elections on the avowed policy of destroying the school system of which some weeks before, he had said that if he were a dictator, he would not change a single disposition of it, he left us no alternative but to accept the declaration of war.

I realize that such a condition of things must be particularly painful and embarrassing to you. On the one hand I know full well that you never approved Haultain's course. On the other hand, the ties of friendship which have grown between you and him, resulting from long association in the same administration, would make it a most invidious task for you to have to oppose him and to fight, with all the firmness which a political contest means in this country, and especially such a contest as is involved in the policy of which he has declared himself the champion.

This consideration of the case has caused me and your friends here a good deal of anxious consideration, for we are all agreed that in the changes consequent upon the new order of things, your long and faithful services to the party, entitle you to the best that may be in the gift of the party.

I have thought it therefore my duty to place at your disposal, one of the two Lieutenant-governorships, that is to say the Lieutenant-governorship of Alberta, as the other is already filled.

Perhaps however for reasons of your own, you would prefer something which possibly might be more convenient. In such a case, I beg you to speak to me freely, and to open me your mind with all freedom, as a friend to a friend. In fact, I will be extremely obliged if you will give me your opinion not only on this one particular aspect of the situation, but upon the whole situation as I have exposed it above.

VI — 19

George Bulyea to Laurier, August 5, 1905:
Laurier Papers, 100386-100388.

Your very kind letter of the 25th ultimo came duly to hand. I have given the matter very serious consideration and have discussed it with Mr. Scott, who only arrived here this morning. I may say that I appreciate very highly the remarks you have made, and am very glad to know that my actions in the past have met with your approval. No one more than myself realized that the difficult position in which I have been placed on more than one occasion during the last few years would only tend to render my position in the provincial contest still more difficult. There were reasons which to the Western representatives of the Liberal party in your Government as well as to local Liberals rendered it advisable that there should not be a local political contest on the Autonomy issue, or a breaking up of the old North-west Government previous to the Federal election of last fall, and I can assure you that had not these reasons appeared to me, as a party man, to be very strong, I could not have refrained from taking the usual constitutional course of resigning when compelled to differ on points of policy with the Leader of the Government of which I was a member. These reasons however are not such as could be publicly used as an explanation of my conduct, and realizing the necessity, from a Liberal standpoint, of establishing a government favourable to yourself in each of the new provinces, and thus preventing, what I have no doubt will be the policy of the Federal Conservative party, throwing the School question again into the Federal arena, I think it is the best of politics to give our friends the freest possible hand, as any attacks on myself on those lines would be embarrassing to them as well as to me.

I am satisfied that our friends will rally around Mr. Scott, and to my mind there is no doubt that he will be able to establish and maintain a good Liberal government in the Province of Saskatchewan.

In the Western province, judging from the report of a large number of our friends who were here on Monday last, there should also be no doubt of the result. My own idea was, and still is, that Mr. Talbot would be the strongest man as Leader there, although there may not be so very much difference between the chances of Mr. Talbot and those of Mr. Rutherford. However, in conversation with Mr. Talbot I found that things had gone perhaps too far, and that the party as a whole might be weakened, in the North particularly, if any change were made now, and Mr. Talbot therefore thought best not to allow his name to go before the Convention as Leader. In view of the fact that West Assiniboia, and possibly Lamont's seat, may be thrown open, the question of opening the Strathcona seat unless absolutely necessary must also be taken into consideration.

Both Mr. Rutherford and Mr. Talbot, who were among the delegation here on Monday last, were kind enough to intimate both to Mrs. Bulyea and myself their sanction and approval of the offer you had made me of the position of Lieutenant Governor of the new Province of Alberta, and the belief that I would be of considerable assistance to them in getting their Government established, as of necessity nearly all the men who will have to do with affairs there for the present will be inexperienced. Both my wife and myself realize the responsibilities of the position and while, under ordinary circumstances, we would have preferred less onerous duties, we know that the difficulties of the situation have been the cause of much anxious thought to yourself and colleagues, and believe that it is our duty to accept the position and do our best to maintain the traditions of that high office, and we trust that your confidence in us had not been misplaced. Had it not been for the solicitation of the Alberta Liberals and of my own belief that I might be of assistance to them I think I would have preferred some other position at your hands, but I trust that the acceptance of this office will not prevent me, at some future time, being of further service to yourself and the Liberal party in some other sphere.

VI — 20

Laurier to Bulyea, August 11, 1905: Laurier Papers, 100393.

I have your favor of the 5th instant, for which I beg you to accept my sincere thanks. I am quite satisfied that you and Mrs. Bulyea will most successfully perform the duties imposed upon you both for the inauguration of the new province of Alberta.

With regard to the selection of a Prime Minister, the opinion of our friends at Ottawa was very strong that you should select Peter Talbot, but this is a matter as to which, of course, your better judgement must prevail. Many reasons were given to me in favor of Talbot, but I will have an opportunity of discussing the matter again with our friend Oliver. I may perhaps again write to you on this subject.

VI — 20

Peter Talbot to Laurier, August 7, 1905:
Laurier Papers, 100422-100427.

. . . There is no doubt that owing to the fact that I am better known in the southern part of the province than is Mr. Rutherford, my selection would be the more popular. But our friends are quite reasonable and I firmly believe will work faithfully for our cause no matter who may be called upon to lead us.

In Calgary I also found a feeling in my favor. The Liberals there look upon Mr. Rutherford as almost an Edmonton man and would prefer me principally on that account.

From Calgary to Leduc there is really no difference to speak of. I think either of us would have as large a following as the other. From Leduc north I think Mr. Rutherford would prove the stronger. The great question in the north is the location of the permanent capital and I think for that reason Mr. Rutherford would be preferred.

Rutherford and I are the best of friends and I had a confidential talk with him. I spoke to him of the Senatorship but I think he is too fully committed to his own constituents for the position of Premier of the Province to now think of withdrawing. At least he did not give any indication of a desire to take anything but the premiership. When I found this to be the case I thought it best to induce my warmest friends to give him their loyal support. This I think they will do. My name did not go before the Convention at Calgary at all, and Mr. Rutherford was chosen as president of our Provincial Association without any opposition. . . .

It is not yet known here what Mr. Haultain will do. I am inclined to think he will run for a constituency in Alberta although some of his political friends say he will remain in Sask.

I hope you are satisfied with our platform which was adopted at the Calgary convention. I would have been better satisfied if Oliver and Scott had been with us in the framing of it, but that could not be.

I consider the Convention was a great success. We certainly have the cream of the settlers of this province with us. And unless Bennett can stampede a greater number than I think he can the election will be a great Liberal victory.

VI — 22

Frank Oliver to Laurier, August 18, 1905: Laurier Papers, 100674-100677.

I am informed that you have officially been made aware of the result of the Liberal convention held in Calgary. Rutherford was the choice, although Talbot would have been preferred and would have been chosen had he not definitely given way to Rutherford. He was influenced in his action I think by the belief that Rutherford had already tacitly been chosen for and had accepted the position, and that to have turned him down would have dissatisfied Rutherford and his friends and thereby promoted a split. On my return in company with Talbot I suggested cautiously a change, but Rutherford would not accept the suggestion, although made as favourable to him as possible. Talbot will largely and earnestly support Rutherford. So I think the only thing to do is have Rutherford called.

The decision of Haultain to remain in Saskatchewan will make things easier in Alberta. And aside from contentions between prospective Liberal candidates matters look very favourable. There is a hope of carrying even Calgary.

P.S. Believe Bulyea appointment will be perfectly satisfactory.

VI — 23

'Mr. Haultain's Choice,' Edmonton Bulletin, August 19, 1905.

Premier Haultain has at last condescended to inform the people of the Territories that he has decided to confer his distinguished services upon the Province of Saskatchewan. While this has for some time been regarded as the probable course of the Honorable Gentleman, the assumption rested on the vague statement of Mr. Haultain that his choice would be decided by professional interests.

This may have been the primary reason for the lot falling upon Saskatchewan, but there are other considerations which doubtless contributed their share of interest to the reflections of the Honorable Gentleman. In the first place the Province of Alberta, a constituency of which Mr. Haultain has represented in the local House for many years, did not display any undue anxiety to be favored by his further presence in an administrative capacity. The 'boom' campaign, which was begun on his behalf by the Calgary Herald at an early stage of the game died a natural death at a very early age, and the course of that journal has not since been of a particularly comforting nature to the Premier.

'Rebellion Brewing' Bennett too, returned from Oxford and London in a fury of adjectives and promises of agitations which gave Mr. Haultain a decided chill. . . . Mr. Haultain too, went back on the Moose Jaw convention in a way which cost him any enthusiasm which might have been felt for him by the

Alberta Conservatives, and the prospect for him in this Province became the unalluring opportunity to figure as third party on a platform of legal technicalities. . . .

VI — 24

'Alberta, a Province,' Edmonton Journal, September 2, 1905.

With glorious Alberta sunshine, amid the cheers of thousands of the strong-armed, loyal and true-hearted citizens of the new province, before a sea of expectant faces of the fair daughters of a fair land, Alberta was proclaimed a province yesterday, a new state in the confederacy of the Dominion, a bright jewel in the constellation of the Empire. With imposing ceremony, amid military pomp and brilliancy and the no less significant and interesting marks of national advancement and prosperity, the Lieutenant-Governor of the new province Hon. G.V.H. Bulyea, was clothed with his authority as the representative of His Majesty, King Edward VII.

The ceremony was pregnant with historic meaning and that was the note of the addresses of the distinguished sons of Empire and of Canada who in felicitious, patriotic terms extended their congratulations to the citizens who were on that occasion granted a fuller measure of self governing powers, and entrusted with greater responsibilities and wider opportunities to work out their destiny.

After the address to His Excellency and the latter's reply had been delivered, the swearing-in ceremony was proceeded with. Mr. J.J. McGee, chief clerk of the privy council made the announcement of the appointment of Hon. G.H.V. Bulyea as Lieutenant-Governor of the Province of Alberta, and Lieutenant-Governor Bulyea then received the congratulations of Earl Grey. Following this at the hour of twelve noon, Privy Clerk McGee read the King's proclamation proclaiming Alberta a province and Hon. G.H.V. Bulyea, His Majesty's representative for the new created state.

In a clear voice His Honor repeated the oath of office, and the register of the crown signed, the vast assemblage heralded him as the representative of His Majesty, and Lieutenant-Governor of Alberta.

Stationed on an historical hill, the bluff that overlooks old Fort Edmonton, the R.N.W.M. Police guns boomed forth a royal salute and renewed cheers proclaimed the end of the formal ceremony.

VI — 25

Speeches by Governor General Earl Grey and Sir Wilfrid Laurier at the Ceremonies Inaugurating the Province of Alberta, September 1, 1905: Glenbow Archives, Edna Shore Collection, Memorial Souvenir Pamphlet.

Earl Grey: I thank you, Mr. Mayor, and your colleagues who represent the City of Edmonton, for the welcome with which you have received me in my capacity as the representative of His Majesty the King, and for your hope that my good fortune may cause me to pay further visits to your city. I cordially reciprocate the wish to which you have given such kind expression. The pleasure I derived from last night's entertainment was in itself sufficient to make me wish to visit you again. When I looked round that magnificent audience, and reflected that that immense gathering of happy looking, handsome and prosperous people, and the grace, refinement and distinction of the performance, and of all the arrangements connected with it were the home growth, were all products of the prairie, I knew that the impressions I had already formed were correct that the future of Alberta was abundantly assured.

I consider it a great privilege to be able to take part as the representative of the King at the coming of age festivities of your people, whose assumption of the high responsibilities and obligations which are inseparably attached to British manhood, you celebrate the day.

The day which marks the addition of a new self-governing province to the Dominion, and thus to the galaxy of self-governing states whose combined brilliance makes the constellation of the British Empire the brightest the world has ever seen, is a red letter day in the history of the Empire. That the Province of Alberta will bring, in ever increasing measure as time goes on, strength and lustre to the British Crown, and prove worthy of the illustrious prince whose name it is your honour to bear, is both my sanguine hope and my confident expectation.

You have referred to the paucity of your population in the past, and to the unborn millions with whom your province is already pregnant. What I have learnt of the fertility of your favoured land causes me to believe your estimate is one to which even the most captious cannot reasonably take exception. Thanks to the invaluable services rendered to your province by your railways, your cold storage facilities, your experimental farms, all of which you owe to the foresight and enterprise of the federal government, happily represented today in the distinguished person of my prime minister, thanks to these aids, and to your own stout energy, you have now proved to the satisfaction of the entire civilized world that you enjoy in this new province of Alberta, and perhaps in a greater degree than is to be found in land of equal extent in any portion of the world outside of the Dominion, the opportunity, which is within the reach of all who can pay their way here, of making for themselves a happy and comfortable home amid pleasant surroundings, with the inspiring feeling of independence which comes with the full ownership of the land you till, in the healthiest of climates, and under the protection of a justice and freedom loving government. This being now proved, you are justified in anticipating a steady flow of settlers into your province. Many who seek to better their condition in the new world as well as in the old, are counting the hours until they can embrace with both hands the riches you are able to offer them from out of your abundant treasury. For the riches you offer are the greatest that nature has to bestow upon mankind: namely, the happiness, health, and well being which your soil, your climate and your geographical position offer as a certain a liberal reward to all who are ready to give honest, persevering and intelligent industry to the cultivation of your land.

That you may quickly assimilate to yourselves all who come to you in the hope of making for themselves a new home in a new country, and that you may grow up a united, prosperous, cultured, God-fearing and righteous loving people, is the prayer which I, as your Governor-General and representative of the King, venture reverently to make for you from the bottom of my heart.

Sir Wilfrid Laurier: I have an advantage over His Excellency, the Governor-General, who visits this city of Edmonton for the first time; I come here for the second time. It is many years since I was here before, so many years that probably you have forgotten it, but I have not, I can tell you to a day. It is just eleven years this month of September. It was in 1894, when it was my privilege for the first time to visit this immense portion of our common country, which extends from the western shore of the Lake of the Woods to the Rocky Mountains, which for two centuries or more was known as Rupert's Land and the North-west Territories, and which today is springing into existence to take its rank and stand in the Confederation of Canada as the two provinces of Alberta and Saskatchewan.

Eleven years have passed and if some one had told me at that time that my next visit to the city of Edmonton would be in connection with the auspicious event which has brought here today His Excellency the Governor-General and this throng not only from the province but from the neighbouring Province of Saskatchewan, from Manitoba, and from the provinces of the east, and I am proud also to say from our neighbour to the South, the American Republic, I am sure if this had been prophesied then, I could not have believed it.

Eleven years have passed, and, as had been hinted a moment ago by the new Lieut.-Governor of Alberta, many and many changes have taken place. In 1894 the expectations which you indulged in of rapid development for this new territory had not been realized. The sun shone, the rain fell, the soil responded generously to the efforts of the farmer, but markets were far, the means of access were few, the profits of the farmer were scanty and small. Agriculture, upon which all industry depends, agriculture, from which all wealth is derived, was sorely depressed, and it being depressed, everything suffered in consequence.

The city of Winnipeg, the pioneer city, after making a splendid start, had reached the rank of a provincial town and seemed to have reached its furthest possibility. The five cities which now adorn the new provinces, Regina, Moose Jaw, Calgary, Edmonton, and Prince Albert were nothing but struggling villages. You know as well as I do that at that time Regina had nothing royal but its name; Moose Jaw was not far removed from the primitive condition which its name implied, a name no doubt in which its inhabitants glory; Calgary had made a splendid start, but stood still. Of Edmonton what shall I say? I am sure I will not offend the pride of any citizen when I say I could count upon the fingers of my two hands all the buildings, public and private, which then constituted your town, now the capital of Alberta. But now everything is changed. Gigantic strides are made on all sides over these new provinces. Only eight years ago I had the honour of representing in Parliament the third largest city in Canada, the old City of Quebec, but now, I am sorry to say I have to take a back seat and that honour now belongs to the city of Winnipeg. But in the name of the people of Quebec let me say I am not jealous, and I may also say that the two largest cities of Canada, Toronto and Montreal, if they are going to keep their supremacy had better look out—or, to use a western phrase, they had better hustle right away.

Nor is this all, Sir, if I look about me in the vast sea of upturned faces I see the determination of a young and vigorous people; I see the calm resolution, the courage, the enthusiasm to face all difficulties, to settle all the problems which may confront this new province. And, if it be true everywhere, it must be more true here in this bracing atmosphere of the prairie that "hope springs eternal in the human breast."

Now, gentlemen, what is the cause of this change? Well, sir, if I were addressing a political audience perhaps I might find many causes for this change. Perhaps also there might be gentlemen on this board platform who cannot agree with me upon these reasons, but this is not a day of political controversy, this is a day of national rejoicing. This is a city where today we only remember one thing,—that we are Canadians and British subjects. Therefore, ladies and gentlemen, I will abstain from going into the causes. But, sir, whether we agree or whether we disagree, there is one thing which we all admit that the prosperity of this new province, past, present, or future, is undoubtedly connected with the question of transportation, with railway facilities. Well, sir, I will not go further, because perhpas, I might trespass upon the ground from which I wish to abstain.

But, gentlemen, in order to bring out this new province to the standard which we expect it to attain it is necessary that we should have the hearty co-operation of all the people, of all the citizens of Alberta. We must have the co-operation of the old settlers, of the pioneers, the old pioneers chiefly from the province of Ontario who came here when the land was a desert and made the desert to smile. We must also have the co-operation of the new citizens who come from all parts of the world, to give to Canada, and to Alberta, the benefit of their individuality, of their energy and their enterprise, and since it happens that I have the honour of occupying the position of first servant of the Crown of this country, let me say on behalf of the Crown and with the concurrence of His Excellency, that to these new fellow-countrymen, to these new subjects of the King, I offer the most cordial welcome. I welcome those of our own kith and kin from the old land, I welcome those from the older portions of Europe, I welcome those who come from the neighbouring, the kindred Republic on the other side of the line.

Let me say to one and all, above all to those newly our fellow-countrymen, that the Dominion of Canada is in one respect like the Kingdom of Heaven, those who come at the eleventh hour will receive the same treatment as those who have been in the field for a long time.

We want to share with them our lands, our laws, our civilization. Let them be British subjects, let them take their share in the life of this country, whether it be municipal, provincial or national. Let them be electors as well as citizens. We do not want nor wish that any individual should forget the land of his origin. Let them look to the past, but let them still more look to the future. Let them look to the land of their ancestors, but let them look also to the land of their children. Let them become Canadians, British subjects and give their heart, their soul, their energy and all their power to Canada, to its institutions, and to its King, who like his illustrious mother, is a model constitutional sovereign.

VI — 26

'Alberta Premier Sworn In,' Edmonton Bulletin, September 2, 1905.

The Lieutenant-Governor announced this morning that in pursuance of the duties of his office he had called upon A.C. Rutherford, M.L.A. of Strathcona, to form the first executive council for the Province of Alberta. Mr. Rutherford had accepted and was sworn in. He had asked for and had been accorded the privilege of a few days delay before submitting the names of colleagues whom he suggested, but in order that there might be as little delay as possible in the transaction of the public business His Honor the Lieutenant-Governor hopes to be able to make an announcement early next week of the full executive council.

The Rutherford government was, of course, but an interim one until elections could be held. Those elections came quickly as a confident Liberal Party sought a mandate from the populace of the new Province. Opposing the Liberals was a rather dispirited and disorganized Conservative Party under the leadership of the mercurial R.B. Bennett. Not surprisingly, as the two party platforms indicate, the Conservatives ran on an anti-Ottawa platform while the Liberals emphasized sound administration and played down the controversial questions of education and control of lands.

There was also a regional overtone to the electoral contests. Officially both Bennett and Rutherford maintained that the choice of the permanent capital was not a partisan matter. Nevertheless, the impression remained, helped by various editorials, that a vote for the Liberals under the leadership of the Strathcona M.L.A. tended to favour Edmonton. Conversely a vote for the Conservatives under their Calgary leader was widely thought to be favourable to that city's interests. In the end, however, the election was a very one sided affair with the Liberals winning a large majority in the first Alberta legislature. A duly elected government now existed and the federal Liberal Party had been successful, at least in the short run, in ensuring that the controversial aspects of the Autonomy bills would not lead to a major federal-provincial confrontation.

VI — 27

**The Liberal Party Platform in the 1905 Election.
Adopted at Calgary in August 1905, Edmonton Bulletin,
August 5, 1905.**

. . . . 3. Resolved that this convention hereby declares its belief that the government of the new province should maintain an efficient system of common schools in order to meet the wants of the settler, and to extend to the children of all classes of the population an equal opportunity to obtain a good primary education, that this system should receive liberal financial assistance from the government revenues, and that all schools receiving such assistance and supported by taxation should be subject in every particular to the direct and continued supervision, regulation and control of the Provincial department of education. . . .

10. Resolved that this convention regrets the necessity which existed for the introduction into the Alberta Act of a clause continuing the exemption of railway lands from taxation: that this convention is in favor of the government urging upon the Federal authorities the advisability of removing the restriction at as early a date as possible. . . .

14. Resolved that this convention hereby expresses its belief that in the establishment of all public institutions and the erection of all public buildings due attention should be paid to the requirements of all parts of the province, and that in selecting locations for the same the government should consider the public convenience and the quick despatch of business. . . .

VI — 28

'The Conservative Party platform in the 1905 Election.'
Adopted at Red Deer in August 1905: Calgary Herald,
August 18, 1905.

3. *Education.* This convention protests against those provisions of the Act creating the Province of Alberta which seek to limit the control of the province over the subject of education and thereby forever preclude the possibility of establishing a national school system, and characterize the same as a flagrant and unwarranted interference with and usurpation of rights of the province under the constitution. The convention declares for such action as will result in the earliest possible reference of these provisions to the Judicial Committee of the Imperial Privy Council with a view to procuring from the court of last resort in the British Empire a decision as to whether they are or are not constitutional and within the power of the Dominion Parliament to enact.

4. *Square Deal in Lands.* This convention declares that the people of Alberta, to the same extent and in the same manner as the people of the other provinces, are entitled to the lands, mines, minerals, forests and other natural resources within its area, and to enjoy the full benefits thereof as well as to administer the same for the advantage of its people; and emphatically protest against our natural resources being unjustly withheld to be exploited by any political party at Ottawa. This convention urges that constant and continued application to and negotiation with the Dominion Government be made for the surrender to the province of the public domain within its boundaries, of which it is now so unfairly and unjustly deprived. This convention further declares that the province is entitled to compensation for lands within its area heretofore alienated for purely Federal purposes.

5. *Distribute the Debt.* This convention declares that the right which the Canadian Pacific railway company enjoys to hold its lands exempt from taxation was a consideration given by the Dominion of Canada in its contract with the company and is an obligation of the whole of Canada which should not be saddled alone on the western provinces. . . .

11. *Capital Location.* Whereas the question of the location of the capital is one entirely outside the realm of party politics, and is one exclusively for the legislative assembly hereafter constituted, resolved that full liberty be accorded every member

thereof to vote on the question in the best interests of his constituency.

In spite of the party positions on the capital question, certain newspapers found it an issue of some use in attacking the Conservatives. Needless to say, this sort of approach was only used in the Edmonton area. In the south Conservative newspapers implied the same biases on the part of the leaders but with different implications in terms of voter interests.

VI — 29

'Capital Location,' Edmonton Journal, September 29, 1905.

Finding the questioned terms of the Autonomy Bill somewhat difficult of either explanation or defence, local Liberal workers have fallen back upon the cry that if Edmonton elects a Conservative in the forthcoming election, we lose the capital. Ignorant and unthinking voters are solemnly warned of the dire calamities to befall this city should the Conservative candidates secure a majority of the votes to be cast in Edmonton riding at the forthcoming election, and discomfitted and distracted Liberal canvassers rest not by day or by night in sedulously inculcating this idea.

It might be well, therefore, under the circumstances, for those electors who question the clauses of the Alberta Bill, and who object to this Province commencing its provincial existence without a foot of land, a pound of mineral, a stick of timber, or a drop of water, and who regard the compensation in lieu thereof to be absolutely inadequate either for our necessities or for the great storehouse of wealth which has been withheld from us, to consider to what extent this question of capital location can be considered an issue in this campaign.

It is to be expected that the thirteen members who will represent the country north of Red Deer will be favorably disposed to Edmonton, notwithstanding their political leanings and that if they are left to vote in the interests of their constituents they will support this city in its claim for the permanent location. It so happens that every Conservative candidate North of Red Deer had pledged himself to support this city, and by most people the question of capital location is considered settled, and that Edmonton is already the capital in fact. . . .

There can, therefore, be but one conclusion, and that is this: The question of capital is neither a question of policy nor party but is entirely a geographical question, and will doubtless be treated as such by the Legislature.

VI — 30

'The Capital is Here to Stay,' Edmonton Bulletin, November 8, 1905.

One of the hard practical issues of the campaign is the location of the Provincial capital.

The temporary location of the capital was made at Edmonton by the Federal Government.

The permanent location of the Capital in this city means the securing of the material and local benefits which belong to capital cities.

But it means far more than this in the distinction which it attaches to the name of the city abroad: in the continuance of the desirable prominence which has come to Edmonton through the Capital being located temporarily here.

The beneficient results of the prestige attaching to the Capital city is evidenced by the campaign being waged in the southern part of the Province, where questions of Provincial administration and general concern have been relegated to secondary places and the opposition candidates pose first and foremost as the advocates of Calgary for the Capital. . . .

Premier Rutherford is pledged to keep the Capital at Edmonton.

Mr. Bennett is pledged, if given power, to remove the Capital to Calgary.

The Capital can be secured to Edmonton only if the Premier is sustained in power by a substantial majority in the House.

Therefore every vote cast for an opposition candidate is a vote against maintaining the Capital at Edmonton. . . .

VI — 31

'Coercionists Sweep Province,' Calgary Herald, November 10, 1905.

By the worst exhibition of Ottawa interference ever displayed in a provincial election, the coercion plot has been forced upon the electors of Alberta. By the influence of the Dominion machine, probably fifteen out of the twenty-five seats have been carried by the Alberta government.

In Calgary, however, in spite of the most outrageous tactics, the Conservative leader has been elected. There can be no question of the accuracy of this statement. Though W.H. Cushing leads, on the face of the returns, by 31, there are some 358 contested votes. They must be counted Tuesday. . . . The Conservative headquarters should be visited at once by every friend of Bennett's whose vote was challenged. They will remain open several days. Some fifty well known Calgary men,—men whose right to vote must have been understood by the Liberal machine which caused their votes to be challenged, appeared at Conservative headquarters last night and received instructions as to the contest. . . .

From the outside the figures at noon are still incomplete. There is no doubt that the Liberals have carried fifteen to sixteen seats. . . .

With the first provincial election complete, the final steps could be taken in the formation of provincial institutions. First and most on the public mind was, of course, the capital site. Calgary seems to have lost hope after the Conservative defeat in the provincial election. Red Deer, however, remained an active and imaginative contender for the honour. That town even paid the way of government officials, Members of the Legislature and various others from Edmonton to view the prospective sites of Red Deer. It was a valiant effort but the Edmonton papers were correct in their assessment of the situation. The capital was likely to stay where it was.

VI — 32

'Great Day in Red Deer,' Red Deer Advocate, April 20, 1906.

The Mayor and Council having invited the Lieutenant Governor and the members of the Legislature to inspect a free capital site in Red Deer on Tuesday last April 17th—by the train from the south reaching town shortly after 11 a.m. the members of the Provincial Parliament began to arrive in Red Deer and at one o'clock His Honor Governor Bulyea accompanied by Premier Rutherford, Minister Finlay and other members of the House reached town in a special saloon car. The distinguished visitors were met by the member for the town, the Mayor and the Clerk of the Legislature, and many introductions were made. Upon His Honor reaching the platform three hearty cheers broke forth and those were acknowledged by His Honor with his usual courtesy.

Mr. J.T. Moore, M.P.P. entertained His Honor, Premier Rutherford and Minister Finlay at luncheon at his residence in Waskasoo Park and the members and representatives of the Press of the Province were provided for at the leading Hotels. Shortly after two the party started out in conveyances to view the town, which they did from many standpoints such as the Hospital Hill, Grand View Park etc., and were driven to the proposed site offered for Government Buildings. . . .

They were shown a site offered by Mr. Jamieson and the special offer of the council consisting of fifty acres north end of Grand View Park. Here the party partook of refreshments and were afterwards shown other positions available for Government Buildings. . . .

The banquet was held in the Arlington hotel and it does the utmost credit to both Mr. and Mrs. Ells, the whole prolonged feast giving unmixed satisfaction in every way to all the assembled guests. Many ladies and others unable to be at the feast came to the hotel to view the tables and elegant decorations. . . . After singing Auld Lang Syne and God Save the King the Company broke up at 4:45 a.m. each and all expressing themselves at the perfect success of the banquet, and the visitors were loud in their expression of pleasure and satisfaction of their visit to the town.

VI — 33

'The Capital Debate Begins Tomorrow,' Edmonton Bulletin, April 24, 1906.

'The Capital Question' comes up for discussion in the House tomorrow and will likely draw to the visitors galleries the banner crowds of the session. From the public point of view there has probably been no more interesting problem requiring solution at the first meeting of the Legislature. The material benefits which result from the erection of large and costly buildings and the presence of a large staff of departmental employees; the practical conveniences to a business community of having the Government offices near at hand; and the prestige which attaches to a 'capital city'; these advantages have been fully recognized and have induced a general and a very active interest in this question as to which of the towns of the Province would secure them.

It may be indeed that this interest has outrun the merits of the cause and that not least among the benefits of the final settlement of the question will be the termination of the discussion to which it has given rise; a discussion which has been waged intermittently on platforms and through the press for more than a year, and which it is to be feared was occasionally more fervid than courteous, encouraged rather the exhibition of local loyalty than the practice of unswerving veracity and accomplished less for the welfare of the Province than for the development of inter-communal prejudice.

The location of the capital is not a matter of Government policy but of individual preference; it will be brought before the House not by a Government measure, but by motions of individual members and in determining it the members will exercise their private judgement without consideration of party affiliation. The matter will come up on a motion of Hon. W.H. Cushing, member for Calgary. Notice of this motion was given on Friday last. Notices of motion in the same connection were given at the same time by the member for Red Deer and the member for Rosebud. . . .

These notices indicate that the debate will take the form of an attempt to remove the capital from Edmonton and that the members favorable to the present location will be on the defensive. The identity of the movers bears out the common assumption that the struggle will be a three cornered fight between Edmonton, Calgary and Red Deer; perhaps it would be better to compare it to successive assaults by the two latter on the former. The unknown purpose of the member for Rosebud suggests the possibility of still another aspirant entering the lists, probably Banff.

VI — 34

'The Permanent Capital,' Edmonton Bulletin, April 27, 1906.

The much discussed question of the permanent location of the provincial capital has been settled by the defeat of the motions proposing its removal from Edmonton. By the Alberta

Act Edmonton was made the seat of capital government until the Lieutenant-Governor in council should determine otherwise. The Government in turn left it to the House to make suggestions for the removal if such were deemed desirable by the members. The House on Wednesday defeated all the proposals for the removal and in so doing expressed to the Government the opinion that the capital should remain at the present location. Having referred the question to the House the Government will of course abide by the decision of the House.

The manner in which the debate was conducted was a tribute to the good sense of the members and a matter of congratulation to the province at large. The subject was of a nature well calculated to lead to a war of words which would have been neither creditable to the Assembly nor beneficial to the Province whose destinies are placed in its hands. The movers of the resolution were placed in the position of seeking to take from one community and give to another a very enviable distinction to which each community felt itself entitled. More than this, the subject had been discussed freely on platforms and through the press in a manner which at times tended very decidedly to the development of sectional feelings. It might very well have happened therefore that had the supporters of the Calgary resolution been men of narrow view their advocacy of the cause of Calgary might have developed into an assault on Edmonton and the northern portion of the province. Such a tack would have doubtless induced replies in kind and the debates would have degenerated into a contest of depreciation of the aspirants for capital honors. Such internecine war whatever its effects on the question in hand would have worked damage of far more consequence to the capital of the province than any good which it could have done the particular place in which the capital might be located and in avoiding these consequences the members gave evidence at once of their own breadth of view and that the welfare of the Province as a whole is of more consequence to them than the distinction of a particular locality.

To Edmonton the majority by which the capital was maintained in its present location is particularly gratifying. The claim that the city has made to the honor has been that the splendid development of the district of which it is the centre has been accomplished practically without railway facilities, that the same handicap has prevented the development which should and would have taken place in the great north country to which it is the gateway and that when these requirements are supplied by the enterprises now actually under way the accelerated progress of these districts will quickly justify the city's claim to be the nearest suitable point to the ultimate centre of population in the Province. Generally speaking the debate Wednesday hinged on future prospects rather than present conditions and the result of the vote is taken by Edmonton as an indication that the members and through them the people of the Province have every faith in the future of the as yet comparatively undeveloped portions of Alberta.

Toward the other cities which aspired, and quite legitimately, to the honor, Edmonton has no ill-will and will indulge in no boasting. Nowhere in the Province more than in this city will there be hearty endorsation of the sentiment expressed by the member for Gleichen when in an eloquent peroration he said:

'Whether the capital sits on the banks of the Bow or the Saskatchewan, as the waters of these two great rivers unite in one magnificent stream, so I hope that the energies of these two cities of Calgary and Edmonton will unite towards the upbuilding and prosperity of the province of Alberta.'

VI — 35

'Site for Legislature Chosen,' Edmonton Journal, October 12, 1906.

The site for the Provincial Parliament buildings has at last been finally settled. The old Hudson's Bay Company's Fort grounds for which the government has been negotiating for months, has been purchased. The deal was completed yesterday in London, England at the head office of the Hudson's Bay Company between the head officers of that company and the agents of the Provincial Government. This morning, Hon. A.C. Rutherford, Premier of Alberta, who is now in Ottawa, accompanied by Hon. W.H. Cushing, Minister of Public Works, attending the Convention of Canadian Premiers, telegraphed the news to M.J. Macleod, Clerk of the· Executive Council, that the arrangements for the purchase of the Hudson's Bay Company fort grounds were completed. . . .

The area purchased is between 21 and 25 acres. The exact delimitation of the block will not be announced until further particulars are received by wire.

Now that the site question is settled, preparation of the plans for the handsome architectural pile will be rushed and no doubt work on the excavation commenced immediately. The structure itself will be probably the handsomest parliament building in the Dominion. It will be 290 feet in length and 200 feet in depth, in the form of an 'I' the front wing being considerably longer than the rear one. The building will be practically four stories in height. The dome or main tower will extend about 140 feet above the ground.

One postscript is necessary to complete this volume. In 1905, during the process of the formation of Alberta, the schools question and land question stood out as major issues. Schools, however, did not remain a controversial problem after 1905. In contrast the federal government control of lands and resources remained an irritating reminder to all of the prairie provinces that they were not quite the constitutional equals of other provinces. Finally, in 1930, the government of William Lyon Mackenzie King transferred control of lands and other natural resources to Alberta.

VI — 36

A Quarter Century Later: Alberta Gains Control of its Natural Resources: The Alberta Natural Resources Act, Statutes of Canada, 1930, Chapter 3.

His Majesty, by and with the advice and consent of the Senate and House of Commons of Canada, enacts as follows:—

1. This Act may be cited as *The Alberta Natural Resources Act.*

2. The agreement set out in the schedule hereto is hereby approved, subject to the proviso that, in addition to the rights accruing hereunder to the province of Alberta, the said province shall be entitled to such further rights, if any, with respect to the subject matter of the said agreement as are required to be vested in the said province in order that it may enjoy rights equal to those which may be conferred upon or reserved to the province of Saskatchewan under any agreement upon a like subject matter hereafter approved and confirmed in the same manner as the said agreement.

SCHEDULE
MEMORANDUM OF AGREEMENT
Made this fourteenth day of December, 1929,

BETWEEN

THE GOVERNMENT OF THE DOMINION OF CANADA,
represented herein by the Honourable Ernest Lapointe,
Minister of Justice, and the Honourable Charles Stewart,
Minister of the Interior,

Of the first part,

AND

THE GOVERNMENT OF THE PROVINCE OF ALBERTA,
represented herein by the Honourable John Edward
Brownlee, Premier of Alberta, and the Honourable George
Hoadley, Minister of Agriculture and Health,

Of the second part

Whereas by section twenty-one of *The Alberta Act*, being
chapter three of four and five Edward the Seventh, it was
provided that "All Crown lands, mines and minerals and
royalties incident thereto, and the interest of the Crown in the
waters within the province under *The North-west Irrigation
Act, 1898*, shall continued to be vested in the Crown and administered by the Government of Canada for the purposes of
Canada, subject to the provisions of any Act of the Parliament
of Canada with respect to road allowances and roads or trails in
force immediately before the coming into force of this Act,
which shall apply to the said province with the substitution
therein of the said province for the North-west Territories";

And Whereas it is desirable that the Province should be
placed in a position of equality with the other provinces of
Confederation with respect to the administration and control
of its natural resources as from its entrance into Confederation
in 1905;

And Whereas it has been agreed between Canada and the said
Province that the provisions of *The Alberta Act* should be
modified as herein set out;

Now Therefore This Agreement Witnesseth:

TRANSFER OF PUBLIC LANDS GENERALLY

1. In order that the Province may be in the same position as

the original Provinces of Confederation are in virtue of section one hundred and nine of the *British North America Act, 1867,* the interest of the Crown in all Crown lands, mines, minerals (precious and base) and royalties derived therefrom within the Province, and all sums due or payable for such lands, mines, mineral or royalties, shall, from and after the coming into force of this agreement and subject as therein otherwise provided, belong to the Province, subject to any trusts existing in respect thereof, and to any interest other than that of the Crown in the same, and the said lands, mines, minerals and royalties shall be administered by the Provinces for the purposes thereof, subject, until the Legislature of the Province otherwise provides, to the provisions of any Act of the Pariament of Canada relating to such administration; any payment received by Canada in respect of any such lands, mines, minerals or royalties before the coming into force of this agreement shall continue to belong to Canada whether paid in advance or otherwise, it being the intention that, except as herein otherwise specially provided, Canada shall not be liable to account to the Province for any payment made in respect of any of the said lands, mines, minerals or royalties before the coming into force of this agreement, and that the Province shall not be liable to account to Canada for any such payment made thereafter.

2. The Province will carry out in accordance with the terms thereof every contract to purchase or lease any Crown lands, mines or minerals and every other arrangement whereby any person has become entitled to any interest therein as against the Crown, and further agrees not to affect or alter any term of any such contract to purchase, lease or other arrangement by legislation or otherwise, except either with the consent of all the parties thereto other than Canada or in so far as any legislation may apply generally to all similar agreements relating to lands, mines or minerals in the Province or to interests therein, irrespective of who may be the parties thereto.

3. Any power or right, which, by any such contract, lease or other arrangement, or by any Act of the parliament of Canada relating to any of the lands, mines, minerals or royalties hereby transferred or by any regulation made under any such Act, is reserved to the Governor in Council or the the Minister of the Interior or any other officer of the Government of Canada, may be exercised by such officer of the Government of the Province as may be specified by the Legislature thereof from time to time and until otherwise directed, may be exercised by the Provincial Secretary of the Province.

4. The Province will perform every obligation of Canada

arising by virtue of the provisions of any statute or order in council or regulation in respect of the public lands to be administered by it hereunder to any person entitled to a grant of lands by way of subsidy for the construction of railways or otherwise or to any railway company for grants of lands for right of way, road bed, stations, station grounds, work-shops, buildings, yards, ballast pits or other appurtenances.

5. The Province will further be bound by and will, with respect to any lands or interests in lands to which the Hudson's Bay Company may be entitled, carry out the terms and conditions of the Deed of Surrender from the said Company to the Crown as modified by the *Dominion Lands Act* and the Agreement dated the 23rd day of December, 1924, between His Majesty and the said Company, which said Agreement was approved by Order in Council dated the 19th day of December, 1924 (**P.C.** 2158), and in particular the Province will grant to the Company any lands in the Province which the Company may be entitled to select and may select from the lists of lands furnished to the Company by the Minister of the Interior under and pursuant to the said Agreement of the 23rd day of December, 1924, and will release and discharge the reservation in patents referred to in clause three of the said agreement, in case such release and discharge has not been made prior to the coming into force of this agreement. Nothing in this agreement, or in any agreement varying the same as hereinafter provided, shall in any way prejudice or diminish the rights of the Hudson's Bay Company or affect any right to or interest in land acquired or held by the said Company pursuant to the Deed of Surrender from it to the Crown, the Dominion Lands Act or the said Agreement of the 23rd day of December, 1924. . . .

FINANCIAL TERMS

20. In lieu of the provision made by subsection one of section twenty of The Alberta Act, Canada will, from and after the date of the coming into force of this agreement, pay to the Province by half-yearly payments in advance, on the first days of January and July in each year, an annual sum based upon the population of the Province as from time to time ascertained by the quinquennial census therof, as follows:

The sum payable until the population of the said Province reaches eight hundred thousand shall be five hundred and sixty-two thousand five hundred dollars;

Thereafter, until such population reaches one million two

hundred thousand, the sum payable shall be seven hundred and fifty thousand dollars;

And thereafter the sum payable shall be one million one hundred and twenty-five thousand dollars.

21. If at the date of the coming into force of this agreement any payment has been made under subsection one of section twenty of *The Alberta Act* in respect of any half-year commencing before but terminating after the said date, a proportionate part of the payment so made shall be taken as having been made under the provisions hereof.

APPENDIX
Glossary of Names

Richard Bedford Bennett: (1870-1947)

Calgary lawyer-businessman and law partner of Senator James Lougheed, Bennett first entered politics in the 1898 Territorial election when he was successful in obtaining a seat as the Member for Calgary. He was re-elected in 1900 and 1902. In 1900 Bennett ran unsuccessfully as a federal Conservative candidate. In 1905 he assumed the leadership of the Conservative Party for the Province but in the election of that year lost his own seat in Calgary. In 1909, however, he was elected as a Member of the Alberta Assembly. In 1911 he entered federal politics and in 1927 would become leader of the federal Conservative Party. In 1930 he was elected Prime Minister and served until his defeat in 1935.

Robert George Brett: (1851-1929)

Born in Strathroy, Ontario and obtaining his M.D. from the University of Toronto, Brett moved to the Territories after practicing medicine in both Ontario and Manitoba. In 1888 he was elected to the North-west Assembly as the member for Red Deer and in 1891 as the member for Banff. He acted as President of the Advisory Council from 1889 to 1891 and was one of Haultain's most prominent opponents in the Legislature. His 1899 election was contested by A.L. Sifton because of alleged corruption. Brett resigned and Sifton won the bye-election.

In 1915 he succeeded Bulyea as Lieutenant-Governor of Alberta, retiring from that post in 1925.

George Hedley Vickers Bulyea: (1859-1928)

First elected to the Territorial Assembly in 1894, Bulyea held several prominent positions on the Executive Council under Haultain. He served as Territorial Secretary from 1899-1905, Commissioner of Public Works from 1903-1905, Commissioner of Agriculture from 1899 to 1905. Bulyea was, in effect, Haultain's Liberal partner in the non-partisan government once J.H. Ross and A.L. Sifton left Territorial politics. In 1905 Laurier turned to Bulyea to take the position as first Lieutenant-Governor of Alberta. Bulyea held that position for two consecutive terms, retiring in 1915.

Edward Henry Crandell: (1859-1944)

Born in Prince Edward County, Ontario, Crandell became mayor of Brampton for several years before moving to Calgary in 1900. Besides his various activities in insurance and realty, Crandell was an active Conservative. In 1905 he was President of the Calgary Conservative Association.

Leverett George De Veber: (1849-1925)

Born in New Brunswick, De Veber was educated at King's College and studied medicine at Bartholomew Hospital in London before moving to Lethbridge where he established a medical practice. In 1898 he was elected to the Territorial Assembly and in 1905 ran successfully for the Liberals in the new Province. He was appointed Minister without portfolio by Rutherford. In 1906 he was called to the Senate.

Frederick William Gordon Haultain: (1857-1942)

A lawyer and politician, Haultain was born in Norwich, U.K. and educated at the University of Toronto. Elected to the North-west Assembly from Macleod in 1888, he quickly rose to prominence in the Legislative Assembly as a leader of the fight for responsible government. President of the Executive Council from 1897 to 1905, Haultain also held the posts of Attorney General, Territorial Treasurer, Commissioner of Public Works and Commissioner of Education at various times in these years.

In 1905 with the creation of the two new Provinces Haultain decided to run in Saskatchewan as leader of the Provincial Rights Party. Personally elected, Haultain's party failed to win office and he thus acted as leader of the opposition until 1912. In that year he was appointed Chief Justice of the Superior Court of Saskatchewan. In 1916 he was created a K.B.

Peter Fidler: (1769-1822)

In 1788 Fidler was apprenticed to the Hudson's Bay Company. He spent the rest of his life in the North West of British North America. Working under the famous Philip Turnor, Fidler became an accomplished surveyor and explorer. His trip to the Athabasca country was one of his earlier explorations.

William S. Fielding: (1848-1929)

A Nova Scotia newspaperman and politician, Fielding became Premier of his native province in 1884. He remained in that position until 1896 when, at Laurier's invitation, he left provincial politics to become Dominion Minister of Finance. He remained Finance Minister until the Dominion government was defeated by Borden's Conservatives in 1911. As the man responsible for Dominion finances Fielding was, with Sifton and Laurier, one of the men primarily responsible for dealings with the North-west Territories. In 1905 Fielding was opposed to the original education clauses of the autonomy bills and rumors circulated that he would follow Sifton in resignation from the cabinet. The redrafting of the bill, however, meant that Fielding was never forced to act.

Fielding would later support the Union Government of Robert Borden and, in the 1920's, serve once again as Finance Minister in the administration of William Lyon Mackenzie King.

Paul Kane: (1810-1871)

Born in County Cork, Ireland, Kane came to York, Upper Canada at a young age. In the 1830's Kane turned his attention to art and after studying in the United States and Europe decided to travel west to paint the natives of that region. His trip took him to the Pacific coast and back between 1845 and 1847 and allowed him to produce numerous paintings and sketches of the peoples of the plains and Pacific slope. They made him one of the foremost Canadian painters of his time and it has often been said that his trip west made him the first tourist to visit the prairies.

John Livingston:
  Editor of the Calgary *Herald* from 1889 to 1892. Livingston was one of the first men in Alberta to support the idea that the region be organized as a district governmental unit. His scheme was premature but the memory of it remained to be revived in 1895.

Senator James Lougheed: (1854-1925)
  Born in Brampton, Canada West, Lougheed attended the University of Toronto. He was called to the bar of the Province of Ontario in 1877. Moving West he established a law practice in Calgary where he soon attained prominence both as a lawyer and a businessman. When Senator Richard Hardisty died, to whom Lougheed was related by marriage, he was called to replace him in the Senate as the Senator for the North-west Territories. A Conservative, Lougheed became leader of the opposition in the Upper House in 1906 and, in 1911, was appointed Minister without Portfolio in the Borden cabinet.

Frank Marriaggi:
  A Fort Saskatchewan hotelier, Marriaggi was proprietor of the Mansion House Hotel in Fort Saskatchewan and of the Alberta Hotel in Edmonton at the turn of the century. An early participant in the movement for Alberta autonomy, he did not remain to see the Province established, moving instead to British Columbia in 1903.

Alexander McBride:
  A Calgary hardware merchant who had come to the city from the east in 1890, McBride was one of the early supporters of the Provincial autonomy movement and was involved in the committee established for that purpose in 1895. In 1896 he became mayor of Calgary.

Maitland McCarthy: (1872-1930)
  Born in Orangeville, Ontario, he attended the University of Toronto and was called to the bar in Ontario and later in the North-west Territories. McCarthy established a law practice in Calgary in 1902 and in 1904 was elected to the federal parliament as a Conservative. He remained an M.P. until 1911. In 1914 he was appointed Chief Justice of the Supreme Court of Alberta.

John T. Moore:
  A Toronto business executive and alderman, Moore came to Alberta in 1902 and settled in Red Deer where he was better able to personally supervise investments in that region. In 1902 he attempted to enter Territorial politics but was defeated by Peter Talbot. In 1905 he went to Ottawa as an advocate of Red Deer's claims to become the capital of the Province. That same year he was elected, as a Liberal, to the Provincial Legislature. He was defeated in the 1909 election.

Frank Oliver: (1853-1933)

Born in Peel County, Ontario, Oliver moved to Edmonton in 1876 and was thus one of the earliest settlers in the area. In 1880 he founded the Edmonton *Bulletin* which he continued to own until 1923. Oliver was first elected to the North-west Council in 1883 but was defeated in 1885. In 1888 he was once again elected and remained in the Territorial Assembly until 1896 when he ran federally as a Liberal and won. In 1905, with Clifford Sifton's resignation, Oliver was appointed to the powerful position of Minister of the Interior. He remained in that portfolio until the defeat of the Liberals in 1911. From 1911 to 1917 he remained in Parliament as a member of the opposition. He was later appointed to the Board of Railway Commissioners by the King administration.

Thomas A. Patrick: (1838-1909)

Patrick was first elected to the Territorial Assembly in 1897 as the Member for Yorkton. He remained in the Legislature until 1905. Patrick was a strong advocate of a two province system with a division on east-west lines.

James Reilly:

Coming to Calgary in 1882, Reilly bought the Royal Hotel in the following year. He was a man who seems to have had an undying enthusiasm for politics. Running first for mayor in 1885, unsuccessfully, he was later elected alderman and then, in 1891, achieved the mayoralty. He then turned his attention to the Territorial level but in spite of repeated attempts was unsuccessful. One of his many causes was provincial status for Alberta and his enthusiasm in 1895 helped revive the idea after it had remained dormant for several years.

James Hamilton Ross: (1856-1932)

Born in London, Canada West, Ross was first elected to the North-west Council in 1883. He remained a member of the Council and of its successor, the Territorial Assembly, until 1903. Under the Haultain administration Ross held the posts of Treasurer, Commissioner of Public Works and Territorial Secretary. His prominent posts and his skills as a politician and administrator made him one of Haultain's most important allies in the on-going controversies with Ottawa. A Liberal in politics, Ross was made Commissioner of the Yukon Territory in 1901. In 1904 he was appointed to the Senate.

Alexander C. Rutherford: (1858-1941)

Born in Carleton county, Canada West, Rutherford was educated at McGill University. A lawyer, he was called to the bar of the North-west Territories in 1895. In 1902 he ran for the Territorial Assembly as a supporter of Haultain and of Provincial autonomy in spite of his Liberal affiliations. In 1905 he was chosen leader of the Alberta Liberal Party and thus became Premier of the Province, a position which he held until 1910. He was personally defeated as an M.L.A. in 1913 and retired to private life.

Walter Scott: (1867-1938)

Born in Middlesex county, Ontario, he became proprietor of the Regina *Leader* in 1895. In 1900 he was elected as a Liberal to the House of Commons and was re-elected in 1904. In 1905 he was chosen leader of the Liberal party in

Saskatchewan and assumed the position of Premier of that Province. He remained in that position until 1916. Scott was a powerful voice for the West in the Liberal caucus and next to Frank Oliver was probably the most influential Member of Parliament from the North-west.

Arthur Lewis Sifton: (1858-1921)

Born in St. John's, Canada West, Sifton was educated at Victoria College. Called to the bar of the North-west Territories in 1883, he moved to Calgary in 1889. An early proponent of provincial autonomy, Sifton's first political appearances were in opposition to Haultain. In 1899, however, after being elected to the Territorial Assembly from Banff, Sifton joined the Haultain administration. From 1901 to 1903 he was Territorial Commissioner of Public Works and Treasurer.

In 1903 he was appointed by Laurier to the position of Chief Justice of the Supreme Court of the Territories and in 1905 Chief Justice of the Supreme Court of Alberta. In 1910 he re-entered politics to succeed Rutherford as Premier of Alberta. In 1917 he joined the Union government as Minister of Commerce and later as Secretary of State.

Clifford Sifton: (1861-1929)

The younger brother of Arthur, Clifford was educated at Victoria College, and in 1882 took up the practice of law in Manitoba. In 1888 he was elected to the Manitoba legislature and from 1891 to 1896 was Attorney General of the Province of Manitoba. He came to national attention in 1896-1897 when he worked as the representative of Manitoba to find a compromise on the controversial schools question with Laurier's federal government. Shortly afterwards he abandoned provincial politics to enter Laurier's cabinet as Minister of the Interior.

Though he resigned as Minister of the Interior in 1905 over the Territorial Schools question, Sifton remained a supporter of the Laurier government until 1911 when he threw his support behind Robert Borden on the question of reciprocity. He was created a K.C.M.G. in 1915.

Charles Allan Stuart: (1864-1926)

Born in Caradoc, Canada West, Stuart was educated at the University of Toronto before moving to Calgary in 1897. In Calgary he opened a law practice and became prominent in the local Liberal organization. In 1905 he was elected to the first Legislature of the new Province of Alberta. In 1908 he was appointed a judge of the Alberta Supreme Court.

Peter Talbot: (1854-1919)

A school-teacher, farmer and politician, Talbot was born in Eramosa, Canada West. Moving to Alberta in 1890 he became principal of the Macleod public school. He later moved to Lacombe where he took up farming. In 1902 he was elected to the Legislative Assembly of the Territories and in 1904 to the House of Commons for Strathcona. He was called to the Senate in 1906.

F. Fraser Tims: (1856-1914)

Tims settled in Fort Saskatchewan in 1888 where he became a Dry Goods merchant. In 1894 he was elected to the Territorial Assembly for Victoria. A Justice of the Peace and prominent local figure, Tims supported autonomy for Alberta. In 1898 he moved to Winnipeg.

Frederick Villeneuve: (1867-1915)

An Edmonton lawyer, Villeneuve was publisher and editor of *L'Ouest Canadien*. From 1898 to 1902 he was a member of the Territorial Assembly for St. Albert. He was a spokesman in that Assembly for French-Catholic interests.

John J. Young: (1868-1923)

Co-owner of the Calgary *Herald* in 1894-1895 and sole owner from 1895 to 1907, Young controlled one of the most powerful newspapers in the Northwest Territories. He was also actively involved in numerous business, realty and mining adventures. He was an early proponent of provincial autonomy and in 1902 was elected a Member of the Territorial Assembly for East Calgary. In 1908 he sold the *Herald* to the Southams.

INDEX